D1739277

LITTLE
COMMON
GROUND

LITTLE
COMMON
GROUND

ARAB AGRICULTURE AND

JEWISH SETTLEMENT

IN PALESTINE,

1920–1948

Charles S. Kamen

University of Pittsburgh Press

Published by the University of Pittsburgh Press, Pittsburgh, Pa. 15260
Copyright © 1991, University of Pittsburgh Press
All rights reserved
Baker & Taylor International, London
Manufactured in the United States of America

Library of Congress Cataloging-in-Publication Data

Kamen, Charles Samuel, 1939–
    Little common ground : Arab agriculture and Jewish settlement in
Palestine, 1920–1948 / Charles S. Kamen.
        p.   cm.
    Includes bibliographical references (p.) and index.
    ISBN 0-8229-3668-2
    1. Agriculture—Economic aspects—Palestine—History.   2. Land
settlement—Palestine—History.   3. Jews—Palestine—History.
4. Jewish-Arab relations.   I. Title.
HD2058.5.K36   1991
338.1′089′92705694—dc20   90-49090
                                                                                                              CIP

Map by Karen L. Wysocki. Reprinted from *The Land Question in Palestine, 1917–
1939*, by Kenneth Stein, © 1984 by the University of North Carolina Press. Reprinted
with permission.

For Sarah Breslow Kamen

CONTENTS

PREFACE

IN THE LATE 1970s I was fortunate to be invited to join a small group of Palestinian Arabs and Israeli Jews who met more or less monthly, mostly in Ramallah but occasionally in Jerusalem, and discussed aspects of the political economy of Israel and of the West Bank. Most of the Palestinian participants were associated with Bir Zeit University, near Ramallah, and most were engaged in work whose goal was to improve the economic, social, and political conditions of life of the Palestinian population in the occupied areas. Most of the Israelis had for some time been involved in research and in political activity relating to relations between Arabs and Jews in Palestine and in Israel.

I had come to Israel in August 1967, after the June war. During my first few years in the country I accepted the conventional liberal analysis of Israeli society, and of the "Israel-Arab" conflict. Not an irredentist, not an adherent of "Greater Israel," I believed in the desirability of reaching a settlement with the Arab countries, but I probably also believed that the impetus for such a settlement had to come from those countries; Israel, after all, I thought, was in no position to make political concessions.

What slowly became clear to me were the consequences of continued Israeli occupation of the West Bank and of Gaza. The parallels between relations between Jews and Arabs in Israel and the occupied territories, between whites and blacks in the United States, between majority and minority—whether racial, national, or religious—in any number of countries became increasingly obvious to me. The destructiveness—personal, economic, physical, social, and political—and growing injustice from which Jews as well as Arabs suffered, though in very different ways, led me to seek ways of becoming politically involved in opposition to existing policies of the Israeli government.

Although I had lived in Israel since 1967, until I began participating in the discussions in Ramallah I had never met Palestinians who were

ix

like me—educated, politically active. That in itself was an indication of
the great gulf between the two peoples; there were few settings in which
individuals like us could naturally come together. Moreover, initiating
and maintaining such contacts was not without problems, in particular
for the Palestinian participants. They were under pressure from other
Palestinian activists to cut their contacts with Israelis and were vulnerable to the activity of the Israeli security forces. Their courage in continuing reflected their committment to seeking a way of overcoming the
division that had been created in 1948.

There were two important results of my participating in these discussions. First, I made friends. Second, I decided to begin investigating
some aspects of the relations between Arabs and Jews about which little
or no published information existed. I realized that my search for an
appropriate form of political activity could best be resolved, for me, at
least, by doing what I had learned to do—academic research. I had, and
have, no illusions about the degree to which such work can affect actual
events. It is, however, important to present information and interpretations which challenge the accepted wisdom, which shed a different light
on subjects that have too long failed to undergo reexamination. This is
especially true with respect to situations, like that of Israel, in which a
particular view of the past is widely used to justify present policies.

Recent years have seen the publication of a number of works on the
history of Palestine and Israel that raise questions about existing under-
standings of political, economic, and social developments. This book is a
contribution to that literature. It is not, however, a book that is "critical"
of the Jews, or of the Arabs, nor do I allocate between them blame or
responsibility. I have tried to understand the situation of Arab cultivators
during the Palestine Mandate, in an attempt to redress what I felt was an
imbalance in the existing analysis of the period. Most of the writing
dealing with Arab Palestine in the period between the two world wars has
focused on the Jewish community of Palestine, or on the political aspects
of the relations among Arabs, Jews, and British. Those works dealing
primarily with Arabs have been more likely to consider the political
rather than the social and economic conditions of the period. As a result,
the accepted interpretation of Arab society in the interwar period has
been strongly colored by the perspectives of those whose main interests
did not lie in providing an account of that society, but for whom it was
primarily a backdrop. In this book Arab society is in the foreground.

I am aware that the very attempt to focus on Arabs is likely to be interpreted as an expression of partisanship and absence of objectivity. The account I have given of how I came to this research may strengthen that interpretation. The irony of such an outcome will be evident on reading this book, for its conclusions give support neither to those who seek justification for a "pro-Arab" nor to upholders of a "pro-Jewish" interpretation. If anything, I have come to believe while writing this book that there was little anyone could have realistically done, given the political, economic, and social circumstances, to bring about a different result in Palestine. Readers may disagree, and I hope that I have provided the material they need to support their disagreement.

I don't think that a similarly pessimistic conclusion should be drawn, however, about the political impasse that began with the June 1967 war, for the circumstances in which Israelis and Palestinians find themselves after three years of *intifada* and a war in the Persian Gulf are completely different from those which existed during the Mandate. It is a mistake to believe, as some do, that the conflict is irresolvable, that the fundamental relationships between Jews and Arabs will never change. I hope this book, by detailing how things were, shows the inadequacy of that view.

This book repays some of the debts I owe to those whose support and friendship encouraged me, and whose work provided me with a standard against which to measure my own. They will know why they are listed here: Judy Blank, Rita Giacaman, Henry Rosenfeld, Shlomo Swirsky. The participants in those meetings in Ramallah which got me started also deserve special thanks. Staff members at the Central Zionist Archives and the Israel State Archives, in Jerusalem, facilitated the collection of the material which forms the basis of this work. Professor Nahum Gross, of the Department of Economics at the Hebrew University, Jerusalem, graciously gave me access to the papers of Alfred Bonné. Seymour Warkov suggested that I spend a year at the University of Connecticut, which gave me the time and space I needed to write, and I would like to thank him as well as members of the sociology department who facilitated my work. Candace Einbeck helped by translating documents from German. The positive comments made by anonymous readers of drafts of the manuscript tempered their criticisms and helped me benefit from them. Catherine Marshall at the University of Pittsburgh Press was a most attentive reader and editor, and I am very grateful to her.

LITTLE

COMMON

GROUND

Introduction

THIS BOOK is the first detailed scholarly analysis of Arab agriculture in Palestine to have been published since the end of the British Mandate. My purpose is to reexamine some of the conventional interpretations of the structure of Arab Palestine between the two world wars. I do so by setting the accepted analyses of Arab Palestine during the British Mandate against an account of the actual social and economic conditions of rural Arab society and the pressures to which that society was subjected. Not surprisingly, perhaps, the results of my own analysis are more ambiguous than partisans might prefer: I conclude that the economic, social, and political context in which Arabs and Jews struggled with their competing claims to the land, and all they implied, greatly limited the available solutions.

There has been in recent years a shift in the emphasis of much research on Palestine and Israel. Investigators are now approaching the study of Israeli society and the history of the conflict with fewer preconceptions regarding the perspective from which their analysis is to proceed. In practice, this usually means that they are less likely to accept what might be called the "official" Israeli view of modern Israeli history, which begins with the founding of the first Jewish colonies in Palestine at the end of the nineteenth century.

Israel is coming increasingly to be seen as a society whose particular history has granted it no immunity from the problems and dilemmas confronted by other countries. The Zionist pioneers often spoke about "normalizing" the situation of European Jewry by creating the homeland which it lacked; a century after the initial steps were taken to found that homeland, Israel is being "normalized" academically as well, particularly by Israeli scholars. Inevitably, perhaps, the scholars undertaking such research are called "revisionists"—an ironic appellation, considering the associations to that term in the history of modern Palestine.[1]

A considerable amount of attention was paid during the Mandate to the question of the effect of Jewish settlement on the Arab population of the country. In a sense, the answer was irrelevant, because no answer would likely have reconciled the Palestinian Arabs to a growing Jewish presence. But the question was nevertheless important, for it provided a focus for the efforts of Arabs, Jews, and government to examine the consequences of Jewish immigration. Therefore, I have chosen it as a point of departure for my reevaluation of Palestinian Arab society. I focus on the countryside, which contained the bulk of the Arab population, and on the agricultural economy, which provided most of them with a livelihood.

What role did Jewish settlement play in the changes that occurred in the social and economic structure of Arab society in Palestine during the Mandate? The Jews argued that in returning to Palestine they enabled the Arab population to better itself far beyond what might have been possible had Palestine remained primarily agricultural, inhabited by a "sparse population living in economic isolation and employing very primitive methods."[2] By developing the enterprises necessary for the building of their national home, the Jews believed they had also laid the groundwork for Arab progress, though this was not, of course, their primary intention. The Arabs often acknowledged the changes that accompanied Jewish colonization. Equally often, however, they denied that the Arabs benefited from them; that they were the result of Jewish, rather than governmental or Arab effort; or that Jewish initiative was a necessary condition of their occurrence. The third party to the conflict, the government of Palestine, refrained from undertaking policies that would deliberately alter the basic order of Palestinian Arab society or compel Jews and Arabs to develop jointly the land they both claimed. At the same time the government initiated, acquiesced in, and carried out measures that nevertheless helped to alter the social and economic structure of Arab Palestine.

There has been a tendency in works dealing with Palestine during the period of the Mandate to dichotomize the society into a "modernizing" Jewish sector and a "traditional" Palestinian Arab sector,[3] and to view the development of Palestine as characterized by the interplay of Jewish "initiatives," such as immigration and land purchase, to take the two most obvious examples, and Arab "responses" to them. This tendency has its origin, perhaps, in the fact that most of the Jews, the Arabs, and the government officials adopted a vocabulary and analysis that assumed this dichotomy. The Jews, as Europeans, saw themselves, were often seen by the British, and were sometimes even seen by the Arabs to be bringing the benefits of civilization to the natives. In addition to believing that their colonization had positive consequences for the Arab population, the Jews were convinced that the demonstration of these benefits was of utmost importance in their efforts to encourage international support for, and in particular British agreement to, the continued expansion of Jewish settlement. Thus, they devoted a considerable effort to collecting material on the presumed benefits to the Arabs of Jewish settlement and presented their arguments in pamphlets, speeches, evidence before investigating commissions, and in meetings with government administrators.

Many Mandatory government officials could agree with the claim that Jewish efforts were improving aspects of the lives of Palestinian Arabs, without necessarily being sympathetic to the Zionist program, or pleased with its consequences. Britain's colonial empire in the period between the two world wars was spread widely, and its administrators grappled with questions arising out of the contact between European settlers and native societies. Jewish settlement in Palestine could easily be viewed in such a context, despite the fact that the settlers were not English, nor were they acting primarily in the interests of a mother country.

There may be some justification for viewing the political history of Mandatory Palestine in terms of "initiatives" and "responses," for politics are carried out by men and women who often act in response to the actions of others. The political history of Palestine, however, unfolded against the background of changes in the social and economic structure of the country which were the result not only of Jewish initiative and Arab response, but also grew out of the independent as well as the joint development of Arab and Jewish society during that period. Dividing Palestine for the purpose of analysis into a modern Jewish and a traditional Arab sector has the effect of neglecting the independent development of Arab society by subordinating it to that of the Jews. Such a division may also, paradoxically, conceal some of the effects of Jewish settlement by focusing attention on the "benefits" brought by the Jews, to the neglect of the disruption to which their settlement led. Rather than

examining the response of Arabs to the progress of Jewish settlement, it
is better to look at the development of Arab society during the Mandatory
period, paying attention to the way in which the conditions created by
Jewish settlement, among other factors, affected that development.
Rather than taking Jewish settlement as the primary factor affecting
change in Arab society, such settlement should be seen as part of the
context within which such changes occurred; it had both facilitating and
limiting effects, direct as well as indirect. Just as the Arabs and their
society comprised part of the conditions for the development of Jewish
Palestine, so the Jews comprised for the Arabs part of the conditions for
their own development.

In the following chapters I examine one aspect of the complementary
relations between Arab and Jewish society: the changing condition of
Arab agriculture. The struggle for control of the land was the most
obvious expression of the conflict between Arabs and Jews; since Arab
Palestine was primarily a rural, agricultural society, the results of that
struggle were bound to have wide-ranging effects on the rural economy.
Zionist ideology emphasized the "return to the land," and even though
the vast majority of Jewish settlers never engaged in agricultural pur-
suits, purchase of land by Jews was, together with immigration, from the
beginning of Zionist settlement one of the two main foundations of the
establishment of the Jewish national home. Ownership of land meant
control of territory, and control of territory on which Jews could build
their villages and towns and settle the immigrants who would arrive was
seen as the basis for the establishment of an autonomous Jewish society.
Whether the goals were explicitly "political," aimed at the establishment
of a Jewish state, or restricted to the founding of a self-governing Jewish
community within some broader, undefined political entity, the acquisition of land was central to all Zionist efforts, and land-purchasing groups
were among the first organizations created by Jews interested in reestab-
lishing a Jewish commonwealth in Palestine.[4]

Jewish land purchases had mixed effects on the Arab population.
Scattered evidence of the beginnings of a reaction to them by a local
nationalist movement was visible in Palestine prior to the First World
War, and especially after the Young Turks seized power in Constantinople in 1908. While the primary concerns of Palestinian nationalists
focused on achieving greater freedom from the authoritarian rule of the
Ottoman sultan, local journalists also expressed their concerns about the

potential danger they saw in such purchases, especially to the rural population.[5] Arab opposition in this early period was based more on the symbolic meaning of these acquisitions than on their practical consequences, for few Arabs were displaced by such transfers. But it was very much to the point, for it implied recognition of the land's symbolic importance to the Jews and, by opposing to this an alternative symbolism, helped to establish the terms in which the argument over Jewish settlement was conducted.

Jewish land purchases received a new impetus following the establishment of the Mandate after the First World War, when the Palestine and British governments increasingly expressed their concerns regarding the political, economic, and social effects of land sales to Jews. Because the Palestinian Arab population was overwhelmingly rural throughout the period of the Mandate, Jewish land purchase and settlement were often seen by Arabs and by government officials as having potentially disastrous consequences for Arab peasant agriculture. In particular, it was feared that Jewish land purchases would become so extensive as to threaten the physical survival of growing numbers of Arab cultivators who would be displaced from their lands. Although a not inconsiderable number of Arab peasants were forced off the land in the process of Jewish settlement, this occurred under circumstances more complex than were implied in the Arab argument.

Jewish land acquisition had positive consequences as well, though it may be difficult to separate them from the effects of Jewish settlement in general or from the activities of the Mandatory government. Probably the most noteworthy Jewish contribution to Palestinian agriculture was the introduction of "scientific" farming practices that could be emulated by Arab cultivators who possessed or were able to acquire the capital necessary to put them into effect. Some of the more important innovations included improvement of the land through crop rotation; the cultivation of fodder for livestock; the introduction of crop strains suitable to local conditions and also profitable; and irrigation. In addition, of course, the existence of a growing Jewish urban population provided an expanded market for the produce of Arab cultivators who were in a position to take advantage of the new commercial opportunities.

But the exemplary character of Jewish innovation in crops, techniques, and equipment has probably been exaggerated. While some Arabs certainly were able to benefit economically from Jewish settle-

ment, most could not, for they did not have access to the economic
resources required to put new techniques into operation. Moreover, in
the absence of agrarian reform, in particular a reorganization of Arab
landholding, there was no possibility for most Arab cultivators to undertake such changes in the working of their holdings even had they wanted
to do so. Most discussions of the agricultural economy of Mandatory
Palestine have understated the complexity of the interplay between Jewish settlement and Arab cultivators. They have stressed one or another of
the most noticeable outcomes—displacement of Arabs, the improvement
of Arab agriculture, the persistence of land sales to Jews—without examining sufficiently their interrelations.

The Zionist historiography of Jewish settlement in Palestine tended to
view Arabs as part of the environment to be overcome. The history of the
Yishuv (the term used by Jewish settlers to denote the organized Jewish
community in Palestine), in this approach, is a history of Jews, in which
Arabs appear only when it is impossible to ignore them—as possessors
or cultivators of land that the Jews wanted for themselves; as a potential
or actual physical threat; as representing a danger, because of their very
presence, to Zionism's political aspirations. But the Arabs of Palestine
were seldom viewed as a people with its own history, worthy of consideration in its own right. One consequence of this approach was the distor-
tion of the history of Palestine from the beginning of modern Jewish
settlement. An outlook developed among Jews that denied Arabs a legitimate place in the country's past (they were "latecomers," unlike the Jews
who were seen to have maintained a continual presence in the country
since biblical times), in its present (the needs of Arabs were subordinated to those stemming from the priority of attaining Zionist goals), or in
its future (expressed in a theme which runs through Jewish settlement,
that somehow the Arab population of the country will disappear).[6]

Writing about the Arabs of Palestine as if their history has independent value, recognizing their existence as a people and a community
confronted with many of the same problems faced by those in other lands
that had come under colonial rule during the same period, is threatening
to one commonly accepted view of the history of Jewish settlement in the
country. By making explicit the nature of Palestinian Arab society, the
effects of Jewish settlement on the development of Arab Palestine, and
the nature of the relationships between Jews and Arabs in the country,
the received view that many Jews and non-Jews in Israel and elsewhere

have had of the modern history in Palestine is undermined. Jews are no longer viewed as prime movers but as participants in a historical process whose initial conditions were set prior to their arrival. The Arabs were also participants in this process, and the actions of both groups affected one another and were carried out in a particular social and economic framework which in the political circumstances of the Mandate could not easily be altered. Only the destruction of Arab society as a result of the 1948 war allowed Jewish settlement in Palestine to break free of some of the limitations set by the country's history, although it imposed others that few had the prescience to forsee. As subsequent events have shown, the basic dilemmas resulting from the joint claims of Arabs and Jews to the same territory have not yet been resolved.

In the following chapters I examine Arab agriculture and rural society in Palestine during the British Mandate, in the context of the changes that resulted from Jewish settlement and government policies. Chapter 2 reviews the demography and political economy of rural Arab Palestine. In chapter 3 I show how political conflict set the terms for the contemporary analysis of Arab rural society, while chapter 4 evaluates the principal attempts to approach Arab Palestine using broader analytic frameworks. Chapter 5 and chapter 6 show in detail how Arab landholding and agricultural practices were affected by Jewish settlement and government policies, and chapter 7 discusses some of the implications of my analysis for the understanding of the history of Palestine and of Israel.

A couple of brief notes about terminology and about sources. I consistently use the terms *Jews*, *Arabs*, and *British* or *government* throughout this work. By doing so I do not intend to imply that each group was monolithic in its perspectives or, in the case of the Arabs and the Jews, in the situation of its members. Indeed, when discussing Arab society I refer in some detail to its various components, identifying differences in their social and economic positions. I don't similarly differentiate, however, regarding what I have called the "views" or "analyses" of Jews, Arabs, or the British government, though I am aware that considerable variation existed within each group. But I am less interested in the process by which "official" policies evolved than in the policies themselves. These policies, in their expression and implementation, created the conditions and defined subsequent interpretations of them. The Jewish Agency and the government of Palestine had policies upon which they acted, whatever disagreements existed in their process of formulation, and however these disagreements affected their implementation.

The absence in the Arab community of any comparable organization whose public positions can be taken to represent the "official" view makes less justifiable the use of the general term *Arabs*. Since I don't read Arabic, it is possible that I have overlooked complexities which may have vitiated or altered my analysis. One of the points I make in the book, however, is that the various analyses of the condition of Arab agriculturalists were put forward, in part, for their political effect. It was important that they be public, and therefore it was important that they be in English. The presumption must be that the Arabs, like the Jews, had every interest in making their case overt, explicit, and widely accessible. It was precisely these aspects which interested me.

Arab Society in Palestine

PALESTINE WAS REMARKABLE in achieving an importance disproportionate to its size, population, resources, and the length of time it existed as a political entity in the modern world. It was a small territory, about ten thousand square miles in area, roughly the same size that Burundi is today, a little larger than the state of Massachusetts. Palestine as a separate country came into existence following the First World War, as part of the process in which protectorates, mandates, and trust territories were established to govern lands, formerly controlled by the defeated countries of the Entente, which the victorious powers were not ready to see independent. Before the war it had been a part of the Ottoman Empire, attached to the *wilayet* of Beirut which extended along the eastern Mediterranean coast from Latakia in the north almost to Jaffa in the south. Palestine had not been a single government entity in Ottoman times; its territory was divided administratively between the *wilayet* of Beirut, covering its northern half, the *sanjaq* of Jerusalem, which included most of the southern portion and most of the Negev, and the *sanjaq* of Ma'an, a part of the *wilayet* of Syria which included the remainder of the Negev. Palestine's separate existence lasted only twenty-eight years; it began with the allocation to Great Britain, on April 25, 1920, of the Mandate for Palestine by the Supreme Council of the Peace Conference at San Remo, and ended on May 14, 1948, when the British administration over the country came to an end in the wake of Great Britain's decision to terminate its responsibilities under the Mandate.

Britain's interest in obtaining Palestine as a Mandatory territory was a consequence of its strategic geographical location adjoining the sea route to India via the Suez Canal and near the expanding oil fields of the Middle East. Economic and strategic concerns merged with others, less

11

clearly defined, resulting from the new Jewish settlement in the country which began in the 1880s in response to the rapidly deteriorating situation of the Jewish population in eastern Europe and in Russia. In November 1917, the British government authorized Foreign Secretary Arthur James Balfour to transmit to Lord Rothschild—as the head of England's most prominent Jewish family and one who had helped the Zionist leaders gain access to the British cabinet—an expression of its support for the establishment of a Jewish "national home" in Palestine, and organized Zionism seemed to have found the great power protector for its colonization which it had long sought.

The two major components of Arab rural society were, of course, population and land, and a discussion of the interaction between them pervades this entire work. In this section, however, I want to delineate the main characteristics of the Arab rural population in Palestine, and of its land, in order to provide the necessary background for understanding the changes that occurred in both, and in the relations between them, during the period under consideration.

People

Between 1922, when the first census of population was carried out by the Palestine government, and the end of 1945, the Arab population of the country more than doubled, from 565,000 to 1,190,000; the number of Jews increased more than sixfold, from 83,800 to 528,700.[1] While the Arab population grew primarily as a result of natural increase, the number of Jews in Palestine depended largely on immigration. Between 1919 and 1947 more than half a million Jewish immigrants entered Palestine. Initially, Jewish immigration was unrestricted, but Arab protests and attacks on Jews led the British government in 1922 to announce a policy under which immigration of Jews would depend on the "absorptive capacity" of the country. Henceforth the number of Jewish immigrants was contingent on a combination of four factors: economic and political conditions in the countries of origin, in particular in eastern Europe; economic and political conditions in Palestine; the number of immigrant visas approved by the Palestine government in its semiannual schedule; and, especially after the rise of Nazism, the number of Jews who could manage to enter or remain in the country illegally. As a result, there were great fluctuations in the annual number of Jewish immigrants. Jewish

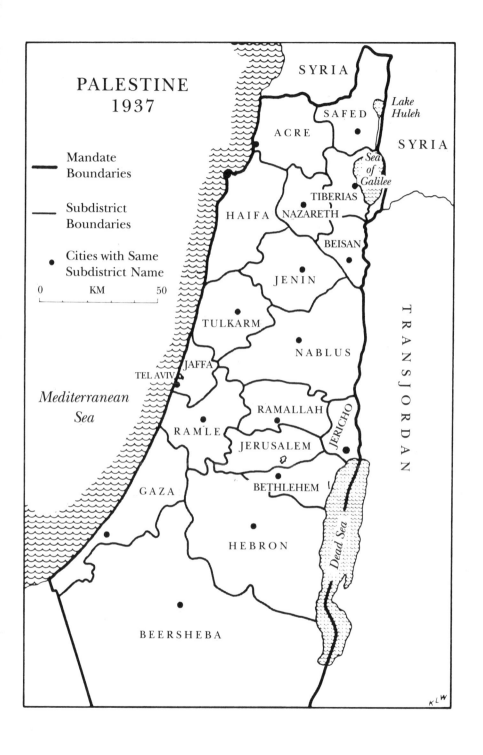

PALESTINE
1937

Mandate
Boundaries

Subdistrict
Boundaries

Cities with Same
Subdistrict Name

0   KM   50

Mediterranean
Sea

SYRIA

SAFED

ACRE

Lake
Huleh

SYRIA

Sea
of
Galilee

TIBERIAS

HAIFA   NAZARETH

BEISAN

JENIN

TULKARM

NABLUS

JAFFA

TEL AVIV

RAMALLAH

JERICHO

RAMLE

JERUSALEM

GAZA

BETHLEHEM

HEBRON

Dead Sea

TRANSJORDAN

BEERSHEBA

K L W

immigration quickly became a bone of contention between Arabs and Jews. Increased immigration was vital for the consolidation of the national home and therefore represented a patent threat to Arab aspirations for political control. In the short run, Arabs argued, immigrant Jews took work away from local Arabs; they also claimed that many Jewish immigrants unable to find employment became public charges, diverting government resources which otherwise could be spent on improving the social and economic conditions of the Arab population. Jews responded that Jewish immigration stimulated economic development, from which both Arabs and Jews benefited.[2]

The most striking characteristic of the distribution of the Arab population during this period was its stability. The relative proportion of the total Arab population in each subdistrict differed only slightly in 1944 from what it had been in 1922 (table 1). The greatest change occurred in the Haifa subdistrict, which had contained 7.3 percent of the settled Arab population in 1922, but whose share increased by 1944 to 10.5 percent; a slightly smaller increase took place in the Jaffa subdistrict, from 7.1 percent of the total population in 1922 to 9.2 percent in 1944. These two subdistricts included two of the three major Arab towns, the growth of which accounted for part, but not all, of the increase in the subdistricts' populations, since their share of the rural Arab population increased as well (the Haifa subdistrict contained 5.6 percent of the rural Arab population in 1922 and 7.3 percent in 1944; the Jaffa subdistrict contained 3.5 percent of the rural Arab population in 1922 and 5.1 percent in 1944). The largest decline between 1922 and 1944 in the proportion of the total Arab population in a subdistrict occurred in the Nablus subdistrict (from 9.8 to 8.0 percent) and in the Hebron subdistrict (from 9.3 to 7.7 percent); the largest decline in the proportion of the total rural Arab population in a subdistrict occurred in the Gaza subdistrict (from 12.6 percent to 10.7 percent) and in the Ramallah subdistrict (from 7.2 percent to 5.8 percent).[3]

If the overall distribution of the Arab population in Palestine changed little during most of the Mandatory period, neither were there dramatic changes in the balance of urban and rural Arab populations. In 1922, 34.3 percent of the settled Arab population was urban; by 1944 this proportion had increased to only 35.9 percent. In the subdistricts containing the three principal Arab towns—Jaffa, Jerusalem, and Haifa—

the proportion of the Arab population which was urban in 1922 was 67.4, 53.1, and 49.7 percent, and in 1944 it was 63.3, 51.6, and 55.3 percent, respectively.

There was considerable variation in the relative increase in the size of the Arab towns, and of the Arab populations of the mixed Arab-Jewish towns, between 1922 and 1944. Three towns—Beit Jala, Bethlehem, and Nablus—grew by less than 50 percent; nine—Gaza, Majdal, Hebron, Ramallah, Jenin, Shafa 'Amr, Nazareth, Acre, and Safad—saw their Arab populations increase by more than half, but not double; nine more towns—Khan Yunis, Beersheba, Jaffa, Ramle, Lydda, Jerusalem, Tulkarm, Beisan, and Tiberias—more than doubled their Arab populations; and that of Haifa more than tripled (table 2). At the same time as the Arab populations of the three major towns were more than doubling in size, they were declining in weight within the towns, compared with the Jewish share: from 84.4 to 70.3 percent in Jaffa; from 45.7 to 38.2 percent in Jerusalem; and from 74.7 to 48.8 percent in Haifa.

Despite the variation in the rate of growth of the Arab towns, the relative distribution of the Arab urban population among the towns of different sizes remained the same between 1931 and 1944 (table 3).[4] Almost half the Arab town population lived in Jaffa, Haifa, and Jerusalem, but the proportion in these towns did not change between 1931 and 1944. The urban Arab population was about one-fourth Christian in 1931 and in 1944; the settled Arab rural population in each of those years was no more than 4 percent Christian.[5] The proportion of Christians among the Arab populations of the three large towns was about one-fifth in Jaffa, almost one-half in Jerusalem, and about two-fifths in Haifa. These proportions remained more or less unchanged between 1931 and 1944.[6] Migration from villages to towns was occurring throughout this period. The rate of natural increase was higher for Moslems than for Christians; Christian villagers must have migrated to the towns more frequently than did Moslems, for the relative proportion of each group in the large towns remained the same.[7]

The data presented above regarding the essential stability of the distribution of the Arab population during the period of the Mandate appears to contradict the accepted view that this population underwent substantial changes during those years. The *Survey of Palestine*, prepared by the government for the visit of the Anglo-American Committee

TABLE 1

The Settled Arab Population of Palestine by Subdistrict, 1922–1944

Subdistrict	Percentage of Total Population			Percentage of Rural Population			Proportion Urban of Subdistrict Population[a]		
	1922 (N=510,651)	1931 (N=794,658)	1944 (N=1,144,370)	1922 (N=374,362)	1931 (N=519,052)	1944 (N=733,870)	1922	1931	1944
Gaza	12.9	10.9	11.7	12.6	9.9	10.7	35.9	40.6	41.3
Beersheba	(b)	0.4	(b)	—	—	—	—	95.6	100.0
Jaffa	7.1	8.9	9.2	3.5	4.2	5.1	67.4	67.3	63.3
Ramle	7.8	8.0	8.2	7.8	8.1	8.5	37.4	33.9	33.9
Hebron	9.3	8.3	7.7	9.9	9.4	8.6	30.4	26.4	28.0
Jerusalem	12.7	12.4	12.3	9.1	9.4	9.3	53.1	50.5	51.6
Ramallah	5.3	4.9	4.1	7.2	6.7	5.8	10.3	11.0	10.7
Tulkarm	6.0	5.9	6.0	8.2	8.0	8.2	9.7	11.3	11.8
Nablus	9.8	8.6	8.0	10.7	9.8	9.4	32.3	25.5	25.3
Jenin	5.9	5.0	5.0	8.3	7.2	7.2	7.8	6.9	7.0
Haifa	7.3	9.1	10.5	5.6	6.5	7.3	49.7	47.9	55.3
Nazareth	3.7	3.2	3.4	3.6	3.2	3.3	35.4	34.7	36.9
Beisan	1.1	1.7	1.4	1.2	1.8	1.6	28.9	28.4	31.2
Tiberias	2.3	2.4	2.3	2.8	3.0	2.8	19.3	29.9	20.3
Acre	5.9	5.8	5.7	7.4	7.3	7.2	18.7	17.3	18.8
Safad	2.8	4.4	4.1	2.7	5.4	5.1	36.7	19.6	20.3
All Palestine	99.9	99.9	99.6	100.6	99.9	100.1	34.3	34.7	35.9

Sources: Data for 1922 and 1931 are based on the censuses of population carried out by the government of Palestine. Data for 1944 are an estimate of the year-end population made by the Department of Statistics.

For total population, 1922: Government of Palestine, Department of Statistics, *Vital Statistics,* p. 3, less tribal population as reported in Gurevich, *Statistical Abstract,* p. 28; 1931, 1944: *Vital Statistics,* p. 6. HM Forces are included in 1922, 1931, but not in 1944.

For rural population, 1922: *Vital Statistics,* p. 5, less tribal population as reported in Gurevich, *Statistical Abstract,* p. 18; 1931, 1944: *Vital Statistics,* p. 8. HM Forces included in 1922, 1931, but not in 1944.

For proportion urban, 1922: *Vital Statistics,* pp. 3–4, less tribal population as reported in Gurevich, *Statistical Abstract,* p. 18; 1931, 1944: *Vital Statistics,* pp. 6–7.

Notes:

a. A subdistrict usually had only one town with a large Arab population, which gave it its name. Additional Arab towns were found in the Gaza subdistrict (Khan Yunis and Majdal), the Ramle subdistrict (Lydda), and the Haifa subdistrict (Shafa' Amr).

b. Less than 0.1 percent.

$Pu = (Tu - Ju) / (T - B - J)$ for each subdistrict, where B = tribal population; T = total population; Tu = total urban population; J = total Jewish population; Ju = total urban Jewish population; Pu = proportion urban Arab population.

TABLE 2
The Urban Arab Population of Palestine, 1922–1944

Town	Population		1944 Population as Percent of 1922 Population	Percent Arab in Mixed Towns[a]		
	1922	1944		1922	1931	1944
Gaza	17,426	34,170	196			
Khan Yunis	3,889	11,220	289			
Majdal	5,097	9,910	194			
Beersheba	2,258	5,570	247			
Jaffa	27,437	66,310	242	84.4	86.1	70.3
Ramle	7,277	15,160	208			
Lydda	8,092	16,760	207			
Hebron	16,147	24,560	152			
Beit Jala	3,101	3,710	120			
Bethlehem	6,656	8,820	133			
Jerusalem	28,607	60,800	213	45.7	43.4	38.2
Ramallah	3,097	5,080	164			
Tulkarm	3,327	8,090	243			
Nablus	15,931	23,250	146			
Jenin	2,630	3,990	152			
Haifa	18,404	62,800	341	74.7	68.4	48.8
Shafa 'Amr	2,288	3,630	159			
Nazareth	7,371	14,200	193			
Beisan	1,900	5,180	273			
Tiberias	2,523	5,310	210	36.3	37.4	46.9
Acre	6,342	12,310	194			
Safad	5,775	9,530	165	65.9	73.0	79.9
Total	195,695	410,500	210			

Sources: Population size, 1922: *Vital Statistics*, p. 4; 1944: ibid., p. 7. Percent Arab in mixed towns, 1922: ibid., p. 4; 1931, 1944: ibid., p. 7.
Note:
   a. Towns for which no figure is given for "Percent Arab" were completely, or almost completely, Arab in composition.

of Inquiry in 1946, discussed in some detail the changes in the geographical distribution of the Moslem, Jewish, and Christian populations. Summarizing their findings, the authors reported that

taking the population as a whole [there had been] a very considerable trend toward urbanization, the urban population having increased by 47 per cent. in 1922–31 and by 97 per cent. in 1931–44, as compared to 32 per cent. and 59 per cent. respectively for the rural population. Out of 100 inhabitants, only 51 per cent. lived in villages in 1944 as compared with 65 per cent. in 1922; meanwhile the share of large towns has gone up from 18 per cent. in 1922 to 32 per cent. in 1944.[8]

But the figures for the population as a whole included the Jews, who were overwhelmingly urban: almost 65 percent of the Jews lived in towns having more than 45,000 inhabitants, and only one-fourth of them lived in villages.[9] The large percentage increase in the urban population was due in part to its small absolute size at the beginning of the Mandate and was accompanied by a large percentage increase in the rural population. Looking only at the period 1931–1944, there was essentially no change in the distribution of the Arab population between villages and towns (table 3).

Although the proportion of Arabs in towns and in the countryside remained stable, it is true that rural Arabs were moving to urban areas. The Arab birthrate was higher in rural areas than in the towns, primarily because the rural population was overwhelmingly Moslem, while the urban Arab population contained a relatively high proportion of Chris-

TABLE 3
Arab Population by Type of Locality
(percent)

| | | In Towns Numbering | | | | |
	In Villages	Up to 5,000	5,000– 15,000	15,000– 45,000	Over 45,000	Total
Villages and towns						
1931	65.3	2.7	9.5	7.1	15.4	99.7 (764,658)
1944	64.1	2.4	9.7	7.2	16.6	99.9 (1,144,370)
Towns only						
1931		7.9	27.8	20.9	45.4	100.0 (246,330)
1944		6.6	27.2	20.0	46.2	100.0 (410,500)

Source: Government of Palestine, *Survey of Palestine,* p. 153.

tians. The Christian birthrate was in general lower than that of the Moslems. Therefore, in order for the relative proportions of rural and urban Arab populations to remain constant, some of the deficiency in the growth of the urban population because of its lower birthrate was balanced by the migration to towns of Arabs from the countryside.

There were factors in addition to differential birthrates and migration patterns which contributed to the maintenance of stability in the geographical distribution of the Arab population during the Mandate. Shifts in population could have occurred either by the movement from one area to another of a portion of the rural population in order to engage in agriculture in the new location, or as a result of even greater migration from the villages to the towns. In the absence of government programs for agricultural resettlement and intensification of cultivation, such as had been advocated by government officials and the reports of investigatory commissions, as well as by the Jews as a way of freeing additional land for Jewish settlement, there was no incentive for Arab peasants to leave the land they cultivated and begin farming elsewhere in the country. Alternative land which could have immediately been brought under cultivation by the peasants was not available, and most of them lacked the capital either to purchase land that might have been for sale or to invest the sums necessary to make it cultivable.

Dispossession of cultivators because of indebtedness or Jewish land purchases was a second factor which might have been expected to result in large shifts in the distribution of the Arab rural population. In practice, however, most of the Arabs dispossessed by the sale of their lands probably remained in the vicinity of their former holdings. This was particularly true of those who lost their lands as a result of indebtedness to Arab creditors, for they often became tenants or hired laborers of the new owner. Nor was the number of those dispossessed by Jewish land purchases in any one area so great as to be able to have a significant effect on the relative distribution of the population among the various regions of the country.

Neither did conditions exist which facilitated or encouraged the migration of rural Arabs to towns and their permanent settlement therein, although such migration increased during the period. Only in Haifa did industrial development take a form that provided significant employment for Arabs in the enterprises undertaken by the government (the port and the railroad yards) or by foreign, non-Jewish capital (the terminus of the oil pipeline from Iraq and the refineries in the Haifa Bay area). Industries established by Jews were almost completely closed to Arabs because of preferential hiring of Jewish workers and the existence of a relatively large population of Jewish immigrants whose industrial labor experience was greater than that of the local, rural Arabs. Even when Arabs possessed the necessary skills, or the aptitude to acquire them, their chances of being hired by a Jewish firm were small because of the exclusionary policies. The amount of Palestinian Arab capital invested in local industrial undertakings was small, and a large-scale market for Arab industrial labor did not develop prior to the Second World War.

The Palestine government actively prevented the influx of rural Arabs into the towns, fearing the creation of a rootless, volatile, and dissatisfied urban lower class. Its efforts to clear the Haifa "tin town," a *bidonville* constructed on the outskirts of the city by Arabs who had come hoping to find employment, was only one indication of government policy.[10] Others included the provision of public works in the vicinity of the villages, mostly in road-building, as a way of reducing the need for villagers to seek work in towns to supplement their inadequate agricultural incomes.

An additional factor which made unnecessary the permanent migration of Arabs from villages to the towns was the small size of the country and the gradual improvement in road transportation. A daily round-trip journey which in most cases could not have exceeded two or three hours allowed many villagers to live at home while working in a town; those unable to make the daily trip could return home weekly, if not more frequently. In fact, official government pay scales for Arab laborers were based on the assumption that these workers were less dependent on urban markets for their food and shelter because of the proximity of their home villages and their ties to them; pay rates were reduced accordingly.[11]

There were, of course, political implications to the size and distribution of population in Palestine. The Jews argued that the increase in the size of the Arab population was greater in the areas of Jewish settlement.[12] The authors of the *Survey* presented data which in their view showed that there had been considerable variation among subdistricts in the increase of the rural Moslem population, such increase having been greater in the subdistricts of the coastal plain—Gaza, Ramle, Jaffa, Tulkarm, and Haifa—than in the interior: "The increase of the rural Moslem population in the coastal plain may probably be explained by the more rapid economic development in those sub-districts resulting in a reduction of mortality, a rise in the rate of natural increase and a movement of immigration from other sub-districts."[13] Yet if the total settled Moslem rural population in these five coastal subdistricts is compared for 1922, 1931, and 1945, their share of Palestine's total settled Moslem rural population was 38.9, 38.0, and 41.2 percent, respectively.[14] Again, there is no evidence for a significant shift in the distribution of the Arab rural population in Palestine as a whole. While it is true that Arabs from the hill districts of Palestine sought work in and around the coastal towns, rather than the reverse, this search for employment failed to result in permanent resettlement.

The Arab population grew primarily as a result of natural increase. Only about 7 percent of the net growth of some 570,000 persons between 1922 and 1944 was due to immigration, although this proportion was quite different among Moslems (4 percent) and among Christians (29 percent). Since Arab Christians were in the minority, their greater representation among the immigrants contributed little to the growth of the total Arab population; moreover, most of the Christian immigrants were non-Arab, came from Europe, and were connected either with religious institutions or the departments of the Palestine government (table 4).[15] Of some 32,000 "authorized" Arab and other non-Jewish immigrants (those who had received permission to enter the country) arriving between 1924 and 1945, only about 20 percent can definitely be characterized as having been attracted to Palestine by the economic possibilities of the country, including those labeled "capitalist," "skilled artisan," and "persons coming to employment". Adding a proportionate number of "dependents" would increase the percentage to little more than onefourth of the authorized immigrants.[16] Many of the Arab immigrants were women from neighboring countries coming to be married to Palestinian men.[17] The extent of "illegal" Arab immigration was the subject of considerable concern among Jews. Immigrants in the categories "travelers registered as immigrants," and "travelers remaining illegally" could have included a certain proportion of persons attracted by economic considerations, but the total number in these two categories was not large (some 25,000 persons). Even if the number of "travelers remaining illegally" was much larger, they would have represented only a small proportion of the increase in the size of the Arab population during the period.[18]

TABLE 4
Immigration and Emigration of Arabs and Other Non-Jews

Total authorized immigration, 1924–1945[a]		32,374
Capitalist immigration, 1926–1945[b]	651	
Skilled artisans, 1926–1945	28	
Those having a minimum income of £P4 per month, 1926–1945	180	
Religious occupations, 1923–1945	3,861	
Students coming to institutions, 1926–1945	1,912	
Persons coming to employment, 1923–1945	5,503	
Dependants, 1927–1945	9,467	
Exempted persons[c]	9,963	
Travelers registered as immigrants, 1924–1945		9,413
Travelers remaining illegally, Sept. 1933–Dec. 1945		15,936
Total		57,723

Country of origin, 1938–1945	Arabs	Others	Total
Middle East and North Africa	3,819	1,824	5,643
Other countries	135	6,830	6,965
Total	3,954	8,654	12,608

Emigrants for more than one year		
1926–1931		8,018
1935–1945		6,532
Total		14,550

Source: Government of Palestine, *Statistical Abstract*, 1944/45, pp. 36–45.
Notes:
  a. The components below do not add to the total of 32,374 because of slight differences in the years covered by the individual categories.
  b. Minimum capital 1926–1929 = £P500; 1930–1945 = £P1,000.
  c. Category names, 1929–1934: "Moslems," "Christians"; 1935–1945: "Arabs," "Others." "Exempted persons" were mostly British police officers, Palestine government officials, and foreign consular officials.

The reasons for the relatively small number of Arab immigrants to Palestine were similar to the reasons for the stability of the geographical distribution of the population. Neither the Arabs in Palestine,[19] the government, nor the Jews desired large-scale Arab immigration. There was no developing industry in which they could be employed, and as a result they found themselves in competition with local Arabs for nonagricultural jobs. To a certain degree they could replace local Arabs as hired laborers on the land while the latter took temporary jobs in road construction or in the towns. But seasonal, subsistence cultivation could not sustain Arab migrants from neighboring lands, and their attempts to settle in the vicinity of the towns were discouraged by the government. Although workers were imported by the government from Egypt during the Second World War, and others undoubtedly arrived without authorization, such migration took place toward the close of the period and had no consequences for the development of Arab society in earlier years.

Between 1926–1927 and 1942–1944 the life expectancy at birth of Moslem men rose from thirty-seven to forty-nine years, and that of Moslem women from thirty-eight to fifty years. This increase was due in large measure to a reduction of 39 percent in mortality during the first five years of life, from 412 per 1,000 to 251 per 1,000. The rate of natural increase for Moslems rose from an average of 23 per 1,000 in 1922–1925 to 38 per 1,000 in 1945.[20] A similar, though smaller, decline in mortality occurred among Christians. At least a portion of the decline in the mortality rate among the Arabs was attributed by government demographers to "actual progress in health conditions," especially among Moslems (part of the improvement among Jews and Christians was due to the changing age structure of these populations which resulted in a relative decline in the number of infants and children).[21] Despite the general improvement in health conditions which these figures imply, there were large local variations. According to the figures for 1942–1944, the Moslem child mortality rate exceeded 300 per 1,000 births in the towns of Majdal, Gaza, Beersheba, Hebron, and Ramle and in the rural part of the Safad subdistrict, while it was less than 200 per 1,000 in the towns of Tulkarm, Nazareth, and Jerusalem and in the villages of the Haifa and Jaffa subdistricts.[22]

One indication of the persistence of poor health conditions among a portion of the urban Arab population was the proportion of deaths attributed to gastric and respiratory ailments, shown by the two illnesses most frequently reported as the cause of death—diarrhoea and enteritis, and pneumonia. The proportion of deaths in towns due to these two illnesses declined from 38.0 percent in 1935 to 31.8 percent in 1945. Table 5A suggests that this decline was in large measure due to the relative increase in the size of the urban Jewish population; this can be seen by looking separately at three Arab towns—Gaza, Hebron, and Nablus—located relatively far from the major Arab urban centers; at Jaffa, the most Arab of the three main Arab towns; and at Tel Aviv, which was almost entirely Jewish. There was almost no change in the proportion of

TABLE 5

A. Mortality from Diarrhoea, Enteritis, and Pneumonia in Selected Towns, 1935–1945
(percent deaths from these causes, of all deaths)

	Gaza, Hebron, Nablus		Jaffa		Tel Aviv	
	Diarrhoea, Enteritis	Pneumonia	Diarrhoea, Enteritis	Pneumonia	Diarrhoea, Enteritis	Pneumonia
1935	29.8	17.8	20.9	25.0	4.3	15.4
1938	29.7	16.2	21.3	20.4	3.7	13.4
1939	32.4	15.0	19.8	19.7	2.7	12.7
1941	31.3	15.1	17.1	17.7	4.6	12.9

B. Mortality in All Towns from Diarrhoea, Enteritis, and Pneumonia by Religion
(percent deaths from these causes, of all deaths)

	Total		Moslems and "Others"		Christians		Jews	
	Diarrhoea, Enteritis	Pneumonia	Diarrhoea, Enteritis	Pneumonia	Diarrhoea, Enteritis	Pneumonia	Diarrhoea, Enteritis	Pneumonia
1944/45	15.8	16.0	24.5	19.9	11.3	12.7	2.7	12.3

Sources: For 1935–1941: Government of Palestine, *Statistical Abstract*, 1936, 1939, 1940, 1942 (table is "Deaths in Each of the Main Towns," although title and page number vary); for 1944/45: ibid., 1944/45, p. 31.

deaths from these illnesses between 1935 and 1941 in Gaza, Hebron, and Nablus. These towns had much higher rates (about 46 percent) than did Jaffa (46 percent in 1935; 35 percent in 1941). Though the proportion of deaths in Tel Aviv from these two illnesses declined only slightly during these seven years (from 20 to 17 percent), it was much lower than in the Arab towns.

These two most frequent causes of death were particularly dangerous for infants and young children. Table 5B compares the entire Moslem, Christian, and Jewish urban population with respect to the percent of all deaths which were attributed to these two illnesses. There are substantial differences between the two Arab (and non-Arab Christian) groups, as well as between them and the Jews, but the most striking figure in the table refers to the extremely low proportion of deaths among Jews from diarrhoea and enteritis, compared with the two other groups. Part of the difference is undoubtedly due to the different age structures of the populations. The Arabs, having a relatively larger proportion of children, would have been more vulnerable as a group to these illnesses. But the fact that almost one-quarter of the deaths among urban Moslems were due to diarrhoea and enteritis is evidence for the inadequacy of public health measures in the Arab towns.

The government did not publish statistics on cause of death for the rural population, since most of the deaths in the villages were not certified by a medical practitioner.[23] Sanitary conditions in the growing Arab slum areas of the towns were probably poor, but whether they were worse than in the villages is difficult to know. Knowledge of appropriate hygiene was most likely to be disseminated through schools and health clinics, both of which were in short supply in Arab villages. According to the 1931 census, there were (outside the four main towns) 91 Moslem and Christian medical practitioners of all kinds, including dentists and veterinary surgeons, and 509 midwives, druggists, nurses, masseurs, and so forth (of whom 435 were female).[24] Although rural Arabs might, in emergencies, have occasionally used the services of a Jewish doctor attending a nearby settlement, they were for the most part dependent on Arab or government medical personnel, access to whom was neither easy nor frequent. The rise in life expectancy during the Mandate was most likely due to a general improvement in health conditions resulting from the economic development of the country, the draining of malarial swamps, the improvement in diet, and some improvement of public and personal hygiene. All these factors affected villagers to some degree, but probably less than town dwellers.

The most striking aspect of Arab rural society during the Mandate was the persistence of wide variations in the conditions of life. The effects of government policy and of Jewish settlement and land purchases transformed the lives of villagers who were able to take advantage of the new commercial opportunities provided by the growing urban population and the market for agricultural produce which it represented. A part of the surplus rural population which could no longer be easily supported on the land, because it had been displaced by inability to repay debts, by the impossibility of further subdividing an already inadequate family holding, or by Jewish land purchases, sought work in the growing towns. Some found employment in construction of shops and dwellings, or on government projects, while others were forced to eke out a marginal existence in the new shantytowns which they put together out of scrap materials. Public works projects in rural areas gave work to villagers who were thereby enabled to supplement their agricultural income while remaining in the countryside rather than adding to the number of urban poor.

At the same time, rural Arabs who lived in areas of the country that were relatively distant from the towns and their markets, or whose lands were not in regions of high priority for Jewish acquisition, were less likely to be affected by the transformations that characterized the coastal plain. Although Palestine was not a large country, its landscape alternated hills and lowland, and road connections were poorly developed to many of the villages in the more mountainous regions of the Galilee and the range of hills running from Nablus south to Jerusalem and then to Hebron. It is misleading, therefore, to speak of changes in Palestine during the Mandate as if they affected all areas of the country equally, and important to keep in mind that many parts of the country were able only with difficulty to participate in the benefits which British rule provided.[25]

Land

Immigration was one principal component of Jewish settlement policy representing a major threat to Arab interests; land purchase was the second. The amount of arable land in Palestine was always a matter of dispute, for it was one of the variables to which Arabs, Jews, and the government repeatedly referred in the ongoing argument over the "absorptive capacity" of the country. This meant the size of the population that Palestine could support, which was considered directly to affect the possibilities for Jewish immigration. The amount of cultivable land was seen to be even more closely related to the country's ability to support a growing population. As with the argument over absorptive capacity, however, the concept of "cultivability" led to considerable disagreement, and the underlying issue was different from that which appeared on the surface. Jewish experts argued that cultivability should refer to the *potential* fruitfulness of the land once available knowledge and techniques had been brought to bear and investment had been made in improvements such as irrigation, mechanization, and changes in cropping practices, thereby upgrading soil quality. The Arabs and the government tended to define cultivability in terms of the existing techniques used in Arab agriculture. As a result, the estimates of the amount of cultivable land presented by Jewish officials exceeded those arrived at by representatives of the government or the Arabs. Hope Simpson, who was sent by the British government in 1930 to investigate conditions in the country, accepted a government estimate of 8 million dunums (a dunum is 1,000 square meters, or about one-quarter acre) out of the 26 million dunums of total area, while Yosef Weitz, who in 1932 became the head of the Jewish National Fund's Land Development Division, arrived at a figure greater by almost half.[26] By 1944 Jews owned almost 11 percent of the land (excluding the Negev), and about 12 percent of the then cultivable area.[27]

The Arab agricultural economy was based primarily on subsistence grain cultivation, which depended for its success on the timing and quantity of the rainfall. The distribution of landholding was unequal throughout the Mandate. A few landowners possessed holdings thousands of dunums in extent; families growing grain could get by on plots of 100 to 150 dunums, but many had less. Most Arab farmers owned the land they farmed, but a large number were tenants on land belonging to others. The peasant standard of living was low because the uncertainty of the harvest, combined with high rental payments and taxes, often left little if any surplus in the hands of cultivators after their obligations had been met. Most had great difficulty in obtaining funds for investment to improve their holdings and were often dependent on moneylenders for loans at high interest rates to tide them over from one season to the next. Inability to repay these debts frequently meant that peasants lost their land or were forced to sell all or part of their holdings.

Though most peasants eked out a hard living, variation in the amount of landholding among villagers meant that some were better off than others. Especially in the hills, where topography and soil conditions were less well suited to growing grain, many villages devoted much of their land to fruit and olives, which were not as sensitive to fluctuations in rainfall. Hill villages may also have held lands in the plains on which they planted grain as well as utilizing level plateaus for this purpose. Extensive citrus groves were planted in the coastal plain, though these were owned by a relatively small number of families, were usually worked with hired labor, and their fruit was exported. Raising vegetables for the market became more important with the growth of the town population, and villagers who lived near towns could get perishable produce to market despite the difficulties of road transportation.

Although no reliable statistics were ever collected regarding the number of landless Arab cultivators, the government, in response to growing Arab protests regarding the spread of Jewish settlement, concluded that the combination of indebtedness and Jewish land purchases was likely to endanger the stability of the Arab agricultural population. Starting in 1929, it introduced a series of ordinances for the "protection" of cultivators, which restricted the ability of creditors to dispossess debtors and required sellers to retain a certain minimum holding for their own support.[28] These regulations were regularly circumvented in transactions among Arabs, and between Arabs and Jews.

The increased pressure on the land which resulted from rural Arab population growth without a corresponding intensification of production exacerbated the agricultural underemployment endemic to the system of extensive grain cultivation. Government public works projects provided employment in the vicinity of villages; opportunities in the towns, particularly in construction of dwellings for the growing urban population, absorbed additional workers, though the regularity of this employment was affected by fluctuations in the number of Jewish immigrants. Gradually, at the same time as agricultural income was rising, so was the number of rural Arabs whose dependence on farming for their chief subsistence was lessening. These parallel developments reached their peak during the Second World War, when the needs of the British forces stationed in

Palestine provided greatly expanded markets for produce as well as thousands of additional nonagricultural jobs in the army camps.[29]

According to information collected by the government in 1932, the area of Palestine (excluding the Beersheba subdistrict—the Negev—which was mostly desert) totaled 13.6 million dunums, of which 62 percent was being utilized for cultivation, grazing, forests, or as state domain. Of this, 3.1 percent, about one-quarter of a million dunums, was irrigated.[30] In general, a higher proportion of the land was utilized in the southern subdistricts than in the northern ones, since the lands in the south were flatter and better suited to extensive grain cultivation. Land suitable for cultivation was in shorter supply in the northern and interior hill regions, where rocky hillsides with shallow soil cover made farming more difficult. The highest proportion of irrigated land was in the Beisan subdistrict (11.7 percent of cultivable land; 44,000 dunums), the Jaffa subdistrict (11.6 percent; 34,000 dunums) and in the Jerusalem sub-district (7.8 percent; 56,000 dunums, almost all in the Jericho region).

Although the figures on irrigated land for 1931 do not differentiate between Arab and Jewish holdings, much of the irrigated land in the Beisan subdistrict was probably in Jewish settlements, while practically all of that in the Jericho region was in Arab lands. Irrigated land in the Jaffa subdistrict was used for citrus and vegetables; Arab and Jewish citrus holdings were more or less equal. Ten years later, according to Jewish Agency calculations for 1941/42, there were 460,000 dunums of irrigated land in the country, of which 53 percent was owned by Arabs. By 1941 citrus exports from Palestine had seriously declined because of wartime disruption of ocean transport, but more than half the irrigated land was still in citrus plantations. Almost 40 percent of the irrigated Arab land was devoted to green fodder, vegetables, and so on, compared with about one-third of the irrigated Jewish land.[31]

Arab rural society was based in villages which ranged in size from less than one hundred inhabitants to a few thousand. Their landholdings were also quite variable; some villages had less than one thousand dunums, while others had tens of thousands. According to Granott, the modal size of the more than 850 Arab villages in Palestine identified in 1945 was between 700 and 800 persons, on 9,000 to 12,000 dunums.[32] The majority of Arab villagers were cultivators, though the proportion engaging solely in agriculture declined during the Mandate as pressure on the land increased.

Although there were large landowners in the country, most of the villagers cultivated small holdings. The modal holding size in a 1936 survey of 322 villages was five to nine dunums; the average holding size was about forty-five dunums.[33] Such holdings were usually inadequate to support a rural family, and the cultivator's difficulty was increased by the fragmentation of the property. Holdings transferred through inheritance were often divided into noncontiguous parcels as a result of the desire to equalize land quality between heirs. In some villages the land was commonly held and repartitioned among the villagers at intervals (*musha'a*); in other villages the land was permanently divided and privately owned (*mafrouz*). The government sought to establish clear title to land and end the system whereby property was held in common in order to create an incentive for property owners to invest in improvements to their holdings, but it did not devote the same effort to the more important, albeit more difficult, task of consolidating scattered holdings into a smaller number of plots in order to increase agricultural efficiency.

Arab rural population pressure on the land rose steadily during the Mandate, primarily because the increase in the size of the Arab rural population was not accompanied by a similar increase in agricultural productivity, and to a lesser degree because of Jewish land purchases: Arabs who formerly worked those lands were replaced by Jewish cultivators. As I noted above, the towns must have absorbed a certain amount of overflow population from the countryside in order for the urban and rural populations to have grown at about the same rate.

The 1931 census provided the only detailed information on Arab agricultural occupations for the period of the Mandate. There were 182,296 Moslems engaged in occupations as "principals"; that is, they provided the primary or major support of the household. Of these, more than half (53 percent) were "ordinary cultivators."[34] About 5 percent of them received income from the rent of land; 65 percent cultivated lands which they owned or leased as tenants; and 30 percent worked as laborers on land belonging to others. The census found it impossible to distinguish "between cultivating and non-cultivating landowners; and between landlords who only receive rent, that is, who are land owners, and landlords who both pay and receive rent, that is who are tenants from a land owner and who have sublet their tenancies to third parties."[35] Nor did the census distinguish earners who were simultaneously owners, lessors, and lessees—cultivating part of their own lands themselves;

leasing out part of their lands to tenants; and themselves leasing as tenants land owned by others—though the data collected on subsidiary occupations provide some indication of such combinations.

Almost 25 percent of all farmers engaged in ordinary cultivation (Moslems, Christians, Jews, and "others"—the overwhelming majority of them Arabs) indicated that they also engaged in a "subsidiary" occupation for at least three months during the year, one that did not represent their principal means of support. In more than nine cases out of ten, the subsidiary occupation was nonagricultural. The likelihood of engaging in a subsidiary occupation was not equal among the various categories of cultivators: 37 percent of those whose principal income was derived from the rent of agricultural land also had a subsidiary occupation, compared with 30 percent of the ordinary cultivators and 7 percent of the laborers. Few of these subsidiary occupations were what the census defined as "ordinary cultivation" (4.5 percent of the landholders'; 2 percent of the farmers'; and 1 percent of the laborers'), but many were in other branches of agriculture. Members of all three groups earned additional income from citrus, fruit, and vegetable cultivation and from stock breeding. There were landlords who also worked as agricultural laborers, and agricultural laborers leasing land to tenants and receiving rent from them. Ordinary farmers were more likely than landowners or laborers to supplement their income with construction work or by hauling goods and produce using camels and mules.

The overall similarity in occupation among the three main groups of ordinary cultivators conceals, of course, the differences in the income which members of each group could expect. Not all landlords were able to live off the rents they received, but some—the proportion is unknown— could. Moreover, the ordinary cultivators, on the average, could expect to make less money than those who specialized in growing citrus, vegetables, grapes, or other such products. The complexity of the various combinations of subsistence arrangements on which particular households depended should not blind us to the fact that most Arab farmers received their principal income from cultivating a limited number of crops and supplemented this income, when necessary, with hired work for others.

Developments in immigration, landholding patterns, and nonagricultural employment should also be seen against the backdrop of government economic and social policy. The primary interest of the Palestine government, reflecting the policies of the British exchequer, was to meet current expenses (as well as recovering costs incurred during the military administration, retire Palestine's portion of the Ottoman Public Debt, and repay the French company that had built the Jaffa-Jerusalem railway) from current revenues and avoid adding to the burden imposed on the British taxpayer. As a result, "human capital" investments, such as in education or in health services, were kept to a minimum, nor did government actively encourage and underwrite agricultural development. The lack of government public welfare activities affected the Arab population in particular. Jewish settlers, through the Zionist organizations and fund transfers from abroad, had created a network of health, educational, technical, and social services which served most of the Jewish population. Arabs, and especially rural Arabs, expected the government to provide such services and were sorely disappointed at its failure adequately to do so.[36]

Peasant Society

Research on Arab Palestine is almost exclusively based on the materials and perspectives collected and developed during the Mandate by government, Jewish, and Arab participants in the political conflict over the future of the country.[37] Although the interests of the three parties differed greatly, they were agreed on the need to transform the conditions of Arab agriculture. All emphasized, in varying degree, the importance of introducing modern agricultural techniques. Some Arab writers expressed their concern over the possible effects of agricultural modernization on the structure of the Arab village community and were suspicious of agricultural innovation because of the possibility that it would make easier the extension of Jewish landholding, and most recognized that changes had to be introduced gradually.[38] But there was general consensus that the government's main efforts should be devoted to agricultural development, despite sharp disagreement between Arabs and Jews with regard to what the focus of this development should be. Thus, most current research on Arab Palestine has taken over the categories that were set by the political argument during the Mandate and has viewed the condition of Arab agriculture almost exclusively in terms of "development."

The focus on the agricultural economy of the Arab village, which has characterized much research on the social structure of Arab Palestine, has the effect of isolating the economic aspects of rural life from their social and cultural context. By making local economic issues primary and neglecting their relationships with broader political and social developments, most researchers have assumed, implicitly or explicitly, that the appropriate way to look at rural Arab society in Palestine during the Mandate was in the terms set by the political argument, in which the central issue was that of economic progress.

An approach that separates the analysis of economic and noneconomic aspects of rural Arab society in Palestine has a number of shortcomings. First, it deals with the economy out of its social and cultural context, and thereby loses the opportunity to understand the meanings of activity, presumably "economic," which appears to be "irrational" in economic terms and is, as a result, dismissed as evidence of backwardness. Second, by neglecting the political and social context it assumes that the economic transformations seen as necessary to raise the peasant's standard of living can be instituted successfully without changes in other areas of the society. Third, in the case of rural Arab Palestine, the categories of analysis were not developed primarily for the understanding of the villagers' social and economic situation, but as part of the conflict over control of the land. They reflect the particular interests of the parties—primarily the Zionist organizations, but also the Palestine government—who had most influence in setting the terms of the discussion.

A more useful approach to the analysis of rural Arab society in Palestine is to view it as a "peasant society" and develop the implications of such a view. Although writers have often referred to the Arab cultivators as "peasants," they have used the term in a familiar, descriptive rather than a technical sense.[39] In retrospect, this is not surprising. During the interwar period "peasant" was seldom used, except by Marxist writers, as a term with a specific meaning stemming from the villager's place in the system of production. Most of the analysis of Arab agriculture in Mandatory Palestine was undertaken by persons affiliated with the Palestine government or with the Jewish Agency, and neither of these bodies was particularly disposed to view agricultural relations in the country in class terms. The farthest they usually went in this direction was to identify what seemed the two main participants in the rural Arab agricultural economy—the "effendi" and the "fellah."[40] Only those associated with a left-wing, socialist, or communist perspective in the *Yishuv*'s spectrum of political orientations presented a more-or-less systematic class analysis of Arab agriculture.[41] Their influence was not great, partly because they tended toward formulations which envisaged the creation of a socialist society in Palestine in which community identification would give way to class solidarity, but more importantly because they were not the ones preparing the official positions of the *Yishuv*.

Nor have contemporary researchers applied the concepts relevant to analysis of peasantry in their work on Arab Palestine, primarily because there has been relatively little work on its social and economic structure. Writers such as Ya'akov Firestone, Sarah Graham-Brown, and Ylana N. Miller have given us detailed descriptions of specific aspects of rural Arab society, but have not concerned themselves specifically with presenting a general view of the Arab peasants.[42] Henry Rosenfeld has perhaps come closest to doing so; though his work has focused on analyzing the situation of Arab society in Israel, he has consistently drawn connections with its situation prior to 1948.[43]

Most rural Palestinian Arabs were not simply country dwellers; they were, as peasants, involved in a complex set of agricultural production relationships which affected the conditions of their existence. In the "ideal" form of peasant society the family is the basic unit of social organization.[44] The family provides all or most of the labor for the farm, and the farm provides all or most of the family's consumption needs and the means for the payment of its duties to the holder of political and economic power. Economic action is closely interwoven with family relations, and the motive of profit maximization in money terms seldom appears explicitly. Land husbandry is the main means of livelihood. A specific traditional culture exists, related to the way of life of small communities. The peasantry is an "underdog," dominated by outsiders, and politically subjugated. "Peasants . . . are rural cultivators whose surpluses are transferred to a dominant group of rulers that uses the surpluses both to underwrite its own standard of living and to distribute the remainder to groups in society that do not farm but must be fed for their specific goods and services in turn."[45] Peasants, moreover, are "essentially powerless in large areas of life, because the basic decisions affecting villagers are made by members of other classes. . . . Economically, peasants are dependent on forces that operate well beyond their local boundaries; only rarely, and under special circumstances, are prices for their products set by village factors. . . . peasants obey; they do not command. They wait to be told, but they do not make major decisions themselves. They are at the end of the lines of communication and authority that radiate from cities."[46]

Peasants, because they are subject not only to the vicissitudes of nature but also to the exactions of landowners and political rulers, operate by what James C. Scott has characterized as a "safety-first" principle, rather than in accordance with the "profit maximization calculus of traditional neoclassical economics." The peasant cultivator "seeks to avoid the failure that will ruin him rather than attempting a big, but risky, killing," and adherence to this principle is what lies behind

> "a great many of the technical social, and moral arrangements of a precapitalist agrarian order. The use of more than one seed variety, the European traditional farming on scattered strips . . . are classical techniques for avoiding undue risks often at the cost of a reduction in average return. Within the village context, a wide array of social arrangements typically operated to assure a minimum income to inhabitants. The existence of communal land that was periodically redistributed, in part on the basis of need, or the commons in European villages functioned in this way. In addition, social pressures within the precapitalist village had a certain redistributive effect: rich peasants were expected to be charitable, to sponsor more lavish celebrations, to help out temporarily indigent kin and neighbors, to give generously to local shrines and temples.

Additional features include a preference for crops that could be eaten over those which must be sold, and for varieties with stable, if modest, yields. Although Scott's fieldwork was done in Burma, and most of his examples are drawn from southeast Asian societies, characteristics of the Palestinian agricultural economy which drew frequent criticism were very similar to many of those which Scott listed: failure to maintain seed quality; fragmentation of holdings; periodic redistribution of land; nonproductive expenditures on ceremonies such as weddings.[47]

Any particular peasant society will diverge to some degree from this ideal type. Moreover, the condition of the peasantry in a particular country is not static; it changes in response to transformations in the economic and social structure of the society of which it forms a subordinate part. The situation of the Arab peasants of Palestine has been frequently described, and general agreement exists regarding the conditions under which they lived at the beginning of the Mandate, though there is less agreement regarding the nature and causes of the changes that occurred in rural Arab society between 1920 and 1948. It is unnecessary here to do more than outline the principal characteristics of peasant society in Palestine during that period.[48]

Palestine at the beginning of the Mandate was a predominantly agricultural country which had undergone a slow but steady development in the previous seventy-five years. During the nineteenth century, villages in the coastal plain which had been abandoned because the government had been unable to protect them from the exactions and depredation of nomadic tribes were gradually resettled, and new villages were established as security improved and a growing population brought additional land under cultivation. There appears to have been no shortage of arable land in Palestine prior to the First World War, and the principal impediment to agricultural progress was the dependence of the peasants on extensive grain cultivation which was extremely vulnerable to variations in the amount and timing of the winter rains. Although exact statistics are unavailable, most peasant households, though perhaps not a great majority, probably owned their own land, especially in the northern and interior hill districts. Even in such circumstances, Palestine was a net exporter of wheat, the principal food grain, indicating that peasants were able to produce a surplus, though the rent and tax obligations, combined with the uncertain harvests, often forced them into debt.[49] Almost all agricultural production was carried out by households on individual holdings, whether owned by the cultivator or cropped on shares. Those with holdings too large to be cultivated by the members of the family could hire agricultural workers with whom they worked together, or rent part of their land to others who may or may not have owned land of their own. Only in the coastal citrus plantations, which were slowly growing in extent, was cultivation based primarily on hired labor.

Nonagricultural production was represented by rural household industry; by enterprises whose raw materials came from agriculture, such as the preparation of olive oil and the manufacture of soap; and by the weaving of cloth which was sold locally as well as exported. Commercial connections between Palestine and Europe were long-standing, maintained by merchants located in major port cities; they received the produce of the interior for shipment abroad and imported basic commodities that Palestine did not produce, such as sugar, tea, coffee, and, toward the end of the century, kerosene. Also imported were manufac-

tured goods; the more expensive products were bought by wealthy urbanites, while the cheaper, mass-produced household goods gradually
spread into the countryside.

Since the peasants produced their own food, and when blessed with
decent harvests retained sufficient produce for their needs during the
coming year, they were not much affected by price fluctuations in foreign
commodity markets. When harvests were bad and peasants could not
meet their tax and rental obligations after putting aside the grain necessary for their subsistence, they were forced to borrow against next year's
crop, at usurious rates, giving their land as security for payment. If the
loan could not be repaid fully it might be extended, but a series of poor
crop yields could result in the loss of the family's holding. In such cases
the peasant was usually not forced off the land, but remained as a tenant
of the new owner.

Ottoman control was weak over the hilly regions of Palestine, where
most of the land was held by those who cultivated it. Road transportation
was poor, and much of the agricultural produce grown there, such as
fruit, was marketed locally. Peasant surplus, both in the hills and in the
plains, was extracted by tax collectors. Up until the mid–nineteenth
century, taxes had been farmed, but subsequently tax-collection was
reorganized and put in the hands of government officials. Taxes were
paid in kind, and usually represented one-tenth of the crop's value;
produce not easily transported was redeemed in money. The cumbersome-
ness and inconvenience of collecting large quantities of grain gradually
led, as elsewhere, to a demand for payment in cash rather than in kind.
Again, as elsewhere, such a demand made peasants more dependent on
those who had access to cash, such as moneylenders and merchants.
While local notables may have been quite powerful in their areas, they
themselves did not necessarily act as links in an economic chain whose
effect was to divest peasant producers of their surplus for the benefit of
more remote markets.

By the end of the Ottoman period, therefore, the Arab peasants,
though living poorly, burdened by debt and continually threatened by the
possibility of losing their land, were not in immediate danger of being
forced out of agriculture or of losing the means of their subsistence. Their
reduced condition was not due to a transformation of agricultural production that made many of them superfluous; indeed, they were indispensable to the continuation of the agricultural economy of the country. So

long as they were tied by debt to the land and had no escape save by trying to bind themselves to another landowner, Arab tenant farmers provided the means for the landowners to maintain their own position. So long as local agricultural technology did not adopt innovations common in less backward countries, owner-cultivators could not easily improve their position. The relative slowness of industrial development provided no alternative to poor peasants who might seek such work in order to escape from their rural poverty. Since there was little interest in the development of large-scale, capitalist agricultural production, except in the citrus groves, there was no threat that a reorganization of Arab peasant agriculture would lead to dramatic changes in the rural economy.

It is difficult to imagine the course of agricultural development in Palestine had not the establishment of the Mandate and the impetus it gave to Jewish settlement transformed the the country's history. Although there were large tracts in absentee ownership, it is not clear to what degree these were inhabited or cultivated. The transformation of Arab agriculture would have had to come about through a combination of debt relief; improvement of agricultural technology; concentration of scattered holdings; the development of export crops; and the growth of urban commerce and manufacturing to absorb the expected surplus rural population. All these changes, however, would have been dependent on the nature of the political regime to be established in the country, and in particular on the question of whose interest it represented. Since an independent Arab Palestine was not established the question is moot, though it might be possible to examine the course of development in neighboring countries whose agricultural regimes were similar in order to infer some possible outcomes.

What is clear, of course, is that the combination of British administration, Jewish settlement, and absence of Arab political power created conditions that made the situation of the Palestinian peasants different from that of other peasant communities, in the region or elsewhere. Although British indecision regarding the future of the country, strengthened by opposing pressures from Jewish and Arab interests, held back the implementation of the policies needed to free peasants from their distress, the lack of a more aggressive policy had some favorable consequences. In particular, it helped delay breakdown of the structure of rural Arab society by keeping the peasants tied to their villages rather than creating opportunities for their migration to urban areas. Such migration, of course, occurred anyway, but to a lesser extent than would have been true had jobs in towns been more widely available, or had market pressures on rural land been greater. Nor were capitalist enterprises in need of large numbers of workers; expansion of citrus cultivation had reached a limit by the end of the 1930s, and Jewish industry had room for few Arabs. The government was able to maintain its policy because there were no major forces undermining the logic on which it was based. In particular, peasants were not being forced off the land in large numbers, and while the basic conditions of Arab agriculture did not greatly improve, neither did they substantially deteriorate.

An important difference between Palestine and other non-European peasant societies which came under the political control of a European power is that the Mandate did not last very long, and there was little time for the effects of any transformation of rural society to become visible. Government opposition to any radical change in agrarian relations, together with the absence of private investment which could have drawn large numbers of peasants from the land, characterized the entire period between 1922 and 1939. The political stalemate over the future of the country contributed to the absence of change in the basic conditions of development.

It was not until the transformation of Palestine into a military staging area in World War II that extensive employment opportunities became available for villagers. One major effect of the wartime economy, however, was to strengthen the economic position of the village: surplus workers found new sources of income; agricultural production greatly expanded to meet the needs of the soldiers stationed in the country; money came into the villages from the workers in the army camps and from the proceeds of the sale of produce at inflationary prices. Thus, although during the years 1940–1945 more villagers than ever before were employed in nonagricultural work outside of their localities, no permanent structure of urban employment and residence was created, and when most of the British forces left the country after the war ended the villagers returned to their homes. In part, this was due to the country's small size, which permitted villagers earning wages in towns and army camps to maintain close ties to their homes; they and their families had less need to leave the village and to move nearer their place of employment. Had postwar developments been different, the effects of wartime economic changes on rural social structure would probably have been great. However, the intensification of the conflict among Arabs, Jews, and British, which led in 1948 to the destruction of Arab society as it had hitherto existed in Palestine, eliminated any possibility of such changes coming about.

Village Social Structure

The social structure of Palestine's Arab villages was inseparable from their economic regime, and the changes in village economy which occurred during the Mandate were reflected in changes that affected important aspects of village social life, in particular family, clan, and political structure and authority. Two problems arise, however, in attempting to describe these changes. First, as I have already noted, the Mandate was short-lived, and the radical reconstitution of Arab society in Palestine after 1948 meant that the processes which had begun to operate between the wars were interrupted and transformed because of the post-1948 conditions. Second, there is an almost complete absence of research on Arab village society during the Mandate, and most descriptions of that society have been, as a result, brief and general.[50]

It is possible, however, partially to substitute later analyses of Arab village society for the material that is lacking. During the 1950s and the 1960s a number of ethnographic studies were made of villages in Palestine, Lebanon, Jordan, and Israel, and their authors included information on the villages' recent past from which a more detailed picture of village social structure can be gained. In the discussion which follows I depend in particular on Henry Rosenfeld's work dealing with Arab society in Israel, because it has the great advantage of combining description with an analytic framework which both permits inferences to be made regarding the structure of village society during the Mandate, and provides a basis for speculation regarding the effects on village life of the changes in the rural economy that occurred during the Mandate.[51]

The description of the structure of Arab village life as it existed during the Mandate should not be taken as representing a social order that had maintained its "traditional" character through the declining decades of the Ottoman period and started to change only after the beginning of Zionist settlement at the end of the nineteenth century and the imposition of British sovereignty after World War I. As I will indicate in my discussion of works dealing with nineteenth-century Palestine, changes were then occurring which affected the economy of the villages, and these must also have altered social relations within them. In other words, the following portrait of village society refers to a system that was slowly changing during at least half a century prior to the start of the Mandate.

Arab village society was organized according to patrilineal, patrilocal lineage groupings (*hamula* or clan) whose members, in principle, traced their descent from a common ancestor. Larger villages would generally have more clans, in part because as village population increased lineage groupings would divide. Lineage solidarity was achieved through marriage patterns, preferably (though by no means exclusively) a cross-cousin match between first cousins who were children of brothers. Such matches were desirable from the point of view of lineage members for two reasons. First, they had the potential for strengthening the lineage's power in the village, since children born to the new couple would align themselves on reaching maturity with the lineage of the husband, and would be lost to that of the wife if it were different. The second reason also was related to the lineage's importance, expressed in terms of the amount of land its members owned. Land was the sole form of property that most villagers possessed. All else being equal, the larger the lineage, the more numerous its holdings, and the wealthier and more powerful it was. Such a lineage could more easily assist, through the provision of employment, for example, members who were less well off, and thereby contribute to the maintenance of its solidarity and its strength.

The household economy was based on the extended family. The family's land was owned by the father, who worked it together with his sons. When the sons married, they brought their wives to the father's house and continued working on the family holding. Sons inherited equally upon their father's death or retirement; daughters inherited only in the absence of sons. Cross-cousin marriage helped insure that land remained within the lineage.

Marriage was the basic element of village social structure, for in addition to affecting the inheritance of property and the future size of the lineage, it created links between families that involved them in sets of mutual obligations which were reflected, for example, in village politics. Desirable marriages created or strengthened bonds between families; conversely, two families who disagreed about the marriage of their children might become estranged, with subsequent effects on internal village political alignments. In principle, potential spouses did not choose one another, but had their marriages arranged. Thus families and lineage members endeavored, by means of the match, to strengthen clan solidarity.

A man who married paid a bride-price which, among Moslems more frequently than among Christians, was appropriated by the bride's father. Normally, the money for the bride-price was provided by the father of the groom, since the latter had neither land nor alternative sources of income which would allow him to raise the necessary amount. The groom's dependence on his father for the bride-price was the tangible expression of dependence on him for the choice of a wife. The desire to keep the resources represented by the bride-price within the clan, rather than lose them to another clan, contributed to the preference for intraclan marriages.

Arab village structure, therefore, reflected the outcome of relationships among families and among clans that were expressed in the exchange of women as the basic mechanism for the creation and maintenance of lineage solidarity. The fact that the only property which existed took the form of land controlled by the household head, who used income from it to pay the bride-price for his son's wife, meant that an unbreakable connection existed between kinship, property, political alignments, and authority, all of which rested on the existing village-based agricultural subsistence economy. Developments affecting any of these elements would have a major effect on the entire structure. The gradual involvement of Palestine in economic relations with European countries during the nineteenth century led to changes in village economy and social structure, though in the absence of the special conditions created by the Mandate these would probably have occurred less rapidly. But the combination of Arab population growth, government land policies, and Jewish settlement worked to undermine the stability of rural Arab society.

The increase of the rural Arab population was not accompanied by an extension in the amount of cultivated land, nor by improvements in agricultural organization or technology which would have permitted the peasant to obtain a higher yield or a greater profit from the same amount of land. Therefore, the pressure of population on the land increased, and the ability of the household to provide for its children, and especially its sons, diminished. At the same time, some of the land was being permanently removed from Arab cultivation by Jewish purchases. Two consequences were evident to all observers: a decline in the size of the average holding, and a rise in the number of rural households who were in fact or in effect landless. As a result, agricultural underemployment became more serious, larger numbers of men sought work in towns, at least seasonally, and the government had to provide public works jobs in the countryside to those who could make a living neither from the land nor from nonagricultural employment in the countryside or in the towns.

There were similarities between this situation and that which Rosenfeld describes for Arabs in Israel after 1948. What characterized both cases were insufficiency of land and the availability of alternative nonagricultural employment. In Israel after 1948 this combination led to a decrease in the dependence of sons on their fathers for the needed bride-price and a consequent reduction in the power of the lineage. But the situation after 1948 differed in an important respect from that prevailing during the Mandate. Though the distribution of property among villagers changed in the interwar years, rural Arab society remained overwhelmingly agricultural prior to 1948. Therefore, the economic basis for lineage solidarity continued to exist, even though many of the villagers were no longer themselves primarily agriculturalists. The agricultural economy of rural Arab society after 1948 was greatly weakened by large-scale expropriation of Arab village lands by the Israeli government, the result being that most rural Arabs found employment in nonagricultural occupations outside of their villages. Sons thus had independent sources of income; even though they may have delivered most of their earnings to their father, they were less dependent on him for the bride-price than they had been previously. Fathers, in turn, were less able to determine who their children should marry. The extent and rapidity of these changes, of course, should not be overestimated; they occurred slowly, but their cumulative effect was to transform the basis of village authority.

Little is known about the consequences for maintenance of lineage authority of increasing differentiation in property ownership during the Mandate. Rosenfeld's work would lead us to expect that it would become more difficult to maintain lineage authority over households whose principal income came from extravillage employment. If so, increased reliance by a segment of the village population on nonagricultural work would lead to internal divisions between them and those dependent on cultivation. On the other hand, Rosenfeld has argued that after 1948 ties among villagers were important mechanisms assisting the transition from rural to urban employment; men seeking work outside the village would obtain jobs with the help of relatives or of fellow villagers who were already established there. This would be a way in which lineage authority might be perpetuated and adapted to the changing economic structure. A similar process would probably have occurred during the Mandate.

Paradoxically, lineage influence remained strong in Arab villages in Israel, despite economic changes. Rosenfeld argues that this persistence had a dual source: the bride-price and the relation between the village and the state. The depressed position of village women allowed the continuation of the bride-price, which made the son dependent on the father's help to marry and hence bound him to the lineage. The Israeli government, through its support of particular lineage leaders and factions, set them up as intermediaries between villagers and government offices capable of granting benefits. The government supported the continuation of lineage authority, since it believed that it was a more conservative force than the alternative which would likely be nationalist and harder to control. The Mandatory government was not confronted with either of these issues, since its policy was to interfere as little as possible with local village life, nor did it have a similar interest in the continued subjugation of the Arab population.

Conclusion

Arab Palestine at the beginning of the Mandate was in large measure a peasant society whose members supported themselves through subsistence agriculture. During the generation of British rule the size of the Arab population more than doubled, leading to increased pressure on the land. Arab agricultural productivity did not increase commensurately, and increasing numbers of cultivators found themselves unable to make a living from their holdings. Some of them found a solution in temporary or permanent migration to urban areas; others were helped to support themselves by government public works projects in the countryside. Growing political controversy between Arabs and Jews during the first two decades was suppressed with the outbreak of the Second World War, which also relieved the pressures on the land by providing greatly expanded employment opportunities for the surplus rural population. This was only a temporary solution, however; with the end of the war the problems of rural Arab society began to reemerge. They were never resolved; instead, the 1948 Arab-Israeli war ended the development of Arab Palestine as it had existed during the Mandate.

In this introductory discussion I have reviewed some of the major aspects of Arab rural society in Palestine. Jewish settlement, as such, had only marginal effects on the basic structure of that society. It neither greatly contributed to nor substantially alleviated the major problems of the Arab agricultural economy—population growth, productivity, and agrarian property relations. The principal effect of Jewish settlement on Arab agricultural development, as I show in the following chapters, lay in complicating the context in which such development was to occur; other effects, whatever they might have been, were secondary in importance. The granting to Great Britain of the Mandate over Palestine made Arab rural development dependent on British policy; the way in which the British government interpreted its "dual obligation" under the Mandate prevented such development. In this sense, Jewish settlement was clearly an impediment to Arab progress, though the Jews can hardly be said to have been at fault.

The development of Arab agriculture during the Mandate took place in the political, economic, and social context set by the British administration, Jewish settlement, and Arab population growth. In the following chapters I examine the changes that occurred in the Arab agricultural situation by focusing on three aspects: how these changes were analyzed, by contemporaries and by more recent writers; the land regime, in particular the interaction between the structure of agrarian relations at the start of the Mandate, the growth of the Arab population, and Jewish land purchases; and Arab agricultural production, paying special attention to the effects on techniques and yields of government policies and Jewish settlement. Throughout, I compare the claims made by the participants in the conflict with the evidence bearing on them.

Arab Progress and Jewish Settlement: Contemporary Analyses

Introduction

IN ORDER TO examine the consequences of Jewish settlement in Palestine for Arab development, it is necessary to look at the changes that occurred in the social and economic structure of Arab society during the period of the Mandate; to evaluate the claims of the Jews, the Arabs, and the government in the light of evidence regarding the changes which occurred during the period; and to draw conclusions both about the changes and about the claims made with respect to them. A notable component of the political conflict over Palestine following the First World War was the utilization of social and economic analyses of the situation of the Palestinian Arabs by the parties to the conflict—Jews, government, and the Arabs themselves. The Jews devoted a great deal of time and effort to collecting statistics about the various aspects of the economy of Palestine, including that of the Arab population, as part of their efforts to convince the government and the British Colonial Office to undertake policies more favorable to Jewish settlement and development. The statistical apparatus of the Palestine government became increasingly comprehensive during the Mandate and was supplemented by the findings of the principal commissions of inquiry on Palestine established by the British government. While the Arabs undertook no comparable fact-gathering operations, they advanced their own analyses of the development of their society.

Current views of Mandatory Palestine are based in large measure on the material collected by the parties to the conflict in the years between the two world wars and depend heavily on their interpretation and analysis, primarily that of the Palestine government and the Jewish Agency.

Thus, in addition to accepting the vocabulary of the time, later writers have also tended to accept the conclusions drawn by Jewish and by government observers.[1] But the interpretations and the conclusions of contemporaries who occupied particular roles in the political struggle were very likely to have been affected by their positions, even if their data gathering was, as in most cases it seems to have been, as free from intentional bias as was possible under the circumstances then existing. An examination of the consequences for Arab development of Jewish settlement must take into account the claims made about these consequences as well as the facts and reexamine both claims and facts in order to arrive at a better understanding of the period.

In the following discussion, I deal separately with government, Jewish, and Arab analyses of the condition of Palestinian Arab agriculture. My description of the government view is based on the basic public documents prepared by Palestine government officials and the commissions of inquiry that examined conditions in the country during the Mandate. In describing the Jewish view, I identify a number of themes which run through the analysis by Jewish Agency economists and others of what they saw as the principal characteristics of the Arab agricultural economy. The Arab view is presented primarily with reference to the responses the Arabs made to the arguments and claims of the government and the Jews.

The justification for the differences in my approach to the views of the major parties to the conflict lies in the fact that, although each was continually aware of, and responded to, the claims of the others, their primary concerns were different, and this in turn affected the way in which they viewed Palestinian agriculture. The government, which bore responsibility for the inhabitants of the country, was concerned to demonstrate the effects of its policies, and the investigatory commissions that visited Palestine were similarly concerned to evaluate the government's actions. Each commission was conscious of operating in the context of the findings of its predecessor. A chronological analysis of their views reflects the development of the dual concern with the conditions of the peasants, on the one hand, and the likelihood that the government would be able to fulfill its obligations under the Mandate, on the other.

The principal concern of the Jews was colonization and the building of their national home. As their numbers grew and the economy of Palestine developed, the social and economic context of their settlement activities changed. Their analyses attempted to take into consideration these changes, but certain basic themes continued to occupy them throughout the period. The Arabs, who never developed a political organization which enabled them successfully to oppose Jewish immigration and land purchases, were continually on the defensive in their discussions of Arab agriculture. They attempted to change the terms in which the discussion of the Arab cultivators was being carried on, which were, in their view, biased in favor of what we might today call the "modernizing mission" of the Jewish colonists, and their analyses were primarily responses to the claims of the Jews.

Government Analyses of Arab Agriculture

Review of the Agricultural Situation, 1922

In 1922 J. Sawer, the director of agriculture in Palestine, reviewed the agricultural situation as it existed when the British occupied the country and described the steps his department had taken since its establishment to improve agricultural conditions. He noted the main impediments to agricultural development, and his analysis was echoed in the series of later evaluations of Arab agriculture in Palestine produced under the auspices of the Mandatory government or of the Colonial Office. Not even the extent of land in Palestine was known for a certainty at that time. While the total area north of 31 degrees north latitude (a line running about seventeen miles south of Beersheba, approximating the line below which rainfall was very uncertain) was estimated at 18.2 million dunums, available records regarding the classification of land in the different regions of the country covered only 15.1 million dunums. Of the classified lands, 7 million dunums were described as having "been written off as uncultivable."[2] After referring to the various undertakings already in preliminary stages of operation for the regeneration of such land—such as experimentation regarding the southern limit of dry cultivation, reforestation, reclamation of swampy areas—Sawer noted that "it may therefore reasonably be hoped the ratio of unproductive land to that capable of returning an economic rent, may be considerably and permanently reduced as a combined result of several distinct lines of action" (p. 2).

In addition to "uncultivable" land, some 3 million dunums of arable land were at least temporarily uncultivated, because "a sparse population living in economic isolation and employing very primitive methods, naturally adopts a farming system based on bare fallowing. Land is cropped without manure until exhausted and then abandoned until a measure of fertility has been recovered" (p. 2). However, changes already underway were creating the conditions for improving the agricultural situation: "Increasing pressure of population, an upward trend in the values of agricultural holdings and produce, the partition of common lands, improved communications and the practical demonstrations of better methods by new settlers are . . . having their effect. Manuring and rotation of crops for the maintenance of fertility, are becoming recognized practices, and based on a system of mixed farming, should solve the problem of closer settlement and financial stability" (p. 2).

Nevertheless, "temporary" obstacles existed to this "natural development," principally "the direct and indirect results of credit, prohibitive prices for all equipment, political and social unrest" (p. 2). Throughout his report Sawer referred to innovations required in order for local agriculture to progress. These included agricultural education, the establishment of experimental farms and demonstration plots; the development of irrigation works; the introduction of modern agricultural machinery in grain cultivation—plowing, harvesting, and threshing—as well as in the processing of agricultural products; and the founding of cooperative organizations of cultivators for production, distribution, and financing. The introduction of such innovations was hindered by the lack of capital and by a shortage of labor. Government funding for the expansion of agricultural extension work was limited; credit for the purchase of machinery was unavailable; the extension of cultivation or the introduction of new, more profitable crops was impossible because of the lack of cultivators in sufficient number to undertake the additional work which would be required.

The absence of agricultural machinery was accompanied by a "serious shortage" of working animals, and those available were incapable of attaining their full potential because of poor nutrition. Even had they been better fed, however, they could usually only keep under cultivation half the 300 dunum potential of "a span of cattle, if well fed and drawing modern implements." "The Palestinian cultivator," Sawer concluded,

is both untrained and unequipped for the production of other than the few simple crops which at present engage his attention. It is consequently a cause of regret that while our Jewish settlements benefit from expert advice and technical instruction in all their undertakings, a vast majority of the rural community remains unguided and untaught, save for the efforts of a single junior member of the departmental staff in each district. That progress lags in the absence of a comprehensive system of technical education is not a matter for surprise, but an inevitable and logical result." (p. 5)

Sawer's report was written only two years after the assignment to Great Britain of the Mandate for Palestine by the San Remo Conference and the subsequent replacement of the military occupation government by a civil administration. It may have been too much to expect substantial progress to have occurred in such a brief period. He did not treat Arab and Jewish agriculture separately, although he recognized the differences between them and more than once referred to the latter as a potential model for the former. He also noted that "economic pressure, in the form of both internal and external competition, is exerting an influence, which can hardly fail in the end to compel mutual effort and assistance. The era of isolation and purely local markets must pass with improvements in communications and commercial intelligence" (p. 7).

Sawer's analysis was based on the experience accumulated by British personnel dealing with the agricultural situation in Palestine following its capture in 1917 and 1918. In subsequent years the Department of Agriculture issued annual reports on the state of Palestinian agriculture based on information gathered in the course of regular departmental activities. The reports, while comprehensive, did not include broader analyses of the agricultural situation in the country. These were to be found, on the British side, in the series of reports issued by special commissions established between 1922 and 1946 to consider the "problem" of Palestine. My discussion of the government analyses of Arab agriculture in Palestine will be based on those reports which have become the basis for all work on the country during the Mandatory period: *Report of the Commission on the Palestine Disturbances of August, 1929* (the Shaw Commission); the Johnson-Crosbie *Report on the Economic Condition of Agriculturalists in Palestine and the Fiscal Measures of Government in Relation Thereto* (1930); the *Report on Immigration, Land Settlement and Development* prepared by Sir John Hope Simpson in 1930; C. F. Strickland's *Report on . . . Agricultural Cooperation in Pales-*

tine (1930); Lewis French's reports on *Agricultural Development and Land Settlement* (1931); the *Palestine Royal Commission Report* (1937) (the Peel Commission); the *Palestine Partition Commission Report* (1938); and the *Survey of Palestine* prepared for the visit of the Anglo-American Committee of Inquiry in 1946.

Although I am treating the reports of the various commissions as representing the government view, it should be clear that the commission members sometimes disagreed among themselves, officials in various government departments held differing views, and there was no necessary unanimity between the conclusions drawn by investigatory commissions whose stay in Palestine was only temporary and those who were entrusted with the ongoing responsibility for carrying out policy in the country itself. Nor did the views of Colonial Office officials in London always coincide with those held by colonial administrators in Palestine. Nevertheless, the reports reflected the "official" British analysis of the condition of Arab agriculture and were extremely influential in determining the way in which it would be viewed.

The Shaw Commission, 1929

In the wake of the riots of August 1929, a commission of inquiry was established to examine their causes. While most of the witnesses examined testified to the specific circumstances and course of the riots, opinions were also heard regarding the social and economic developments which were said by Arab spokesmen to have created conditions favorable to the outbreak. The commission devoted most of its report to the specific events of the riots, but it also prepared a brief analysis of the situation of Arab cultivators.[3] The main concern of the commission in this section of its report was the danger that Jewish land purchases would create a substantial class of landless Arabs. In its view, the landless comprised two groups: those who were themselves displaced by Jewish purchases; and the descendents of the existing Arab population who would be unable to find a place in agriculture because of the increased pressure on the land caused by a combination of reduced area available for settlement and a larger Arab population in need of it. The commission saw no alternative to the continued settlement of this population on the land: "The British Administration has brought improved sanitary conditions and with them a lower death rate. The net excess of births over deaths may be expected within the next thirty years to increase the population of the country by some 300,000 people of whom, in the absence of staple industries, most must look to the land to provide them with a living" (p. 123). The commission viewed as inadequate the ordinances introduced by the Palestine administration for the protection of cultivators, believing that they failed to prevent the dispossession of Arab peasants. Its members attached no blame to the Jews for the dispossessions, since the latter acted "with the knowledge of the Government," and even paid compensation to tenants without being required to do so by law (p. 118).

The commission summarized its analysis of Palestinian agricultural prospects: For the country to support a substantially larger agricultural population, agricultural methods would have to change radically and intensive cultivation would have to become widespread; the rate of introduction of such cultivation would have to take into account local and foreign markets for the produce; credit would have to be made available to permit the cultivators to develop their property; the introduction of intensive cultivation should not be permitted to displace existing peasants unless alternative land was found for them; and that "even with improved methods and intensive cultivation, the Government of Palestine, in deciding the rate at which newcomers are to be admitted to agriculture, should have regard to the certain natural increase of the present rural population" (p. 123). Concluding that future dispossessions would inevitably swell the landless population because no land was available for the resettlement of those forced to leave their holdings, the commission urged the government to undertake "further protection of the position of the present cultivators and some restriction on the alienation of land" (p. 124).

The Johnson-Crosbie Report, 1930

In the two years following the 1929 riots, four major government reports were published containing much information on the condition of Arab agriculture in Palestine. The first of these presented the results of a survey of 104 Arab villages which had been carried out under the direction of two senior officials of the Palestine government, W. J. Johnson and R.E.H. Crosbie. They provided an estimate of the income and expenditures of the villagers included in the survey and proposed a series of short- and long-term fiscal measures designed to ease the burden of the Arab cultivators. Johnson and Crosbie's principal recommen-

dations included the replacement of the tithe and *werko* (a tax on land
and buildings) by a low annual land tax; the institution of a progressive
income tax; reduction in the commuted tithes payable by agriculturalists
in order to provide temporary relief; immediate issuing of short-term
agricultural loans; and restricting the importation of wheat, flour, unre-
fined olive oil, and sesame seed in order to maintain the prices of local
produce.[4]

But the authors did not restrict themselves to a narrow analysis of the
financial position of the cultivators. Noting the lack of available
cultivable land, the investments required to make additional land
cultivable, the uncertainty whether the resulting agriculture would be
profitable enough to justify these investments, and the fact that most
peasant cultivation was aimed at the needs of the household rather than
oriented toward the market, Johnson and Crosbie stressed more fundamental tasks to be carried out if Arab agriculture was to be improved:

> The principal difficulty here, as in most other countries, is the general
> lack of organisation of cultivation and of marketing, and the reluctance
> of credit institutions to finance agriculturalists. There is a great need
> for the training of cultivators in simple and economical methods of
> cultivation. . . . The rural population, which forms the bulk of the in-
> digenous population, could not easily be industrialized even if there
> were industries to absorb it. (p. 41)

Believing that the "foremost need of the agricultural industry is ra-
tionalisation" (p. 41) they also recommended the establishment of village
cooperatives to deal with credit, purchasing, and marketing, and called
for the partitioning of *musha'a* land (pp. 44–46, 56, 58).[5]

The survey found that the average holding included 56 dunums,
providing an annual net return of £P11 (Palestine pounds). The minimum maintenance cost of an average peasant family was estimated at
£P26, and the average burden of family debt of £P27, with annual
interest charges amounting to an additional £P8. The authors concluded
that the minimum holding required by owner-cultivators was 75 dunums,
and by tenants 130 dunums (since a portion of the tenant's crop went to
the landlord). In the villages studied there was practically no difference
between the average size of holdings cultivated by tenants and those
cultivated by their owners (pp. 20–22).[6]

The Hope Simpson Report, 1930

The Johnson-Crosbie report was completed in time to be utilized by Sir John Hope Simpson in his survey of immigration, land settlement, and development, though his concerns were much broader than the financial situation of Arab cultivators. His analysis attributed to government inaction much of the responsibility for the continued underdevelopment of Arab agriculture, mentioning in particular the structure of rural taxation; the lack of widespread agricultural extension, experimental, and demonstration activities; the inadequate growth of elementary education and agricultural education in the villages; the insufficient development of water resources and irrigation; the failure to encourage the creation of cooperative societies; and the absence of adequate credit facilities (pp. 60–91 passim).

Unlike previous analyses, which limited themselves to describing the policies governing Jewish settlement and accepting the claims of the benefits accruing to the Arabs as a result, Hope Simpson took issue with the principle of permanent inalienability of land owned by the Zionist settlement organizations and with the prohibition imposed on the employment of Arabs on that land. "It is impossible," he wrote, "to view with equanimity the extension of an enclave in Palestine from which all Arabs are excluded" (p. 56). He distinguished between the older colonies of the Jewish Colonization Association (ICA, later PICA) whose settlers employed Arabs, and the newer ones established by the Zionist organizations which did not. His objections to these policies were not rooted in an analysis of their economic effects, but focused rather on their political implications. In addition to representing, in his view, a violation of article 6 of the Mandate (which dealt with the facilitation of close settlement by Jews while not prejudicing the rights of the Arabs), he felt the exclusionary policies were damaging relations between Jews and Arabs in the country (pp. 50–56).

Hope Simpson believed that the Arab peasants had the capacity to improve their condition, if they were provided with the necessary assistance: "The fellah is neither lazy nor unintelligent. He is a competent and capable agriculturalist, and there is little doubt that were he to be given the chance of learning better methods, and the capital, which is a necessary preliminary to their employment, he would rapidly improve his position" (p. 66).

In holding this belief he was similar to other administration officials and British commission members who investigated agricultural conditions in Palestine. He was also similar to them in another way: like most of the others, Hope Simpson stressed the necessity of insuring that the cultivator remained on the land and retained land in his possession. Thus, the ordinances introduced by the Palestine administration for the protection of cultivators were, in Hope Simpson's view, inadequate, and he recommended the introduction of "an effective provision for occupancy right in favour of the tenant," to be accompanied by the establishment of a register of tenants that would provide the basis for the implementation of such a right (pp. 37–38).

Hope Simpson's most important conclusion was that, with the exception of reserves held by Jewish land-purchasing organizations, no additional land existed in Palestine for Jewish settlement so long as Arab cultivation techniques were not improved (p. 141). This conclusion was based on estimates of the total amount of cultivable land in Palestine, the size of the rural Arab population, and the amount of land needed to support a family of Arab cultivators. These estimates were immediately challenged by the Jewish Agency; nor were they accepted by the subsequent Royal Commission inquiry in 1936.[7] Hope Simpson emphasized the need to improve techniques of peasant cultivation and to undertake the consolidation of peasant holdings in order to free land for further Jewish settlement (p. 143).

Strickland's Report on Cooperative Institutions

While Hope Simpson was examining the agricultural situation in general, C. F. Strickland, an official in the Indian Civil Service, toured Palestine in the course of an investigation whose purpose was to recommend how cooperation could best be introduced into Palestinian agriculture. Strickland differentiated between the Jewish and the Arab agricultural economies, and he believed that government efforts should be aimed primarily at encouraging cooperation among Arab peasant cultivators, leaving the Jews to continue the independent development of their own institutions. Perhaps because of the nature of his subject, Strickland attributed greater importance than did the authors of the other reports to the "character" of the Arab peasant and the difficulties this placed in the way of developing successful cooperative societies.[8] Nevertheless, he recognized that the "backwardness" of peasant agriculture was due not only to "instability of character," but resulted also from "a lack of opportunity as well as lack of security in the past . . . and to the load of debt which hampers all [the peasant's] operations" (p. 3).

Strickland's report noted the same deficiencies in Arab agriculture that had become commonplaces of the British analyses, though he also pointed to aspects which had not been previously mentioned. Thus, for example, in discussing the need to consolidate fragmented peasant holdings, he noted that government efforts to regularize title to village lands, known as "land settlement," tended to prefer villages where the land had already been permanently divided among the peasants, whether through formal *ifruz* (division of the village lands into holdings no longer redistributed among the villagers) or informal arrangements which had the same effect. Strickland believed that it was easier to convince peasants in *musha'a* villages, whose lands were periodically redistributed among the shareholders, to accept three large blocks of land than to have to reallocate the holdings in individual possession of villagers where *ifruz* had already been carried out. He hinted that the priorities of the land settlement officers were the reverse of those he advocated, since progress in settlement was demonstrated more rapidly by concentrating on those villages which had already reached agreement on the division of the lands, leaving to the settlement officer little more than the task of registering the holdings. Thus, in Strickland's view, a relatively easy opportunity to consolidate holdings was lost, and was unlikely to return (pp. 43–44). In another example, Strickland referred to the policy, which was strongly urged by Jewish spokesmen, of encouraging peasants to sell a portion of their irrigable land in order to obtain capital to develop the remainder. Though supporting it, he pointed out that such a policy might be difficult to realize: "(1) an arrangement for irrigation cannot often be made for single individuals; (2) a redistribution of holdings will be necessary if water is not to be wasted; and (3) the amount of debt, required to clear the old creditors and also pay for development, will be such as to overburden some of the borrowers" (pp. 39–40).

Strickland's main concern, of course, was to recommend ways of freeing the peasants from the recurrent need to undertake short-term obligations at usurious rates of interest, and to propose a method whereby the long-term debts could be cleared as well. Village credit societies were to provide alternative sources of short-term credit to the cultivators, while long-term credit was to be provided by a government

loan fund. Strickland proposed a radical solution to the problem of the
peasants' long-term debts: cessation of payments to creditors, forcing the
latter to seek a remedy in the civil courts, which he believed would
probably "fix installments and in any case [bring] down the interest to a
lower rate" (p. 9). The implementation of such a proposal would have
required agitation among the villagers to convince them to undertake
such a course, as well as at least tacit support of the government.
Strickland called his remedy "heroic" (p. 9), indicating perhaps that he
did not believe it could be put into effect.

The French Report, 1931

Lewis French arrived in Palestine in August 1931 to take up his
duties as director of development. Formerly with the Indian Civil Service, he was appointed to the position created as a result of Hope
Simpson's recommendations. French's first task was to report to the
colonial secretary concerning the number of landless Arabs and the costs
of their resettlement; the extent of lands which could be made available
for Jewish settlement; the situation of the Arab peasants in the hill
districts; the provision of agricultural credits for both Arab and Jewish
cultivators; and the reclamation of uncultivated lands. His principal
conclusions were that no uncultivated lands of any extent existed which
could be made available for Jewish settlement: state lands which might
have been included in that category were all occupied or allocated, and
French's own inquiries revealed only about 15,000 dunums of privately
owned dry-farming lands possibly suitable for purchase.[9] If "surplus"
lands were redefined as those which were at the time under extensive
cultivation but which could by the introduction of irrigation and new
crops be made to support a much larger farming population, such lands
would have to be purchased or expropriated in order to make them
available for intensive settlement. French implied that were such steps to
be undertaken, the beneficiary should be the growing Arab population,
which was finding it increasingly difficult to obtain sufficient land for its
needs, rather than the Jews (p. 60).

French favored a plan whereby the government would develop tracts
of land and make them available for settlement by Arabs, who would
repay the development costs over a period of years. He believed that the
government should retain control over such land, and over its water
resources. In this way the dispossession of the cultivators could be

prevented, and their lands would be "inalienable" along the model provided by the settlement activities of the Jewish National Fund (JNF) (p. 18). French believed that security of tenure was the principal requirement for the amelioration of the condition of the peasantry in the hill districts, for it alone would have permitted the development of the holdings and the intensification of cultivation. He suggested two policy changes which he expected would result in immediate benefits—granting permission for the cultivation of land which had previously been uncultivated (*mewat*), and the distribution by government of fruit trees (p. 90). He proposed that legislation be enacted to insure that the peasant retained a minimum holding and that sale of Arab lands to Jews be restricted (pp. 20, 101ff).

Though advocating intensification of cultivation of Arab lands, French believed that financial, legal, social, and cultural difficulties stood in the way: "The transitional period [from the extensive to intensive cultivation] is not an easy one for the tenant. He is called on to change entirely his traditional methods of extensive farming for the restrictions of intensive cultivation; and at the same time, while waiting for his small grove to reach maturity, to seek his livelihood by casual labour on other lands or some other kind of manual labour, eked out by the produce of a vegetable patch which has been reserved from his young orchard" (p. 61). Moreover, even the acquisition of land for resettlement by purchasing it from existing owners "is a task of the greatest difficulty," for such land must satisfy a number of conditions: it should "be of cultural value; . . . yield a good title; . . . be purchasable at a reasonable price; . . . be within reasonable distance of drinking water; . . . be so situate as to be reasonably congenial to the new settlers; . . . be clear of tenants, or be capable of being so cleared satisfactorily; already proved to be under contract" (p. 62).

For French, intensive cultivation meant the growing of oranges or, at the most, grapefruit and bananas (p. 65). While he noted the danger of the expansion of citrus cultivation, both from the point of view of finding overseas markets for the produce and the risks of crop failures due to plant pests, he concluded that the citrus industry would be Palestine's principal source of revenue for the forseeable future. It is interesting that he seemed to give little importance to the intensive cultivation of vegetables, particularly in the districts where the major towns were located; when the Jews spoke of the intensification of Arab agriculture in the cereal-growing areas they frequently had vegetable cultivation in mind. French could not, however, have forseen the great increase in the size of Haifa, Tel Aviv, Jaffa, and Jerusalem during the 1930s, nor the expansion of the produce market during the Second World War.

Although French referred more than once to displacement of Arab cultivators as a result of *Arab* (as opposed to Jewish) land purchases (pp. 19–21, 63), he did not provide a detailed analysis of its extent or the circumstances under which it occurred. He believed that purchases in the hill districts by the "Arab *effendi* or capitalist landlord" led to as many dispossessions as resulted from Jewish land acquisitions (p. 19). In later years many Arab cultivators submitted claims against Arab landlords under the Protection of Cultivators Ordinance, but such displacements always remained an issue secondary to the effects of Jewish land purchase.

The Palestine Royal Commission Report, 1937

The Palestine Royal Commission (the Peel Commission) was appointed in 1936 as a result of the Arab rebellion which began in April of that year. It was charged with "ascertaining the underlying causes of the disturbances," investigating the operation of the Mandate and determining whether the Jews or the Arabs held legitimate grievances regarding its conduct, and recommending steps to remove such grievances (p. vi). The commission concluded that the contradictory obligations required by the Mandate toward Arabs and toward Jews rendered it unworkable and recommended partition of Palestine between the two national groups. The longest section of the report was devoted to the question of land; the background to its consideration of that issue was set out in the review of Palestine's development since 1920. The Royal Commission briefly restated the main drawbacks of Arab peasant agriculture at the beginning of the British Civil Administration:

> The outstanding characteristic of the peasant class was its poverty. For this there were several reasons—the poorness of the soil, especially in the stony hills where most of the villages were situated, and the lack of water; the heavy load of debt which robbed them of most of their earnings and deprived them of the capital required for the better irrigation of their land or the improvement of its crops; the lack of knowledge of intensive methods of cultivation; the cramping effect of the antiquated land-system and the general insecurity of tenure; the lim-

ited markets for country produce and the badness of the means of access to towns. (p. 44)

It constrasted that situation with developments during the five years preceding its arrival in Palestine:

> The economic position of the Arabs as a whole continued to improve. Wages rose, markets for country produce expanded, more roads and bridges and schools were built. And in due course the new measures determined on in 1930 for safeguarding and advancing Arab interests came into operation [establishment of a Department of Development; the landless Arab inquiry; enactment of new Protection of Cultivators Ordinances; encouragement of Arab cooperative societies; introduction of a self-government ordinance for municipalities]. (p. 80)

Nevertheless, the condition of the majority of Arab cultivators remained perilous, despite the general advance of the Arab population. In 1936,

> the standard of living among the *fellaheen* is still low. . . . they have suffered from the world-wide fall in prices [and] from severe and re-peated droughts and consequent bad harvests. Some of the obstacles to their progress have been partially removed. Some of the cramping *mash'a* [*musha'a*] system of land-tenure has been replaced by individ-ual ownership. Their burden of debt has been eased. The Government has done much to relieve them by reducing and remitting taxation and providing loans. Tithe was reduced, commuted, and finally replaced by a more equitable tax on rural property. [Cooperation is slowly develop-ing, and] . . . there is evidence . . . that some *fellaheen* are at any rate on the way to becoming better cultivators. If the great majority are still wedded to their old primitive ways, there are some who are learning better methods, using better seed and better tools, under official guid-ance and inspection. (p. 127)

The commissioners were able to conclude that "despite the disproportion between their numbers and the amount of cultivable land they occupy, the *fellaheen* are on the whole better off than they were in 1920," this progress having been due in no small measure to the services provided by the Palestine government to the country as a whole and to the rural Arab population in particular (p. 128).

The commission supported a policy of prohibiting sales to Jews of Arab

lands in the hill districts, where congestion was greatest, and of control-
ling such sales elsewhere. As did its predecessors, it recommended the
consolidation of small, scattered parcels into larger holdings through the
establishment of large-scale projects, thereby permitting intensification of
cultivation and irrigation (p. 226). The choice of focus for its comprehensive review of developments in Palestine during the Mandate may have
been influenced by its conclusions regarding the workability of the Mandate itself, for in its recommendation for partition it left untouched the
basic problems of the Arab cultivators, those remaining in the territory to
be assigned to the Jews as well as those included in the area intended for
the Arabs. The commission addressed in only a limited way the issue of
agricultural development in the context of partition. It recommended that
a study be made of the feasibility of finding sufficient land which, after
development, would provide room for the resettlement of some 225,000
Arabs who the commissioners believed would have to be moved from
territory assigned to the Jews. It did not deal with the conditions of their
resettlement, such as the nature of their tenure on the new lands, but only
recommended that the plan should remain under British control and direction until its conclusion (pp. 390–92).

The Palestine Partition Commission, 1938

The recommendation of the Peel Commission that most of the country
be partitioned into Arab and Jewish states, with the remainder assigned
to the control of a Mandatory power, was accepted by the British government, and another commission was established to recommend boundaries for the new political entities, as well as to consider the economic
and financial consequences of partition. While the report of the Palestine
Partition Commission, which was published in October 1938, devoted
most of its attention to the question of boundaries, it also addressed the
issue of the viability of the two proposed states, and was not optimistic
regarding their prospects. Consequently, it recommended that the new
entities should be linked in a customs union whose fiscal policies would
be determined by the government designated by the League of Nations to
take over the position of Mandatory in the areas of Palestine scheduled to
remain under such supervision.[10]

The pessimism of the Partition Commission was greatest regarding
the prospects of the future Arab state, and its reasons reflected contemporary British views of the condition of Arab Palestine. Because of the high

rate of Arab population growth, "the economic position of that population will be menaced in the future unless one or other of the following developments should take place: an increase in the standard of cultivation, enabling a larger population to be maintained on the land; an increase in industrial activity, providing opportunities for secondary employment; a limitation of the size of the family; or migration" (p. 242). The commissioners did not believe that any of the first three developments was likely, and thus migration to seek work in the Mandated territories adjoining the Arab state would provide the only relief of population pressure on the land, since Arab labor migration to the Jewish state would presumably be forbidden by its government. The amount of employment available in the Mandated territories would depend "first upon the amount of capital introduced by Jewish immigrants into those territories, and secondly, upon the fluctuations between prosperity and depression brought about by Jewish immigration policy in general" (p. 243). In other words, the Partition Commission envisaged that the economic stability of the Arab state would be at least in part dependent on the ability of its growing surplus labor force to find employment as migrants on enterprises established by Jewish capital in a territory where discrimination in employment on the basis of "race" would be prohibited.

These expectations on the part of the commission were based on its views of the condition of Arabs in Palestine. While the average standard of living of the "whole community" was higher than it had been before the war, and there was as yet "no pressure on the means of subsistence" as indicated by the declining death rate, still "it seems certain that the amount of land now under cultivation, by the present methods and on present standards, is insufficient to support the same percentage of the total Arab population to-day as in 1922" (p. 28). The commission's computations indicated that the average holding of an Arab peasant family was far below the admittedly rough estimate of the "lot viable"— the minimum amount of land necessary for its support. As a result, Arabs were already dependent on supplementary employment for their subsistence; the demands for such employment would increase because of the growing population even in the absence of further Jewish land purchases; and since the bulk of the capital needed to provide such employment would be supplied by Jews, the future of the Palestinian Arab population was tied to the continuation of Jewish immigration and capital import (pp. 29–30).

The series of commissions, committees, and investigations which considered, among other issues, the condition of Arab cultivators, thus gradually arrived at the conclusion that, whatever advantages had been gained from the activities of the Palestine government, and whatever benefits had accrued from Jewish settlement, the future prospects of Arab peasants were extremely uncertain. While all investigations noted an improvement in their standard of living, it was not seen as having been due primarily to agricultural development, but to the supplementary income earned by peasants or members of their families in what were referred to as "subsidiary" occupations.

It could be argued that if, as the Arabs claimed, Jewish settlement was responsible for the depressed condition of the Arab peasants, it was not for the reasons usually adduced—the displacement of rural Arabs because of Jewish land purchases. A better case could be made for the claim that the Arabs were prevented from finding their own solutions to their agricultural problems by virtue of the British commitment to the policy of the Jewish national home, which prevented it from granting sovereignty to Palestine while not itself undertaking policies of agricultural reform. It is, of course, impossible to determine whether the government of an independent Arab Palestine, untroubled by Zionist aspirations backed by a major European power, would have been able to bring about the needed transformation in land policy and agricultural development.

The Survey of Palestine, 1945

The Palestine government prepared, at the end of 1945, a comprehensive survey of conditions in the country for the use of the Anglo-American Committee of Inquiry which had been established to recommend a solution to the dispute regarding the future of Palestine. Unlike previous reports, the material prepared by the government was intended to describe the background and current situation of the country's inhabitants, rather than attempt to answer specific questions. The *Survey of Palestine* based that portion of its analysis which dealt with land tenure and agriculture (chapter 9) almost entirely on published government sources, primarily the regularly published statistics prepared by the relevant departments. The paucity of detailed knowledge regarding the conditions of Arab cultivators which had hampered the commissions established during the 1930s had not been much remedied by 1945, as the material made available to the Committee of Inquiry clearly indicated. The major new source of information was the "Survey of Social and Economic Conditions in Arab Villages, 1944," conducted in five villages in the Ramle subdistrict. Some of the results of that inquiry were presented to the committee.

The data on land tenure and agriculture presented a mixed picture. On the one hand, there was no evidence of any fundamental change in the conditions of Arab cultivators insofar as the security of their tenure on the land was concerned. On the other hand, the *Survey* noted changes in agricultural production as Arab cultivators responsed to the opportunities offered by the local market because of the wartime conditions. They were, however, concentrated in certain sectors of the agricultural economy. For example, the authors of the *Survey*, and others, noted the great increase in Arab vegetable growing, as well as the increased use of tractors and deep plowing (pp. 313, 325). Yet progress in animal husbandry, particularly dairying, had been more limited, nor had there been much increase in the planting of fodder crops for animal feed and for improvement of the land (pp. 311, 314, 332).

The most important change in the conditions of Arab peasant agriculture noted by the *Survey* was the reduction of debt. Rising agricultural prices during the war enabled many cultivators to reduce or repay entirely their debts to moneylenders, or to replace them with bank loans (pp. 364ff). The authors of the *Survey* based their conclusions on interviews with bankers, district officials, and members of Arab cooperative societies in 88 villages. The results of their investigations were not, however, unambiguous. Jewish and Arab bankers disagreed on the extent of peasant indebtedness to moneylenders and merchants; reported indebtedness varied considerably among the districts; and almost one-fifth of the members of cooperative societies in the Arab villages studied were current holders of usurious loans. Since only 135 Arab villages, at the most, had cooperative credit societies in November 1945 (p. 362), and since cultivators in *musha'a* villages had difficulty obtaining bank loans because of the joint-tenure system (p. 354), it is likely that the degree to which peasants continued to resort to moneylenders was greater than the 18 percent estimate obtained in the villages selected.

The *Survey* listed the principal activities undertaken by the government to improve agricultural productivity since the establishment of the Mandate (pp. 342ff). Only the first one mentioned, the survey and settlement of title, affected the relations of the cultivators to the land and to each other. The others all had to do with technical assistance, afforestation, and agricultural education. Between 1919 and 1945 the government loaned to cultivators almost £P1,764,000; prior to 1940 the loans were in large measure a response to hardship resulting from crop failures, while during the Second World War they were offered in order to increase food production. One-third of the total amount was loaned between 1919 and 1923; almost half was loaned between 1940 and 1945, two-thirds of it going to Jewish farmers (one-third of the total) (pp. 349, 353, 354). The government-supported Agricultural Mortgage Bank, which commenced operations in 1935, had by 1938 loaned £P425,000, mostly to citrus growers; Arabs and Jews obtained approximately equal proportions of the total funds (p. 351). It does not appear that agricultural credits provided by the government could have helped the Arab peasants to do more than hang on in bad years, and it is by no means clear how many were able to benefit even from that limited assistance.

Jewish Analyses of Arab Agriculture

Arab agriculture was a major concern of the leadership of the Jewish Agency, because the possibilities of Jewish settlement quickly became linked with, and were often made dependent upon, the situation of the Arab cultivators. The two basic Jewish settlement goals—land purchase and immigration—rapidly became identified by Arab spokesmen, and often by government officials as well, as the major threats to the agricultural economy of the Palestinian peasant. The Jews vehemently denied that their colonization was injuring the rural Arab population and argued their case in detailed memoranda which were usually prepared for submission to government, or which were responses to public statements of government policy and to reports of official investigating commissions. The Jewish analysis had much in common with that prepared by the Palestine government, especially regarding the basic causes of the "backwardness" of the peasant economy, but it differed radically in its view of the desirable future organization of Palestinian cultivation. The Jewish analysis had various components, and consensus did not always exist among those who developed and presented the arguments. If this was true within the Jewish Agency, it was even more true with respect to the divisions in the Jewish community in Palestine as a whole. But a number of major themes can be identified in the "official" Jewish analysis of

Arab agriculture which run throughout the entire Mandatory period. These formed the basis for later historical analyses of Arab agriculture in Palestine between the two world wars.

The "Dual Economy"

The Jewish analysis of the economy of Palestine began with a distinction between the Jewish and the Arab "sectors" as a fundamental reality. This distinction was basic to almost every analysis of social and economic conditions in the country. In the early stages of Zionist settlement the emphasis was placed on the difference between the Jewish settlers and the Arab population in terms of their background, their motivation, and their potential for transforming Palestine into a progressive, European society. As Jewish settlement grew and became increasingly diversified, the emphasis shifted to comparisons of the "backward" condition of the Arabs with the achievements of the Jews. Indices of development were presented to demonstrate the great disparity between the Jewish and Arab economies; these included indices of health and mortality; occupational distribution; agricultural productivity; educational attainment; relative contribution to the revenue of the country; as well as others. A 1938 survey by David Horowitz and Rita Hinden argued that "the usual economic problems of capitalism—trade fluctuations, finance, inflation and deflation, balance of payments—are almost completely absent from the Arab economic organisation, which is centered—up to 60–65%—on more or less self-sufficient agriculture."[11] They seemed to equate the economy of Palestine with that of the Jewish sector: "We are here dealing mainly with the Jewish sector, which has already developed as a modern capitalist economy. The Arab economic sector is still in the transition stage towards modern capitalism, and the trends peculiar to its circumstances will be discussed in a separate chapter."[12]

A number of factors contributed to the Jewish view of the dual nature of the Palestine economy. The differences between the Jewish immigrants and the Arab population were undeniable. The ability of the former to mobilize capital and modern methods of technology and of organization, especially after the establishment of the Mandate provided a more favorable field for Jewish activity than had existed under Ottoman rule, led the organized Jewish community in Palestine on a path of development that increasingly differentiated it from most of the Arab population.

A second reason for the development of the conception of a dual economy was the overwhelming importance to Jewish analysts of developments in the Jewish community, rather than in Palestine as a whole. Although Jewish organizations usually collected and presented data on the entire country, this was often done in order to demonstrate the contribution that the Jews were making to its development, or to compare the Jews with the Arabs. The collection of data about the Arab population was directed by the specific political relevance of the information, such as the number of landless Arabs, the area of cultivable land, relative contributions of each community to government revenue, and so forth. The collection of information about the Jewish community covered a much wider range of topics. For many purposes of Jewish analysis, the condition of the Arabs was irrelevant.

A third reason had to do with Jewish policy regarding economic integration with the Arab sector. For a number of reasons, such integration was actively—and often bitterly—opposed by the Zionist organization in Palestine. In practice, therefore, the interrelations between the Jewish and the Arab sectors were not emphasized, and separate analysis of the two sectors was consistent with the policy of economic exclusiveness.

Nevertheless, Jewish Agency economists recognized that substantial links connected the Jewish and Arab sectors. Alfred Bonné, who directed the Jewish Agency's Economic Research Institute, took issue in 1936 with the view that Palestine had to be considered as having two separate economic systems:

> Despite certain indications pointing in the opposite direction, this country has one common system of economy. Naturally like in every other country, there are very considerable differences in the degree of economic development between the various districts and sections of the population. . . . these differences are no more and no less than those to be found in other countries between the quiet and backward economic activities of poor and remote provinces and the intensive activities of centrally-located districts. . . . There are Jewish places and settlement areas as well which were hardly touched by the wave of prosperity; some even show a retrograde trend of development. . . . Post-war conditions in Palestine . . . have tended to favour the coastal zone, more particularly the two harbour cities and their vicinity with the inevitable concomitant of considerable differences in the economic development of the various parts of the country. It cannot be too

strongly emphasized, however, that this favourable development was by no means limited to the Jewish sectors; thanks to its dynamic force this wave drew the Arab sectors into its orbit as well. This alone would serve to show that the Arab economy is part of the general economy of the country, and benefits more particularly by any boom produced by Jewish effort.[13]

Bonné listed the principal economic relationships in the agricultural sector between Jews and Arabs: Jewish markets for Arab produce; emulation of Jewish farming methods; Jewish land reclamation projects which also had a beneficial influence on Arab land in the vicinity; capital provided by Jewish land purchases; the consequent reduction of peasant indebtedness.[14] The items on this list were often adduced as evidence of the benefits that Jewish colonization brought to the Arabs; Bonné was using them as evidence for the existence of a single agricultural economy in which Jews and Arabs played different parts.

An example of the difficulty of separating analytically the two sectors is provided by Horowitz's 1945 work on the effects of Jewish colonization on Arab development. He argued that for these effects to be traced the Palestinian economy had to be separated into two parts, although the differentiation he proposed was already implicit in his initial formulation of the problem. Nevertheless, according to Horowitz, the two sectors were in contact at various points: the market; emulation of technological and organizational innovation; and revenue transfer mediated by government taxation policies.[15]

Despite Jewish efforts to promote economic exclusiveness, the nature of the interrelationship between the Jewish and Arab sectors changed as time passed, affected by temporary setbacks in the connections between them such as that caused by the Arab revolt between 1936 and 1938. Jews were concerned about possible competition from Arabs—in marketing of produce, or in gaining employment in Jewish citrus groves and on government construction projects, for example—and in their attempts to reduce such competition they pressed for increased separation of the two sectors. But a 1945 analysis by L. Samuel of agricultural production and marketing suggested that direct competition was being replaced by sectoral differentiation, especially after 1936. Production and marketing were carried out almost exclusively within the two national communities, with the exception of Jewish Jerusalem, which because of local settlement patterns remained heavily dependent on Arab produce. However, the intensive mixed farming which was almost completely Jewish was gradually becoming a major consumer of surpluses from extensive Arab agriculture in Palestine and in neighboring countries, particularly cattle feed and fodder, surplus organic manure, and cattle for breeding and crossing purposes:

> This relation between intensive and extensive farming reveals the com-plementary character of both forms of agriculture from the point of view of production, whereas consumption by the Jewish urban population of food, produced on extensive farms, provides an important outlet for extensive agriculture with respect to meat and poultry, eggs, vegetables and fruit. . . . Already for an extended period [the competition for mar-kets] has gradually been replaced by division of markets seasonally, territorially and with regard to products.[16]

Samuel recommended the development in a planned manner of this replacement of competition by market differentiation, but the formula-tion of future policy became increasingly difficult as the growing anticipa-tion of the expected termination of the Mandate took precedence over other concerns. Nevertheless, his analysis suggests that one possible line of development might have been increasing market differentiation, as Arab agriculture met needs that the Jews could not economically fill, because of their higher production costs.

The Effect of Jewish Colonization on the Arab Population

The Jews devoted much effort to demonstrating the beneficial effects which they believed Jewish colonizing activities were having on the Arab population. Evidence was presented comparing the current condition of the local population with its situation prior to the First World War and with Arab populations in neighboring countries. The main points which the Jews repeatedly stressed, as I have already noted, included improve-ment of health conditions; provision of capital (by means of land pur-chases) to Arab cultivators enabling them to reduce their debts and intensify their cultivation; setting an example of innovative agricultural techniques; providing tax revenues to government which were subse-quently used for expanding services to the Arab population; and provid-ing Arab producers, particularly farmers, with a growing urban market of new consumers.

While the Jews hoped that the Arabs would themselves realize the benefits they could expect from Jewish settlement, and that this realization would temper their opposition to Zionist colonization, they addressed most of their arguments to government officials, in Palestine and in England. Since the decisions on policy toward Jewish immigration and land purchases were made not by Arabs but by British officials, the Zionist arguments combined demonstrations of the successes of Jewish colonizing and the effects of Jewish settlement—on the country as a whole and on the Arab population in particular—with severe criticism of what they believed was the failure of British policy to carry out the intention of the Mandate. In particular, the Jews denied that the Palestine administration was doing all it could to, in the words of article 6, "facilitate Jewish immigration . . . [and] . . . encourage . . . close settlement by Jews on the land."[17]

The Jewish arguments dealt in detail with the effects of colonization on Arab agriculture. The claim that Jewish land purchases were dispossessing large number of Arab cultivators focused most of the debate on rural Palestine. The Jews specifically addressed this claim, in addition to their more general analysis of the advantages their immigration brought to the Arab population. They denied that Jewish colonization was responsible for the depressed condition of Arab agriculture. They pointed to the relations between the peasants and the regime during Ottoman rule as the principal cause of the impoverishment of the rural population, noting specifically the burden of debt which the small cultivator found almost impossible to avoid. They denied that Jewish land purchases had led to a worsening of the condition of those who formerly farmed those lands and stressed their policy of compensating tenants who were forced to leave lands sold by their owners. They also argued that in the evaluation of overall benefits it was necessary to view Palestine as a whole; thus, Jewish activities that led to overall improvement in the condition of the country were to be seen as counterbalancing cases in which individual Arabs suffered.[18]

Much of the argument about the effects of Jewish settlement focused on the amount of land available for Jewish colonies. This argument was complicated by the lack of any accepted estimate of the extent of "cultivable" land in Palestine, nor was there agreement on how "cultivable" land was to be defined. The working definition adopted by the government referred to "land which is actually under cultivation or which can be brought under cultivation by the application of labour and

the financial resources of the average Palestinian cultivator."[19] The
Jews rejected this definition, primarily because it defined the "average
cultivator" as the average *Arab* cultivator and thus unnecessarily restricted the amount of land that could be brought within the definition
because of the limited financial capabilities of the typical Palestinian
peasant. In the Jewish view this definition was in essence a definition
of *cultivated* land, since Arabs had brought into cultivation almost all
the land that could be farmed using techniques in common employ.
Most damaging, from the Jewish point of view, was that the definition
omitted areas "which through the application of modern agronomical
progress [were] on the way towards becoming cultivable," and made no
allowance for "technological progress, education, skills, markets and
capital."[20] The Jews also criticized the methods used by government
agricultural experts to arrive at the estimates of the amount of cultivable land even under the definition to which they objected, arguing
that they led to underestimation of the actual area.

The determination of the extent of cultivable land was important to
the case regarding the effects on the Arab population of Jewish settlement, since the larger the estimate, the more land was available for both
Jews and Arabs. The Jews, however, did not give equal weight to present
Arab land needs and those of future Arab generations.[21] In its memorandum to Hope Simpson the Jewish Agency argued that "in no country in
the world is land for the development of which capital is available
deliberately left idle or uncultivated with the object of providing for
future generations. Every new generation must make the improvements
which are necessary for its needs."[22] A. Granovsky (Granott), the managing director of the JNF, believed that the Jewish land-purchase program
should be based on the anticipated needs of future immigrants and not
content itself with current needs.[23] But he also argued that "it would
hardly be possible to set aside land reserves for future generations [of
Arabs]. No state in the world is able to adopt measures for assuring the
economic status of posterity."[24] Maurice Hexter, a member of the Jewish
Agency executive, tended to agree with him:

> It is a most difficult point. In the Hope Simpson era we were all op-
> posed to [taking into account the land needs of future Arab cultivators]
> on the ground that it was impossible to hold rural areas in reserve for
> coming generations. On the whole I am still inclined to that view.

Furthermore, it has the difficulty that it is an unlimited quantity; the future is infinite in time, the area of land is fixed in space, and the future demands of an increased rural Arab population unknown."[25]

There was also opposition to providing land to existing Arabs, such as agricultural laborers (*harrathin*), who had not previously been landholders. "If the Government were out to provide every inhabitant of every village in Palestine with land," noted the Jewish Agency in response to the report by Lewis French, "the problem would become insoluble—quite apart from any Jewish settlement policy. Besides, the working of larger farm units would become impossible unless a rural labourers' class were 'recreated.' "[26]

The issue of the amount of cultivable land was related to the question of the "lot viable," which was defined by the government as "a holding sufficient for the subsistence of a farmer and his family, [enabling him] . . . to maintain a decent standard of living."[27] The Jews claimed that there was no shortage of land in Palestine, on condition that cultivation be carried out in a rational and a progressive manner, which was not the same as the method of cultivation then current among the majority of Arab peasants.[28] The concept of the lot viable was used to estimate the number of farming households that could be supported on a given area, usually by dividing the estimate of the amount of cultivable land by the area of the lot viable. Official estimates were often based on a lot viable which assumed extensive cereal cultivation, such as the figure of 130 dunums used by Hope Simpson.[29] The resulting number of households which, according to the calculations, the land could support was lower than it would have been had separate estimates been made of the carrying capacity of lands of varying quality and suitability for the main crops grown in Palestine. Estimates of the lot viable in various regions of the country were presented to the 1936 Royal Commission; they ranged from 10 dunums of citrus land to 400 to 600 dunums of hill land.[30] In the absence of an agreed-upon definition of what constituted "cultivable" land and a detailed, countrywide survey of the amount of land of different types actually available for cultivation, estimates of the number of agricultural households that could be supported in Palestine were bound to be controversial.

For the Jews, the issues of the amount of cultivable land, the size of the lot viable, and the estimate of the carrying capacity of Palestine's agricultural land were inseparable from the development program which they viewed as crucial to the continuation of their colonization and as equally beneficial to them and to the Arabs. By consolidating scattered holdings, undertaking irrigation projects, and adapting to intensive cultivation, the Arab farmer would improve his situation, using as capital the proceeds of the sale of part of his lands to the Jews, who would thus acquire additional areas for settlement. For such a program to succeed, it had to be carried out on a large scale, and repeated approaches to the government were made by representatives of the Jewish Agency in an attempt to obtain support for its implementation.

Evidence presented by the Jews regarding the beneficial effect of their colonization was not limited to conditions in Palestine. Statistics describing other countries in the region were compared with data for Arab Palestine in order to demonstrate the potential for development as well as the progress that had been made thus far. Bonné compared the situation of the Palestinian peasant with that of peasants in Syria, Cyprus, Egypt, and Iraq.[31] Horowitz looked at a wide range of conditions in neighboring countries and in Palestine and attempted to demonstrate that the degree of rural "congestion"—persons per unit of cultivable land— in Palestine was lower than in other countries such as Japan where agricultural development was much more intensive.[32]

Comparisons with other countries, in addition to supporting claims made regarding the benefits to Arabs from Jewish immigration, were used to demonstrate the inevitability of many of the changes that were occurring in Palestine, whether or not they were due specifically to Jewish settlement. The impact of capitalist development, it was argued, was felt in Palestine as it was elsewhere in the region. Among its results was migration from rural to urban areas and the growth of an industrial labor force.[33] As these examples showed, capitalist development did not affect Jews and Arabs equally, for it was the latter who in Palestine migrated to the urban areas, while the former comprised the growing industrial labor force. The benefits of Jewish settlement were thus viewed as part of a process occurring on a much larger scale, cutting across national boundaries:

> The consequences of the break-up of the small holdings are neutralized by the new possibilities which a development of the country opens up before the rural population. In Palestine the beneficial aspect of eco-

nomic modernisation has been accentuated by the special influence of Jewish colonisation. . . . The towns have gained at the expense of the villages as wages rose and employment facilities increased to the surplus rural population, which in other Near Eastern countries, weighs heavily on the whole structure of the economy. . . . The semi-feudal, closed structure of the. Arab rural economy is tottering under the impact of the new capitalist forces which have penetrated into the Near East since the World War. But in Palestine, the impact has been softened by the vast new possibilities opened up by the colonisation of the country. These have compensated for the loss of the meagre livelihood which was all that the primitive, self-sufficient Arab farm could yield to its cultivator. The real development of the Arab economy is the resultant of these two divergent forces.[34]

The Place of Arabs in the Development of Palestine

Jewish plans for the development of Palestine implicitly assigned to the Arabs a continuation of the primarily rural character of their society. The Jews were interested in the improvement of Arab agriculture in order to free land for Jewish settlement. Based on their analysis of the condition of Arab agriculture and its relation to their colonization needs, the Jews repeatedly outlined the main elements of a plan for the development of the Arab agricultural economy which was to be carried out by the government. It was not a program for agricultural reform, for it was not intended to affect existing property relations. Owner-cultivators would continue to own their land, although it was hoped that they would sell some of it to the Jews. Large landowners whose holdings were worked by tenants would also remain proprietors as before. Tenants would not become property owners, nor would the landless acquire holdings of their own. The Jews envisaged the division of agricultural land between them and the Arabs and believed that improvement of Arab agriculture was an indispensable condition for this to come about, but they did not call for more far-reaching alterations in the land regime.

In response to French's report, Granovsky listed a series of proposals which included agricultural education; introduction of fertilizers; improvement of seed and livestock; development of additional markets abroad for Arab produce; the creation of a countrywide irrigation network; reduction of the agricultural interest rate; tax reform; agricultural credit extended through credit unions; the creation of producers' and

consumers' cooperatives; and the partition of *musha'a* lands together
with settlement of title throughout the country.[35] Thirteen years later, in
1945, similar proposals continued to be made.[36]

The Jews expected that they would be the ones to modernize Palestine, and they hoped to create a Jewish economy which would be as self-
sufficient as possible. "Intersectoral exchange" was to be minimal, in
order to provide the maximum opportunity for the development of the
Jewish economy. While recognizing that the large Arab population could
provide a market for inexpensive, locally produced consumer goods, they
believed the future of the country lay in

> modern economic development based upon heavy capital investment
> and up-to-date technical equipment, the establishment of manufactur-
> ing industries, the expansion of the scope and purchasing power of the
> home market, and a transition to intensive and diversified cultivation,
> also involving a heavy capital outlay. Those who are anxious to provide
> for the future of the growing Arab population of Palestine can, there-
> fore, from the economic point of view, do nothing better than promote
> Jewish immigration, capital import, and the technical advancement of
> manufacture and agriculture. . . . the more rapid the pace of economic
> progress, the greater the total population which will be finally absorbed
> and maintained in the country.[37]

Thus, the predominantly rural character of Arab society was to be maintained, while its agricultural economy was being transformed by the
concentration and intensification of the holdings.

The Structure of Rural Arab Society

The complexity of relations among the various classes in rural Arab
society based on the system of land tenure was never fully addressed
either by the Jews or the government. Persons might have rights to land
as owner-cultivators, with or without hired laborers, or as owners who
leased part or all of their land to tenants. They might live in the village
where their lands were located, have lands in other villages as well, or
might live in a town inside or outside Palestine and visit their property
seldom if at all. Tenants might hold land owned under one or more of
these arrangements, or might combine cultivation of land they themselves owned with tenancy on land owned by others. Part of the land

might be in *musha'a*, while other holdings were *mafrouz*. Both owner and tenant holdings might range in size from very small to very large. Owners and tenants might also work as laborers on lands held by others, in addition to cultivating their own holdings. Some landless laborers worked for the same households for many years, while others had much less security of tenure and moved around frequently. Some of the Arab tenants or laborers worked lands which had been bought by Jews but on which the Jewish settlements had not yet been established.

The Jewish analysis of Arab agriculture tended to trichotomize Arab rural society into absentee owners (the Jews often characterized them as "effendis"), owner-cultivators, and tenants. The emphasis placed on one or another of these groups depended on the period under consideration and the type of argument that was being made. Especially in the early analyses, stress was placed on the two groups whose interests were presumed to be most opposed to each other, the absentee owners and their tenants. Discussions of the impoverishment of the Arab peasant emphasized the accumulation by powerful rural and urban notables of lands that had formerly been in the possession of cultivators who lost control of them during the second half of the nineteenth century. The opposition between absentee owners interested only in immediate returns from their lands, and tenants ground down by their inability to eke out more than a bare subsistence from season to season, provided an appropriate background against which both the need for, and the benefits to be expected from, Jewish settlement could be convincingly demonstrated.

After the establishment of the Mandate, and especially after 1930, the emphasis of the Jewish analysis shifted to the owner-cultivator. Whereas in the earlier period the Jewish land-purchasing organizations had been able to acquire large tracts from individual owners, such large holdings subsequently had become much less common. Jews were increasingly likely to buy land from owner-cultivators, and the analytic emphasis on this group was linked to the shift in the sources of available land. Formerly the Jews had pointed to the vast tracts of uncultivated land in the possession of wealthy absentee owners, worked by tenants living in small, scattered villages who could not possibly exploit the full potential of the holdings; later they emphasized the wasteful nature of intensive cereal cultivation and the relatively small return it brought to peasants working their own land. The Jewish development proposals that envisaged a transformation of Arab agriculture through concentration of holdings and intensification of cultivation coincided with the increasing emphasis on acquiring land from individual owner-cultivators.

Stressing the opposition of interests between "effendis" and tenants allowed the Jews to present themselves as a force for progressive change in rural Palestine. The absentee owner, in the Jewish view, had few if any redeeming characteristics, and once freed of their "feudal" ties the lot of the tenants could only improve. While recognizing that the circumstances leading to the concentration of holdings in the hands of a small class of absentee owners might have justified the actions of nineteenth-century Palestinian peasants in relinquishing title to their lands, the continued existence of such holdings perpetuated the backward condition of the peasants and represented a serious impediment to Jewish settlement (though also, by virtue of the possibility of acquiring them, a tremendous opportunity).

The view of the owner-cultivator that the Jews presented in their analyses was of a peasant capable of, and used to, making rational calculations regarding his land—its cultivation and its disposition—in order to improve his situation: "Even the simplest Fellah is an intelligent, shrewd and business-like person who is well capable of discerning what is and what is not in his own interest."[38] Thus, if it were up to him, the Arab owner-cultivator would be quick to take advantage of the opportunity provided by Jewish readiness to purchase part of his land in order to upgrade the remaining portion. This view fit in well with Zionist settlement goals.[39] But as I note elsewhere, even though the Arab peasants possessed (presumably in common with peasants everywhere) the ability to recognize what was in their interest and what was detrimental to it, the Jewish analysis could have applied to only a relatively small part of the independent owner-cultivators: those living in the areas targeted for Jewish purchase and owning sufficient land to be able to sell a portion and support themselves on the remainder, using the proceeds to repay their debts and make the necessary capital investments to improve the remaining land.

The lack of systematic data makes it difficult to determine the degree to which the concentration of holdings in *Arab* hands continued during the Mandate. Although the national Jewish land-purchasing organizations replaced the wealthy Arab absentee landowners as the principal holders of large tracts of agricultural land in Palestine, some evidence suggests that Arabs continued to lose their land to other Arabs who were accumulating substantial holdings.[40] Horowitz and Hinden in 1938 referred to the polarization occurring in the Arab village between large landowners and landless peasants who had become laborers because of inability to repay their debts to usurious moneylenders.[41] They meant to describe current conditions, not the historical circumstances half a century earlier. Periods of prosperity which enabled peasants to repay debts alternated with successive seasons of poor harvests or setbacks in the Jewish colonization effort which reduced the amount of capital coming into the country and forced cultivators to reincur obligations to creditors. Even the great improvement that was widely noted in the situation of Arab cultivators as a result of the wartime demand for produce between 1940 and 1945 was viewed by some Jewish experts as potentially transitory unless appropriate steps were taken to strengthen the position of these farmers:

> It might be assumed that the profits obtained during the last few years have enabled Arab farmers to repay their debts and to accumulate even cash reserves. Such a favourable state of affairs, undreamed of for a long period, does, however, in no way, provide a guarantee against a return of indebtedness. . . . Without very careful handling of the whole situation the dependancy of the majority of Arab farmers on the big landowners is bound to be restored. The danger of such a development is particularly serious because of the fact that a few thousand Effendi families must have at their disposal the repaid debts of the small farmers, an amount of some £P1,500,000 and the war profits, say 25% of total Arab profits during the war, an amount of another $1\frac{1}{2}$–2 million."[42]

The Jews often viewed themselves as competing for land with wealthy Arabs who were also accumulating holdings. Both were taking advantage of the deteriorating condition of the peasants, though the Jews, at least, argued that their purchases would ultimately lead to improving the peasant's lot. The Jews tended to claim that purchases by Arabs were usually made for the purpose of speculative resale to them at inflated prices. Though this may have been true in regions where the Jews were known to be buying land, French's comment about Arab land purchases in the hill regions, where the Jews were not buying, suggests that there were motives other than the expected increased value upon resale.[43] In 1930 F. H. Kisch, head of the Jewish Agency's Political Department, suggested that the position of the "effendi landlord" was declining; he seemed to accept Strickland's view that tenants increasingly were becoming indebted to merchants rather than to landlords.[44]

Extremes and Average Values

In addition to selecting now one, now another segment of rural Arab society as the focus of analysis, the Jews relied greatly on average values for the computations they made to demonstrate the feasibility of their proposals. Because of the general lack of information on the distribution of land tenure in Palestine, the sources of data available to official investigators were no more comprehensive than those of the Jews. This was probably due at least in part to the lack of detailed data on Arab land tenure, but the effect of this approach was to create an "average" owner-cultivator whose characteristics were neither typical nor modal. At the same time, the Jews were able to draw upon the extensive information they had collected about their own colonization activities in order to refute claims made by government officials or the conclusions of investigatory commissions which they believed were mistaken.

The Jewish reliance on average values, particularly with respect to the proposals for combining Jewish land purchases from owner-cultivators with intensification of cultivation on the remaining holding on the assumption that the total area before the sale measured ninety-five dunums, contributed to an undifferentiated approach to the analysis of Arab agriculture. Just as the restricted focus first on absentee owners and tenants and then on owner-cultivators oversimplified the actual conditions, so the reliance on average holding size led to the formulation of a development program the feasibility of which was impossible to evaluate. The Jews made clear that such a program could not be implemented on a level lower than that of the village as a whole, or even that of the local region, in order for the necessary irrigation works to be introduced, for it was prohibitively expensive to irrigate individual holdings when those adjacent remained unimproved. But no mention was made of the manner in which the highly skewed size distribution of holdings would affect the ability of individual owner-cultivators to benefit from the change. Nor was mention made of the widespread social and structural effects on the village to which the implementation of the proposed development plan would almost certainly lead.

Much of the reason for this one-sided approach was undoubtedly the "impractical" nature of the Jewish proposals, in the sense that there was little possibility of obtaining government support for consolidation of Arab holdings. Since no general program for Arab agricultural development was ever undertaken by the government of Palestine, and no systematic information on landholding existed, there was no compelling reason for the Jews to make the tremendous effort to try and obtain information whose immediate practical value was extremely questionable. It was also far from likely that they would have been successful in their attempts to collect the data, because of noncooperation by government departments and the impossibility of the Jews themselves carrying out such data collection in the villages.

In cases where they had the detailed data, however, the Jews marshaled it skillfully to oppose conclusions inimical to their interests, as in their criticisms of the Hope Simpson report, Arthur Ruppin's comments on French's report, or the Jewish Agency memorandum to the Royal Commission.[45] On the one hand, therefore, the Jewish proposals for agricultural development that were intended to free Arab land for Jewish settlement were based on average values for landholding which, on the evidence of the British surveys, were not representative of the holdings of a majority of the Arab cultivators. On the other hand, the Jewish analyses of the data presented in government and other official documents that supported conclusions opposed to Jewish interests dealt in great detail with the variability in the circumstances of the Arab peasants. It may be that the data presented by the Jews were never seriously challenged because there was never any real possibility for implementing a development scheme such as the one they proposed. The Jewish Agency's analysis of Arab agriculture was in large measure irrelevant to the formulation of agricultural policy in Palestine, since the government was not about to implement it, and the Jews lacked the authority to do so. The government analyses, whether accurate or not, were important less for their consequences for the improvement of Arab agriculture, since they led to no comprehensive development schemes, than for their effects on Jewish settlement, for they were used to justify restrictions on immigration and land purchase. That is why, of course, the Jews devoted so much effort to refuting them.

The Arab "Mentality"

The view of the agricultural economy of Arab Palestine as backward and undeveloped was accompanied by a complementary view of the "mentality" of the Arab peasant. The condition of Arab agriculture was seen as due not only to the structural changes in rural Palestine between the middle of the nineteenth century and the First World War, but also as a consequence of Arab peasant culture. Jewish impatience at the apparent willingness of the government to accept the continuation of the underdevelopment of Wadi Hawarith, north of Hadera, in order to avoid disrupting the Bedouin who were occupying the lands, clearly expressed the link they saw between Palestinian peasant culture and agricultural backwardness: "Here, indeed, we have a classic example of the issue of goat *versus* man—swamp pasture against orange plantation."[46] And on the same topic, after criticising the Shaw Commission for concluding that Palestine could not support a larger agricultural population unless cultivation techniques changed radically, a Jewish Agency pamphlet by Leonard Stein complained that despite this conclusion the commission was "apparently prepared to let an area fit for orange growing remain grazing land merely because its present occupants claim to need it for their flocks, 'know nothing of irrigation,' and because, in case of transfer, 'it seems likely that the tribe will lose its identity as a tribe and become a scattered community.' "[47]

The Jewish view of the mentality of Arab peasants and of their capacity for self-improvement was not without contradictions and inconsistencies. These stemmed from the basic duality of the attitude of the Jewish settlers toward the Arab population. On the one hand, Arabs occupied the lands on which the Jews hoped to establish the national home and thereby represented a serious obstacle to the success of their endeavor; on the other, there was a strong belief among many of the settlers that their coming would benefit the local population and that it was both possible and desirable for Jews and Arabs to live peacefully together. The Jewish analysis of Arab agriculture necessarily included an evaluation of the peasants' capacity to adapt themselves to the expected transformation of the countryside, to recognize the opportunities it provided them and, by implication, to accept the inevitability of Jewish colonization.

Yosef Weitz, from 1932 director of the JNF's Land Development Division, responding to Hope Simpson's pessimistic analysis of the possibility of widespread colonization in the hill country of Palestine, disagreed with his explanation of why the peasants living in the hills had not developed their holdings. It was neither their lack of capital nor their inability to forgo income from land while they waited for fruit trees to bear that accounted for the backwardness of cultivation in the hills:

> For, notwithstanding Sir John's testimony, based on hearsay, that the Palestine fellahin are not lazy, we who know the fellah well, know better than to accept it as strictly conforming to reality. The fellah has many admirable qualities: he is keen, peaceable, polite, hospitable, etc., etc.; but he lacks one fundamental quality: the love of work. The fellah works, and works hard, but only as much as he is compelled to by the immediate pressure of hunger, and insofar as he can see a prospect of immediate reward. But he never does the work of the future, not even of his own future, and never does he do any work which will profit him only indirectly.[48]

Bernard Joseph, who was then legal advisor to the Jewish Agency's Political Department, writing a few years later in connection with proposed restrictions on Arab land sales to Jews, had a different opinion:

> It must be remembered that the Arabs are by no means comparable to natives of the African jungles who may be said to be fit subjects for protection in their own interests by their governors carrying the 'White Man's Burden.' . . . He is frequently poor but that is because he has never been able to throw off the burden of debt resulting from the accumulation of interest on loans, and has had no one to teach him to use improved methods of agriculture in order to get more out of his land. The Fellah of Palestine is not known to be traditionally improvident.[49]

One of the contradictions in the Jewish view of the Arab mentality was expressed in a claim that Jews repeatedly made to demonstrate the positive effects on the Arab population of their settlement activities. Arabs living in villages in the vicinity of Jewish settlements, it was frequently said, had, by emulating the techniques of their Jewish neighbors and by taking advantage of the markets provided by the nearby Jewish population, managed to improve their own agricultural techniques and, as a result, their standard of living, health conditions, and so on. In a sense, one of the main Jewish arguments in justification of their colonization depended on the ability of the local Arab population to benefit from Jewish settlement precisely in the way the Jews claimed they did, thereby enabling the Jews to claim that they themselves were the motivating factor in the change.

At the same time, however, there were those such as Ruppin who believed that improvement could only come about gradually: "The chief cause of the fellah's plight lies in the backwardness of his methods, which have not yet been adapted to modern agricultural requirements. . . . Only those fellahin have improved their condition who have gone over to fruit crops or are raising irrigated vegetables in the neighborhood of the cities and the large Jewish colonies. . . . This is not, of course, to imply that the transformation from extensive to intensive farming can be made overnight. The fellah's rooted traditions bar the way to abrupt changes."[50] Even in this example, however, Ruppin refers both to the "objective" conditions which hindered the development of Arab agriculture and to the "subjective," "rooted traditions" which did not, however, prevent change occurring where conditions were favorable.

This dual theme of objective and subjective reasons for the backwardness of Arab agriculture appears again in a 1945 analysis by David Horowitz of the effects of Jewish colonization on the Arab population. After describing the advances made in Arab agriculture as a result of Jewish capital import and Jewish technical superiority, he continued: "It takes a long time to transform a primitive and self-sufficient agriculture of predominantly feudal character into more intensive agriculture with scientific production methods. Apart from the capital required for the improvement of production methods and for the shifting over to more valuable crops and animal products, a change in the human attitude and in the social conditions must also take place."[51]

Neither Horowitz nor other Jewish analysts specified what changes were necessary in the peasant's "attitude," nor did they indicate how such changes might be brought about. Their proposals referred almost exclusively to the need for technical education, agricultural credit, intensification of cultivation, settlement of title, and the other structural changes which all observers of Palestinian Arab agriculture had been recommending for decades. Apparently it was not necessary to wait for the Arab cultivator also to develop an appropriate mentality as a precondition of his modernization. Samuel, writing in 1947, was satisfied that Arab farmers were then capable of adapting themselves to the necessary changes, if they were provided with the resources they required: "In summing up, it seems desirable to point out that the Fellah must be considered as quite prepared and able to adjust his farm to changing outside conditions in a comparatively short period, provided that this change does not surpass his financial means. Therefore the belief that the Fellah, given capital and adequate education, would make a much larger progress in the future than in the past, is fully warranted."[52]

Arab Analyses of Palestinian Agriculture

Unlike the government of Palestine or the representatives of the Zionist organizations, whose analysis of the situation of Palestinian Arab agriculture was carried out with reference to the terms set by the Mandate, the Palestinian Arab analysts were confronted with a dilemma. Most of the Arab leadership rejected the terms of the Mandate, believing that it subordinated the interests of the existing Arab majority to those of the Jews who represented, at the end of the First World War, little more than one-tenth of the country's population. Much of the argument regarding conditions in Palestine was, however, phrased with reference to the clauses of the Mandate: the Jews repeatedly claimed that the government failed to live up to its obligations regarding immigration and settlement, while the Arabs stressed that Jewish gains were being made at their expense, thereby vitiating the Mandate's provisions aimed at protecting the rights of the existing population. The Jews saw the Mandate as providing them with an opportunity to establish the national home in Palestine and claimed that their efforts to that end benefited not only their own community, but the Arabs as well. The latter, although denying the validity of the Mandate, were drawn into an argument about the effects of Jewish settlement in order to counteract Jewish claims regarding its benefits. Since the Mandate was in operation, and there was little likelihood that changes could be made in its key provisions, the Arab emphasis on its validity left open to the Jews the opportunity to demonstrate the advantages of their colonization. In order to counter the Jewish claims, the Arabs attempted to deal with them on their own ground.

But this approach also had its disadvantages. The Arabs had no organization devoted to the collection and analysis of social and economic information, nor did Palestinian Arab society possess centralized institutions which could easily have accommodated themselves to the activities needed for such data to be collected. The establishment of such institutions would in any case have been difficult in a society without experience in research and information-gathering based on a European model, but it was made harder by the political divisions within the Arab community that hindered cooperation on a national level. The Arabs were thus at a considerable disadvantage in comparison to the Jews, who were well organized as a community and who devoted much effort to collecting information about Palestine, both as part of their colonization activities and for its use in the debate over the future of the country. The Arabs were dependent on material collected by government departments, on reports of the various investigatory commissions, on material collected and published by Jewish organizations, and on the personal experience of local Arabs. While partial analyses of the condition of Palestine were prepared by Arabs throughout the Mandatory period, the most comprehensive and sophisticated document appeared only in 1946, as evidence submitted to the United Nations Special Committee on Palestine (UNSCOP).[53] But the Arabs consistently and emphatically denied the claims made by the Jews and presented evidence which was intended to support their arguments.

These preliminary remarks should be kept in mind in order to understand the difference between the Arab analysis of Palestine agriculture, on the one hand, and that of the government and of the Jews, on the other. While the government as well as the Jews portrayed the improvements in the condition of the Arab cultivators and attributed them to their own policies, the Arabs tended to stress the deterioration of the rural agricultural economy which they attributed to these same policies. In 1924 a memorandum from the Palestine Arab Congress to the Permanent Mandates Commission of the League of Nations recognized the impoverished state of the rural cultivators and attacked the government for continuing to tax them beyond their ability to pay, while failing to provide them with basic services such as schools, roads, and public security.[54] In a separate memorandum, which dealt with the first four years of the civil administration, the Executive Committee of the Palestine Arab Congress specified its grievances regarding the economic policies of the government as they affected the Arabs. It argued that the land policy was encouraging Arab land sales to Jews by depressing prices and reducing even further the ability of farmers to live off their produce; it also repeated the argument that the bulk of taxation fell on the farmers while they received few benefits in return.[55]

These arguments were developed and reiterated, with variations, in a series of articles that appeared between 1929 and 1931 in the English edition of *Falastin*, published in Jaffa by Issa Daoud el-Issa. The Arabic *Falastin* first appeared in 1911, and was the second Arabic newspaper in Palestine to appear on a continuing, if irregular, basis. According to Shim'oni, the paper would shift its editorial support to the predominant party or faction in Palestinian Arab politics at any particular time.[56] While such frequent shifts might have seemed opportunistic, they were also attempts to maintain a position of influence in the Palestinian Arab movement. In 1929 the Arabic edition, which had been appearing two to three times a week, moved to daily publication, and soon afterward a weekly English edition began to appear. Its editor, Muhammad Roshan Akhtar, wrote most of the articles analyzing the condition of Arab agriculture in the country, but his tenure ended in June 1932, when he died of pneumonia.[57]

For Akhtar, the indebtedness of the Arab peasant was the "root cause" of the major threats to the Palestinian Arab agricultural economy: transfer of land; nondevelopment of holdings; depressed trade in agricultural products, and the increase in criminal activity in the rural areas. But, in his view, the influence of the "root cause" was not unidirectional, as can be seen from his specification of the causes of the indebtedness itself, a combination of the characteristics of the land and climate, the structure of the agricultural economy, and the behaviors of the Arab cultivators themselves. The causes of the indebtedness included the undeveloped state of the holdings (which was, of course, also one of the results); uncertainty of crops because of variations in rainfall; heavy government taxation on small holdings; recourse to moneylenders, out of desperation; the failure of government to provide agricultural credit; the rise in land prices because of Zionist purchases which, by enabling peasants to increase their borrowing, also increased the burden of their indebtedness; excessive, costly, and time-consuming litigation over boundary disputes and village feuds; and unnecessary expenditure on ceremony and on ornament.[58]

Akhtar held the government of Palestine responsible for the continuing shortcomings of Arab peasant agriculture. Making liberal use of the findings of the various government commissions, as well as studies such as Volcani's monograph on the fellah's farm,[59] carried out under the auspices of Jewish institutions in Palestine, he criticized the authorities for their inaction. Referring only by implication to his fundamental opposition to the expansion of Jewish settlement at the expense of the Arab population, he listed the basic policies required of the government if Arab agriculture was to be put on a sound footing: substantial reductions in the tithes on produce and in the taxes paid by cultivators; establishment of a comprehensive system of agricultural education in the schools and the expansion of agricultural extension work; development of new, more profitable crops; and creation of a system of agricultural credit.[60] Akhtar preferred a government-run agricultural bank as the principal means of supplying credit to the small cultivators, rather than cooperative credit societies in the villages, as Strickland recommended, and was concerned that the funds required for the establishment of the latter would come at the expense of the bank. But he reported at length on Strickland's recommendations regarding the need for village credit societies and reprinted excerpts from Strickland's writings.[61]

The fundamental difference between the Arab analysis of the effects of Jewish settlement and that advanced by the Jews can be seen in the Arab response to the report by Lewis French. In a theme that recurred in many subsequent documents, the Arabs distinguished between the consequences of Jewish settlement for individual Arabs in particular localities, and the consequences for the Arab "nation" in Palestine.[62] By making this distinction, the Arabs were indicating their recognition of the fact that the link between the economic and political consequences of Jewish settlement was as clear to them as it was to the Jews, and they were taking issue with the Jewish argument that stressed the beneficial effects of colonization for individual Arabs while not referring to its effects on the Arab nation as a whole. By focusing on the beneficial consequences of Jewish settlement for individual Arab cultivators and villages, the Jewish argument implicitly denied that there could be negative consequences for the Arab population as a whole. The Arabs, however, denied that the benefits to individual Arabs could be summed in order to claim an overall benefit for the entire country.

The Arabs also denied that the proper object of analysis for the evaluation of the effects of Jewish settlement was the "country as a whole." In his rebuttal of the basis for the Royal Commission's statement that advances in social services provided to Arabs were due to the establishment of the national home, George Mansur, a prominent Arab trade union leader, rejected the argument that the import of Jewish capital had a "fructifying effect" on the economic life of the whole country. Mansur believed that the relevant issue was the effect of Jewish capital on the *Arab* economy.[63] While recognizing, for example, that Arab citriculture expanded by virtue of the capital obtained from land sales to Jews, he argued that the relevant question was whether, in the absence of such sales, the necessary capital could have been obtained elsewhere: "The industry might indeed have developed more slowly . . . [but] if there had been no National Home, Arab labour would never have been driven out of the groves and from the Arab national point of view it would have been far more advantageous for them that the capital invested should not be so overwhelmingly Jewish" (p. 23).

Mansur pointed to similar dangers with regard to other sectors of the economy where Jewish investments were said to benefit Arabs. Although it was argued that the employment of Arab labor had increased in urban areas, especially in the port towns of Jaffa and Haifa, because of Jewish development and enterprise, Mansur noted the squalid living conditions of Arab workers in those two towns and pointed to what he believed were broader consequences of their rapid growth: "The too rapid development of these towns has in many ways had a prejudicial effect upon the smaller towns such as Safad, Tiberias, Gaza and even Nablus. Any check in the ports results in the return to the smaller towns and villages of a large surplus population, partly proletarianised, for whom there is no surplus land available to cultivate" (p. 25). He also denied the Jewish claim that the marked increase in the urban Arab population in the areas of Jewish settlement was due to the improvements introduced by the Jews. Haifa, Jaffa, and Jerusalem would have been expected to develop more rapidly than other towns even had there been no national home, since Jaffa was the terminal for the citrus trade, Haifa was a major port and terminus of the oil pipeline from Iraq, and Jerusalem was the capital. Moreover, "the fact that these three cities have developed disproportionately to other Arab cities is also partly because the landless workers inevitably drift to the big towns and partly on account of the neglect of the Arab interests [in other towns, e.g., the soap industry in Nablus and the curio manufacture in Bethlehem] on the part of the Government" (p. 27).

Frequent attempts were made to explain why the Arabs sold land to Jews, since such sales seemed a fatal contradiction of the Arab national claim. The explanations typically distinguished between sales by absentee landowners who lived outside Palestine and sales by local cultivators. Those sales which were consummated prior to 1914, it was argued, were carried out before the political or social implications of such transactions were fully realized.[64] George Antonius, who had been the assistant director of education in the Palestine government, told the Royal Commission that many of the large landowners found themselves cut off from their holdings by virtue of the new boundaries in the region established after the First World War, which had the effect of lowering the value of these lands to those residing outside the country.[65] The peasants, it was said, sold only when they could not avoid it, and in most cases their lands were first taken over by moneylenders or by Arab intermediaries who then resold them to the Jews.[66]

In contrast to the Jewish analysis of the agricultural situation of the Arab peasantry, which was primarily concerned with the development of proposals that would free land for Jewish settlement by enabling the existing Arab rural population to raise their incomes while decreasing the size of their holdings, the Arab analysis began with the proposition that the existing area of cultivable land was already inadequate to support the agricultural population that depended on it. Any improvement in the methods of cultivation would have to be devoted, above all, to improving the condition of the present cultivators and to providing land for their children. The Arabs denied, in response to the French report, that lands already acquired by Jews could be viewed as "surplus," supporting their claim with reference to Hope Simpson's estimate of the proportion of landless Arabs.[67] They also implied that the breaking up and redistribution of large holdings might be possible under certain circumstances: "An Arab landowner may hold an area of thousands of dunams although one hundred or, say hundred and fifty dunams may be sufficient for his own cultivation. In this case the remaining part of this land cannot be considered as 'surplus', unless it is in excess of the needs and requirements of the Arab community as a whole."[68]

Nor did the Arabs submit that upgrading of land through intensification of cultivation could provide a short-term solution. In the face of the Jewish proposals, the Arabs claimed that "insurmountable difficulties" stood in the way of intensifying cultivation, "chief of which are the lack of markets, lack of water, lack of capital, the serious doubts whether the land is at all suitable, the fact that intensive cultivation entails a period of waiting and can at the best be only a very slow process."[69]

While the government and the Jews emphasized the structural conditions that created the existing Arab agricultural economy and continued to perpetuate it, the Arab analyses reiterated that it was the responsibility of the government to alter these conditions so that the lot of the rural cultivator could be improved. Although the Arabs believed that restrictions on Jewish settlement, immigration, and land purchase would in and of themselves benefit the Arab population, they did not limit their criticisms of government policy to anti-Zionist arguments. The Arabs repeatedly faulted the government for the inadequacy of its investments in rural education, agricultural credit, technical assistance, encouragement of cooperatives, and agricultural development in general. The Jews also pointed to the government's inactivity in these areas, but linked their recommendations for government action with policies designed to free land for Jewish colonization. The Arabs attacked the government for not undertaking the policies that would have enabled them better to resist Jewish settlement.

The Arabs also denied that Jewish colonization was an appropriate model for their own development, thus attempting to negate a powerful theme in the Jewish arguments and one that was clearly evident in the government's own analyses. While recognizing the accomplishments of the Jewish settlers, Arabs were skeptical regarding their relevance to themselves:

> No one is silly enough to deny what the Jews have done for themselves in Palestine in a quarter of a century; but to hold this up to the world as proof that the Arabs are unfit to develop their country is a gross misrepresentation. For development must proceed along the lines indicated by the needs of the individual or nation. . . . If we are to arrive at a true evaluation of the Arab's progress we must relate his achievements to his needs and to his individual means. [70]

> Jewish achievements in agriculture are an indication of what money and government help can do. That Arab progress lags far behind implies that he commands neither. . . . The lack of capital and the absence of opportunity of learning better methods necessarily warp any conclusion drawn from a comparison of the respective achievements of Arabs and Jews. [71]

In this view, the peasant's supposed traditionalism and the fact that he seemed to display little initiative or capacity for innovation were seen as rational responses to his objective situation:

The fellah's fatalism and laziness are often advanced by his detractors as the cause responsible for the economic plight in which he finds himself; and casual observers unduly stress them. But one should not be hasty in passing judgement. The fellah's holding seldom exceeds the *lot viable* while on an average it is smaller. He therefore cannot allow any part of it to remain fallow save the area which may be necessary for his crop rotation. It follows that he cannot carry out any extensive work of improvement without suffering a diminution in his annual return which he can ill afford. . . . His fatalism is observed only in adversity when circumstances beyond his control deprive him of his meagre means of livelihood. . . . In reference to anyone but a fellah such an attitude would compel admiration as fortitude in adversity, but where a fellah is concerned it is downright fatalism.[72]

Conclusion

The series of government commissions, committees, and investigations that considered, among other issues, the condition of Arab cultivators, gradually arrived at the conclusion that, whatever advantages had been gained from the activities of the Palestine government, and whatever benefits had accrued from Jewish settlement, the future prospects of Arab peasants were extremely uncertain. While all investigations noted an improvement in their standard of living, it was not seen as having been due primarily to agricultural development, but to the supplementary income earned by peasants or members of their families in what were referred to as "subsidiary" occupations.

What is remarkable about the government analyses is their consistency and their similarity during the period between 1920 and 1936. "Three main problems connected with the land in Palestine" were identified by the Peel Commission:

1. The fulfilment of the instructions in the Mandate regarding "close settlement by Jews on the land," combined with the obligation of safeguarding "the rights and position of other sections of the population."

2. The area available for cultivation by residents or immigrants, due allowance being made not only for waste land, but for that required for afforestation or grazing and the means by which it may best be developed in the interest of both races.

3. The extent to which extensive can be replaced by intensive cultivation and the water resources in Palestine can be developed.[73]

While different in emphasis from the major points raised in earlier documents, in that the so-called dual obligation to Jews and Arabs was mentioned first, the two major issues of the amount of available land and the condition of Arab agriculture continued to be of primary importance. Indeed, the Peel Commission recognized that it was following "a well-beaten track" in its inquiry on the land question and referred to the series of reports which preceded its own investigation.[74]

The inquiries of the Peel Commission, like those of its predecessors, were seriously hampered by the absence of reliable and comprehensive data on the situation of Arab cultivators. Throughout the period references to the same limited number of quantitative studies continually reappear: the report of the committee on the partition of *musha'a* lands; the Johnson-Crosbie survey; and the efforts to determine the number of landless Arabs. Errors in interpretation of the results of one survey were often perpetuated in subsequent official documents: the amount of village *land* estimated in 1923 to be held in *musha'a* tenure became the proportion of *villages* in such tenure; similarly, Hope Simpson's conclusion, based on a misreading of a table in the Johnson-Crosbie report, that 29.4 percent of the Arabs were landless, continued to appear despite repeated attempts to discredit it. Indeed, the Peel Commission complained that "after 15 years' administration of Palestine by the Mandatory Power, [it had not] been presented with a really final and reliable statement either of the waste lands, the Government Domains, or of the cultivable area,"[75] although it recognized the difficulties faced by the Palestine administration in collecting the necessary information.

Subsequent analyses have not substantially improved our knowledge of the period since they have, in large measure, been based on the inadequate information contained in the official reports, supplemented by data and estimates provided by the research departments of the Zionist organizations in Palestine. Historical research has been hampered by the disruption of Palestinian Arab society in the 1948 war and the destruction of most Arab villages, together with their local records, in the area in which Israel was established. Moreover, only recently has empirical research on Arab Palestine begun again to address questions of social and economic conditions, rather than focusing on political developments.

The information whose lack was regretted by the Royal Commission, although still of interest, was more important for its contemporary concerns than it would be today. Since so much of the political argument between Jews and government depended on the amount of land available for settlement, which in turn was seen as determining the amount and rate of permitted Jewish immigration, the unavailability of reliable data on the distribution of land and its quality meant that no agreement could be reached even on the basic facts underlying the differences over land and immigration. Even had such data been available, however, and accepted by both government and the Jewish Agency, the major issue was not *how much* land existed, but rather what should be done with the land and the Arabs who occupied it in order to make room for more Jewish settlers. This was, of course, an argument between the Jews and the government, the Arabs rejecting its premises.

It is therefore somewhat surprising that so much attention was devoted to the *extent* of the land available, since both the Jews and the government agreed that the continuation of large-scale Jewish settlement would be possible only if lands in Arab ownership were to be transferred to Jewish hands. That was only possible, as both the Jews and the government realized, if basic changes were made in the techniques of Arab peasant agriculture, in particular regarding the intensification of cultivation which would free land for Jewish settlement.

Given that the real issue was the demand of the Jews for a restructuring of Arab peasant society, it is possible to specify what information would have been required to plan such a policy. At the very least, data would have had to be collected in order to provide detailed statistics on the main problems which all agreed confronted the Arab peasant: (1) the distribution of holdings by type of tenure and by size, and the number of persons included in each category, principal earners as well as dependents; (2) the degree to which ownership of land was concentrated in the hands of large estate owners, and the geographical distribution of the lands owned by such persons; (3) the degree to which *musha'a* tenure with repartitioning continued to exist, as well as the extent of informal as well as official *mafrouz;* (4) the distribution of the burden of peasant debt; (5) the incidence of nonagricultural labor among peasants, as a supplement or to substitute for their agricultural income; (6) the extent of labor migration within Palestine. Such information was never gathered, however, except to a very limited extent, because the policies that would have justified its collection were incapable of implementation in the political conditions of Mandatory Palestine. There was no possibility that the government would undertake a program of agricultural reform at the expense of the Arab landholders, both effendi and fellah, in order to transfer land from the Arabs to the Jews, even if the lot of the peasant would have been greatly improved as a result.

The Palestine administration often excused its inability to provide better statistics regarding the land question on the grounds of the anticipated costs of obtaining the required information more rapidly than had been planned, or of obtaining additional information whose collection had not been budgeted. The various investigating commissions sympathized with the administration's financial embarrassment and recommended to the cabinet that the necessary funds be made available. It is difficult, in retrospect, to see what use could have been made of the findings, had such data collection been undertaken, since the policies they would have been designed to serve were clearly impossible of execution. This, rather than the financial difficulty, may have been the underlying reason for the lack of comprehensive statistics on the social and economic condition of the Arab cultivators.[76]

The British analyses of the condition of Arab agriculture in Palestine contained incompatible elements which were never successfully reconciled. Again and again reports noted the principal impediments to agricultural development and recognized that the pressure on agricultural land was increasing because the growth of the rural population was not accompanied by a commensurate growth in the amount of new land available for cultivation, or by the transformation of existing land and techniques so that more persons could be supported in the countryside. The reports consistently attached to the policies of the Palestinian government the major portion of the blame for the continuation of a situation which their authors felt was clearly unsatisfactory. The fiscal policies of the British government, which failed to provide the money that was necessary to begin development on a broad scale, made the task of the local administration almost impossible. Yet the authors of the reports continued to stress the need to keep the peasants on the land and maintain them as agriculturalists.

Everything in Palestine was working in the opposite direction. The rural population was increasing and holdings were growing smaller;[77] new land for Arabs was not being brought into cultivation; the total

amount of Arab-owned land was diminishing because of Jewish purchases; the farming tools and methods used by the majority of Arab
peasants had not been significantly improved; agricultural credit on a
large scale was not being provided, by either public or private institutions, and moneylenders continued to be a major source of funds for
peasants; the efficiency of produce marketing by most of the villagers
had not improved; major construction and the many public works projects undertaken by government were drawing thousands of men away
from their villages for shorter or longer periods of time; and Jewish
construction in the towns provided employment for many more, especially during periods of increased Jewish immigration. These factors,
and others whose effects were less far-reaching, pulled more and more
persons in the countryside away from depending primarily on agriculture
for their subsistence.

It does not seem that Jewish land purchases were, in themselves, a
crucial factor in undermining the rural Arab agricultural economy,
though they certainly contributed toward speeding up the process of
change. If the Jews' claims were correct, part of the money they paid for
the land they bought was used by the sellers for the upgrading of the
remaining part of their holdings, although, as I shall discuss below, it is
uncertain how many sellers of lands that they themselves cultivated
could have benefited in this manner. Much of the land had in any case
been purchased from large landowners, many of whom were not residents
of Palestine, and led to the displacement of a relatively small number of
persons. Given the conditions of life for a tenant farmer in Palestine,
some might even have been better off in their dispossession, according to
the amount of compensation they received, than they could have been
under existing conditions on the land. In the absence of government
agricultural development programs, there would have been little future
for them in farming.[78]

In these circumstances, Jewish land purchases and Jewish immigration were salient issues not only for nationalistic reasons. They were the
visible embodiment of a process occurring, in greater or lesser degree,
throughout Palestine. The Arab response to the spread of Jewish settlement has been linked by many writers to the behavior of members of the
Arab political elite who were themselves, along with their relatives and
friends, privately selling land to the Jews while publicly condemning
Jewish settlement. By attributing to them dishonest motives and accusing

them of stirring up trouble in order to conceal their own role, the implication was made that a similar duplicity of motive was general in Palestinian Arab society regarding land sales to Jews. But it should not be forgotten that both the activities of the government and the spread of Jewish settlement created conditions that facilitated the transformation of Arab rural society, without providing the means for insuring that the changes would be to the benefit of the majority of the peasants. While it is undoubtedly true that many prominent Arabs were able to reap both the political and the economic advantages of their positions, they were a small minority of the landowning population.

The Jewish analysis of the condition of Arab agriculture also foundered on the political realities. Moreover, whether or not the Jewish proposals for the development of Arab agriculture were implemented in full, in part, or not at all, the Jewish view contained an inherent contradiction. The Arab rural population was expected to continue to increase in size, and the Jews opposed setting aside reserves of land for future generations of Arab cultivators. The surplus Arab rural population would have had to find other employment in the countryside, or migrate to the towns for work. Possible jobs for those continuing to live in the countryside, other than on Arab holdings, included public works projects; commuting to towns without establishing permanent households there; work as hired laborers on private Jewish agricultural holdings; and nonagricultural employment in rural Arab localities, though only a small number of persons could have been absorbed in this way without a transformation of the economic basis of village life.

In order for migration to the towns to absorb those who could no longer find land to cultivate, employment had to be made available by Arab, by government, by Jewish, or by "international" enterprises (such as the petrochemical industry in the Haifa Bay area). But government policy attempted to minimize the number of Arabs moving to urban areas, and Jewish exclusionary economic policies opposed the hiring of Arabs by Jewish employers. Building booms provided only temporary employment. The expansion of government services could have been an important source of employment, but not necessarily for unskilled, uneducated villagers. For Arab firms to have provided the needed jobs would have required the expansion of existing small-scale workshops and manufactories, but the capital required for such expansion was not yet forthcoming.

The implementation of the Jewish proposals for the development of
Arab agriculture would have been possible only in a political context that
recognized Jewish claims in Palestine as primary, for it would have
required state action to bring about the concentration of holdings, which
was the prerequisite for rational intensification of Arab agriculture. The
Palestine government had shown little willingness to carry out the Jewish
proposals, and the Jews were, of course, without the authority to do so.[79]

The Arab analysis involved a more fundamental dilemma than did
that of either of the other two parties to the conflict. It was expressed not
in the specific conception it presented of the conditions and future of
Palestinian agriculture, but in the very necessity of accepting the terms
of an argument that was set by others. Just as the Arabs had to choose in
their political activity between accepting the Mandate and relinquishing,
for the forseeable future, the possibility of achieving an independent
Arab Palestine, or rejecting the Mandate and weakening their chances of
influencing government policy, so they had a similar choice to make
when preparing their analyses of the social and economic changes occurring in the country.

Although they were hampered by the lack of data independently
generated and specifically addressing their concerns, this handicap was
secondary. More important was the fact that the terms of the argument
over the social and economic condition of Palestine were set according to
the standards of the colonial administration, which stressed "development," "progress," what in more recent times has come to be called
"modernization." These standards fit perfectly with the interests of the
Zionist movement, which saw itself as the harbinger of such changes.
The Arabs, on the other hand, often argued they could achieve "development" and "progress" on their own, without help from the Jews or the
necessity of their example. They stressed the consequences of the
changes brought by Jewish settlement for the traditional structure of
Palestinian Arab society. They searched for a way to demonstrate the
negative consequences for Arab society as a whole of the social and
economic developments which were taking place, while being forced to
agree that in many cases they were clearly beneficial to individuals.

Views of Palestine:
Feudal Society, Colony, Dual Economy

THE TERMS for the accepted analysis of Palestine's Arab economy were established in the half century preceding the outbreak of the Second World War by economists on the staff of the Jewish Agency and by members of the British commissions which from time to time investigated conditions in the country. The two groups often differed sharply in their views of existing economic opportunities, and in the political conclusions to which they were led. But they shared a general outlook according to which the future development of the country was dependent on overcoming the stagnation and backwardness resulting from Ottoman policies favoring wealthy landowners at the expense of peasant cultivators. Both government and Jewish analyses usually began with the conditions in the country as they existed when members of each group first arrived. The Jews took as their reference point the situation in the 1880s, at the start of modern Jewish immigration. The British referred back to their occupation of Palestine in 1917, and in particular to the beginning of their civil administration under the terms of the Mandate. Very little concern was shown with the details of social and economic development in Palestine prior to renewed Jewish settlement and British occupation.

The implicit assumption that Palestine had been for hundreds of years in a condition similar to that in which it was found at the end of the nineteenth century was congenial to both Jewish colonists and British officials. One important component of Zionist ideology stressed the renewal of the productive capacity of the land; adherents saw a clear link between its revitalization and the renaissance of Jewish society and culture. Although Palestine may not have been, in this view, "a land without people," it was surely a land whose people had failed to develop it; their moral claim to possession was therefore weaker than that of the

Jewish settlers committed to its refructification. While British interests in Palestine differed from those of the Jews, their stewardship of the land could be accommodated easily within the framework of colonial rule over native peoples. Once established in the country, British officials saw little evidence to contradict the view that, with respect to the Arab population, their role was to be similar to that of colonial administrators in other lands.

This approach was an early example of what Roger Owen has referred to as a tendency of many writers on Palestine to treat its history "as almost entirely *sui generis*, that is as something with its own special logic requiring its own special mode of historical analysis and explanation." Owen attributed this tendency, in part at least, to "the constant play of passion and political calculation" in which information about Palestine's history "has been used to support this or that tendentious argument, this or that piece of special pleading." He argued that most writers who studied the economic and social transformation of Palestine during the Mandate adopted one of three approaches: "Stated briefly, these are the views that Palestine was a typical European colony with a typical European settler minority, the view that Palestine contained two communities with their own quite separate political and economic arrangements, and the view that the situation was best analysed as one in which a capitalist sector (identified largely with Jewish industry and agriculture) came to dominate a pre-capitalist (predominantly Arab) one."[1] There was also a fourth view, which Owen doesn't mention, put forward by some left-wing Jewish analysts of the political economy of Palestine. Their approach stressed what they believed to be the "feudal" character of Arab society; they focused on the changes that occurred even prior to the beginning of Jewish settlement as a result of the growing influence of European commercial interests and on the consequences for portions of the local economy of their gradual incorporation into trade relations with European lands.

Prior to 1948, most of the analyses of Mandatory Palestine's social and economic structure were put forward by parties to the conflict, although a number of attempts at appraisals intended to provide a balanced view of conditions in the country and future prospects were sponsored by organizations not directly involved in the political dispute.[2] Most of these works were intended to affect policy, and those which appeared under the auspices of the Jewish Agency or the British government represented, to a considerable extent, the "official" positions of these institutions. After 1948, the dissolution of the Mandate and the establishment of Israel altered the nature of the argument over Palestine, and a shift in focus occurred in the research dealing with the period of the Mandate (called, in Israel, the period of the *Yishuv*). Most analyses of social and economic conditions in Mandatory Palestine were undertaken by Israeli scholars, either as a historical backdrop to a discussion of contemporary Israeli society, or as topics worthy of attention in their own right. Few attempts were made to place discussion of the social and economic development of Palestine society in a context broader than that provided by the internal history of the *Yishuv* or the consequences for that history of the deteriorating condition of European Jewry. Arabs were considered to be a separate entity, external to the *Yishuv*, and were seen as an impediment to the realization of Zionist goals.

Since the 1970s, however, there has been a resurgence of interest in the analysis of the social and economic structure of Mandatory Palestine. Much of the newer work has been undertaken by non-Israeli scholars who were influenced by intellectual currents that focused on the political economy of development in western and nonwestern societies. The reevaluation of the Mandatory period is also due in part to changing perceptions of the relationship between Jews and Arabs in Israel that resulted from the continuing Israeli occupation of territories captured in the 1967 war. This provided an additional impetus for a reconsideration of the accepted view of development in Palestine.

In addition to these studies, there also exists a considerable body of work on the economic and social structure of Palestinian Arab society which originally appeared during the Mandate period. Most of the authors were Jews who were writing not only from an "academic" perspective but out of ideological commitment to a particular view of the eventual shape of the Jewish society then under construction, and the place of Arabs within that society. There has been a tendency to neglect this body of work, perhaps because its authors belonged to political factions that failed to gain hegemony in the institutions of the *Yishuv* and therefore could not effectively advance nor subsequently implement policies which followed from their analyses.[3]

There have been three perspectives from which the analysis of Arab society during the Mandate has been viewed, in addition to what might be designated the "mainstream" approach represented by the British and

the organized Zionist institutions. The first of these, historically as well
as in the order I discuss them, argued that Ottoman Palestine was essentially a "feudal" society, and that Jewish settlement provided the catalyst
for the necessary capitalist transformation that would eventually lead to
the modernization of the country and the improvement of the conditions
of life for the Arab peasantry. The second, more recent, sees Mandatory
Palestine as an example of a colonial society. The third, most similar to
the "mainstream" analysis, stresses what it believes to be the most
important aspect of the country's economic structure, the existence of
what such writers called a "dual economy." Each of these perspectives
provide important insights into the economic and social structure of rural
Arab Palestine. This division is slightly different from Owen's, probably
because it stresses more than did Owen the views of those writing during
the Mandate.

Palestine as a Feudal Society

In the previous chapter I described the "official" Jewish analysis of
Palestinian Arab agriculture and noted that alternative analyses were
presented by those whose view of social and economic conditions in the
country differed from the position held by the Jewish Agency. Their
approach was Marxist, and they tried to understand both current conditions in Palestine and the country's future prospects by seeking the roots
of the existing situation in the development of agrarian relations during
the preceding two or three centuries. But even these radical interpretations could not completely escape the ideological constraints of their
Zionist beliefs. Their authors also claimed that Jewish settlement was
beneficial for the country as a whole, but they supported their view with
arguments that followed from their own political-economic analysis.

Two succinct but comprehensive examples of an alternative analysis
of the social and economic history of Palestine to the end of the nineteenth century appeared in 1936 and in 1940 in *HaShomer HaTza'ir*, the
biweekly journal of the movement bearing the same name.[4] Written over
fifty years ago and based primarily on contemporary evidence and published secondary sources, these analyses sometimes reached conclusions
that are not supported by more recent research. Nevertheless, their
arguments are worth presenting, not only because they are much less
well known than the "official" views promulgated by the Jewish Agency,

but also because they provide an understanding of Arab Palestine which implicitly argued against the notion that the country's modern history could best be understood by viewing Arab and Jewish society in isolation from each other.

In 1936 Binyamin Greenbaum, a member of kibbutz Gan Shmuel, published a three-part article reviewing the agrarian history of Palestine, assimilating it to contemporary analyses of the development and dissolution of European feudalism.[5] He began with the Ottoman capture of Palestine from the Mamluks. Most of the land was the property of the state, which leased it to dignitaries who were responsible for collecting and remitting the taxes due on it and in turn received from the peasants a portion of their crop. The peasants supplied all their own household needs and had no contact with a market.

The undermining of these "typical" feudal relations began in the seventeenth century, when foreign merchants established themselves in Palestine and provided the estate-holders with capital by purchasing from them for export the produce they received in ground rent. Greenbaum argued that the desire of the estate-holders to increase their money income led them to squeeze more out of the peasants who worked their lands. The new commercial relations gradually undermined the peasants' "natural economy," as the landlords' need for cash to meet their tax obligations, and their desire to purchase imported luxury goods, led them increasingly to demand cash payments from their tenants, rather than continuing to accept payment in kind.

Throughout the nineteenth century cheap imported domestic goods gradually displaced household production and increased peasant dependence on the market. Their growing need for cash drove peasants to moneylenders, but this only drew them further into a cash economy in order to repay the loans. The monopolization of trade by merchants granted concessions by the government insured that peasants would receive low prices and prevented them from clearing their loans.

The effect of the penetration of the village by commercial capital was the reconcentration of landholding, but through a process that differed in essential respects from the creation of large holdings in the "feudal" period. Whereas the "feudal" estates were created by grants from the government whose purpose was to assure the regular collection of taxes, large estates were created in the nineteenth century as a result of the investment of commercial capital in the purchase of agricultural land. No

clear differentiation occurred between "feudal" and commercial wealth:
the initial capital of many of the wealthy local merchants came from the
proceeds of estate-holding, and the monopolization by the state of commercial concessions made investment in agricultural land the only possible use for the profits gained from local trade. In such a setting, no
conflict could arise between agricultural and commercial interests.

The reconcentration of landholding which was the result of the joint
operation of "feudal" and commercial capital finally led, in Greenbaum's
analysis, to the stratification of the village community. The traditional
unity of the village community, characterized, he believed, by mutual aid
and the sharing of a common fate, came to be replaced by a structure in
which individual peasants and their families were forced to face alone
the consequences of the social and economic transformation of rural
society. This was the condition of Arab peasant society as Jewish settlement began.

Two articles by Simha Flapan built on Greenbaum's argument.[6] The
first, "On the Development of the Arab Village," is similar to Greenbaum's in that Flapan also sought the causes of the current condition of
Arab agriculture in Palestine in the historical development of production
relations, though he criticized Greenbaum for using the term "feudalism"
without specifying what Flapan believed were important differences between feudalism in Europe and in the Middle East, in particular the
different role played by the towns in the development of commercial
capital. This disagreement with Greenbaum, however, had no effect on
his discussion of the Palestinian Arab economy.

Flapan's analysis of the effects of Jewish settlement on village social
structure in Palestine was based on his view of the development of the
links between feudal and commercial interests in the Middle East.[7] He
believed that Jewish settlement provided the impetus and created the
fundamental conditions without which no alternative was possible to the
dominance of commercial capital and its stultifying effects on agricultural development. Although processes were occurring in rural Arab
society which, because they were similar to those which had occurred in
rural Europe as the feudal order was breaking down, could be interpreted
as heralding a similar transformation in Palestine, the underlying conditions were very different.

The appearance of capitalistic elements in agriculture—a cash economy, production for the market, the replacement of collective by individ-

ual ownership of land—were not, according to Flapan, themselves evidence of economic development. On the contrary, the imposition of "modern" economic forms on the primitive village economy allowed the traditional exploitation of the peasant to continue in a manner more easily concealed. As before, almost all the surplus value produced by peasants was taken out of their hands—no longer in the form of produce, but in the form of cash rental payments. Nor did the creation of a class of landless peasants represent, in and of itself, a progressive factor. In Europe, urban industry provided jobs for those who were forced off the land or chose to abandon it, and the growing urban population provided farmers with an incentive for the development of rational, capitalist agriculture. But in Palestine there was no industrial alternative for landless peasants, who had no choice but to remain in the villages competing with each other for positions as tenants, thereby driving up the price of land leases and the interest on loans they needed to survive.

> Commercial capital only produces a closed circle of exploitation, immiseration and atrophy. The more that the immiseration increases, so do the possibilities for exploitation also increase. The existence of masses of displaced and poverty-stricken peasants—who have no choice other than to lease a plot, or to obtain loans, under the worst possible conditions—enables the landowners and the creditors to increase the exploitation without mercy. Under these circumstances, special mechanisms of political repression are unnecessary. Equal political rights can be granted to the peasants; democratic government can be established; complete freedom can be allowed in all areas of life—without in the least reducing the profits of commercial capital. Economic retardation, the absence of industry to absorb the surplus labor power in the villages, the lack of an internal market for agricultural products, the shortage of productive capital desirous of expanding agricultural and industrial production—that is the secret both of feudal exploitation and feudal rule.[8]

The effect of Jewish settlement in Palestine, according to Flapan, was to undermine the existing structure of exploitation by infusing into the country productive capital which it used to establish industrial enterprises and develop intensive agriculture utilizing scientific principles and technology. The growth of the urban Jewish sector based on industry and commerce spurred the development of the country as a whole, including the expansion of road transport, the utilization of raw materials, the growth of internal and external trade, and the creation of new productive branches. Jewish immigration undermined the hegemony of commercial capital. The spurt in urban building, the expansion of employment in government enterprises, and the intensification of cultivation created a great demand for labor; this provided alternative sources of livelihood for displaced and landless peasants, who were able to free themselves from exploitative tenancy contracts. Peasant owner-cultivators took advantage of the new urban markets to reduce their dependence on the usurious loans that were an integral part of the peasant's grain cultivation economy. Jewish land purchases provided the capital needed by Arab owners of large tracts to expand capitalist agricultural production, especially of citrus, and enabled smallholders to obtain capital to intensify production on their own lands. Nevertheless, the primary factor in undermining the power of traditional commercial capital in Palestine was not Jewish land purchases, but the impetus that Jewish immigration gave to the proletarianization of the landless peasants, and this was the basic cause for the opposition of feudal landed and commercial interests to Zionist settlement.

But despite its profound effects, Jewish colonization in Palestine could not, by itself, bring about the complete transformation of traditional agricultural relations in the country. Jewish immigration to Palestine, the principal force in undermining the existing agricultural order, was subject to sharp fluctuations. When the number of immigrants declined, so did employment opportunities outside the village; the movement of villagers to the towns was reversed, and landless peasants were again forced into disadvantageous tenancy agreements. Even had Jewish immigration continued at uniformly high levels, however, the economic consequences would not be sufficient to eliminate the remnants of the old order. The central issues for small peasants had to do with access to land and freeing themselves from debt, and alteration of the existing structure of relationships could only come about by means of government action that would create new rights in land for peasants at the expense of the landed merchant class which controlled much of the country's agriculture.

Flapan's analysis of the effects of Jewish settlement on the Arab village, against the background of the condition of Arab Palestine prior to modern Jewish immigration, can be summarized as follows. Though the traditional economy of Palestine was affected by the incursion of market forces and capitalist production in the form of a money economy, production for the market, and the transition from collective to individual ownership of land, this was insufficient to bring about general economic development. The forms of the relationship between the tenant and the landowner had changed: landownership was no longer the monopoly of a single social class; the peasant was not subjected politically to the land- owner; there was private property in land; tenancy was individual and not collective, and defined by contract. Nevertheless, the basic relation between the landholder and the peasant which existed under the feudal regime continued after its transformation: the landowner expropriated most of the peasant's production. Since the landowner was not interested in rationalizing production for the market, but only in continuing to obtain land rent, the changes in the form of agricultural relations did not lead to an alteration in their content.

Nor did the creation of a class of landless or semilandless peasants lead to a basic change in the economic structure of Palestinian society. Such a change could have come about if those forced off the land were absorbed in urban industrial production and contributed to its further development. The growth of an urban working class would also have encouraged the rationalization and intensification of agricultural produc- tion in order to provide food for the expanding urban market. But land- holders and merchants were not interested in industrial investment and did not create enterprises that could have provided work for peasants pushed off their lands. The masses of displaced peasants had no alterna- tive but to attempt to maintain themselves in agriculture by accepting increasingly disadvantageous lease contracts on land owned by others, or by moving to the towns in the hope of finding work, while being too poor to provide the market which would encourage the growth of agricultural production.

These analyses of the transformation of Arab peasant economy and the movement from a "feudal" to a "commercial" base are valuable for the perspective they provide on the development of the agricultural economy of the country and the way in which they identify the underlying relations between the principal social groupings involved in this transfor- mation. While Greenbaum devoted his discussion to agrarian relations among Palestinian Arabs prior to the revival of Jewish settlement, Flapan examined the effects of such settlement on Arab society and agriculture from the beginning of the century until 1940. Both these discussions, by

identifying existing agrarian relations as the principal impediment to
Arab progress, reached conclusions differing little from those which
followed from the British or the official Zionist analyses. Moreover,
though this could not have been their intent, by tracing the origins of
current conditions to a period which predated by centuries the beginning
of modern Jewish settlement in Palestine, they implicitly relieved Jewish
settlement of responsibility for the deteriorating condition of Arab peasants. Improvements could come about only through the reform of rural
property relations, which was the responsibility of the government. Jewish settlement might furnish economic opportunities enabling individual
Arabs to break the bonds of poverty and debt, in particular through
providing nonagricultural employment, but only a relatively small proportion of the peasants could be absorbed in such jobs.

Analyses such as those of Greenbaum and Flapan were less optimistic than those of the Jewish Agency regarding the power of Jewish settlement to transform Arab agriculture. They recognized the need for reform
of agrarian relations, a policy which, if implemented, might seriously
have hampered the continued ability of the Zionist land-purchasing organizations to acquire additional holdings, and thus endangered the success of Jewish settlement in the country. A "radical" analysis such as this
was impractical in the existing political circumstances, based as they
were on the continued separation of Jews and Arabs in the country.

More recent research on conditions in nineteenth-century Palestine
provides information not available to Greenbaum or to Flapan. Roger
Owen's *The Middle East in the World Economy, 1800–1914* provides a
systematic discussion of the economic relations between Europe and the
countries of the region, including Palestine but, as he himself notes, the
paucity of information makes his conclusions tentative.[9] Scattered evidence regarding the increase in production of various Palestinian crops
between 1850 and 1880 indicates that "given the opportunity to sell his
produce for cash, the local peasants were as quick to respond to market
advantage as those anywhere else in the Middle East," but the available
material was insufficient to show the mechanisms by which the peasant
was able to respond. Nor was Owen able to estimate the effects on the
cultivators' standard of living of the additional income that they must
have received. Although much of it went to rents and taxes, some remained with the peasants. Of the portion expropriated by merchants,
moneylenders and other controllers of land living in the towns, part was

used to buy Ottoman bonds, part to invest in the expansion of citrus cultivation (which Owen found "surprising" for the Middle East), and part was devoted to "the struggle for wealth and power." Owen argues that economic growth continued between 1880 and the First World War and supports his claim with data on population increase, the expansion of the cultivated area, growing foreign trade, especially in grains and oranges, and craft/industrial production. Whereas prior to 1880 the Palestinian economy was an Arab economy, subsequent developments summarized by Owen reflect the effects of Jewish immigration as well as the expansion of Arab enterprise.[10]

Alexander Schölch's study of European economic penetration into Palestine during the nineteenth century concluded that "Palestine experienced a remarkable economic upswing in the two and a half decades following the Crimean War."[11] The cultivated area of the country was extended; an agricultural surplus was provided for regional and for European markets; production remained diversified; many of the towns experienced considerable growth and relative prosperity.

One wonders whether Schölch was referring to the same country to which the Jewish settlers came in the 1880s, for the terms of his description are very different from those used by Zionist writers and by British officials who came after the First World War. But Schölch also noted that "neither in the sphere of agriculture nor of manufacture did hitherto unknown products or new methods of production make their appearance. . . . no basic economic restructuring through European penetration took place" (pp. 55–56). Nevertheless, the expansion of trade led to the integration of Palestine into an international market dominated by the capitalist economies of Europe, which had two important effects on the future development of the country. One was the creation of large areas of landed property, and the other was the growing and significant infiltration of commercial capital into the sphere of agricultural production. The effects of this process, Schölch concluded, was to establish "the preconditions for a peripheralisation of the economy . . . in so far as these social groups were destined to take the lead along the path towards that predominantly outward orientation of 'underdeveloped' economies which results in foreign control and in the increased emphasis on the import of luxury goods" (p. 57). Though Schölch used terms that would not have been familiar to writers in the 1930s, his conclusions are not very different from Greenbaum's.

Greenbaum did not devote much attention to the effect of Jewish settlement on Arab society, but Flapan's extension of Greenbaum's analysis considered the question in detail. In Flapan's view, Jewish settlement created the conditions that made possible the undermining of the feudal-commercial hegemony and the creation of an Arab industrial labor force and stratum of independent small farmers. Sarah Graham-Brown's study of conditions in the Jabal Nablus region during the Mandate provides information which can be set against Flapan's argument.[12] Her principal concern was to examine the way in which the economy of the local region became integrated into the international capitalist structure. She looked in particular at "the adaptation of tenure relations, productive processes and labour power to the development of market forces at various economic levels," and their effect on the social structure of the rural areas and on the socioeconomic differentiation of the villages. The area she studied was not one that contained Jewish settlement. It can thus serve as a crucial case for an examination of the general effects of such settlement on the Arab population.

According to Graham-Brown, the most important external forces affecting economic life in Jabal Nablus during the Mandate were the influence of the government, the establishment of the Jewish national home, and the reactions to these circumstances of the class of local merchants and landowners. British officials in Palestine acted as if they were governing a colony, especially with respect to fiscal and budgetary policy. But the Mandate's prohibition of trade discrimination against any member of the League of Nations exposed Palestine to the dumping of cheap foreign manufactured goods while preventing the authorities from retaliating against high tariffs imposed by most industrial countries. Such policies severely disadvantaged local manufacturing.

The major consequence of Jewish settlement, and of the British obligation to facilitate the building of a nation home, according to Graham-Brown, was that it "superimposed" on the existing economy, which was characterized by noncapitalist agriculture, a community with "access to a substantial volume of capital and skills with which to build up an industrial and agricultural sector that was generally capitalist in its relations of production and geared to selling goods for exchange on both local and international markets" (p. 94). Although she claims that the growth of Jewish economic interests was accompanied by pressures on the government to accommodate them, Graham-Brown never explicitly

argues that economic policies implemented in response to specific Jewish demands had negative effects on Arab enterprises. The only exception is her reference to the lifting of duties on some imports needed by
new Jewish industrial enterprises, and the imposition of tariffs on others
in order to protect Jewish firms (p. 97). Her conclusion that the government's policy of maximizing revenue and budget-balancing combined
with its obligation to the establishment of the Jewish national home
"militated against concentration on the development of indigenous agriculture" does not attribute to Jewish settlement the failure of government
to implement such a policy (p. 98).

Nor does it appear from Graham-Brown's analysis that landowners
and merchants were greatly affected by "the impact of the mandatory
state and Jewish colonization" (p. 100). She claims that one major blow
to their position was the elimination of tax farming, but by the late
Ottoman period that source of income was less important than the rent
payments received from tenants. Reduced access to posts in the government administration was a second consequence of the British takeover,
though the number of Arab officials slowly increased. A third result was
a curtailment of the role of landowners and merchants as the main
providers of rural credit. But their role could not have been reduced very
much, for commentators during the entire Mandatory period continued to
note the pervasive influence of moneylenders on rural agriculture, and it
was not until the price inflation of the Second World War that peasants in
any substantial number were able to free themselves, briefly or for a
longer period, from their indebtedness.

Graham-Brown's analysis leads to the conclusion that in areas such
as Jabal Nablus, which were relatively distant from the major urban
centers, capitalist transformation of the rural economy occurred only
slowly. Relations between landowners and tenants were not greatly affected by the growth of the urban markets, and the government took little
action to reduce the tenants' dependence. Local manufacturing did not
diversify to take advantage of new opportunities, and Nablus's major
industry, soap-making, continued to operate with the same techniques
which had been used for generations. Potential investors still preferred to
put their money in land and in lending. Nor did Arab labor outside
agriculture develop to the point of creating a sizeable proletariat. Jewish
enterprises were under pressure to hire Jewish workers; there were not
enough Arab enterprises to provide work for more than a small number of

workers; and there were very few extensive operations which could have attracted large numbers of laborers—the Haifa port and the railroad were notable, though isolated, examples.

In contrast to its effects in other parts of the country, Jewish settlement had only a minor influence in the Jabal Nablus region. More important for social and economic change in the area was government policy regarding land and industrial development, which permitted the existing relations between landlord and tenant to continue and did little to increase the attractiveness of industrial investment as compared to investment in land. Graham-Brown's work, therefore, provides a useful correction to Flapan's analysis of the "progressive" effects of Jewish settlement in Palestine insofar as concerns the development of Arab society. While they may have created the conditions for extension of capitalist relations throughout the country, Jewish enterprises restricted the degree to which Arabs could participate in them directly. In regions relatively remote from the main centers of Jewish settlement, the effect of colonization was minor. Though Flapan recognized that without legislative action to free peasants from dependence on landowners no fundamental change in agrarian relations was possible, he seems not to have seen that, failing such a change, the "progressive" influence of Jewish settlement had necessarily to remain limited.

Palestine as a Colonial Territory

There has been some controversy regarding the "colonial" status of Palestine, especially with respect to the relationship between the Jewish and the Arab populations.[13] Israeli policies toward Arabs in Israel and, after 1967, in the occupied West Bank and Gaza have sometimes been likened to the system of relationships between Jews and Arabs in Palestine. But the interesting question is not whether Palestine (or Israel, for that matter) can appropriately be described a "colonial" situation, but whether a comparison between the situation in Palestine and that in other colonial territories can help understand the development of the country during the Mandate. Since Palestine was under British rule, the most relevant comparison would seem to be between British colonial policies in Palestine and elsewhere.

On the surface, there appear to be many similarities between Palestine after the First World War and colonial territories, especially those in

Africa which contained indigenous populations settled on the land while attracting European settlers who sought to displace them. Palestine was widely, if not always closely, settled at the beginning of the twentieth century. There were areas, such as the Negev in the south, which were sparsely populated, but Arab villages could be found throughout the arable regions, and agricultural production, even with the techniques of cultivation then in use, was capable of supporting a larger population on the land.

The British administration confronted in Palestine problems similar to those which had been met in British colonies elsewhere, and the experience gained in other parts of the world was useful to the officials in the Colonial Office and in Palestine in attempting to define and deal with them. But there were significant differences between Palestine and other British colonies, especially regarding British investment and settlement. British enterprises found few investment opportunities to interest them. Palestine had no natural resources so valuable as to make their exploitation immediately profitable. Great returns could not be expected from extensive cereal cultivation, and the potential area of citrus cultivation was relatively limited. The terms of the Mandate hindered foreign investment (except by Jews) which might have harmed the position of the Arab population.

Nor was Palestine a target for British settlement. The great age of colonization had come to a close with the war, and whatever attraction Palestine may have had for European immigrants had been limited by Ottoman resistance to such incursions. At the start of the Mandate, almost 90 percent of the population was Arab, and while there was a small non-Arab Christian population of merchants, the largest European community in the country was that of the Jews. Unlike the Europeans in other overseas colonies, the Jewish population of Palestine was not able to look back to a "mother country" whose interests it could be said to have been representing. Although the capitulation agreements between Ottoman Turkey and the European powers had granted certain rights to Jewish (and other) residents of Palestine who were citizens of those countries, these were in no sense the vanguard for an expected wave of additional settlers from a "home country." The early history of political Zionism, until the Balfour Declaration and the establishment of the Mandate, may be seen, in large part, as the search for a European power that would be willing to act in the role of a "mother country" for Jewish settlers. Political Zionism represented an attempt to fit Jewish settlement in Palestine into the existing framework of colonial expansion. It failed in this aim, for three reasons: the wave of settlement colonization, on which it hoped to ride, was ebbing; the Jews as potential colonists had no "natural" European guardian; and many of the potential settlers, unlike the leaders of the movement, rejected the colonial model.

Palestine was the last colonial country in the world, in the sense of being a land with a long-established, settled native population to which colonists came under the auspices of a European power able to permit or deny them entry regardless of the desires of the non-European population of the country. But the terms of the Mandate, which gave Britain that power, had the potential to restrict the use of it, in that Britain was obliged simultaneously to consider the rights of the Jewish colonists and the Arab inhabitants. Since Britain was not acting on behalf of its own nationals in overseeing Jewish settlement in Palestine, it could not have been expected to act as forcefully to guarantee the position of Jewish colonists as it did on behalf of British settlers in other colonial lands.

Despite these differences, there were also similarities, and the problem of land was one of the most important. Without attempting an exhaustive taxonomy, there were at least two main types of British overseas territories: those, such as India, in which no attempt was made to establish a British settler population dominant over the indigenous peoples; and those, such as the African colonies, which attracted settlers from England. At first glance, problems of land policy may seem to be different in the two types of territories. In the first, where the principal colonial interest lay in the extraction of value from native production, the main effort was devoted to establishing production relations that supplied the materials in which overseas investors were interested. Colonial land policy in such cases, to the degree that it existed, concentrated on trying to transform the existing agrarian society in order to facilitate incorporation of local producers and land in new forms of agrarian relations oriented to export agriculture. They did not, however, require that European producers replace local cultivators. They had only to control the latter's labor in production for export.

In settler colonies, on the other hand, competition for land between the indigenous population and the newcomers was present from the outset. This was especially true in cases where settler agriculture was oriented toward an export market and profitability could be maintained or increased only by expanding the scale of production. Indigenous agriculture was usually based on nonintensive use of land, because of its relative abundance in comparison with population and the restriction of production to what was necessary for subsistence. Under such conditions, much of the land's productive capacity often appeared "wasted" to settlers, since their own production plans required more intensive utilization of the land. While the settlers may have desired to employ local labor, and may indeed have been unable to avoid doing so, they had a major interest in gaining ownership over the land they worked, as a way of protecting their investment and as an expression of their commitment to their colonization and a justification of its legitimacy. As a result, existing rights to land inevitably came into conflict with settler demands, and the resolution of the conflict typically left the indigenous population with less land than it had before.

Despite these apparent differences, both types of colonial situations often had very similar outcomes as far as native landholding was concerned. The introduction of capitalist production, whether based on settlers or on overseas investors, was extremely disruptive of existing social and cultural systems, especially where traditional peasant cultivation gave way to capitalist agriculture as the result of policies that compelled native participation in plantation production. These usually required expropriation of land, severe restrictions on its use, or heavy tax impositions that forced cultivators to work in the new, large-scale agricultural enterprises in order to obtain cash to pay the taxes.

A major review undertaken in the 1930s of colonial land policies in Africa identified three distinct types: "There is, first, the group of states which have been influenced in their policy by the demand for land for European colonists or for mining interests; secondly, the group which has sought development mainly through the agency of the native cultivator; and, thirdly, the group which has endeavored to develop the resources of the territory by giving to Europeans large-scale concessions of land or of monopolies for the collection or sale of produce."[14] In the first group the authors included the Union of South Africa, Northern and Southern Rhodesia, Kenya, and Nyasaland; the second group included the remainder of the British territories; and the third comprised the Belgian and French colonies, though they noted that the concessionaire system had practically ceased to operate.

Palestine could not have been placed in any of these categories, primarily because British business had no economic interests in Palestine that required a large local labor force. The commercial importance of Palestine for British enterprise was restricted to the goods which could be provided to the local population—Arab, Jewish, and British—and since the total population was small Palestine did not represent a significant market for British exports. The major private British enterprise in the country was the complex of refineries near Haifa at the terminus of the pipeline from Iraq, but this was, by its nature, not capable of easy expansion. The country's agricultural prospects were not such as to attract significant overseas investment aimed at creating a profitable export industry; citrus cultivation was already in local hands and was not easily capable of great expansion. Although there were a number of concessions granted in Palestine, such as those for the development of the Huleh area and for mineral extraction from the region of adjoining the Dead Sea, the terms of the Mandate as well as government policy led them to be granted to local Arab or Jewish companies, rather than to overseas firms.

The establishment of colonial rule had consequences not only for the distribution of landownership, but also altered the very conception of rights in land. Tribal societies usually had no "private" rights in land, which was either held in common or was under the control of a chief who was bound in his disposal of it by custom. But colonists, whether primarily interested in investment or in settlement, desired assurances about the future of their endeavors and brought with them a model of private property ownership developed in Europe. Colonial legislation gradually superceded tribal land law in areas of the country suitable for investment and settlement. Common land became "Crown" land; sales of tribal lands to settlers became recognized in law; and the indigenous population gradually lost control over the land.

Tribal land law prevailed in most of the areas of colonial settlement in Africa. Land was held in common, and private property rights in the European sense were unknown. The situation in Palestine was different. Palestinian Arab cultivators were settled in villages to whose land they had a legal title recognized by the Jewish colonists and by the governments that ruled the country—first the Ottomans, then the British military and civil administrations. The question of their dispossession by fiat almost never arose, except in wishful thinking by some Zionists who thought the expulsion of Arabs from Palestine would be a solution to the national problem, and in deliberations of the Partition Commission regarding the exchange of Jewish and Arab populations in order to create homogeneous territories. Since the country was small, and there was hardly any cultivable area without Arab villages, except for the Negev, it was impossible to delineate large tracts of uninhabited land for Jewish settlement. Jewish colonies were established only on lands that could be purchased, and although priorities existed regarding the order in which various regions of the country should be settled, it was often necessary to buy land simply because it was being offered for sale, and not because it was located in a region of current interest. Nor was the government of Palestine under pressure to facilitate transfer of land from native owners to British settlers, as were colonial governments elsewhere, such as in East Africa. There was no British settler movement to Palestine, and the government hardly viewed Jewish immigrants as a proxy for English colonists.

The ideological component of Labor-Zionist settlement also made developments in Palestine differ from those in other colonial countries. Rejecting Arab hired labor on Jewish land hindered the establishment of Arab "squatter" populations on lands bought by the Jewish national institutions. Although the close proximity of Arab villages to potential sources of employment would have worked against the development of permanent settlements on or near Jewish agricultural lands, it was not inconceivable that such encampments would come into existence. Village Arabs drawn to Haifa and to Jaffa in the hope of finding employment created shantytowns (called "hutments" by the British) on the outskirts of those cities, and had employment on Jewish land been possible they might have sprung up in the countryside as well. (In fact, in Israel after 1967 Arabs from the West Bank and Gaza employed as agricultural workers on land owned by Jews built shacks adjacent to the fields and lived there, often with their families.) The so-called private Jewish agricultural sector had fewer compunctions about hiring Arab labor, and the Jewish owners of citrus groves and vineyards depended on Arab workers during all stages of cultivation. Most of the workers were drawn from villages in the vicinity, however, and "squatter" camps did not develop.

The land situation in Palestine was similar to colonial countries that attracted a settler population intending to engage in agriculture. Jewish settlement in Palestine was carried out in the framework of an ideology that posited a mystical link between the Jewish settlers and the land.

This belief had its origins in the religious significance of the land of Israel for observant Jews, which was capable of evoking strong feelings even among others who were themselves less committed to the details of ritual behavior. The early colonists who developed the ideology of Labor Zionism added to the religious significance of the land a secular interpretation of its importance which was linked to their analysis of the condition of European Jewry. In this view, the return to Palestine was to be accompanied by a return to basic productive occupations, agriculture in particular. The rights of Jews to own land in Eastern Europe and Russia, the home of the largest European Jewish populations and those whose survival was the most threatened, were severely limited. Forced into secondary and tertiary occupations, Jews lacked the firm connection that only productive activity on one's own land could provide. This social and economic analysis combined with the religious significance of the land of Israel to imbue settlement and acquisition of land in Palestine with powerful emotional meanings which could be drawn upon and incorporated into a political program.

Although Zionist leaders devoted much effort to arguing for the beneficial effects of their settlement in Palestine, and attempted to allay Arab fears regarding the future, an inherent conflict of interest existed between Arabs and Jews regarding control of the land. Settlement needs combined with ideology to justify unrestricted expansion of Jewish control over territory. If land acquisition by Jews was limited only by shortage of funds to purchase new portions, many Arabs believed that it could only be a matter of time before the Arab population would be facing the possibility of becoming a minority shareholder in the property of the country.

In many countries of European colonial settlement the newcomers acquired land through force. In others, where tribal law prevailed and European legal conceptions of private property were unknown, settlers often obtained land from local chieftains at the expense of other members of the native community. In Africa, for example, where colonists were extending imperial interests, they could usually count on the courts and the military to support their displacing the African population, especially in the earlier period of colonization. Though growing government concern for the African population gradually led to restrictions on the ability of Europeans to gain control of African lands, such limitations were introduced in the later stages of colonization, after much of the desirable land had already been taken over.

Neither expropriation of land, nor purchase from tribal chiefs, were options available to Jewish settlers in Palestine. They did not have the power to take land by force of arms or of law from the local Arab population. Nor was there a legal "vacuum," in the sense that the local categories of landownership were unrecognizable in European law. All land in Palestine could, in principle, be classified according to its ownership, and Ottoman land law continued in force following the British occupation. Jewish land purchasers in Palestine were dependent for their acquisitions on the willingness of Arab sellers. The only way for Jews to acquire land was by purchase from its Arab owners or, on a much smaller scale, by obtaining Crown lands from the government. Though Arabs sometimes complained that the Jews were able to bid up prices to such a degree that cultivators had no choice but to sell, there was still a considerable difference between sales for economic reasons and expropriations based on political or military power. Crown lands, moreover, were usually not located in the areas on which Jews set greatest priority and were often poorly suited to agriculture; nor was the government, fearing Arab reaction, eager to release them for Jewish settlement.

Unlike the typical colonial situation, in which the colonial power supported the settlers in their takeover of native lands, either through positive action or by benign inaction, the Mandatory government soon felt obliged to set restrictions on Jewish land purchases. A series of ordinances for the "protection of cultivators" imposed limitations on the ability of Arabs to sell their lands to non-Arabs. The purpose of these regulations was to intervene in the free working of the land market in Palestine and act as a counterweight to the ability of Jewish purchasers to pay steadily increasing prices for land. The government was required by the terms of the Mandate to insure that the rights of the non-Jewish population were protected, and the possibility of widespread transfer of land from Arab to Jewish hands, whether real or imagined, could easily be defined as a danger to the rights of the Arab population. Moreover, the growing resistance by Palestinian Arabs to Zionist settlement, expressed through remonstrances, demonstrations, and violence, gradually convinced British officials, both in Palestine and in London, that restrictions on Jewish land purchases were necessary in order to prevent further deterioration of the situation.

When Zionist settlers arrived in Palestine they found that a market in land already existed. The country's land was not held by tribes (except among Bedouin), but by individuals. Even in those villages where land was regularly repartitioned or reapportioned, individuals had rights to well-defined shares of the common property, if not to particular plots of ground. Since landowners in Palestine had unquestioned legal rights to dispose of their property, no legal objection could be raised to the sale of land by its legal owner, although appeals for "justice" were frequently made by tenants dispossessed when the land they worked was sold over their heads. Thus, no one with rights in land could lose them because of the action of others, except in the case of fraud or expropriation for public purposes. Land was a commodity; it could be bought and sold, mortgaged to secure debts, and taken over in the wake of default. Although Jews and Arabs, buyers as well as sellers, often found it convenient to circumvent Ottoman, and later British, restrictions on land sales, it was not necessary for them to transform land into a salable good as was done in many countries where private ownership of land had been unknown.

Jewish purchases were not the only, or even the principal, threat to Arab landownership in Palestine, even though the government devoted most of its efforts regarding control of land transfers to those involving Jewish buyers and Arab sellers. The conditions of Arab cultivation were such that many farmers were in continual danger of losing their lands to moneylenders, and the transformation of a smallholder into a tenant or a landless person was a frequent event, especially in years of poor harvests. In the Punjab, the British administration attempted to prevent the continued growth of a landless class by requiring that debtors be allowed to retain a certain minimum holding in their possession. The government of Palestine promulgated but never successfully implemented similar regulations.

There was, of course, a considerable difference between a case in which Arabs sold land to Jews which the sellers had themselves been cultivating, and the case in which an Arab family lost its land to an Arab creditor. Contracts for sales were freely undertaken, though the absence of institutions that could provide credit to Arab cultivators undoubtedly weakened the position of some farmers who might have preferred to continue on the land but lacked the necessary capital to repay their indebtedness or improve their holding. Loss of land to creditors, however, was completely involuntary. There are no statistics available on the number of foreclosures which resulted in Arab cultivators losing their land, but they were certainly common.

Land transfers in Palestine and in the African colonies also differed in their scope. By the end of the Mandate, Jews had acquired about 6 percent of the total area of the country (representing about 11 percent of the area north of the Beersheba subdistrict that contained almost half the land area of the country and was mostly desert), and about 12 percent of the "cultivable" area, as defined by the Jewish Agency.[15] In comparison, areas reserved for Africans in the territories of the Union of South Africa represented, by 1936, 12 percent of the country's total land; in South West Africa in 1935, 37 percent of the land was in European possession; so, by 1907, was 62 percent of the area of Swaziland; by 1935 about half of the land of Southern Rhodesia was in European hands; European-owned lands in Northern Rhodesia in the 1930s represented about 62 percent of the total area.[16] One important reason that African colonists were able to take over large areas of land was that many of the tribal peoples were not permanently settled on it, but depended on grazing and shifting cultivation, which could create the impression of vast unused areas available for settlement. In Palestine north of the Beersheba subdistrict, on the other hand, the Arab population was settled on the land, and had been so for generations.

In Palestine there was little vacant land that could have been easily brought under cultivation, and the land at issue was already cultivated by Arab farmers. There was no question of establishing "native reserves" for the Arab population, in the African sense of land in actual or intended possession of the indigenous population. There were continuous Jewish efforts to obtain Crown lands for new settlements, though the government was unwilling to accede to these requests. If anything, the Jews believed that reserves should be set aside for their own future expansion. But one of the considerations that applied to land policy in the African colonies was also relevant to Palestine, though it took there a different form. The demarcation of "native reserves" in many African colonies made provision, to whatever degree, for anticipated needs of future generations.[17] Arabs in Palestine also believed that government land policy had to take into consideration the land needs of future generations of Arab cultivators. This was an additional argument for restricting the right of Jews to buy land.

Although the land conflict in Palestine was very different from that in the African colonies, the government of Palestine eventually issued regulations regarding land transfers that recalled these previously put into effect in Africa. The establishment in 1940 of zones in which land sales by Arabs to Jews were restricted represented the culmination of a policy that had gradually restricted the free working of the land market whose unfettered operation would have benefited Jewish settlement. The government was thereby following a policy that had been used in the colonies to restrict sales by Africans to Europeans. The policy viewed the Jews as a colonial population and the Arabs as "natives" in need of protection. In Africa it was the British presence that permitted, encouraged, and often initiated the takeover of African lands, and the later restrictions on land transfers from Africans to Europeans were intended to prevent a continuation of the damage that British rule had caused. In Palestine the government had done no more than permit willing Jewish buyers and Arab sellers to find each other. It discovered, however, that the economic inequality between the two groups which was caused by the conditions of Palestine agriculture was in danger of creating an outcome similar to that which had been brought about in Africa by force.

I have compared at length government land policy in Palestine with similar policies in other British colonial countries in order to examine whether it is useful to view Jewish settlement as an example of colonial incursion. Jewish settlers cannot be seen as surrogates for colonial immigrants, because of the substantial differences between conditions in Palestine, on the one hand, and other, more "typical" colonial countries, on the other. There were, however, aspects of British rule in Palestine, other than land policy, which were more similar to the experiences of its colonial territories elsewhere. The government was concerned to maintain social stability; it was guided by a policy of fiscal conservatism and biased against development. Policies that elsewhere expressed themselves in the preservation of tribalism became in Palestine "the politics of notables," and the welfare of the Arab population came to be identified with that of the members of existing national and local elites who became functionaries and officials in the administration. These policies, according to Rachel Taqqu, were consistent with the doctrine of "indirect rule" advanced by Lord Lugard after the First World War.[18]

One of the purposes that members of the League of Nations hoped to serve by establishing Mandated territories was to assist in the economic and social development of their populations. In the British case, how-ever, these goals conflicted with the fiscal conservatism of the Colonial Office, which believed that colonies should be self-sufficient economi-cally and not impose a burden on the home treasury. There was also an inherent conflict between development and attempts to prevent social disorganization by preserving traditional structures of authority. One of the effects in Palestine of this contradiction was to restrict efforts aimed at improving the condition of Arab agriculturists.

Viewing Palestine as a colonial territory, therefore, can help us under-stand government development policy, but it cannot offer much assis-tance in an analysis of the relationship between Arabs and Jews in the country. Although the basic element of a colonial relationship—political control by a foreign government—was clearly present, the correlates of that feature which have usually been taken as defining characteristics of colonialism were absent. There was little economic exploitation of the country's population or resources, nor did settlers, encouraged and backed by the colonial power, attempt to take over the land. This is not to deny the insights which can be obtained from a comparison between Mandatory Palestine and colonial lands, but the special character of British rule in Palestine prevents us from adhering too closely to the colonial parallel.

Economic "Dualism" in Palestine

Writers on Palestine generally agreed that there were substantial differ-ences between the social and economic conditions of the country's Arab and Jewish populations. The wealth and variety of colonial experience during the preceding century provided a conceptual framework to which the analysis of Palestinian society could be easily assimilated. As I noted earlier, the Jewish analysis of Arab agriculture was based in part on the argument that a "dual economy" existed in which the Arab "sector" was the traditional, backward element and the Jewish "sector" the modern and progressive. There was even controversy regarding the degree to which the Arab and Jewish sectors could legitimately be regarded as comprising a single economy.

In its original formulation, the concept of the dual economy referred to a colonial society in which a clear distinction could be made between two different social and economic sectors. Harold Brookfield summarized the essence of the dualist analysis of non-European societies: "The Western or Westernized element in the economy is materialist, rational, individualist; much more than in European countries themselves, it is the epitome of exploitative and unyielding capitalism. The Eastern element, by contrast, is pre-capitalist, characterized by a prevalence of self-employment, fatalistic, unresponsive to variations in prices and wages to the extent of being characterized by 'backward-sloping supply curves of effort', and is not profit-oriented."[19]

J. H. Boeke, whose discussion of the contrast between "Western" and "Eastern" social structures as it appeared in Indonesia is considered to be the earliest systematic formulation of the notion of the dual economy, saw clear parallels with Toennies's distinction between *Gemeinschaft* and *Gesellschaft*. Boeke's principal concern was not simply to delineate the existence of these two sectors of the typical colonial economy, for they had been noted by Malthus and by Marx, as well as by innumerable travelers, administrators, and scholars. Boeke particularly emphasized that the fundamental differences between precapitalist and capitalist social and economic structures made inappropriate the application to precapitalist settings economic theories developed to account for the functioning of capitalist economies.[20]

Boeke's original notion of dualism was based on the argument that economic theories developed for market societies were inappropriate for the analysis of societies in which market relations did not dominate economic life. His detailed discussion of the way in which the capitalist sector affected the working of the indigenous economy showed how the intrusion of western economic relations transformed the traditional social and economic structure.[21] His argument regarding the necessity of understanding the indigenous economy in its own terms was correct so long as that economy remained viable. But as the spread of capitalist production and marketing undermined the traditional economy and compelled the participation of the local population in a market that transcended local and even national boundaries, Boeke's point of view necessarily lost much of its force. More recent discussions of dualism ignore the epistemological issue, now moot, and use the concept as an aid to the study of sectoral differences between "haves" and "have-nots" within and between national economies.

Economic dualism in Palestine did not have the same meaning as it had in colonial lands. The typical colonial dual economy was one in which an exogenous capitalist sector imposed itself on local labor and productive capacity, purposely breaking down preexisting economic relations in order to obtain commodities that could be marketed abroad, as well as creating markets for imported consumer goods. In such economies, "dualism" refers to the perpetuation of a primary producing sector whose members are not fully integrated into the market economy. Their contact with it is peripheral, through the mediated sale of their production and their purchase of mass-produced consumer goods that replace products formerly obtained through traditional market arrangements. In Palestine, however, the Zionist leadership, and in particular the Labor-Zionist faction, supported a radical separation between the immigrant and the native economies, for ideological as well as practical reasons. Zionists argued that only through the "self-labor" of settlers could the bond between the Jews and their land be renewed and transformed into the basis for the creation of a national entity. The need to provide employment for Jewish immigrants required minimizing the number of jobs held by Arabs in Jewish enterprises, though unwillingness of Jews to work as hired farm laborers meant that private Jewish farmers employed mostly Arabs.

Unlike most colonial societies, in which the growing control of foreigners over production and marketing led to a transfer of wealth from the indigenous population to those who imposed themselves from without, political realities prevented a similar outcome in Palestine. In fact, representatives of the *Yishuv* repeatedly argued that the net resource transfer between the two communities, Arabs and Jews, benefited the former at the expense of the latter. Zionist economic policy was consistent with the Jews' inability to exercise control over the economy of the country, either under the Turks or under the British.[22] Dualism in Palestine, for most Jewish writers, meant separation of the Arab and Jewish economies, and their work was in large part devoted to a consideration of the "Jewish sector"; if they referred to the Arab economy it was usually to compare its development unfavorably with that of the Jews. Only infrequently were attempts made to view the economy of the country as a single unit and to specify the interconnections between the two "sectors."

If the essence of economic duality lies in the integration of local precapitalist production and labor into a system dominated by foreign capital and the resulting transformation of traditional village society, then clearly Palestine was not a dual economy in the original sense of the term.

There were three principal types of foreign capital investment in the country which were important during the Mandate. The first was by wealthy Arabs from neighboring countries, particularly Lebanon and Egypt, who purchased large tracts of land, either with existing villages or on which new villages were established, from whose inhabitants they collected agricultural rents. The second was the result of Jewish investment, both in land purchase and in industrial production, with funds supplied both by the immigrants themselves and by the "national institutions" established by Zionist bodies to undertake investment in the country. The third was British, and included government investment in infrastructure (such as the Haifa port and the railroad), and private investment in the oil installations in the Haifa Bay area at the terminus of the pipeline from Iraq.

Each of these three types of investment had only limited effects insofar as the transformation of the traditional Arab village economy and social structure was concerned, for none of them required for their success changes in behavior of large numbers of peasants. Wealthy Arabs who invested in land assumed that their return would come from a continuation of peasant cultivation. Most Jewish productive investments were aimed at creating an independent Jewish economy. Although they bore the potential for transformation of traditional economic relations, the exclusion of Arab labor from most Jewish enterprises meant that such potential would remain unfulfilled. British investment, both public and private, did not discriminate between Arab and Jew, and it established enterprises that by any standard were "modern." But their nature and scope limited their potential to transform a traditional peasant society. The railroad and the port were public enterprises, serving a defined market, and their possibilities for expansion were limited. While the government preferred they show a favorable balance, their public character meant that profit was not the principal consideration in their operation. The refineries in Haifa Bay, though privately owned, were in effect an adjunct to the productive capacity of distant oil fields, and not suited to continual expansion.

In short, none of the main types of investment present in Palestine led to the creation of a system of economic relations based on productive enterprises that would gradually undermine the traditional economic order. Most Arab landowners lacked, for various reasons, the incentive or the ability to transform their holdings into capitalist farms and thereby failed to create the conditions that elsewhere drove villagers out of the countryside. Most enterprises established by Jews were not large and did not provide many opportunities for unskilled labor. Jews preferred hiring other Jews as skilled workers, thereby restricting the opportunities for Arabs with the necessary qualifications to move into such positions. Even had Jewish hiring been nondiscriminatory, skilled positions were few in number relative to the surplus Arab population, and they were inappropriate for the skills of most of the peasants seeking work in towns. There were only a few sectors of the Palestinian economy—citrus cultivation, for example, or residential construction—in which Jews could provide wage-paying jobs for relatively large numbers of unskilled workers. Even here, however, although the proportion of Arabs among those employed was relatively high, their absolute number was small, because of the small scale of the activities themselves. Moreover, the volume of residential construction fluctuated greatly according to the amount of Jewish immigration and could not provide a stable source of work for underemployed or displaced villagers. Finally, the lack of natural resources for which an export market existed, or of exportable products capable of being produced in great quantity, meant that Palestine was unlikely to develop the typical characteristics of a dual economy.

"Separateness," rather than "duality" in the original sense of the concept, might seem to be a more appropriate description of the relation between the two major components of the Palestine economy during the Mandate. A substantial degree of communal segregation of Arabs and Jews existed in the country, visible to a greater or lesser degree in patterns of settlement, social relations, economic behavior, political institutions, and cultural life. The British viewed their obligations under the Mandate as requiring them to consider the best interests of the country as a whole in their formulation of policy, but it soon became clear that the national conflict was so fundamental that it impeded efforts to deal with the population of the country as a single entity. The terms of the Mandate, which provided for the building of a Jewish national home, legitimized Jewish separatist goals. The British accommodated their activities to the basic communal division, and thereby contributed to reinforcing it.

Jews separated themselves geographically from the Arab population by establishing new towns and villages and, following the anti-Jewish riots during the 1920s, they tended to concentrate in all-Jewish quarters of the principal mixed towns, Jaffa, Haifa, and Jerusalem. The geographical segregation, combined with the differences of religion, language, and culture, made many contacts between Arabs and Jews superficial and transitory. The refusal of the representatives of the Jewish and Arab communities to agree to various government proposals regarding the establishment of a legislative council meant that the creation of a potential point of contact was forestalled. It is true that there were individuals from both communities who succeeded in developing friendships across national lines, and small groups of Arabs and Jews whose personal and political beliefs enabled them to transcend the basic enmity existing in the country managed to establish themselves. But on the whole, it was only in the economic sphere that Arabs and Jews met on a continuing basis for long-term, sustained interaction.

Just as the notion of a "dual economy" as applied to Palestine is inappropriate, it is also questionable whether "separateness" is the most useful approach to understanding economic relations between the two communities. A number of Israeli economists have investigated the economic structure of Mandatory Palestine with particular reference to the relationship between the Arab and the Jewish "sectors."[23] Their work demonstrates that, despite the authors' assumptions of duality and separateness, Arabs and Jews were joint participants in a single economic system. What distinguished Arabs and Jews economically was their different positions in the national economy, but it is clear from these studies that the mutual influences of Arab and Jewish economic activity were great.

This is not simply a question of semantics. No one would disagree that so long as Arabs and Jews were free to enter into economic relations with one another, and were subject to a government whose fiscal powers applied to all citizens, they were by definition jointly involved in a single economy. The issue of duality or separateness in Palestine obviously refers to the degree to which Arab and Jewish economic life can legitimately be viewed as independent of each other. I would argue that this issue is a spurious one, and by raising it the researchers are forcing their analysis in a direction which guarantees that their results will implicitly confirm their assumption of separateness. The effect is to reinforce the view of Mandatory Palestine as comprised of two societies, a view that is consistent with the Zionist emphasis on creating an autonomous community distinct from its demographic and social surroundings. Obviously there were great differences between Arabs and Jews, but there were also many similarities.[24]

The analyses by Sussman, Metzer, and Kaplan of Palestine's economy during the Mandate show how subtle were the effects of Arab and Jewish economic activity on each other and on the economy as a whole.[25] Sussman describes how the existence of a large Arab labor pool for unskilled work complicated the efforts of the Histadrut to enforce a minimum wage for Jewish workers which would insure them an acceptable "European" standard of living. Even though many employers hired Jews rather than Arabs, the willingness of Arabs to accept lower pay set a limit on how much Jewish workers in unskilled jobs were likely to be paid.[26] Metzer and Kaplan call attention to some of the similarities between the Arab and the Jewish sectors in 1935, in particular the share of net national product represented by foreign exports and the dominance of citrus among commodities exported.[27] They also note that utilization of cultivable land increased by about 40 percent between the 1920s and the 1930s. On the Arab side, this increase was due to the expansion of markets for produce, and among the Jews it came about as lands purchased from Arab sellers were put into cultivation.[28]

Metzer and Kaplan analyzed the Arab-Jewish intersectoral trade balance in 1921 and 1935; by the latter year, 14 percent of the Arab product (excluding land sales) was purchased by Jews, in particular agricultural produce, transport, trade, building materials, and rental of Arab-owned dwellings. Their conclusions also confirm, however, the limited utility of the "dualistic" approach: "contrary to what one would expect in a growing dual economy, the proportion of Arab labor services bought by the Jewish economy, while rising, was still relatively small in 1935. The phenomenon was closely related to the high rate of Jewish population and labor force growth, and to some extent to Jewish economic nationalism, which attempted to minimize the entry of unskilled Arab labor to the Jewish labor market."[29]

In a separate article, Metzer addressed the question of resource transfer between Arabs and Jews as this resulted from government fiscal policies. He concluded that "the government brought about a net transfer of resources from the high-income (and high-resource) Jewish sector to the low-income Arab sector," which implied that "the fiscal system as a whole was progressive between the two national communities."[30] Zionist

writers made similar claims during the Mandate and used them to support their contention that Jewish settlement benefited the Arabs of Palestine, while at the same time they criticized the government for what they
felt was a lack of proportion between Jewish revenue contributions and
government expenditures on services to the *Yishuv*. Metzer shows that the
Jewish criticisms of the distribution of government expenditure were
based on the assumption that the only relevant items to be considered
were "nationally earmarked" outlays on health, education, and transport
(such as roads to Jewish and Arab localities), and the distribution of Jews
and Arabs employed in government public works. But Metzer's own
analysis allocates to the Arab and the Jewish sectors general government
expenditures on administration, internal security, defense infrastructure,
and other economic services, not according to the relative weight of each
group in the total population but differentially according to specific
criteria for each expenditure category. He concludes that between 1926/
27 and 1935/36 "the change in the composition of [government] expenditures was in the direction that favored the Jewish sector—chiefly through
the rise in the weight of economic services."[31]

It seems clear that the conclusions reached both by contemporary
and subsequent analyses of economic relations between Arabs and Jews
in Palestine depended a great deal on the initial assumptions made by
the analysts regarding the structure of the Palestinian economy, and that
these assumptions, in turn, were strongly affected by the political views
of those who made them. In my discussion of how government, Arabs,
and Jews viewed Arab agriculture I described in detail how political
considerations affected analysis; Metzer does the same in his consideration of the political context of the debate over relative Arab and Jewish
contributions to government revenue and benefits from government expenditure.[32] I think that the same point can be made regarding recent
attempts to impose on Mandatory Palestine an analysis based on the
presumed dual nature of its economy. Since the major characteristic of a
dual economy, the integration of a native labor force in enterprises
established with foreign capital and oriented toward production for an
export market, was absent in Palestine, the use of the dualism model
seems to be a translation into modern social-scientific terms of the Zionist view that the development of the Jewish community should be as
separate as possible from that of the Arabs.[33]

Conclusion

Even though I have argued that Palestine during the Mandate cannot justifiably be characterized simply as a feudal society, as a colony, or as possessing a dual economy, it clearly had aspects of all three. That does not mean that Palestine was in some sense "unique," except in the sense that is true of any society at a particular point in time. I would not wish to be accused of committing the error referred to by Owen, of viewing the history of Palestine during this period as *sui generis*. On the contrary, the discussion in this chapter is based on the many parallels which can be drawn between the situation in Palestine and that existing elsewhere.

The contemporary analyses of Arab agriculture were responses to the political, economic, and social conditions existing during the Mandate; they were prepared as part of the political struggle for control of the country, and were intended to affect it. The more general discussions of the political economy of Palestine, whether written during the Mandate or in later years, made clear what many of the contemporary analyses had failed to emphasize: the history of Palestine since the revival of Jewish settlement should be seen as bound up in broader historical processes.

It would, of course, be quite unfair to accuse contemporaries of neglecting completely events outside Palestine. Government officials, Jews, and Arabs were quite sensitive to the potential effects on their aspirations of the international political context in which they were operating. The British were concerned with the response of other Arab countries to their Palestine policy, while at the same time they were subject to domestic and foreign pressures regarding events there. The Jews long sought international support for their return to Palestine, which they justified in part by an analysis that saw no future for the Jewish masses in Eastern Europe and in Russia. Palestinian Arabs were increasingly affected by the rise of Arab nationalism, in one form or another, elsewhere in the Middle East and North Africa. But this awareness of the importance of external political forces was usually not matched by the realization that social and economic developments within Palestine had parallels elsewhere, and that the experience in other countries might shed light on what was likely or possible in Palestine.

Should our goal be to develop an alternative, more comprehensive model of Palestine society, one that would be less vulnerable to criticisms such as those presented in this chapter? I think not. Each of the approaches reviewed here highlights particular aspects of the country's social structure, and their value is twofold. On the one hand, they allow us to identify the parallels between the situation in Palestine and conditions elsewhere. This helps counteract a tendency to see the period of the Mandate as unique because of the unusual circumstances of Jewish settlement. On the other hand, the competing and sometimes incompatible approaches enable us to clarify the differences that existed nevertheless between Palestine and other countries, differences which become evident when we try to apply each model to the details of Palestinian political economy.

We are much less likely today to view the course of a country's social and economic development in isolation from its relation to other, more powerful societies with which it is in contact. Much of this changed perspective comes from the recognition that political decolonization in Africa and Asia did not lead to the economic and social decolonization which many had hoped for. As scholars sought to understand the antecedents of existing political, economic, and social structures, they turned to historical analysis, and our knowledge of Mandatory Palestine has benefited as a result. But care must be taken in applying to the Mandatory period concepts such as "feudal society," "colony," or "dual economy" which were developed in response to situations differing in essential respects from those found in Palestine.

Landholding: Transformation and Continuity

Introduction

IT WAS common in the analysis of Palestinian Arab society during the period of the Mandate to describe the impediments to progress under which the peasant cultivator labored. Seen from the perspective of British colonial administrators or Jewish agricultural experts, the backwardness of the peasant agricultural economy was evident, and the reasons for it were clear. Palestine's underdevelopment was a consequence of its location within the decaying Ottoman Empire. Its distance from Constantinople and its proximity to the desert regions with their marauding nomadic tribes made it difficult for the Porte to maintain continuous and effective administrative and political control over the country. Thus, after the middle of the nineteenth century, powerful local officials achieved considerable independence of action and were able to grow wealthy by subordinating to themselves the peasants in the villages. The latter, it was claimed, sought protection from raids by Bedouin who met with no serious obstacles in their incursions, and wished to evade taxation by agreeing to have the land they cultivated registered in the names of village chiefs or urban notables.

Peasant cultivators were often heavily in debt. Interest rates were usurious, and holdings passed from the hands of owner-cultivators into those of their creditors, the former owners often continuing to work them as tenants. Wolf has summarized the conditions leading to high interest rates for peasant cultivators, and his analysis applies to Palestine as well:

> the poverty of the population itself compels cultivators to use the income derived from production to feed themselves. Poverty implies that

133

subsistence takes priority over investment, and renders many cultivators unable 'to make ends meet.' Hence they must seek to get money through loans, and must often use such money to cover their subsistence. The moneylender, however, does not get his benefits from the consumption of his creditors, but from their production. Both the aggregate demand of many cultivators for loans and the desire of the moneylender to maximize his returns from their production tend to drive up interest rates. Lending to such a population with only a minimal capacity for repayment, moreover, freezes capital; that is, the moneylender cannot always or easily recover his money whenever he needs it. This situation again acts to drive up interest rates.[1]

Few large landowners intervened in the agricultural practices of their tenants, beyond insuring the payment of the share of the crop due them at harvest time. They did not seek to make their holdings more profitable by increasing yields or introducing crops that could earn them higher returns. The cultivators themselves, engaged in subsistence farming and living on the edge of failure, lacked the knowledge, the resources, and the incentive to introduce changes in their traditional methods of cultivation. These were well adapted to the circumstances in which they found themselves, although they resulted in low yields and no surplus which would have allowed them to escape from their chronic indebtedness. The Ottoman government did not undertake to better the condition of the peasants, and their techniques of farming could do no more than maintain them in their precarious existence.

Arab peasants were not legally bound to remain on the land and were, under Ottoman rule, free in principle to leave whenever they chose. They were responsible for the tax and rental payments, however, and in years of bad harvest, or as the result of disorder in the countryside, when they were unable to meet their obligations, peasants often fled their villages to avoid forcible collection of their debts. Freedom to leave the land was, of course, limited by the lack of alternative sources of income. Peasants who abandoned their villages could only resettle on other land, usually as tenants of the landowner. There was apparently no shortage of cultivable land in Palestine prior to the First World War. Although all the land was owned, either by the state, by large landowners, or by owner-cultivators, the density of settlement varied greatly, and there were areas that could support a larger population.

Under these conditions, landless peasants were forced to reach an accommodation with a landowner in order to survive. They were most likely to find a plot on the holding of a large absentee landowner, since the owner-cultivators would likely have only a limited amount of land and find it difficult to set some of it aside for a tenant. But the tie to the absentee landowner was quite tenuous, and the relation between the peasant and the holder of the land was usually restricted to meeting the latter's demands for rent payments in the form of a portion of the yield. There was little active interference by the landowners or their representatives in the day-to-day operation of the tenant holding or in the communal life of the peasant village. The income earned from sale of the produce they received as rent was great enough to permit the holders of large estates to maintain a position of wealth and power in the country and have influence at the Ottoman court.

By the same token, there was little interest in improving the condition of peasant agriculture, for doing so would have meant a profound alteration in the nature of the relationship between the landowner and the cultivator and necessitated the introduction of technical as well as organizational rationality into peasant farming. The improvement of peasant agriculture by modern methods of farming, with production oriented toward the world market, would have required much closer supervision of individual cultivators than was necessary when landowners were content to collect rents; it would have involved a revolution in social relations as well as in agricultural techniques.

The Effects of Musha'a Tenure

Under the Ottoman Land Code, which was taken over, with adaptations, by the British authorities, most of the agricultural land of Palestine was in the permanent ownership of the state, though heritable rights of possession were granted to individuals on condition that they maintain the land under cultivation. Such land was known as *miri*.[2] *Miri* land could also be transferred from one registered holder to another, and large tracts could be accumulated for the reasons described above. In addition to the large estates, whose lands were was worked by tenants, there were extensive *miri* holdings by villagers. There were typically of two kinds, *musha'a* and *mafrouz*. *Musha'a* lands were held in common by the inhabitants of a particular village and redistributed by them at more or less regular intervals, so that individual plots did not remain in the uninterrupted possession of a particular household. *Mafrouz* lands had been permanently assigned to individual households and were no longer redistributed.

Musha'a tenure was repeatedly singled out by government and by Jewish analyses which emphasized its presumably detrimental effects on agricultural development. Because the peasants' right to cultivate a particular parcel of village land was only temporary, it was argued that there was a disincentive for them to improve their holdings by using fertilizers, terracing against erosion, draining the fields, planting trees that would bear fruit only after the land had again passed from their possession, or undertaking irrigation works.

The proportion of *musha'a* land in Palestine declined continually. Although the Ottoman land legislation of 1858 had required the partitioning of such land and the establishment of individual title to holdings, the breakup proceeded slowly. No comprehensive survey was ever carried out of the extent of *musha'a* holdings, though repeated estimates of its prevalence were made throughout the Mandate period. According to Granott, practically all the land in Palestine was *musha'a* when the Ottoman land legislation was promulgated;[3] in 1917 *musha'a* lands comprised 70 percent of the total;[4] six years later their extent was estimated at 56 percent;[5] in 1926 half the villages were said to be *musha'a*;[6] the survey undertaken for the Johnson-Crosbie committee in 1929 estimated the proportion of *musha'a* land in 104 cereal-growing villages at 46 percent;[7] French believed that the extent of *musha'a* had by 1931 declined to less than 40 percent.[8] A 1932 analysis by Arthur Ruppin of the reasons for the relative backwardness of agricultural development on Arab holdings in the hill regions did not mention *musha'a* as one of the impediments to the planting of fruit trees;[9] this suggests such tenure was by then much less widespread in those areas. By 1940 only about 25 percent of Arab lands were said to be *musha'a*,[10] though Granott claimed in 1947 that at least half the Arab villages were still officially registered as such.[11] In practice, however, many of them had long been partitioned. Moshe Smilansky argued that villages which undertook de facto partition were more likely to be located in the vicinity of Jewish settlements.[12]

There were a number of reasons for the decline in the prevalence of *musha'a* tenure. Its disadvantages for the development of cultivation, which had been noted by foreign observers, were also evident to the peasants. With the growth of local and foreign markets for agricultural produce there was a growing incentive for individual cultivators to free themselves from the restrictions of communal cropping. The expanding market in land sales, to Jews as well as to Arabs, was an additional factor, since purchasers, especially Jews, preferred to acquire defined holdings whose boundaries were not subject to change rather than shares in the common land. The Palestine government encouraged the partition of *musha'a* lands, and its settlement-of-title activities gradually required their permanent division among villagers who held shares in them.

A number of explanations have been proposed to account for the origin and persistence of *musha'a* tenure, though no comprehensive study was ever carried out. Wolf argued that *musha'a* represented a choice made by the peasant community in confrontation with pressures toward internal differentiation in the distribution of resources, primarily land; the *musha'a* system could "reduce the strength of the selective pressure[s] falling upon any one household . . . by leveling their impact . . . [through the periodic redistribution of land, rather than letting the] differentiation take its course . . . maximiz[ing] the success of the successful, and . . . eliminat[ing] those who cannot make the grade."[13] Since, however, there was more than one possible criterion for determining the amount of land each shareholder was entitled to receive, some allocation procedures preserved rather than minimized inequality among villagers.[14] Moreover, in villages such as those in Palestine which were organized according to lineage descent groups, the larger *hamula*s (clans) necessarily received larger shares of the lands.

Doreen Warriner sought the origins of *musha'a* tenure in an original allocation of lands among members of a nomadic tribe which had settled in one place, combined with a periodic reallocation in order to maintain equality among the tribesmen. She attributed the persistence of the system, despite its clear disadvantages for the development of cultivation, to the fact that "the peasants cannot reach any agreement as to how to equate the different categories of land" in the event of a final partition.[15] The extent of de facto partitioning of *musha'a* land in Palestine, however, even in advance of government settlement-of-title operations, suggests that disagreement among the peasants was not an important factor in maintaining *musha'a* tenure and that its breakdown had more than one cause. In the village of Zar'een, for example, only one or two reapportionments were carried out after the First World War, "a contributory factor being . . . [the] expectation of imminent surveyed settlement of title to the lands."[16] Gabriel Baer suggested that the economically stronger groups in the village were more interested in the permanent partition of common lands, in order to minimize uncertainty regarding the value of their investment. He argued that inequality of landholding increased as a result of permanent partition. If Baer is correct about the motives of wealthier villagers, then their support of permanent partition of village lands may be more than a way of minimizing uncertainty; it would also serve to strengthen their economic and political position.[17]

Various explanations have been advanced linking *musha'a* tenure to the type of cultivation carried out; the resettlement of lands once abandoned and the need to allocate them among the settlers;[18] or the needs of villagers living in an unstable transitional zone between permanent settlement and nomadism, whose lands held in common could be made available to the entire community returning after having been forced to abandon them in fear of attack or because they were unable to pay the taxes.[19] Similar systems of periodic repartitioning were known elsewhere: in Persia the reallocation was carried out by the owner of the villages in order to prevent the cultivators from obtaining a vested interest in a particular holding;[20] in the Russian peasant commune land was periodically reallocated, but the serf was tied to the land in a way the Arab peasant was not.[21]

The close parallel between *musha'a* in Palestine and the periodic redistribution of land in the Russian repartitional commune led Ya'akov Firestone to suggest that the system came into existence in order to equalize as much as possible the burden of impositions.[22] In his view, *musha'a* was not a survival of some archaic equality among members of the community, for that would have led to a desire to equalize consumption among them. The reallocation of land under *musha'a*, however, served to equalize production. It was carried out under a regime that imposed tax obligations on the community as a whole, but was indifferent to how they were distributed internally. *Musha'a* was a way of insuring that the tax burden was spread as equally as possible, among the maximum number of members, in order to minimize its incidence on each of them. By equalizing holding size and quality, the *musha'a* system reduced the likelihood that any particular household would fail to meet its obligations because its holding was too small to permit it to survive.

By the end of the Ottoman period, however, and certainly during the Mandate, the economic relations between villagers and the owners of their lands, in those cases where the villagers were not themselves independent cultivators, were individual rather than collective. Nor were taxes imposed collectively, on the village as a whole, but were based on the production of individual holdings. Firestone's explanation of the origins of *musha'a*, therefore, suggests an additional reason for its gradual decline—the individualization of the tax regime.

Even though Palestinian Arabs recognized the disadvantages of *musha'a* for the development of agriculture, support for partition of village lands was not unequivocal. Since *musha'a* land was less attractive to prospective purchasers because of the uncertainty regarding when the share could be transformed into an individual plot, Jewish buyers preferred *mafrouz* land. Thus, *musha'a* was seen by Arabs as well as by Jews as an impediment to the extension of Jewish land ownership.[23] Observers also claimed that *musha'a* tenure, whatever its disadvantages, strengthened the communal life of the village by making manifest the interdependence among the peasants.[24] Peter Kolchin notes a similar effect of communal tenure in the Russian peasant commune:

> The practice of communal repartition served to fortify the collective mentality of the peasants. "Their" land was held collectively by the whole community rather than privately by individual peasants. . . . Critics of the communal system argued that it undermined individual initiative and inhibited the development of the concept of private property among the peasantry. But communal landholding and the communal responsibility engendered by the tendency of pomeshchiki [landowners] to deal with the mir [the peasant commune] collectively through its leaders rather than with peasants individually also reinforced the serfs' sense of solidarity with each other, their recognition that their fate was bound up with that of their fellow villagers.[25]

When obligations ceased to be collective, as in the case of Palestine, we would expect the sense of solidarity arising out of communal tenure to decline, because it would no longer be reinforced by the need to equalize impositions. But reallocation of land continued for many years after the original justification for it disappeared, and this undoubtedly helped maintain communal solidarity despite the changing economic and social

circumstances. Indeed, Arabs opposed to Jewish land purchases valued
musha'a as an obstacle to them, not only because Jews were reluctant to
buy undivided shares in village lands, but perhaps also out of a belief
that the communal structure made such sales more difficult. For the
same reason, of course, Arabs who wished to sell land, to Jews or to
others, supported the permanent partition of village holdings. In her
study of Jabal Nablus, Graham-Brown argues that *musha'a* not only
helped maintain communal solidarity, but also acted as "a kind of safety
net which temporarily retarded the effects of market mechanisms for
those peasants still living near the margins of subsistence and unable to
respond positively to the market. For many peasants, who had no capital
to invest anyway, the disincentives to invest in land and capital stock as
commodities, which seemed to many people inherent in the *mushaa*
system, were largely academic."[26]

Baer's analysis of the development of *musha'a* and the changes in the
system over time suggests that criticisms of it as preventing agricultural
development have to be reassessed. The implications of his description
are that *musha'a* was not always a rigid system; that many villages
adapted it to their needs; and that whether or not such adaptation occurred might have been due more to the specific social, political, and
economic conditions in the individual villages than to the characteristics
of the system itself. *Musha'a* was certainly not a framework that encouraged individual entrepreneurial activity oriented to the market, but it
could have been adapted in specific cases. Such adaptations, of course,
would have weakened it. One could conclude that *musha'a* as a system
retarded agricultural development oriented toward increased production
and desirous of taking fuller advantage of market opportunities; individual villages were, on the other hand, more or less able to overcome
musha'a's restrictions and find ways of permanently allocating all or part
of their land if the villagers wished to do so. The question then becomes,
of course, what made it likely that some villages would, and others would
not, make the necessary adaptations. Relevant factors would certainly
include proximity and ease of access to markets; the kinds of crops
which could be grown; and pressure from potential land purchasers. But
it is clear that the consequences of the *musha'a* system were more varied
than the blanket condemnation of it as a principal contributor to agricultural backwardness would imply.

In 1928 a Land Settlement Ordinance was enacted whose purpose was to establish a cadastral survey of Palestine and to fix the title to the land defined by that survey. Following settlement of title to lands in a particular village they passed out of *musha'a* tenure and were no longer subject to redistribution. Settlement of title progressed slowly, and by the end of 1935 operations had been completed in only 107 villages.[27] The Arab revolt in the following three years, and the outbreak of the Second World War, seriously hampered the subsequent progress of title settlement. Some Arabs recognized the value of delaying settlement as a way of hindering land sales to Jews,[28] while settlement of title facilitated such sales by those who wished them to proceed.

Fragmentary information collected at different times by government and by Jewish bodies provide some idea of the distribution of *musha'a* and *mafrouz* villages in various parts of Palestine. Of ten villages specified in a 1933 report on partition operations in advance of settlement of title in the Tiberias subdistrict, four were in fact *musha'a;* four more were registered as *musha'a* but their lands had not been redistributed since the original registration thirteen to fifteen years earlier; and most of the lands of the remaining two villages were in *mafrouz* ownership of the Palestine Land Development Company (PLDC), one of the major Jewish land-purchasing bodies.[29] Four years later the Jewish Agency provided to the Palestine Royal Commission a list of thirty-one villages in which the public Jewish land-purchasing companies had bought or leased land in *musha'a* tenure; they were located in the subdistricts of Haifa, Tiberias, Safed, and Beisan, and totalled 58,400 dunums.[30] In March 1938, an official of the Jewish National Fund (JNF) applied to the commissioner for land and surveys requesting that settlement-of-title operations be commenced in the village of Tayiba in the Beisan subdistrict, on whose lands the Jewish settlement of Moledet had been established. Tayiba consisted of eleven blocks of *musha'a* land, totaling approximately 8,700 dunums, of which the JNF owned about one-fourth. The Jews wanted to be able to develop the land, and the villagers were reported to be willing for settlement of title to proceed.[31] Of twenty-one selected villages in the Tulkarm subdistrict in the early 1940s, all but four were *mafrouz*, and in these four at least half the land was still being periodically redistributed.[32] At the end of 1944 Jews held shares in *musha'a* land in at least twenty-eight villages, most of them in the Acre and Safed subdistricts. The Jews' share of the village *musha'a* lands ranged from 5 percent or less, to 90 percent, and the median share was 18 percent, indicating that the Jewish *musha'a* holdings represented a minority of the total. Some of the non-*musha'a* land in these villages, however, may also have been in Jewish ownership.[33]

A rough estimate of the distribution of Jewish and Arab landholdings in some of the villages between *musha'a* and non-*musha'a* property was made by comparing for each of twenty-two villages for which information was available the proportion of the *musha'a* land held by Jews with the proportion of total village land in Jewish hands. In thirteen villages the proportions were approximately the same, suggesting that all or almost all of the village's lands were still held under *musha'a* tenure. In seven of the remaining villages, the Jewish holdings were concentrated in the *musha'a* lands.[34] In April 1946, the official in charge of settlement of title operations in the Galilee forwarded a list of twenty *musha'a* villages in which such operations were underway. The persistence of active *musha'a* tenure was apparently not a rarity even by the end of the Mandate, though the phenomenon seems to have been more common in the hilly, northern subdistricts than in the coastal plain. The greater value of plains land, which was closer to the centers of Jewish settlement—and hence worth a higher sale price—and also more suitable to crop production for the market, particularly vegetables and citrus, was probably the main factor explaining why *musha'a* tenure declined sooner in those areas than in the hill regions.[35]

Even villages in which we would expect *musha'a* to have been eliminated after settlement of title had been completed sometimes retained remnants of the earlier system. In one of the five villages included in the 1944 Department of Statistics' survey, there were a total of 268 parcels owned by two or more persons. Of these, 54 percent were permanently partitioned, though still reigstered in joint ownership; 22 percent were unpartitioned and jointly cultivated by co-owners or leased out; 18 percent were unpartitioned, belonging to relatives living in the same household; and 4 percent were redistributed by rotation every two years.[36] Joint ownership, of course, was different than *musha'a*, nor was it an outgrowth of it. Joint ownership was usually resorted to by heirs as a way of avoiding the disadvantages resulting from the disivion of land into ever smaller plots. It would be a mistake, however, to conclude that settlement of title freed village lands for easy sale on the market. As this example suggests, a substantial portion of village lands (almost half in this case) continued to be held by more than one person, making their sale potentially more difficult than it might otherwise have been.[37]

Both the Palestine government and the Jews sought to reduce the extent of *musha'a* and eventually to eliminate it. The government hoped that by so doing one of the serious obstacles to Arab agricultural development would be removed. The Jews also pointed out the disadvantages of *musha'a* for peasant agriculture, but their main interest in its abolition was connected to their settlement plans. They preferred not to buy *musha'a* land, for no permanent tracts for settlement could thereby be obtained. Thus, the Jews pressed the government to institute settlement of title to land, and after settlement operations had begun they pressed the authorities to hasten their progress.

Many villagers also realized the negative consequences of *musha'a*, and a slow but continuous transition to *mafrouz* tenure had been underway even prior to settlement-of-title operations. Individual villagers would apply to have their portions of the land removed from the periodic reallocation; the intervals between redistribution increased until there were villages in which de facto *mafrouz* had been in effect for years; upon application by a defined proportion of the villagers, the lands of the entire village would be permanently allocated among its inhabitants.

Settlement of title alone was able to do little toward improving the condition of Arab cultivators even when they owned their land. In most cases, land settlement fixed the existing division of holdings in the village, which was often characterized by extreme fragmentation of plots, making cultivation both difficult and inefficient. The fragmentation was a result of the working of inheritance rules on village lands divided into categories of different quality, in such a way that heirs received portions of holdings in the various sectors of village land. For agricultural development in the villages to have been significantly advanced, settlement would have had to be accompanied by consolidation of plots. The government did not link the two and never introduced an ordinance requiring consolidation, although its representatives were in some cases able to bring about voluntary consolidation in particular villages. The Jews strongly supported consolidation of Arab landholdings. In addition to their belief that such consolidation was necessary for the improvement of peasant agriculture, it was vital to their program for Jewish settlement, for it would have led to the release of additional lands for purchase.[38]

Estate Agriculture in Palestine

A portion of Palestine's agricultural land was owned by wealthy proprietors whose holdings comprised tens of thousands of dunums. No reliable
data regarding the distribution of landed property in Palestine exist prior
to the second decade of the Mandate, when findings from a survey of
landholding in 322 villages were summarized by the Department of
Statistics. By then, many of the largest estates had been broken up as
their owners sold some or all of their holdings to Jewish land-purchasing
organizations. But estimates of the extent of large landholding exist from
the end of the nineteenth century. Some of these were provided by
travelers to the country; others were prepared by representatives of Zionist bodies who were engaged in acquisition of land for Jewish settlement.

The Jews were interested in knowing how much land was concentrated in large estates because it was much easier to purchase large tracts
from single owners than to negotiate with dozens of smaller proprietors in
order to obtain an equivalent area. The lands of the large estates had the
additional advantage of being contiguous; Jewish settlements could then
be established in blocs without Arab villages interrupting the territorial
continuity. The figures provided in the estimates are only approximate,
but they give an idea of the extent of large landownership in Palestine at
the beginning of the Mandate. According to one estimate, 138 estates
were identified, each of at least 2,000 Turkish dunums in area, together
totaling more than 1.4 million Turkish dunums.[39]

The total land area of Palestine, excluding the district of Beersheba,
was about 13.7 million metric dunums, and the estimate of the cultivable
area, about which considerable disagreement existed, was between 6.5
and 9.2 million metric dunums.[40] Since some of the large estates were
located in the Beersheba region, and about 400,000 dunums of land
were in 1919 owned by Jews,[41] the owners of estates whose area was least
2,000 Turkish dunums held between 13 and 18 percent of the Arab-
owned cultivable land.[42] Ruppin estimated that 20 percent of Arab land
in the coastal plain was in 1932 in the hands of large landowners and
worked by tenants, though he did not indicate how big the holdings of
such landowners were.[43] Applying to the 95 dunum average holding of
owner-cultivators in the coastal plain the ratio of minimum holdings
presented by the Johnson-Crosbie committee, which concluded that an
owner-cultivator required 75 and a tenant 130 dunums,[44] there were at

least 2,500 tenant families in the region. Since the mean tenant holding was probably smaller than the minimum required for subsistence, the actual number of tenants was probably greater. In 1936 a survey of 322 Arab villages found that holdings of 2,000 or more metric dunums each represented 23 percent of the total land area (cultivable and uncultivable) of those villages (see table 6).[45]

Another list of large estates from the period of the First World War indicates where the owners lived. Since it included only estates exceeding 5,000 Turkish dunums in area (with one exception), the number and area of the estates is lower than in the 1936 survey. There were also some inconsistencies between the two lists regarding the areas of estates which appeared in both. Of fifty owners, thirty-one lived in Palestine and held slightly more than one-half million Turkish dunums; nineteen lived outside Palestine—in Beirut, Alexandria, or Damascus—and owned about 434,000 Turkish dunums.[46] Twelve years later the total amount of land in the country owned by Palestinian and non-Palestinian landlords residing outside of Palestine was estimated at 118,000 metric dunums,[47] less than

TABLE 6
Large Holdings in 322 Villages, 1936

	Number of Holdings	Gross Area of Holdings (dunums)	Average Area of Holding (dunums)
Size of holding (dunums)			
1,000–1,999	92	135,195	1,470[a]
2,000–2,999	23	54,408	2,366
3,000–3,999	15	50,545	3,370
4,000–4,999	7	30,541	4,363
5,000 +	13	624,435	48,033
Total holdings, 1,000 dunums or larger	150	895,124	5,967
Total holdings of all sizes in the 322 villages	71,789	3,252,735	45.3

Source: Government of Palestine, Department of Statistics, "Survey of Social and Economic Conditions in Arab Villages, 1944," *General Monthly Bulletin of Current Statistics*, January–March 1946, p. 55.

Note:

a. The average area of the holdings in this category is given in the source as 1,328.46 dunums. Dividing 135,195 by 92, however, gives 1,469.51. There are no apparent errors in the source table that would resolve this inconsistency; its most likely cause seems to be an error in division.

one-third of what it had been at the start of the Mandate. Most of the
difference was due to the purchase by Jews of large tracts in the Jezre'el
Valley and elsewhere, and not from the transfer of land from larger to
smaller Arab landowners.[48]

Most of the owners of large estates who were themselves residents of
Palestine lived in the district where their lands were located, or in a nearby
district. The portions owned by large landowners not resident in Palestine
were all located in the northern subdistricts—Tiberias, Acre, Haifa,
Nazareth, Jenin, and Tulkarm. No non-Palestinians were listed as owning
large tracts in the Nablus, Jaffa, Jerusalem, or Gaza subdistricts.[49]

Though the amount of land owned by absentee owners residing outside Palestine may have greatly declined after the First World War, the
proportion of Arab land in such estates remained large. According to the
1936 survey of 322 villages, more than one-quarter of their lands was
found in holdings of 1,000 dunums or more, which represented less than
one-tenth of 1 percent of the total number of holdings in these villages
(table 6). Assuming that the 322 villages in the sample represented about
40 percent of the villages in the country, more than 2.2 million dunums
of land were held by about 375 landowners whose holdings averaged
almost 6,000 dunums.[50]

These were large holdings for a country the size of Palestine, which
did not have vast areas of plains land where huge plantations could be
established. Even though part of the land was probably not fit for cultivation, much if it was likely devoted to agricultural crops. Since, except for
citrus growers, Arab owners of large estates did not usually engage in
capitalist agriculture, employing large numbers of hired workers on a
permanent or even a seasonal basis, most of these lands must have been
worked by tenants. Assuming that a peasant family using the prevalent
techniques and implements could cultivate an average of 100 dunums,
there could in 1936 have been some 20,000 tenant families in the whole
country working on holdings of 1,000 dunums or larger; if the average
holding was smaller, the number of tenants would have been even
greater.

Although there has been general agreement among most writers on
the Palestinian agricultural economy regarding the process by which the
large estates were created, Haim Gerber has argued that this consensus
is unjustified. He listed the accepted explanations as follows:

1. The villagers needed the city notables to protect them from the Bedouin menace and to represent them in their dealings with the government. In lieu [*sic*] of these services they were willing to register their lands in the names of these powerful urbanites.

2. Peasants were chronically in debt to city moneylenders and often could redeem their debts only with their lands. Such peasants would then remain on the land as serfs of the urban landlord.

3. The peasants were afraid to register the lands in their own names, lest this bring down on them heavier burdens of conscription, taxes, and extractions. They preferred to have the land registered in the name of a city notable.

4. Sometimes they acted out of ignorance because the whole business of registration was beyond their understanding.

5. Bedouin shaykhs played a major role by registering tribal lands in their own names rather than in the names of individual tribesmen; their actions proceeded from the shaykhs' total political superiority over their tribe.[51]

On the basis of his own research, however, Gerber concluded that most of these reasons were unsupported by evidence. Though he thought it likely that the fifth reason was correct, and he did not rule out the possibility that the others might have been true in particular cases, he denied that they provided a complete explanation of the formation of large estates. Gerber argues that the Ottoman Land Law of 1858, which for the first time made it possible "to purchase land on paper at the offices of the government and to make a profit from these lands (a previously unheard-of activity) whetted the substantial appetite for landlordism of the autochthonous Arab elite of Palestine."[52] Large tracts were purchased, settled with tenants, and, as happened with the Jezre'el Valley, which was purchased by the Sursoq family, later sold to Zionist land-purchasing organizations. Gerber's analysis suggests the creation of large estates was more complex a process than has hitherto been assumed and one that may have led to the extension of cultivation to previously barren land.

It may not always have been the case, therefore, that feudal grants of land originally made by the Ottoman conquerors of Palestine in order to assure the regularization of tax collection from the existing population slowly became transformed into private ownership of large estates. Nor was estate ownership in the form which it took in Palestine necessarily detrimental to agricultural progress. Though sales such as those to the Sursoqs have been seen as fraudulent and corrupt, enabling the purchasers to enrich themselves at the expense of the public treasury, Gerber argues that this view neglects the barren condition of the land sold. In fact, the Ottoman government "most likely made an excellent deal. It sold worthless land to an energetic entrepreneur who not only paid a price for it but undertook to put it under cultivation (as in fact he did), thereby increasing not only public security and the general volume of business in the country but also cash revenues through the tithe paid on the produce."[53]

It is worth asking why the accepted explanation for the creation of large estates in Palestine was not questioned earlier. I think there are two main reasons. The first has to do with the general lack, until recently, of research on the social structure of Arab Palestine. The second may be the result of the compatibility between Zionist views of Arab Palestine and the explanations adduced for the creation of the large estates. As can be seen from the list above, the accepted explanations all depend on ignorance, corruption, and oppression of the peasant landholders by those who held political or economic power. Such explanations were additional evidence, in Zionist eyes, of the backwardness of Palestine, and provided by implication additional justification for Jewish settlement.

The system of large landholding in Palestine was similar in some respects to that in agrarian regimes elsewhere, but there were also important differences. In combination, they gave Palestinian estates a particular character which affected the development of the country's agriculture. The fact that the large estates in Palestine were usually owned by persons who did not live on their land, and frequently did not even live in the country, has often been adduced as a reason for their agricultural shortcomings. But absentee ownership, in and of itself, need not represent an impediment to running an efficient and successful enterprise. Many of the Russian estate owners, for example, did not live in the countryside, but they were nevertheless frequently involved in the details of the operation of their holdings, either directly or through a staff of officials and stewards. Those with extensive holdings had no other choice, especially if their lands were divided among estates that were not territorially contiguous. The geographical distance between the Moscow or St. Petersburg residences of large landowners in Russia and the fields on which their serfs toiled was many times greater than that between the Beirut effendi and his land south of Jaffa. Critics of absentee ownership in Palestine seem to have assumed that the physical distance was accompanied by psychological distance and that the separation between the landowners and their property led to indifference regarding its condition.[54]

Such a criticism may have sometimes been true, but in general it was misplaced because it judged the relationship between the absentee landowners and their tenants according to a combination of ideological and instrumental criteria that were foreign to their own outlook. Neither maximization of profit, nor considerations of the most efficient use of productive resources, was central to the landowners' concern so long as no alternative use was available for the capital locked up in their property. Nor could the estate-owners easily have increased the productivity of their holdings, for relations between them and their tenants were characterized by an almost complete absence of interference in the day-to-day running of the individual tenant farms. Unlike the Russian estates on which production for the market was primary and whose organization and daily round was, at least in theory, centrally controlled, or the plantation in the American south on which production for the market was directed by owners who almost always lived on their holdings, the absentee owners of estates in Palestine extracted as much as they could of the peasants' grain production, but did not, at the end of the nineteenth century, attempt to alter the mix of crops that were usually grown. Had Palestinian agriculture developed unaffected by Jewish settlement, peasants might have been forced by landlowers to produce crops that were more profitable in overseas markets, but those developments never came about. Greenbaum and Flapan argued that exactly such a process occurred two hundred years earlier, with the incursion of European merchants into Palestine after the sixteenth century. That led to pressure on the peasants to abandon cultivation of crops used in household production, and a shift to grains that could be exported to European markets. Palestinian agriculture continued to be characterized by grain cultivation until the beginning of the First World War, and except for grain exports to neighboring countries, primarily Syria, melons to Egypt, and citrus, few attempts were made to adapt it to the commercial possibilities of international trade.

In 1936 the largest holdings provided subsistence for only a small minority of all peasant families in Palestine. Although comprehensive data is lacking, available material suggests that the majority must have lived on small or moderate holdings. In most cases the landowner culti-vated a portion of the land with members of his or her family and the rest was worked by the tenants. Most of the country's Arab cultivators proba-bly owned the land they worked, though since the average holding was small they controlled a minority of Palestine's land.

The Market for Agricultural Land

Prior to the final decades of the nineteenth century, the market for agricultural land in Palestine was primarily local, and the holdings in-volved were small. In the absence of large-scale commercial agriculture, land remained in the hands of the villagers or was accumulated in nonmarket transactions by wealthy persons who were able to benefit from the Ottoman land legislation of 1858 by transferring title to peasant holdings to their names. The enlarged holdings continued to be worked by household units, and no benefits of scale accrued from the concentra-tion of land in large estates.

The desire of the Jewish settlers to purchase land, and the prices they were able to pay, created a very different market. The Jews viewed the transformation of the land market as one of the benefits which their colonization had brought to the Palestinian Arabs, in that the rise in land values had provided the latter with a "capital reserve of 30 to 50 million pounds, or even more."[55] Initially, the principal beneficiaries of this new land market were the owners of large tracts. They were not engaged in commercial agriculture and usually had no intention of developing their holdings to make them more profitable, although Suleiman Nassif Bey, who was Sursoq's agent, had begun to make improvements on the lands of Nuris village, near Beisan. Jewish land-purchasing institutions pre-ferred to acquire large tracts and were able to offer higher prices than could otherwise be obtained. The early Zionist settlers had been able to acquire holdings in various parts of the country. PICA, the Palestine Jewish Colonization Association, for example, had by 1914 purchased 265,000 dunums in the Safed, Tiberias, and Haifa subdistricts.[56] Soon after the reopening in 1920 of the land registers—they were closed in 1918 by the British when they occupied the country—transactions affect-ing land in the Jezre'el Valley and the Acre Plain totaled almost one-quarter million dunums. While the average PICA colony included an area of about 10,600 dunums,[57] not all of which had necessarily been purchased from a single landowner, the villages bought as part of the Jezre'el and Acre transactions averaged 16,000 dunums.[58] As is well known, most of these lands were sold by the Sursoq family.

In the succeeding years the relative amounts of land sold by large landowners probably declined, although there are no published statistics available. The Peel Commission reported that most of the £P854,796 paid by the Jews in 1933 for the purchase of Arab land went to owners of "large estates," though it is not clear how extensive were these holdings.[59] The Jews consistently argued that in purchasing part of a smallholder's property they enabled him to improve the remainder, and while the Arabs denied that the improvements could be made they did not deny that the sales were occurring. There were in later years fewer opportunities to purchase large tracts, since these were no longer being created, although cases were reported of Arab middlemen buying up the lands of villagers in order to offer them for subsequent sale to the Jews as a single continuous holding.[60] Kenneth Stein presents data on Arab land sales to Jews between June 1934 and August 1936 which indicate that more than one-quarter of the land sold was in parcels not exceeding 100 dunums in size.[61] In 1931 French noted that Arab "*effendi* or capitalist landlords" were buying up land in the hills and thereby either displacing Arab cultivators or weakening their ability to remain on the land.[62] Ruppin did not believe that the Arabs were purchasing these lands in order to resell them at a higher price to the Jews, since the Arabs knew the Jews were not buying land in the hills.[63]

Between 1920 and 1945 the extent of Jewish landholding increased by almost 940,000 dunums;[64] by the end of 1945 the total amount of land in Jewish possession, not counting government concessions, was almost 1.5 million dunums.[65] While comprehensive data on land transactions for the entire Mandatory period have not been published, it is clear that large sums of money were transferred to Arabs as a result of land sales. Table 7, which is drawn from a variety of sources, shows that Jews paid at least £P5.7 million for the land they acquired since 1878, and the actual sum was probably greater. Most of the acquisitions were made after the beginning of the Mandate and followed the major purchases of large tracts of land that characterized the early stages of Jewish land acquisition. The payments for land purchased from foreign owners were taken out of Palestine, while those made for purchases from local Arabs

TABLE 7
Amount and Value of Land Purchased by Jews, 1878–1945

| | Net Amount of Land Sold by Arabs and Acquired by Jews | | Rural Land Acquired by Jews | | |
	Dunums	Total Price (£P)	Dunums	Total Price (£P)[a]	Average Price per Dunum (£P)
1878–1900			218,170	141,811	0.650
1901–1914			199,930	235,917	1.180
1920–1927	427,547	2,585,758	446,550	1,181,125	2.645
1928–1936	333,031	5,202,886	367,196	2,149,933	5.855
Total 1876–1936			1,231,846	3,609,309	2.930
Total 1920–1936	760,578	7,789,644	813,746	3,331,058	4.093
1937–1945	178,339	4,342,370	288,062[b]	2,012,668[b]	6.99[b]
Total 1920–1945	938,917	12,132,014	1,519,908[c]	5,721,454[c]	3.76[c]

Sources: Gurevich, Statistical Handbook, pp. 135–37; Government of Palestine, Statistical Abstract, 1939, p. 162; ibid., 1942, p. 144; ibid., 1944/45, pp. 277–78; Government of Palestine, Department of Statistics, General Monthly Bulletin of Current Statistics, various issues.
Notes:
 a. Based on that portion of the transactions for which data are available, and on applying the average price per dunum to the entire amount of land acquired. For the whole period, data is available on 69.9 percent of the transactions (1878–1900: 75.6%; 1901–1914: 64.4%; 1920–1927: 88.5%; 1928–1936: 47.0%).
 b. 1940–1944.
 c. 1878–1936; 1940–1944.

remained in the country. The proportion of sales by foreign owners was greater before the First World War and during the Second World War. The proportion of sales by local Arabs was greater during the mid-1920s and early 1930s, years of economic prosperity, large Jewish immigration and consequently a greater demand for land.[66]

What became of this money? According to the survey of 104 villages reported by Johnson and Crosbie in 1930, the average net return to an owner-cultivator was £P35.20, and to a tenant, after subtracting the portion due the landlord, £P20. The estimated annual cost of living for a family of six averaged between £P26 and £P38, not including £P8 for interest on debt, which averaged, according to their calculations, £P27 per family.[67] The Jews paid more than £P2 million for land purchased between 1928 and 1936, enough to pay off the debts of 74,000 families. That was almost the total number of Arab earners in Palestine engaged in 1931 in ordinary cultivation, or in intensive agriculture other than citrus growing.[68]

But the Jews' land purchases were concentrated in nine of Palestine's eighteen subdistricts, and the total number of rural Arab families in those subdistricts did not exceed 42,000.[69] Since subsequent reports on the condition of Palestinian agriculture continued to emphasize the precarious position of the Arab peasant cultivators,[70] it is clear that most of the money paid for Arab land was not received by the smallholders. Part of it was probably invested in the expansion of Arab citrus cultivation, which added 115,000 dunums between 1928 and 1936. Some must have also been used by Arab growers to introduce and expand vegetable production for the market. Between 1921 and 1935 vegetable production as estimated from tithe returns and by the Department of Agriculture increased from 7,742 to 56,399 tons, which represented approximately 34,000 dunums.[71] It is difficult to know how many cultivators grew vegetables, or the area each cultivated, but if a total of only 34,000 dunums (about 1,360 acres) were used by Arabs for growing vegetables in 1937, not much of the proceeds from land sales could have been spent for this purpose. The Jews claimed that their land purchases were providing the resources for improving Arab cultivation, but this does not seem to have been the case.

Displacement of Arab Cultivators

In November 1918, the British military administration in Palestine closed the land registry offices, thus halting all transactions in land, including transfers from Arabs to Jews. The main reason for the closure was the administration's fear that unrestricted land sales to Jews would lead to the creation of a class of landless Arabs whose numbers would be continually increasing. Their concerns were shared by those Arabs who, even before the war, had opposed land sales to Jews on nationalistic grounds.[72] In 1920 the first Land Transfer Ordinance was promulgated. Its aim was to insure that tenants of long standing would not be evicted upon the sale of the lands they cultivated.[73] Neither the 1920 ordinance nor subsequent attempts to protect cultivators by legislation limiting unrestricted land transfers were successful in preventing extensive sale of Arab land to Jews, because ways were always found by Arab sellers and Jewish buyers, and Arab purchasers as well, to circumvent the regulations. But the danger to Arab Palestine from land sales to Jews did not lie only in the dispossession of tenants, or even in the "voluntary" self-creation of a class of landless Arabs who had formerly been owner-cultivators. It lay also in the creation of a base "for the acquisition and establishment of a Jewish national territory upon which a state could function and in which a population could survive."[74]

Considerable controversy existed regarding the effects of Jewish land purchases on the Arab cultivators, and in particular regarding the degree to which such purchases were displacing or dispossessing the tenants. The question of displacement was more complex perhaps than the parties to the political struggle were willing to admit. The sale of Arab lands to Jews occurred in many different kinds of circumstances, and the creation of a market for land provided cultivators with opportunities which had not previously existed. The development of a land market in Palestine was not accompanied by the creation of nonagricultural industrial jobs which could have provided the foundation for the growth of an Arab urban labor force, since most industrial establishments employing more than two or three workers were owned by Jews, who usually did not employ Arabs. Given the depressed state of many of the peasant cultivators, whether owners or tenants, and the absence of any substantial government or other assistance which would have enabled them to improve production on their holdings, the chance of being freed of the burden of their land might have seemed quite attractive.

The complexity of the circumstances attending the sale of Arab land to Jews can be appreciated by examining the list of exclusions from the category of "landless Arab," as it was defined for the purpose of the inquiry into Arab dispossession carried out by the government in 1931 and 1932:

> 1. Persons who owned land other than that which they cultivated as tenants
> 2. Persons who had found land other than that from which they were displaced and were now cultivating it as tenants
> 3. Persons who, subsequent to the sale of the land from which they were displaced, obtained other land, but, on account of poverty or other reasons, had since ceased to cultivate it

4. Persons who, at the time of sale, were not cultivators, such as laborers and plowmen

5. Persons who had themselves sold land to Jews

6. Persons who, although landless, had obtained equally satisfactory occupation.[75]

These limitations may, as Stein writes, have reflected more than anything "a Jewish Agency political victory," but they also suggest the changes that were occurring in rural Arab society at the time. The categories described part of the range of conditions in which peasants for one reason or another were unable or unwilling to continue cultivating the land they had once worked. A total of 3,737 claims were submitted for inclusion in the register of landless Arabs; 899 were finally recognized. The categories of ineligible applicants clearly included those who were displaced by the sale of the land they cultivated, and there may have been additional persons who did not apply even though they were in fact qualified.[76]

It is possible to estimate, very roughly, the maximum number of Arabs who could have been displaced by Jewish land purchases by utilizing data that Stein presents on the sale of Arab land to Jews between June 1, 1934, and August 31, 1936.[77] Of 121,617 dunums of land purchased during that period, 27.7 percent represented holdings of less than 100 dunums; 28.6 percent holdings of 100 to 150 dunums; and 43.7 percent holdings of more than 500 dunums. The total land bought by Jews in 1930–1939 was 331,619 dunums, and from 1940 to 1945 Jews bought 93,167 dunums.[78] The maximum number of persons who could have been displaced by these sales can be estimated by applying to the total land purchased in each period the proportions obtained for 1934–1936, computing the number of sales in each size category by applying the mean holding size from the 1934–1936 data, and multiplying the number of sales by an average of five persons per peasant family. The results are shown in table 8.[79]

According to the estimate, a maximum of 41,000 persons could have been displaced by Jewish land purchases.[80] This estimate is undoubtedly too high: not all the land was cultivated, many sellers certainly retained part of their holdings, and others may no longer have been living on them when they were sold. Together with the 3,737 claims submitted to the landless Arab inquiry, not all of which were valid even by criteria less strict than those applied, the maximum number of displaced Arabs could

TABLE 8

Estimate of the Maximum Number of Arabs Who Could Have Been Displaced by Jewish Land Purchases, 1930–1945

Size of Sale (dunums)	Percent of Total Sales	Mean Area of Sale (dunums)	1930–1939			1940–1945			Total, 1930–1945		
			Dunums	Number of Sales	Maximum Number of Persons Displaced	Dunums	Number of Sales	Maximum Number of Persons Displaced	Dunums	Number of Sales	Maximum Number of Persons Displaced
Less than 100	27.7	15.76	91,858	5,829	29,145	25,807	1,638	8,190	117,665	7,467	37,335
100–500	28.6	212.21	94,843	447	2,235	26,646	126	630	121,489	573	2,865
More than 500	43.7	1,297.07	144,918	112	560	40,714	31	155	185,632	143	715
Total			331,619	6,388	31,940	93,167	1,795	8,975	424,786	8,183	40,915

Sources: Stein, *Land Question in Palestine,* p. 181; *Survey of Palestine,* p. 244; see also notes in text.

have reached 60,000 persons. A more reasonable estimate of the number of persons actually displaced by Jewish land purchases might range between 10,000 and 30,000, or between 2,000 and 6,0000 households. This would include owner-cultivators who sold their own lands, as well as tenants whose lands were sold from under them.

In effect, Jewish land purchases contributed to the process of breakdown of traditional rural Arab life in Palestine whose principal causes were the growth of the rural population and its inability to support itself on the land because of outmoded techniques and of the way in which peasant agriculture was financed. Government distress at the creation of a class of landless Arabs was rooted at least in part in the desire to prevent any radical changes in existing Arab society, but the administration did not receive the funds it would have needed to put Arab farming on a profitable basis. By providing employment on public works in rural areas, the government attempted to ameliorate the hardships faced by the peasants, without solving the basic problems which they confronted.

The land transfer regulations were an additional means by which the government sought to lessen the effects of the transformations underway in the countryside. The 1920 Land Transfer Ordinance restricted the size and the value of land involved in sales. It was criticized by Arabs, by Jews, and by government officials, and amended the following year to remove restrictions on the area and value of the land to be sold, and on purchases by persons living outside Palestine. The "speculative" purpose of a particular transaction ceased to be a ground for refusing approval of it, and what protection the ordinance afforded extended only to tenants-in-occupation, but not to agricultural laborers or to owner-cultivators. Various devices were employed to circumvent the limitations on sales of land occupied by tenants; and in recognition of the failure of the purpose of the 1920 ordinance and its amendment, new regulations were instituted. The 1929 Protection of Cultivators Ordinance allowed the substitution of monetary compensation for the requirement that tenants retain sufficient land for their maintenance. In 1933 a new Cultivators (Protection) Ordinance combined the provisions of the 1929 law and subsequent amendments to it, and in its main points remained in force until the end of the Mandate. According to the 1933 law any tenants, specified relatives, or heirs, as well as hired laborers who received a portion of the produce in compensation for their work, who had occupied and cultivated land for at least one year, were protected from eviction.[81]

In 1940, following the recommendations of the Palestine Partition Commission, land transfer regulations were instituted that restricted or prohibited entirely in most of Palestine the sale of Arab land to Jews, on the grounds expressed in the 1939 White Paper:

> The reports of several expert Commissions have indicated that, owing to the natural growth of the Arab population and the steady sale in recent years of Arab land to Jews, there is now in certain areas no room for further transfers of Arab land, whilst in some other areas such transfers of land must be restricted if Arab cultivators are to maintain their existing standard of life and a considerable landless Arab population is not soon to be created.[82]

The Jews' policy regarding land purchase stressed the accumulation of holdings even if they could not be immediately settled or cultivated. Since possession of land was viewed by the Jews as crucial to the establishment of their national home, their efforts were divided between settling land already in their hands and acquiring additional land for future settlement. The Arabs, on the other hand, stressed the current consequences of Jewish land purchases. Although they frequently voiced their apprehension about the possibility of the eventual transfer of all Arab lands to Jewish hands, such arguments, however deeply felt, were presented rhetorically rather than substantiated with detailed evidence. Both the Jews and the government recognized the connection between agricultural development and the size of the population that could be supported on the land. The report of the Palestine Royal Commission noted that "unless there is a marked change in the methods of cultivation, the land in Palestine is unable to support a large increase in the population."[83] In 1939 the Partition Commission wrote that "it seems certain that the amount of land now under cultivation, by present methods and on present standards, is insufficient to support the same percentage of the total Arab population today as in 1922." The Jews submitted numerous memoranda to demonstrate how much land could be freed for Jewish settlement by the introduction of intensive cultivation.[84]

The future land needs of the Arab population of Palestine did not receive detailed attention. Although the increase in the size of the Arab population since the beginning of the Mandate was repeatedly noted and used as evidence for the improvement of conditions in Palestine, seldom was consideration given to the problem of reserve lands for Arabs, in contrast to the attention paid to future land needs of the Jews. While Jewish Agency representatives sought to arrive at a position regarding the issue of land reserves for Arabs, the absence of any long-term government agricultural development policy meant that no appropriate context existed in which future Arab land needs could be explicitly discussed.[85]

It is, in a sense, remarkable that the connection between the growing Arab population, on the one hand, and diminishing Arab landholdings, on the other, was not made explicitly either by the government or, even more, by the Arabs themselves. Both opposed the transfer of Arab lands to Jews, though not for the same reasons. The most likely explanation for Arab silence on this matter may have been the absence of any effective organization to speak for the interest of the peasants, who were most affected by the decline in the amount of available land. It may also have been the case that the combined effects of population increase and reduction in available land had not yet begun to make themselves felt seriously in the twenty years between the beginning of the Mandate and the outbreak of the Second World War. The increased opportunities for nonagricultural employment, as well as the extension of irrigated vegetable cultivation during the war may have postponed the more serious consequences of increasing population pressure on the land.

The Distribution of Arab Landholding

Analysis of land tenure in Palestine during the Mandate has always been hampered by the absence of systematic data on the distribution of holdings in the individual villages. While there has long been agreement as to the extent of land sales by Arabs to Jews for the country as a whole, resolution of the controversy over the effect of Jewish settlement on the Arab population depends on detailed information on particular localities in which patterns of landowning changed over the years. An equally interesting question, but one that has received even less attention, involves the degree of inequality of landownership among Arabs themselves and the changes in the distribution of Arab landholding during the Mandate. It seems to be agreed that, in the 1920s and earlier, large tracts of land—many tens of thousands of dunums in extent—were owned by Arabs who lived outside the country, but no one has ever investigated in detail what became of most of these lands or of the people who lived on them. French commented at the beginning of the 1930s that the concentration of hill property in the hands of Arab owners had accelerated in recent years, but we do not know whether these lands had been cultivated, if peasants were made landless, or whether they were forced out of their villages entirely.

The regulations for the protection of cultivators introduced and subsequently revised and expanded by the government may have been aimed primarily at mitigating what were seen to be the harmful effects of Jewish land purchases, but their provisions were also used by Arab cultivators against Arab landowners in cases where sales to Jews were not an issue. Between 1932 and 1938 Arabs sold to other Arabs approximately one-quarter million dunums, which represented almost half of the lands sold by Arabs during those years.[86] It is unlikely that the net result of these transactions was neutral regarding the distribution of Arab landholding, but there is no way of knowing at present whether they reduced or increased inequality of landownership among Arabs.

One factor which most observers expected to work in the direction of reducing the average holding size was the distribution of family property among heirs following the death or retirement of the household head. Whether or not the heirs actually split the holding into separate parcels, or continued to cultivate it jointly in order to achieve greater efficiency, the result was the same: a reduction of the amount of land available to each household, and a decreasing likelihood that its members could continue to subsist from agriculture without changes in crops and techniques of cultivation. Increasing fragmentation, however, might gradually be likely to bring about an opposite trend. We would expect that under such circumstances growing numbers of persons would seek alternative employment, as in government public works projects. The absence of data makes speculation unavoidable, but it is likely that, as holdings became smaller and families devoted less time to their cultivation, there was a growing incentive to sell them to other villagers who still had sufficient land and could afford to extend their holdings. Thus, over the long run, two opposing processes could have continued simultaneously: fragmentation of family holdings because of inheritance, leading to a reduction in mean holding size, and agglomeration by purchase of impracticably small holdings, leading to an increase in mean holding size.

Only twice, in 1936 and 1944, did the government undertake surveys to collect information that might have shed some light on the question of the distribution of Arab ownership. In preparation for the visit of the Royal Commission, the Department of Lands and Surveys and the Department of Statistics excerpted from the land registry books data on 322 Arab villages throughout Palestine which included the number of holdings in the village, the size of the holdings, the amount of land registered in the mukhtar's name, and the amount registered as *waqf*,[87] state land, and in Jewish ownership.[88] In 1944 a detailed analysis was carried out of social and economic conditions in five cereal-growing villages in the Ramle subdistrict. The only published results of the 1936 investigation appeared in the report on the 1944 survey, which included a table showing the distribution of holdings by size for the 322 villages.[89] Some information on landowning in the early 1940s is also available for a number of villages in the Nablus, Jenin, and Tulkarm subdistricts.[90]

Neither the Israel State Archives nor the Public Record Office in London could locate additional material from the 1936 survey, but what is apparently a summary of a portion of its findings was contained in one of the files of the Central Zionist Archives, Jerusalem.[91] The tables in the file refer to four subdistricts in the northern part of Palestine—Haifa, Nazareth, Acre, and Safed. While there is no indication on the file copies of their origin, there could be no other source than the government investigation for such data on individual villages. The Jews did not have free access to the land registry books and had frequently to make official requests for information they needed in the preparation of memoranda for submission to the government. Nor could they conduct surveys in the villages in order to obtain such statistics. It is probable, however, that the Jewish Agency was able to obtain a copy of the results of the survey—thanks to official assistance or unofficial connivance the agency had received other material, whether or not confidential, prepared for or directed to the Palestine government. The partial results of the 1936 survey preserved in the Zionist archives are thus a unique source for the study of the conditions of land tenure in the mid-1930s.

A number of difficulties exist which require that these summaries be used cautiously. They cover only about one-third of the settled area of Palestine, and most of the villages included are located in the Galilee. Thus, they completely omit the large areas of cereal cultivation farther to the south. They also include little citrus area. The state of the land registry books from which the data were extracted is not clear. Settlement

of land title had been underway in some of the subdistricts, particularly
Haifa, though most of the area of the four subdistricts had not even been
surveyed by the end of 1936.[92] The Turkish land registration was not
cadastral (based on a survey defining plots on the ground), and there may
have been inaccuracies in the determination of the size of holdings,
though probably not in the statement of their number. Moreover, as
described in note 88, the distribution underestimates slightly the average
holding size, although the difference is probably too small to be of any
significance.

There were 102 localities for which information was collected in the
four subdistricts; the analysis that follows is based on 88 of them. Two
types were excluded: those which were clearly tribal areas, rather than
villages, and those whose population was very small but whose landholdings were very large. Both were very unlike the great majority of the
villages in the four subdistricts.[93] Table 9 summarizes the information
from the villages in the four subdistricts and compares the distribution of
holdings with that obtained for the entire sample of 322 villages. Overall,
the two distributions were very similar, though there were differences
among the subdistricts. Safed had a higher proportion of holdings
smaller than five dunums, while Haifa and Nazareth had a relatively
greater number of larger holdings. Very little land in these villages had
been registered in the name of Jews (the largest proportion, 4.3 percent,
was in the Haifa subdistrict), and since the survey predated settlement of
title only a small area had been registered as state lands.

About one-fourth of all the land in the four subdistricts was registered
in the name of the village mukhtar. There was relatively less land of this
type in the Safed subdistrict, and relatively more in the Nazareth
subdistrict. It is most likely that, prior to settlement, this was *musha'a*
land,[94] though the data would not have reflected cases in which such
land had in fact been permanently allocated among the villagers without
it having been registered as such. The amount of true *musha'a* land
which was still being periodically reallocated among the villagers was
certainly less than the amount indicated by the 1936 survey. Twenty-nine
of the 88 villages had either none, or less than 1 percent, of their land
registered in the mukhtar's name. While no village had all of its lands so
registered, 80 percent of Yanuh's lands, a village near Acre, and more
than 70 percent of the lands of six other villages, most in the Acre
subdistrict, were in the mukhtar's name.

TABLE 9
Distribution of Holdings in Arab Villages, by Size of Holding and by Subdistrict, 1936 Survey

A. TOTAL LAND IN THE VILLAGES, INCLUDING TRIBAL AREAS *(dunums)*

		Subdistrict			
	Total	Haifa	Nazareth	Acre	Safed
Number of villages	102	21	10	38	33
Total land	1,424,467	438,835	182,802	488,751	314,079
In Arab ownership[a]	1,340,921	374,599	177,470	480,470	308,382
Registered to mukhtar (%)	26.2	23.4	32.8	29.8	19.0
Registered to individuals (%)	73.8	76.6	67.2	70.2	81.0

B. DISTRIBUTION OF HOLDINGS, EXCLUDING TRIBAL AREAS

	Total, 1936 Survey	Total, 4 Sub-districts	Subdistrict			
			Haifa	Nazareth	Acre	Safed
Number of villages	322	88	21	10	35	22
Arab land registered to mukhtar (%)	NA	28.0	23.5	32.8	31.0	25.3
Total land registered to individuals (dunums)	3,252,735	898,975	286,618	119,259	324,863	168,235
Total number of holdings	71,789	20,803	3,932	3,276	9,032	4,563
Mean size of holding (dunums)	45.3	43.2	72.9	36.4	36.0	36.9
Distribution of holdings (%)						
1–4.9 dunums	31.9	36.5	29.2	38.3	32.2	50.1
5–9.9	15.1	13.4	13.4	12.7	15.0	10.6
10–19	15.9	13.2	14.6	12.2	14.9	9.1
20–49	29.1	17.6	17.6	15.8	20.9	12.3
50–99		10.1	11.1	12.1	10.0	7.8
100–499	7.7	8.5	12.6	8.2	6.3	9.4
500 or more	0.6	0.8	1.5	0.8	0.6	0.7

C. PUBLIC LAND AND LAND IN JEWISH OWNERSHIP
(percent of the total land in 102 villages and tribal areas)

		Subdistrict			
	Total	Haifa	Nazareth	Acre	Safed
Public land	3.8	10.2	2.5	0.7	0.3
Land in Jewish ownership	1.5	4.3	—	0.4	—

Source: CZA/A202/150, Number of Owners by Size of Holdings in Metric Dunums (in Hebrew).
Note:
    a. Excluding 9,197 dunums of *waqf* land.

It should be possible, in principle, to obtain an estimate of the number of landless Arab households in the surveyed villages by comparing the number of landowners with an estimate of the number of households in those villages, based on the figures for village population from the 1937 *Village Statistics*. Unfortunately, as table 10 demonstrates, such a comparison has little utility. The total number of landowners in the four subdistricts in the 1936 survey exceeds by almost 50 percent the esti-

TABLE 10

Relation Between Number of Landowners and Estimated Number of Households in Four Northern Region Subdistricts, 1936

		Subdistrict			
	Total	*Haifa*	*Nazareth*	*Acre*	*Safed*
Number of villages	81	19	9	32	21
Number of Arabs	65,288	16,738	9,579	27,935	11,036
Estimated number of households					
(Arabs/5)	13,058	3,348	1,916	5,587	2,207
Number of landowners	19,334	3,083	3,126	8,927	4,198
Relation between number of households and number of landowners[a]					
Number of villages with:					
More households than landowners	17	8	3	5	—
Equal number of households and					
landowners	9	7	—	—	2
More landowners than households	56	4	6	27	19
Total number of households and landowners according to whether there were:					
More households than landowners					
Households	1,989	1,294	293	402	—
Landowners	1,362	752	377	233	—
Equal number of households and					
landowners					
Households	1,270	1,169	—	—	101
Landowners	1,261	1,159	—	—	102
More landowners than households					
Households	9,799	885	1,623	5,185	2,106
Landowners	16,711	1,172	2,749	8,694	4,096

Sources: For number of households: Government of Palestine, *Village Statistics,* 1937; for number of landowners: CZA/A202/150.
Note:
   a. The categories are based on differences of at least 10 percent between the estimated number of households in a particular village and the number of landowners.

mated number of households obtained by dividing the Arab population of the villages by five.[95] Only in the Haifa subdistrict were there more households than landowners. The most reasonable explanation for the apparent shortage of households lies in the fragmentation of holdings due to inheritance, and the fact that a single holding was registered to one or more individuals, not to a household. Thus, a single household could be represented more than once in the count of holdings, so that a simple comparison of the number of holdings and the number of households fails to provide the desired information. (It is difficult, on this explanation, to account for the figures from the Haifa subdistrict.)

Table 11 presents a number of characteristics of the distribution of landholding in the eighty-eight villages. When the mean size of holding was large, this was generally because there were relatively many very large holdings rather than many medium-sized properties. In nineteen of the eighty-eight villages at least 50 percent of the landowners held areas of less than five dunums. In more than 40 percent of the villages, less than 10 percent of the land was registered in the name of the mukhtar; in the Haifa subdistrict most of the villages had between 10 and 50 percent of the land registered in this way, while in most of the villages in the Acre and Safed subdistricts this proportion was less than 10 percent.

A rough measure of the concentration of village landownership in larger holdings can be obtained, in the absence of data for individual properties, by comparing the mean and median holding size for each village. In a symmetrical distribution the mean equals the median; the mean is greater than the median when the distribution is skewed upward, and less than the median when the distribution is skewed downward. The greater the value of the ratio of mean to median size of holding (in only one village was the mean less than the median), the greater the concentration of larger holdings in the distribution of village land. Section D of table 11 summarizes the comparison: landownership was most concentrated in larger holdings in Safed, next in Haifa, and least in Acre (the Nazareth subdistrict was excluded from the comparison because data was available on only ten villages).

There was some relationship between the proportion of village lands registered in the mukhtar's name and both the mean size of individual holdings and the ratio between the mean and median size of holding (table 11, section E). The greater the proportion of land registered to the mukhtar, the smaller the mean size of individual holdings; all else re-

TABLE 11
Selected Landholding Characteristics for Eighty-eight Villages in Four Subdistricts, 1936

A. MEAN SIZE OF HOLDING, BY SUBDISTRICT (*percent*)

Dunums	Total (88 villages)	Haifa (21 villages)	Nazareth (10 villages)	Acre (35 villages)	Safed (22 villages)
Less than 20	14.8	9.5	—	22.9	13.6
20–29.9	21.6	14.3	40	14.3	31.8
30–49.9	26.1	14.3	30	34.3	22.7
50–99.9	19.3	28.6	10	14.3	22.7
100 or more	18.2	33.3	20	14.3	9.1
Total	100.0	100.0	100	100.1	99.9
Mean size of holding	43.2	72.9	36.4	36.0	36.9

B. PROPORTION OF INDIVIDUAL HOLDINGS LESS THAN FIVE DUNUMS IN AREA, BY SUBDISTRICT
(*absolute numbers*)

Proportion of Holdings	Total (88)	Haifa (21)	Nazareth (10)	Acre (35)	Safed (22)
0–24.9 %	24	9	2	13	—
25–49.9	45	11	6	18	10
50–74.9	13	—	2	2	9
75–100	6	1	—	2	3
Total	88	21	10	35	22

C. PROPORTION OF ARAB-OWNED LAND REGISTERED TO MUKHTAR, BY SUBDISTRICT (*percent*)

Proportion of Land	Total (88)	Haifa (21)	Nazareth (10)	Acre (35)	Safed (22)
None	33.0	14.3	(10)	42.9	45.5
Less than 10%	10.2	14.3	(10)	5.7	13.6
10–29.9	15.9	28.6	(20)	11.4	9.1
30–49.9	18.2	28.6	(50)	8.6	9.1
50–69.9	14.8	9.5	(10)	20.0	13.6
70–100	8.0	4.8	—	11.4	9.1
Total	100.1	100.1	(100)	100.0	100.0
Percent registered to mukhtar	28.0	23.5	32.8	31.0	25.3

D. CONCENTRATION OF LAND OWNERSHIP IN LARGE HOLDINGS:
RATIO OF MEAN SIZE OF HOLDING TO MEDIAN SIZE OF HOLDING, BY SUBDISTRICT *(percent)*

Ratio of Mean to Median Size	Total (88)	Haifa (21)	Nazareth (10)	Acre (35)	Safed (22)
Less than 1	1.1	4.8	—	—	—
1.0–1.9	22.7	9.5	(10)	40.0	13.6
2.0–2.9	22.7	19.0	(30)	31.4	9.1
3.0–4.9	21.6	33.3	(40)	14.3	13.6
5.0–9.9	17.0	19.0	—	5.7	40.9
10.0 or more	14.8	14.3	(20)	8.6	22.7
Total	99.9	99.9	(100)	100.0	99.9
3.0 or more	53.5	66.7	(60)	28.6	77.3

E. RELATION BETWEEN PROPORTION OF LAND REGISTERED TO MUKHTAR, MEAN SIZE OF
INDIVIDUAL HOLDING, AND RATIO OF MEAN SIZE OF HOLDING TO MEDIAN SIZE OF HOLDING,
BY SUBDISTRICT *(Pearson r)*

	Relation Between Proportion of Land Registered to Mukhtar and:	
Subdistrict	Mean Size of Individual Holding	Ratio of Mean to Median Size of Holding
Haifa	− 0.57	0.14
Nazareth	− 0.57	− 0.50
Acre	− 0.42	− 0.25
Safed	− 0.26	− 0.41

Source: CZA/A202/150, "Number of Owners by Size of Holdings in Metric Dunums" (in Hebrew).

maining equal, that land was not available to be taken over by individuals. The relationship suggests, however, that as *musha'a* land was permanently allocated among villagers, its distribution probably reinforced the existing inequality of landownership in the village rather than ameliorating it. In three of the four subdistricts, there was also a negative relationship between the proportion of land registered to the mukhtar and the measure of concentration of village landholding. This suggests that there was relatively less concentration of landownership in *musha'a* villages, and is consistent with the inference that the permanent allocation of *musha'a* land increased the holdings of larger landowners proportionately more than it did those of smaller landowners.[96]

The desire of the Palestine government to eliminate *musha'a* as an impediment to agricultural development, and the Jews' belief that it hindered their land purchases, was one more factor in the weakening of the village community, while at the same time it was a reflection of the changes that had already taken place within its bounds. Here was an additional example of the contradictions in government policy toward rural Arab society: while opposed to policies that would have improved the condition of the peasants at the expense of their landlords and creditors, it undermined the traditional institutions that helped that society maintain itself. The data also suggest that in 1936 *musha'a* tenure might still have been fairly widespread.

There seems to be no relationship between the characteristics of landownership summarized in table 11 and the geographical distribution of the villages. Except for the proportion of land registered in the mukhtar's name, with villages having less than 5 percent of their lands in that category being concentrated in two groupings northeast of Acre and north of Safed, there were no clear concentrations of villages according to mean or median size of holding; the proportion of holdings less than five dunums in area; or the ratio of the mean to the median holding size. This suggests that the circumstances affecting the structure of landholding in a particular village were likely to be specific to it, rather than applying more generally to a wider area, and that the explanation for a particular pattern should be sought in the history of the individual village.

Although the 1936 survey of holdings was to provide information for estimates of the subsistence area required by a peasant family, the Department of Lands and Surveys was unable to prepare them. According to testimony before the Royal Commission, the difficulty arose in determining to what extent any particular peasant was in fact living from his holding. The survey showed that about 35 percent of the holdings were under five dunums in size, and the witness noted that "it is perfectly certain that no one can live on that area and that consequently a very large proportion of the rural population of Palestine is actually doing something else besides agriculture. In these particular cases it would appear that the main occupation is non-agricultural."[97] If holdings smaller than 5 and larger than 500 dunums were excluded, the average holding size was 33 dunums. "The only inference is that a very large number of the agricultural population have a subsidiary means of subsistence, since this area of 33 dunums does not agree with our experience of what is necessary for a man to live on if he is doing nothing but agriculture."[98]

The figure of thirty-three dunums applied to all cultivable land. For Rural Property Tax categories 1–3 and 5–8 (the citrus and better quality crop land) the average was nineteen dunums. The survey was undertaken to determine how many families could have been settled on certain areas of land, but officials of government departments were unable to "found any practical conclusions" on the results.[99] In part this was because there had been substantial changes in landholding since the 1931 census, but it was also because no reliable information existed on the number of agriculturalists who currently had additional means of livelihood.

The data on the Nablus, Jenin, and Tulkarm villages in the early 1940s refer to a more restricted area than the 1936 survey, and the information collected is different.[100] Though Kendall's work does not include data on landholding, we can learn something from it about other kinds of inequality in the villages (table 12). Most of the localities considered were small (only six of the twenty-three had 1,000 or more inhabitants), though the average population of those in the Nablus subdistrict was twice that of the villages in the Tulkarm subdistrict. What is most interesting for our purposes is the average number of livestock per household, and the proportion of men working outside the village. Kendall's data refer to the summer of 1941, almost two years after the start of the war, by which time the British military presence in Palestine had greatly increased, and the opportunities for work in British army camps had multiplied.[101] Yet in seven of the twenty-three localities there were no men employed outside the village in nonagricultural jobs. Most of those who had found outside work, on the other hand, had jobs which were paid for by public funds: the railways, the departments of Public Works and Education, the police, the postal services. Only in a few cases were villagers engaged in commerce (those from Dannaba, for example, were cart and stall owners in Jaffa) or employed in agriculture (from Anabta and from Ramin). Although some villages had very few men in outside employment (Shuweiqat, with 2,800 inhabitants, had only 12), most had at least 20 percent.[102] Many of the village households, therefore, were clearly dependent on income from outside jobs.

The other side of the coin is the relative absence of livestock, especially cattle and other work animals, which suggests that the families whose men worked outside the village no longer actively engaged in cultivation, for there were not enough work animals in the villages to provide each household with a team for ploughing. The same holds for

TABLE 12
Characteristics of Villages in Nablus and Tulkarm Subdistricts

	Nablus	Tulkarm	Total
Number of villages for which data is available	15	8	23
Total population	10,380	12,118	22,498
Mean village population	692	1,515	978
Mean number of households[a]	108	237	153
Livestock per village			
Sheep and goats	419	581	475
Cattle	203	279	229
Other work animals	62	125	84
Livestock per household			
Sheep and goats	3.9	2.5	3.1
Cattle	1.9	1.2	1.5
Other work animals	0.6	0.5	0.5
Range of livestock per household, all villages			
Sheep and goats	1.0–21.9	0.4–6.7	
Cattle	0.4–4.4	0.1–9.9	
Other work animals	0.3–5.3	0.3–1.3	
Men working outside village			
Total	918	660	1,578
Percent of all men[b]	35%	22%	28%
Range of percent working outside, all villages[c]	19%–60%	2%–53%	

Source: Kendall, *Village Development in Palestine*, pp. 49–52.
Notes:
   a. Population/6.4, size of household in 1944 village survey; see Government of Palestine, Department of Statistics, *General Monthly Bulletin of Current Statistics*, July 1945, p. 433.
   b. Assuming men aged fifteen or older represent one-fourth of the population.
   c. Six of the Nablus villages and one of the Tulkarm villages had no men working outside.

sheep and goats; the range across villages is great, indicating that many families could not have kept more than one or two goats whose milk they consumed at home or sold. Such families were either very poor or had relinquished agriculture and husbandry for dependence on wage labor.

    Another view of the same general region is provided by the data which Granott collected, apparently to use in his book on the Palestine land regime. His files contain information on twenty-five villages; fourteen of them were *mafrouz* while seven still had all or part of their lands in *musha'a* tenure; there was no information about land tenure in the four remaining villages. In seven of the villages there were no large landowners, though in others there were individual holdings which were hundreds of dunums in size; some exceeded one thousand dunums. Granott considered holdings up to 100 dunums as "small"; from 100 to 500 dunums as "medium"; and above 500 dunums as "large."[103]

The average size of the holding owned by villagers who were not large landowners was twenty to fifty dunums. Many of the villages had part of their land in the hills and part in the plains. Even if the entire holding of fifty dunums was in the plains, it would have been too small when put under grain to provide sufficient yield for a family's needs. The file indicates that some villages raised vegetables; that might have provided an alternative to grain by requiring a much smaller area, but it would also have required irrigation. We must conclude that many of the villagers held little or no plains land and depended primarily on income from orchards and especially from olive groves. In eight of the eighteen villages for which such information was available, there were no landless families; the number of such families in all the other villages, except one, was small, ranging from two to twenty (the latter in a population of 3,000 people). Only Qalqilya was an exception; it had one hundred landless families, though no mention was made of their means of livelihood. Most of the landless in the other nine villages worked as agricultural laborers or as day laborers in nearby towns like Tulkarm.

The larger landowners leased all or most of their lands to tenants, though some cultivated a portion of them with hired labor. It is noteworthy that, for the most part, the landowners continued to receive rent in kind, as a predetermined proportion of the crop, and not in cash, even in the 1940s. It is difficult to imagine that a money economy had not penetrated to villages between Nablus and Tulkarm. It is more likely that tenant cultivators still had no easy access to markets and were unable themselves to sell their crops and pay their obligations in cash. This suggests that despite the general increase in prices for agricultural products during the war, many tenants were unable to alter the conditions under which they had previously leased land. Although it seems to have been generally accepted that many Arab cultivators were able dramatically to improve their circumstances and free themselves from debt as a result of rising wartime prices, it is hard to see how tenants who continued to pay their rent in kind could have benefited from these changes. Since yields did not increase, nor did holding size, the lot of tenants farming land belonging to others could not greatly have improved.

The third source of systematic information on Arab landholding describes five villages in the Ramleh subdistrict in 1944. Title to village lands was settled during 1933–1935, and almost all the cultivable area (25,685 dunums) was in private hands. Most (88 percent) of the 781 private landowners lived in the village where their land was located; another 9 percent lived in nearby or more distant villages; and the remainder lived in towns. More than three-quarters of the holdings (77.9 percent) were completely within the village, and another fifth were split between the village and other villages. About 15 percent of the area of village holdings was outside the village.[104] The man holding size of cultivable land was 32.8 dunums; for resident owners it was 30.3 dunums; for owners in other villages, 23 dunums; and for owners living in towns, 136.1 dunums.[105] More than half (53.3 percent) the holdings in the five villages were no larger than 20 dunums, and 95 percent were smaller than 100 dunums. Most of the land was devoted to field crops; in the one village for which such data were presented, only 3 percent (212 dunums) of the arable land was devoted to orchards, and four-fifths of this was in the *hawakir* area of groves and gardens adjacent to the village's built-up area.

The land in the five villages was divided into 2,522 parcels (3.2 parcels per owner), and the parcels were in turn divided into 6,871 shares (2.7 shares per parcel; 8.8 shares per owner). Half (1,274) the parcels in the five villages were jointly owned and half were not; since there were only 781 owners this meant that many of them must have been the sole owners of a portion of their holding and joint owners of another portion. It was found in the one village for which such data were analyzed by the survey's authors that larger parcels had more co-owners than did smaller parcels, although there were many examples of parcels that did not conform to this pattern. Of the jointly owned parcels whose co-owners were not members of the same household, more than one-quarter were leased out or jointly cultivated, about 5 percent were repartitioned every two years (despite the fact that title had been settled more a decade earlier), and the remainder were permanently partitioned among the co-owners. Land transactions were infrequent; in the one village for which such information was collected only thirty transactions involving eighty-six dunums had occurred in the decade preceding the survey.[106] Whatever changes in the distribution of landownership may have occurred during that period were due almost entirely to inheritance.

Publication of the survey's findings was discontinued in early 1946 with the end of the regular appearance of the *General Monthly Bulletin of Current Statistics*, in which the findings were published, as a result of cutbacks in government activities in preparation for British withdrawal from the country and from the Mandate. Although information must have been collected on leasing arrangements and occupation as well as on demographic structure and land tenure, it was never made available to the public. Still, a comparison of the results of the 1944 survey with the data from the villages in the Tulkarm area two years earlier, and with the 1936 survey data from villages in the northern subdistricts, suggests that the war had not brought any fundamental alterations in the distribution of village landed property. The average holding was still too small to support a family. About 40 percent of the land was in holdings larger than 100 dunums. Even if we assume that all the land owned by nonresidents who lived in towns was in holdings greater than 100 dunums (the average size of their holding was 136 dunums), almost 30 percent of village lands were concentrated in the hands of a relatively small number of residents. Since there were almost no land transactions for ten years, the inequality of landownership in these villages must have been fairly long-standing.

The lack of detailed information on individual villages showing changes in patterns of landholding over time makes it very difficult to evaluate the conflicting claims regarding changes in the condition of Arab peasant cultivators. The fragmentary evidence which has been reviewed in this section, however, does not indicate that substantial improvements occurred in their ability to make a living from agriculture. The farmers who were able to adapt themselves to new market opportunities arising out of the war do not stand out in these chance studies. Although they undoubtedly existed and may well have flourished, the true extent of their operations remains unknown.

Upgrading of Arab Lands

A portion of the uncultivated land in Palestine at any time was capable of being brought under cultivation, and a portion of the cultivated land was capable of being upgraded so as to permit the production of more valu-

able crops. The extent of such lands was a matter of continuing controversy between the government and the Jews, for the degree of "cultivability" of unproductive land was determined by the characteristics of
the land itself in combination with the investment required to make it
productive. Since the major obstacle to the cultivation of much land in
Palestine was the lack of water, the cost of irrigation by wells or by
natural streams was a major component in the calculation of the resources required. Land that might have been cultivable given the needed
resources, which the Jews possessed, was not cultivable by Arabs who
lacked them.

Systematic efforts to extend the amount of cultivable land in Palestine had begun toward the end of the nineteenth century, with the beginning of modern Jewish settlement. These efforts continued throughout
the period of the Mandate, undertaken by Jews, by the government, and
by Arabs. Land was brought into cultivation as a result of the draining of
malarial swamps; unirrigated land suitable only to cereals was made
more productive by irrigation; previously uncultivated hill lands were
terraced and planted. A basic argument made by the Jews throughout the
period of the Mandate was that the size of the population that could be
supported on the land could be greatly increased by the intensification of
cultivation on Arab lands, the consolidation of scattered holdings, and
the establishment of Jewish settlements on the land thus "freed." Although no government program was undertaken to transform Palestinian
Arab agriculture, the Jews frequently claimed that such a process was
occurring on a smaller scale in many areas where they were buying land.
Their purchase of part of an Arab's holding, so their argument ran,
enabled the seller to repay debts and invest the balance of the sale price
in the development of the remainder of the holding, thereby making a
better living than before on an area smaller than was previously required.

It is unclear to what extent such transactions actually led to the
intensification of Arab cultivation. The Jews often gave examples of
villages where such a process had occurred, but no systematic information seems ever to have been collected.[107] Leonard Stein, who was in
charge of preparing evidence for presentation to the Palestine Royal
Commission, asked Bernard Joseph, legal advisor to the Jewish Agency's Political Department, whether additional examples were known
that could be cited to help buttress the claim.[108] Joseph himself said
in his evidence to the Royal Commission, "I do not know whether we

have proved that point to the satisfaction of the Commission or not, but I say that that, at any rate, gives [the villager who sells part of his land] a chance, and certainly some people have benefited; of that there can be no doubt. Possibly not everyone can benefit in that way, but if you stop the thing [land sales to Jews] entirely nobody has a chance . . . of improving their position."[109] At least one government witness before the Royal Commission was skeptical as to the extent of such improvements.[110]

Some evidence is available from published government statistics reporting the area of land in each tax category. This data, based on the Village Notebooks, refers to the distribution of land by village according to broad categories of the Rural Property Tax Ordinance. The upgrading of land could have been reflected in a change in the distribution of the total amount of land among the tax categories, for the country as a whole as well as for individual villages. Data is available for 1938 and for 1944/45,[111] and comparison of the two periods should show the degree to which the wartime need for increased production led to an upgrading of Arab lands as a result of Jewish purchase.[112]

Table 13 shows the distribution of all land in Palestine for 1938 and 1944/45, by the land tax categories. There was a slight shift upward in the quality of the land as represented by its distribution among the categories. The amount of "plantation" lands (categories 5–8) increased by about 6 percent, and the amount of taxable cereal lands (categories 9–13) increased very slightly (1.3 percent), to the extent of 60,000 dunums.[113] It would be useful to be able to account for the "source" of 134,000 dunums added to tax categories 5–13 between 1938 and 1944/45, but that would require access to records for individual villages and individual parcels of land within them. Thus, it is difficult to know whether the evidence of upgrading found in table 13 reflects a change on the ground or was merely due to reclassification for other reasons, including errors of categorization.

It would be desirable to examine separately the changes in the amount of lands held by Jews and by Arabs in each of the Rural Property Tax categories in order to seek evidence of upgrading of land. Unfortunately, although statistics on landholdings by tax category are available for Jews and Arabs separately for 1937, 1943, and 1945 in the *Village Statistics* series, changes in the classification of ownership during that period makes it impossible to utilize for comparative purposes the data

TABLE 13
Distribution of Land According to Categories of the
Rural Property Tax Ordinance, April 1, 1938, and 1944/45 (dunums)

Land Tax Category[a]		1938	1944/45	Difference, in Dunums	Percent Change
1–2:	Citrus land	275,715	283,335	7,620	2.8
1		267,369	274,586	7,217	2.8
2		8,346	8,749	403	4.8
5–8:	Higher grade irrigated land, fruit plantation, and ground crop land	1,135,164	1,210,211	75,047	6.6
5		4,490	7,508	3,018	67.2
6		220,966	298,748	77,782	35.2
7		594,149	592,220	− 1,929	− 0.3
8		315,559	311,735	− 3,824	− 1.2
9–13:	Lower grade irrigated land, fruit plantation, and ground crop land	4,661,143	4,719,836	58,693	1.3
9		222,701	233,852	11,151	5.0
10		845,037	802,844	− 42,193	− 5.0
11		736,924	715,174	− 21,750	− 3.0
12		977,713	980,266	2,553	0.3
13		1,878,768	1,987,700	108,932	5.8
14–15:	Lowest grade irrigated land and ground crop land[c]	959,214	952,773	− 6,441	(b)
14		744,244	733,268	− 10,976	− 1.5
15		214,970	219,505	4,535	2.1
16:	Nonagricultural land	6,469,309	6,322,662	− 146,647	2.3

Sources: Government of Palestine, Statistical Abstract, 1942. p. 142; ibid., 1944/45, p. 272.
Notes:
   a. Not including Beersheba subdistrict, the Hula Concession, and the urban areas.
   b. Less than one-tenth of one percent.
   c. These categories of land were first taxed in 1944/45.

on Arab holdings. The extension of government activities in settlement of title to land resulted in the reclassification as state land many holdings which had formerly been recorded in Arab ownership. The total amount of land held by Arabs declined by 1.7 million dunums between 1937 and 1945, while that recorded as held by Jews increased by only one-tenth of that figure.[114] Most of the difference was due to the reclassification of 1.3 million dunums of "uncultivable" land from Arab to government ownership. The transfer to government ownership of cultivable land included 26,000 dunums of "plantations," 304,000 dunums of taxable cereal land, and 70,000 dunums of untaxable cereal land which, notwithstanding the category name, had begun in 1944/45 to be taxed as well. The changes are summarized in table 14, which shows that, of almost 400,000 Arab-owned dunums of cultivable land in categories 5–15 in 1937, 57 percent had by 1945 been reclassified as state land and 43 percent had been transferred to Jewish ownership.[115]

Some of the deficiencies of the published statistics for the country as a whole, or for the various subdistricts, may be avoided by examining data on changes in landownership for individual villages. It is possible to

TABLE 14
Change in Arab and Jewish Landownership, 1937–1945
(dunums; excluding Beersheba subdistrict)

1. Arab land, 1937	12,370,396	
2. Arab land, 1945	10,638,499	
3. *Difference*	1,731,897	
4. Arab uncultivated land, 1937	6,151,297	
5. Arab uncultivated land, 1945	4,813,289	
6. *Difference*	1,338,008	
7. Decline in the amount of Arab-owned cultivable land, 1937–1945 (line 3 minus line 6)[a]	393,889	
8. Decline in Arab-owned land in tax categories 5–15, 1937–1945[a]	399,208	(100%)
9. Amount of line 8 representing increase in recorded Jewish landownership	171,394	(43%)
10. Remainder (probably land transferred to government ownership after settlement of title)	227,814	(57%)

Source: Government of Palestine, *Village Statistics*, 1937; ibid., 1945.
Note:
   a. The estimates of the decline in the amount of Arab-owned cultivable land in line 7 and line 8 differ by less than 1.5 percent. This difference is probably due to minor changes in the categorization and estimates of areas between the two periods, though I cannot account for them in detail.

identify villages whose total area did not decline between 1937 and 1945, indicating that government did not claim part of their lands. By determining whether, in such villages, Jewish landownership in 1937 was associated with a change in the distribution of Arab land in the various tax categories between 1937 and 1945, we may be able to obtain some evidence of the extent to which Arab lands were upgraded.

The results of the comparison are shown in table 15, which presents data for forty Arab villages. In twenty-seven of these villages Jews owned land by 1937, and in an additional thirteen villages Jews had acquired land by 1943.[116] The first three lines of the table show the total of all village lands, and of the lands in categories 1, 2, 5–16 of the Rural Property Tax Ordinance, classified by Arab and Jewish ownership. The second section presents, for each pair of years, the distribution of Arab-owned land among the tax categories. Data for the twenty-seven villages that included Jewish-owned land in 1937, and the additional thirteen villages with such land in 1943, are first presented separately, and then combined. Overall, the amount of land owned by Jews in the forty villages doubled between 1937 and 1945, from about one-eighth of the area not built upon, to about one-fourth. But there were only very slight changes during this period in the distribution of Arab-owned land. The proportion in the poorer categories of land declined from 29.1 to 24.7 percent of the total, and the proportion of better land showed a comparable increase. The absolute amount of land in each broad category which remained in Arab hands in 1945 was lower than the amount held by them in 1937 or 1943, with the exception of citrus land, which increased in area by 856 dunums.

It would be wrong, of course, to draw far-reaching conclusions from the date in table 15 regarding the effect on the Arab cultivators of Jewish land purchases. The information in the table refers to only 40 of the 282 Arab villages in which Jews were registered landowners by 1945. Restrictions on Jewish land purchases prevented the registration by Jews of additional lands which might have been purchased in evasion of them after 1940. The groups into which the land tax categories were combined in the published *Village Statistics* were broad and do not permit identification of changes in the distribution of tax categories within groups. It may also be that the tax categories themselves, once assigned, were infrequently altered to reflect changes in the condition of the land, or were insufficiently sensitive to reflect such changes, despite the require-

TABLE 15

Distribution of Land in Selected Villages Where Land was Purchased by Jews, According to Categories of the Rural Property Tax Ordinance: 1937, 1943, 1945 (dunums)

	27 Villages				13 Villages				40 Villages			
	Absolute Number		Percent		Absolute Number		Percent		Absolute Number		Percent	
	1937	1945	1937	1945	1937	1945	1937	1945	1937	1945	1937/1943	1945
Total land	292,001	292,770	(a)	(a)	94,832	94,742	(a)	(a)	386,875	386,743	(a)	(a)
Arab-owned	253,176	194,372	87.6	74.5	80,945	70,048	86.5	76.8	334,121	291,911	87.3	75.5
Jewish-owned	35,775	66,468	12.4	25.5	12,675	21,138	13.5	23.2	48,450	94,832	12.6	24.5
Distribution of Arab-owned land according to Rural Property Tax categories												
1–2: Citrus	6,627	7,483	2.7	3.5	268	268	0.3	0.4	6,895	7,751	2.1	2.7
5–8: Plantations	20,070	19,310	8.1	8.9	21,073	20,057	26.2	28.8	41,143	39,367	12.5	13.8
9–13: Taxable cereal	147,685	133,062	59.2	61.4	38,361	35,262	47.6	50.6	186,046	168,324	56.4	58.8
14–15: Untaxable cereal	19,788	14,471	7.9	6.7	2,224	1,294	2.8	1.9	22,012	15,765	6.7	5.5
16: Uncultivable land	55,090	42,276	22.1	19.5	18,630	12,752	23.1	18.3	73,720	55,028	22.4	19.2
Total	249,260	216,602	100.0	100.0	80,556	69,633	100.0	100.0	329,816	286,235	100.0	100.0

Sources: Computed from Government of Palestine, *Village Statistics,* 1937; ibid., 1943; ibid., 1945.

Note:

a. Percentages are based on the total amount of land in categories 1–2 and 5–16, *not* on the total amount of village land.

ment that the tax authorities be notified of any changes in land quality. Nevertheless, the information in table 15 does not suggest that Jewish purchase of land in Arab villages, in and of itself, led to any widespread upgrading of the land remaining in Arab hands in those villages.

The Jews themselves may not have been entirely convinced by their claims regarding the benefits that land sales would bring to Arab cultivators. In a 1945 analysis, L. Samuel of the Jewish Agency's Economic Research Bureau made the following comment in the context of a discussion of the absence of any overall government agricultural policy embracing intensive as well as extensive cultivation: "It is nevertheless quite true that a few outstanding personalities like the late Dr. Ruppin indicated that large-scale Jewish colonisation in Palestine would enable Arab farmers to adopt modern methods of production through the capital acquired by sale of part of their land. . . . But, in reality, all this was remote and did not lead to a conception of a real policy for agricultural development."[117]

Another way of examining the claim is to look at estimates of the cost to Arabs of upgrading their holdings and the potential income that the owner-cultivator could have realized from sale of his lands. Ruppin prepared some basic computations in connection with his proposals for the agricultural development of Palestine.[118] He assumed that the average Arab cultivator owned ninety-five dunums. His plan envisaged purchase of thirty-two dunums for £P150 (£P4.69 per dunum) and the cultivator's disposition of this sum as follows:

£P30   for payment of debts;

£P30   invested as his share in a village irrigation scheme which would enable him to irrigate six dunums;

£P30   to plant three dunums of citrus trees, at a cost of £P10 per dunum;

£P15   for improvement of his livestock;

£P45   for subsistence during the three years until the citrus trees started bearing.

The villagers would eventually expand the area under irrigation to include twelve to fifteen dunums; together with the citrus, about two-thirds of the land would be irrigated.

Ruppin's plan envisaged the widespread implementation of the development scheme, along with consolidation of individual holdings and concentration of the lands left in the possession of the villagers in such a way as to make room for the establishment of Jewish settlements on the lands sold. Development undertaken by individual cultivators, not in the context of a general scheme, would necessarily be more expensive, especially with respect to the basic investments for preparation of the groves and the introduction of irrigation.

According to the 1936 survey of 322 villages, the average holding was 45.31 dunums, just about half the size Ruppin estimated, and about 90 percent of the holdings were less than 95 dunums in area.[119] While the size of holdings may have declined somewhat because of land sales between 1933 and 1936, even in 1933 the situation of the Arab cultivators would have prevented the vast majority of them from benefiting from Ruppin's scheme. It seems clear, therefore, that those cultivators who were able to sell part of their lands to Jewish purchasers, pay off their debts, and upgrade the remainder of their land were found among the small minority of 10 percent whose holdings were at least 100 dunums in extent. It was the larger landowners who possessed surplus land, and they were the only ones who could have benefited from Jewish land purchases in the way Ruppin proposed. It is possible, of course, that proceeds from land sales were not used to repay debts, but to make investments whose returns would allow the debt to be paid. Bonné believed that

> a large number of the fellahin in Palestine could undoubtedly have
> discharged their debts during the past few years if they had applied
> their surplus earnings to the purpose. In the large majority of cases,
> however, they preferred to extend and intensify their farm-holdings and
> to raise their standard of living. Nevertheless, the reduction of debt
> has been so striking in certain districts that Government, which used to
> underline this point in every report, expressly emphasises the improve-
> ment. According to the Report of 1935 (p. 25), the indebtedness of the
> fellahin in the Northern District has diminished by no less than
> 60%.[120]

Arie Avneri presents some examples of such land sales, but they refer to large areas, not to small holdings.[121] During 1936–1939 the JNF bought land from villagers in Tira, Tayibe, Tamra, and Na'ura, in the Nazareth subdistrict. According to Avneri, the sales were at the villagers' initiative and were intended to enable them to free themselves from debt and prevent their lands from falling into the hands of their creditors. In Tayibe eleven owners sold an average of 542 dunums each and retained an average of 291 dunums; five more sold all their land, an average of 253 dunums each. The latter received an average of £P7.11 per dunum, paid their debts, and bought land elsewhere. Assuming an average debt, according to the Johnson-Crosbie report,[122] of £P27 per family on an average holding of 59 dunums, or £P2.185 per dunum, these five families would have had an average debt of £P553 and would have retained after repaying it an average of £P1,245. Whatever land they purchased would almost certainly have cost them less than the £P7.11 per dunum selling price. The sale of their holdings and their purchase of new land would have enabled them to retain their position among the small minority of large landowners. The other examples presented by Avneri in the same chapter are all of holdings much larger than the 50 dunum average, or than the 95 dunums assumed by Ruppin in his development plan. It would have been almost impossible for small cultivators to pay for planting oranges or introducing irrigated vegetable cultivation with the proceeds gained from the sale to Jews of part of their lands.[123]

Data supplied by PICA and presented to Hope Simpson provide additional evidence regarding the status of Arab cultivators who were able to benefit from land sales to Jews. According to PICA, 131 Arabs in villages near Petah Tiqwa had in the late 1920s planted 8,144 dunums of orange groves, an average of 62 dunums per planter. The capital costs of such planting were at least £P620, and if they were underwritten by the proceeds from land sales, which were also used to repay debts, then each planter would have had to have disposed of considerably more than 100 dunums. They were thus not poor proprietors even prior to the sale of part of their lands. During the same period, 97 cultivators in the area of Rehovot and Rishon le-Ziyyon planted an average of 36 dunums each of orange groves.[124]

The memorandum submitted to Hope Simpson by the Jewish Agency contained calculations regarding the additional number of Jewish families who could be settled in agricultural colonies on the coastal plain, between Hadera in the north and Rehovoth in the south. It assumed an average selling price for land of £P4.375 per dunum and an average debt of £P50 per Arab cultivator.[125] The average cultivator would have had to sell about 11.4 dunums of land to pay the debt and would have to sell more in order to have the money to invest in developing his holding. But, according to the 1936 survey of holdings, almost half were smaller than 10 dunums, and an additional quarter were between 10 and 30 dunums. Even if the holdings in the coastal plain were larger than the average in the country as a whole, only a small proportion of the cultivators would have had sufficient land to sell and still retain enough for their future needs.

There is reason to believe that the size of the peasants' holdings in the coastal plain may have been smaller than they were elsewhere. The authors of the Jewish Agency memorandum noted that their calculations applied only to lands owned by the village.[126] Sale of lands worked by tenants would not necessarily improve the position of those among the latter who remained on the unsold portion of the holding, if such existed. The proportion of land in the coastal plain owned by "effendis" was not known, but estimates made by the Jewish Agency ranged from 25 to 40 percent.[127] Most of these lands were reported to have been leased to cultivators who owned land in neighboring villages and worked the leased lands in addition to their own. If the estimates were correct, the size of the average private holding of villagers other than "effendis" would have been smaller than that given in the 1936 survey, and would have been even less likely to provide through sale the means of freeing the peasants from debts and enabling them to upgrade the land that remained.

A draft of the memorandum ultimately submitted to Hope Simpson made explicit the type of peasant holding on which the Jewish argument was based. It contained 100 dunums, of which 80 would be sold and the remainder brought under intensive cultivation.[128] Volcani made a similar assumption in his 1930 discussion of the Arab peasant farm and its transition to more intensive cultivation.[129] Two years later, in a memorandum prepared in response to the report by Lewis French, Granovsky estimated that Arab cultivators in the Sharon plain had planted 10,000 dunums of orange groves with money they had received from Jewish land purchases.[130] If the establishment of one dunum of orange grove cost at least £P10, and the average price of land in the Sharon up to 1936 was £P3.42 per dunum,[131] at least 30,000 dunums of land had to be sold to underwrite the investment in the citrus plantations, in addition to the land whose sale covered the outstanding debts of the cultivators.

Land Sales to Jews and the
Situation of Arab Cultivators

The Jews argued that their land purchases did not harm Arab cultivators. They based this claim on their belief in the benefits that would accrue to the landowners who sold part of their holding and used the proceeds to free themselves from debt and to improve their remaining lands. Officials of the Jewish Agency also pointed to their policy of compensating tenants forced to leave lands that had passed into Jewish ownership, whether purchased from absentee Arab owners resident elsewhere in Palestine or in neighboring countries, or from landowners who themselves lived in the villages and were directly involved in cultivation. This compensation was paid in order to minimize as far as possible resistance by the tenants to their relocation as well as subsequent conflicts between the tenants and the Jewish settlers. Such payment was also seen by the Jews as helping to blunt criticisms of their land acquisition policy, and some viewed it as a moral duty. Nevertheless, the Jews preferred the lands they purchased to be free of tenants and all dealings with them on questions of compensation to be concluded by the Arab owners prior to the transfer of the land to Jewish hands.[132] In 1931 doubts were raised about the wisdom of this policy, and the Palestine Executive of the Jewish Agency polled representatives of land-purchasing bodies and others on possible alternatives.[133] After 1936 such conditions were standard in land purchase contracts.[134]

Material collected by the Jewish organizations in connection with the determination of the amount of compensation paid to the displaced tenants, and with attempts to demonstrate to government officials and to British investigating commissions that the circumstances of these former tenants had not worsened, or had in fact improved following their removal from the lands they cultivated, provides some information regarding the condition of these cultivators. Unfortunately, similar information is not available regarding purchases from owner-cultivators, since these sellers were seen to be acting of their own free will and were assumed to be the best judges of their own interests. Although the legislation designed to protect cultivators required at various periods that owner-cultivators selling land retain a minimum area for their own subsistence, and obliged government officials to certify that such was the case before the transfer could be registered, it is generally accepted that these regulations were ineffective in preventing peasants from disposing of larger portions of their holdings than the government felt was desirable. In any case, the Jewish organizations saw no need to collect detailed information regarding the circumstances of such sellers.

On the eve of the British occupation of Palestine in 1917, Jews owned approximately 590,000 dunums of land.[135] By the end of 1930 Jewish landholdings totaled more than 1 million dunums.[136] About 415,000 dunums had been bought by PICA, 69 percent from absentee landlords and the remainder from owner-cultivators.[137] In 1930 PICA officials provided, in connection with Hope Simpson's investigation, details regarding the sellers of 262,000 dunums, most of which had been acquired before the First World War. Almost three-quarters of this land had been bought from absentee owners. Thirty percent had been acquired in villages where absentee owners were the only sellers; 63 percent had been acquired in villages where twice as much land was bought from absentee owners as from owner-cultivators; and only 7 percent of the total had been purchased in villages where land was sold only by owner-cultivators.[138] The proportion of PICA lands bought from absentee owners after the First World War (about 64 percent) was lower, but until 1930 most of PICA's acquisitions continued to be from absentee owners. In 1930 the holdings of the JNF totaled some 270,000 dunums; 90 percent of these lands had been purchased from absentee owners.[139]

Between 1910 and 1930 the Palestine Land Development Corporation (PLDC) purchased 420,000 dunums of land from Arabs north of the Beersheba subdistrict; 93 percent of this was acquired from large landowners. In the five years after 1930, an additional 93,000 dunums were purchased noth of Beersheba; 69 percent of this was bought from large landowners.[140] Of the 503,015 dunums bought by PLDC between 1921 and 1935, 72 percent were sold by absentee large proprietors, 20 percent by resident large proprietors, and 8 percent by smallholders (though "large proprietor" was not defined).[141] In the same five-year period PICA acquired about 14,000 dunums, 35 percent from large landowners.[142] In 1930 Granovsky, who was then managing director of the JNF, argued that the distribution of Jewish land purchases was evidence refuting the criticisms made of Zionist land policy: "Since the [JNF] purchases from fellahin represent no more than 9.5% of its total possessions, and since these purchases, almost without exception, were made from Arab villages wishing to dispose of a part of their land which they could spare, there can be no question of dispossession in such instances."[143]

"Absentee" landowners and "large" landowners were not necessarily the same people, though in the period before and immediately following the First World War there was a great deal of overlap between the two categories. Although Granovsky does not indicate how much land made someone a "large landowner,"[144] such a person might not hold more than a few hundred dunums. In terms of the distribution of landholding in Palestine, however, those property owners would have been found in the upper tenth of the distribution of holdings by size. No systematic data exist regarding the continued creation of large holdings after the First World War, but it is clear that the total extent of such holdings diminished because of Jewish purchases although, as French and others noted, cultivators were always in danger of losing their lands to their creditors.[145] The amount of land in Palestine owned by absentee landlords in March 1932 was reported by the PLDC to be 118,000 dunums, of which almost 70 percent was located in the Acre, Safed, and Tiberias subdistricts.[146]

Between 1933 and 1942 Jews bought from Arabs 334,490 dunums of land in 6,207 separate registered sales. Eight percent of these sales were for holdings of 100 dunums or larger. The size of the average holding sold during these years was 54 dunums.[147] This was slightly smaller that the average size of a holding in the 1936 survey of 322 villages, which found 8.9 percent of the holdings to be 100 dunums or larger.[148] Thus, the distribution by area of land sales to Jews during this period was similar to the distribution of size of holdings.[149]

These data can be compared with those describing the size of tenant holdings on lands bought by Jews. The mean size of tenant holdings on 261,000 dunums bought in the early 1920s in the Jezre'el Valley and the Acre Plain was about 1.4 feddans, or 210 dunums.[150] These lands had been used for subsistence cereal cultivation, and the entire area of the holdings was sold. The mean holding size would have been greater than it was in later years. Compensation was paid to 690 of the displaced tenants, and information subsequently collected by the Jewish Agency in connection with the Shaw Commission's hearings on the 1929 riots revealed that half of them had formerly cultivated holdings (they were described as fellahin). Of these, 89 percent continued to cultivate holdings in their new locations. Only 5 percent of those who had not been cultivators became fellahin in their new locality. Most of the others were found in occupations that were probably quite similar to those they had followed prior to their dispossession and that did not involve responsibility for cultivating a holding as a tenant, such as shepherds or agricultural laborers *(harrathin)*; other laborers accounted for 44 percent of those dispossessed, the same proportion as those who continued as fellahin. [151]

Before the sale of the lands they worked, the average locality had 32 families. After their dispersal, the average number of former Jezre'el Valley and Acre Plain families in their new locations was 7.6, less than one-fourth of their former numbers. Nineteen families moved to localities to which none of the other dispossessed came, and there were fifteen localities which took in 2 families each. On the other hand, 14 families or more were found in each of nine new locations, including 37 in Haifa, 48 in Nazareth, 52 in Mejdel, [152] and 70 each in Shafa 'Amr and in Ma'alul (where the former tenants had been given land to cultivate as tenants of the Jewish purchasers, with an option to buy at the price paid by the Jews, an opportunity of which they were unlikely to be able to take advantage). [153]

Information is available for some of the former tenants who subsequently applied for inclusion in the register of landless Arabs set up by the government in order to certify claims that would entitle dispossessed Arabs to obtain leases on government lands. The applications went first to government officials for a preliminary investigation of the claim. Information regarding those who seemed to have a legitimate case was then transmitted to the Jewish Agency, which reviewed it and presented whatever evidence was in its possession regarding the legitimacy of the claim. [154] The Central Zionist Archives contain 200 of these applications, from claimants who had indicated that they had been dispossessed from villages which were part of the Sursoq holdings in the Jezre'el Valley. Based on the entries in their application forms, the former tenants from Jidru, Kufritta, Mejdel, and Dar el-Beida, whose households averaged 6.7 persons, had cultivated an average of 251 dunums each. They reported that they had received an average of £E0.28 per dunum, [155] or £E70 per household, as compensation for "disturbance." [156] This fits with Granovsky's report that the Jews paid compensation at the rate of £E20–£E45 per feddan (150 dunums); [157] tenants from the four villages for which data is available received an average of £E42 per feddan, or £E70 for their holding.

Granovsky stated that the average tenant family received about £E38, which he estimated was equal to its earnings during a year or more and was almost two-thirds of the amount Hope Simpson estimated was

required to settle a fellah family on the land.[158] Villagers in the four
localities for which I have data received almost twice as much in compensation as the average reported by Granovsky, so there must have been
considerable variation among the localities. Data summarized by an
official of the PLDC showed that the compensation per dunum in eleven
localities whose tenants received cash payments rather than leaseholds
ranged from £P0.17 to £P0.33 per dunum, and the compensation per
tenant household ranged from £P25 to £P93.[159] Since no information is
available regarding the debts owed by these tenants, it is impossible to
estimate how much money they had left after repaying them. Only about
one-fifth of the tenants were later reported as owning land, buildings, or
other property, and some of these were probably merchants or others who
had reestablished themselves in the towns.[160] The number of dispossessed tenants who were able to use their compensation to buy land could
not have been great. Reports throughout the period of the Mandate
suggest that many cultivators preferred to receive compensation in cash
rather than in land,[161] but it is not clear whether this preference was
based on a desire to buy land in areas of the cultivator's choice rather
than being compelled to resettle on a government tract, or whether the
preference for cash was due to a desire to stop farming and undertake
another occupation.

The applications of villagers from Mejdel and Kufritta for inclusion in
the register of landless Arabs contain information on whether 105 former
residents of those two villages were leasing lands at the time of their
application. The mean area previously cultivated by those who reported
they were currently leasing land was twice as large (327 dunums) as that
reported by those who were not leasing land at the time they applied (160
dunums).[162] This suggests that tenants with larger holdings prior to dispossession were better able to continue in agriculture than those with
smaller holdings. It is not clear whether the compensation the tenants
received allowed them to do more than maintain their previous status.

There were 167 tenants who received compensation for dispossession
from the villages of Kurfitta, Jidru, Dar el-Beida, and Mejdel. Comparison of the names on the list of those who received compensation with
those of the applicants for admission to the register of landless Arabs
shows that sixty-three persons (23 percent) who had received compensation subsequently wished to be considered "landless." The reported
mean former holdings of those on both lists was somewhat greater than

that of the applicants to the register who did not appear among those who received compensation (309 vs. 246 dunums). The fellahin among those who received compensation were more likely than the others to appear among the applicants to the register (Q=.52), but little difference was found regarding those receiving compensation who were identified as owning property. Although this comparison refers to only about 40 percent of those who received compensation in the four villages, and to an even smaller proportion of applicants to the register, it suggests that the payment of compensation for dispossession did not end the efforts of many former tenants to obtain land from the government.[163]

Between 1933 and 1936 tenants in the area of Qiri-Qamun, on the land southeast of Haifa where the Jewish settlement of Yoqne'am was established, received compensation for dispossession. Information is available regarding 146 payments averaging £P29. Of these, 40 percent amounted to £P10 or less, and an additional 22 percent were between £P11 and £P20. The file does not indicate the size of the individual holdings, but a document from 1923 listing village lands offered for sale indicates that 20,000 dunums were on the market.[164] The total compensation received by the tenants was almost £P4,300, averaging £P0.21 per dunum if the entire area had been purchased by the Jews and if there were no tenants other than those on the list. That amount was similar to the compensation per dunum reported ten years earlier in the sale of the Sursoq lands.[165]

The government had, in the 1920s, reached an agreement with tenants and other claimants to state lands in the Beisan area which had formerly belonged to the sultan and had passed to its control. Tenants received long leases and could eventually purchase the land on very favorable terms. Critics of the agreements argued that in many cases persons had received land in excess of their capacity to cultivate it and that others had benefited from grants of extensive areas to which they were not entitled. In many cases tenants were not making the annual rental payments as required.[166] Eventually the government relaxed restrictions on the sale of these lands, and Jewish land-purchasing organizations were able to acquire many of them. Detailed information is available on such purchases in the Ghazariyya and the Ghor-Mudawarra tracts.[167]

There were originally forty-one holders of land in Ghazariyya, and their average holding was 198 dunums. Of the 8,100 dunum total, about

38 percent was bought by the Jews. Twenty-nine landholders sold all their property in Ghazariyya, and of the twenty-seven who had 58 dunums or less, twenty-four sold all their land. Each seller, large or small, received about £P2.45 per dunum. The effect of the Jewish purchases in Ghazariyya was to concentrate the Arab-held land in the hands of the larger cultivators.

A different pattern of sales appeared in the Ghor-Mudawarra area. The sixty-two landholders had almost 13,000 dunums and sold on the average 40 percent of their holdings. None of them sold out completely: five were left with less than one-quarter of their original land; thirteen retained between one-quarter and one-half; twenty-nine kept between one-half and three-quarters; and the remaining fifteen sold less than one-quarter of the land they had received from the government. Although the mean price paid per dunum for the Ghor-Mudawarra lands was almost the same as that paid in Ghazariyya (£P2.40 vs. £P2.45), the price range for the individual holdings was much greater. Twenty sellers received less than £P2 per dunum; twenty-seven received between £P2 and £P3; and fifteen received £P3 or more per dunum (two of these received between £P4 and £P5). There was no relationship between the size of the original holding and the proportion of the land that was sold, nor was there any relation between the size of the original holding, or the amount of land sold, and the price received per dunum. Nor did the tendency toward concentration of landholding in the hands of the larger cultivators, which was clear in the Ghazariyya area, appear with equal clarity in Ghor-Mudawarra. Although the mean remaining holding size represented an increasing proportion of the mean original area in three of the four categories of original area, it declined in the largest category (115–138 dunums: 57 percent; 142–186 dunums: 60 percent; 203–272 dunums: 68 percent; 275–558 dunums: 57 percent). The largest landholders sold proportionally more land than did the others, though some evidence of increasing concentration of holdings was visible among the other three categories.[168]

The entire area of state lands in the Beisan region totaled about 264,000 dunums, of which slightly more than half (54 percent) was irrigated. The mean area per household (excluding nonfarmers in Beisan and the large village of Samakh on the southern shore of Lake Tiberias) on the irrigated lands was about 110 dunums; on the nonirrigated lands it was about 185 dunums.[169] According to the various calculations made by government and by Jewish experts in connection with possible development plans, these holdings should have been large enough to support the cultivators.

Between 1939 and 1945, 1,062 tenant households in forty-eight localities were evicted from lands that had been bought by Jews. The area they had occupied totaled almost 80,000 dunums, and the average tenant household cultivated approximately 75 dunums. In eighteen localities the mean holding size was 50 dunums or less, and in another seventeen localities it measured between fifty-one and one hundred dunums. The average compensation received by the tenants was £P3.32 per dunum, or £P316 per household, but there was a considerable range of values among the different localities. In sixteen localities the tenants received less than £P2 per dunum, and in eleven they received £P4 or more. These variations probably reflected differences in the market and the quality of the land. According to the material prepared by Yosef Weitz, almost all the dispossessed tenants continued as cultivators, in their home village or one nearby. Many of them may have been owners of village land and worked in addition as tenants on other land before the latter was sold.[170] The file does not contain information regarding the amount of land remaining to those who had to relinquish at least a portion of their holdings, so it is not possible to evaluate the effects these purchases had on the concentration of Arab landholding.

Conclusion

The changes in patterns of Arab landholding during the Mandate reflected the joint effects of Jewish land purchases and the pressures of rural population growth. Much of the land was privately owned in small and medium-sized tracts, title to which was legally recognized by the administration. Land sales by Arabs to Jews were widely publicized, and though they represented about half the land transactions, by the end of the Mandate only about 5 percent of Arab lands had passed into Jewish hands. At the same time, a quieter but continual process of fragmentation and consolidation of Arab holdings was occurring: on the one hand, lands were divided among heirs; on the other, parcels sold because they were too small to support a household were purchased by other landowners who thereby increased the size of their own holdings. The available information does not enable us to determine whether these sales increased or lessened inequality in the distribution of Arab landowning.

Land transactions during the Mandate occurred in a particular political and economic context. It is ironic that the Jewish land-purchasing agencies replaced wealthy families such as the Sursoqs as the holders of the country's largest estates, though the relations between PICA or PLDC and the settlements established on their lands were quite different from those between the Sursoqs and their tenants. In a sense, the most important feature of the land regime during the Mandate was something that was missing: large-scale dispossession of tenants and owners due to the introduction of capitalist agriculture requiring consolidation of extensive tracts of land under a uniform production regime. Such an outcome failed to occur for at least two reasons. Arabs held their lands not under "traditional," tribal tenures with no immediate parallel in the British system of land law, but in legally recognized private ownership. Any alteration in the rights of landowners would have required government action. The Palestine administration, however, interfered as little as possible in the structure of agrarian relations. Only through purchase could large tracts have been created, and the anticipated profitability of agricultural production once such an investment had been made did not justify attempting it.

Although their political and symbolic significance was great, Jewish purchases of Arabs lands were not a major factor in the transformation of Arab rural society. The concentration of Jewish purchasing efforts in an attempt to create contiguous holdings, their growing preference for tracts whose acquisition did not require displacement of Arab cultivators, their emphasis on buying land along the coast and in the Galilee and their chronic shortage of funds to buy additional territory, meant that large areas of Palestine were unaffected by local Jewish land purchases.

Villagers adapted as best they could to their changing demographic and economic circumstances, but they were limited in their responses by the lack of government initiative and support for agrarian change. *Musha'a* tenure was apparently no obstacle to agricultural development in many villages with access to markets for their produce: villagers often arranged among themselves to cease the redistribution of plots. Employment in towns and in local public works projects enabled them to maintain their rural base while supplementing an inadequate agricultural income. Some of those who sold land, to Jews or to Arabs, were able to use the proceeds to continue farming on a firmer footing; others took the opportunity to move out of agriculture; still others received too little to enable them significantly to change their condition. But the absence of fundamental change in the land regime during the Mandate meant that such adaptations could only offer temporary solutions to problems whose root causes were never addressed.

Agriculture:
Subsistence, Innovation, and Debt

Introduction

A G R I C U L T U R E   R E M A I N E D the basis of the Arab economy of Palestine throughout the Mandate. A majority of the Arab population lived in rural areas, and most of the Arab labor force worked the land. Many of the Arabs employed in towns had come from villages, to which they regularly returned for visits or used as a fallback when urban jobs were hard to find. The condition of Arab agriculture and rural society was a central concern of government policy, and the acquisition of Arab agricultural land was a main goal of Jewish settlement policy. The growing burden of population on existing holdings, in the absence of commensurate increases in yield and value of crops, forced increasing numbers of cultivators to seek nonagricultural work, but the lack of industrial jobs prevented them from severing their connection with the land.

Arab agriculture supplied the much of the foodstuffs for the growing urban populations, Arab as well as Jewish. The market these provided allowed some cultivators to take advantage of new commercial opportunities and provided both incentive and funds for altering traditional cropping practices. Palestine was a small country, and during the Mandate the rural hinterland was drawn slowly into a closer relation with the towns, as these grew in size in response to increasing commerce and migration from the countryside. Despite these changes, however, most Arab cultivators did not see fundamental modifications in their circumstances.

The development of Arab agriculture in Palestine during the Mandate was very uneven, with considerable variation according to the principal crops grown. Substantial changes occurred both in the total area devoted to different crops and in their yields. The value of the different crops also

194

changed greatly during this period, but these changes were due more to the effects of world prices than to local Palestinian factors. The relative share of subsistence agriculture in the economy of Arab cultivators declined during the Mandate, as a greater proportion of the total agricultural product, whether measured by quantity or by value, was derived from intensive forms of cultivation rather than from dry cereal farming. Most cultivators, however, continued to depend on grain crops.

Intensive agriculture was irrigated, and its product was destined for the market. The major crop was citrus for export, until restrictions on shipping following the outbreak of the Second World War put a temporary end to Palestine's trade in these fruits. The other major market crop was vegetables, grown primarily for local consumption. No systematic information is available regarding the organization of Arab citrus and vegetable production at the local level. While all the citrus groves were irrigated, this was not true of the vegetables. Introduction of irrigation required investment which, in the case of citrus groves, would not bear fruit for at least four to five years. Other crops were often raised on the citrus land while the trees were maturing. Irrigated vegetables gave immediate returns, but most small landowners, much less tenants, lacked the resources to bring water to their fields by sinking a well and installing the pump and pipes necessary for irrigation. They were more likely to be able to purchase water from an adjacent well-owner, but little detailed information is available about the arrangements employed during this period for financing the irrigation of crop land.

The agricultural practices of most Arab cultivators were, in large measure, an unavoidable consequence of the existing relations of production in the countryside. The combination of subsistence farming, dependence on cereals, too small holdings, tenancy, and debt was too great an obstacle for most cultivators to overcome. They devoted their energies to hanging on to what they had. Some, however, more fortunately situated, were able to benefit from new market opportunities, from technical assistance and demonstrations provided by government agricultural extension programs, from the example of Jewish farming, or through government loans. Most Arab peasants, however, were not so fortunately situated, and in the absence of fundamental changes in the system of agrarian property relations they had little hope of improving their condition.

The Major Crops

Arab agriculture in Palestine throughout the Mandate was almost completely dependent on the weather for the success of its main crop, cereals. Cereals took up more than half the cultivated area of the country throughout the Mandatory period, although the amount of land devoted to them declined between 1937 and 1944 from 4.5 million to 3.2 million dunums of wheat and barley, and from 1.1. million to 0.7 million dunums of durra (Indian millet).[1] Cereals provided the principal income for the majority of Arab peasant cultivators, those who had neither citrus groves nor commercial plantations or fruit trees or olives, nor raised large crops of vegetables for the market. Cereals also provided the basic subsistence for most village families, since a portion of the crop was retained for the household's needs during the year.

The agricultural year was divided into two main seasons: winter, from late October to mid-April, when the rains fell, and summer, when they did not. Cereal cultivation was carried out on a one-, two-, or three-year rotation; by the 1940s the latter was most common.[2] The three main cereal crops were wheat, barley, and durra. Wheat or barley was sown in November–December and harvested in May–June, followed by a fallow until April of the next year. The land was then sown with durra or sesame, which was harvested in August and followed again by wheat or barley (or by a legume in a three-year rotation).[3] In the late 1920s a two-year rotation might have been more prevalent: half the cropped area was set aside for summer planting and half for winter crops.[4] The timing of the first winter rains, their spacing, the advent of hot weather, the outbreak of plant diseases, and the depredations of locusts or field mice all combined to create great uncertainty regarding the success or failure of a particular season's crop in one or another region of the country. The precarious position of the cereal-growing peasantry was due in part to their almost total dependence on the vicissitudes of nature and their lack of any recourse other than the landlord or moneylender when nature failed them.

Because Arab cereal crops were not irrigated, annual variations in the amount and timing of the rains led to great differences in crop yields. Between 1922 and 1939, per capita yields of these crops varied greatly (table 16).[5] To some degree, poor yields of winter crops were compensated by better yields of summer crops, and vice versa, but since most of

TABLE 16
Yield of Principal Grain Crops Per Capita
of Arab Population, 1922–1939 (kg)

	High (year)	Low (year)
Wheat	135 (1925)	43 (1938)
Barley	90 (1926)	28 (1932)
Durra	62 (1938)	10 (1933)
All three	263 (1937)	96 (1933)

Source: Computed from data on grain yields and population, Government of Palestine, *Statistical Abstract*,
various years.

the cereals were grown in the winter, failure of the rains could have
disastrous consequences for villagers. The Johnson-Crosbie report estimated that an Arab village family of six persons required about one ton of
grain (wheat and durra) to live on for a year, or about 160 kilograms per
person. Between 1922 and 1939 there were two consecutive years (1932
and 1933) when the per capita total crop yield of wheat, durra, and
barley was only about three-fifths of what was required. If we consider
only the yield of wheat and durra, since barley was used for bread only if
absolutely necessary, six of the eighteen years between 1922 and 1939
had inadequate yields, of these three in a row (1931–1933). Grain
imports partly supplemented the shortfalls, though they were not sufficient to assure that per capita consumption levels would reach the estimated subsistence level. Annual yields, imports, and consumption per
capita between 1927 and 1939 are shown in table 17.

Writers on Arab Palestine frequently noted the poor grain yields that
the villagers obtained from the soil and attributed them to overutilization
of the land. The Arab cultivators failed to leave the land fallow long
enough for it to regain its fertility, nor did they compensate for the short
fallow by fertilization or by growing green manure crops. Most writers
recognized that a major obstacle to improving the fertility of soil was the
lack of sufficient fertilizer at a price the average cultivator could afford.
Imported chemical fertilizers were much too expensive, and their proper
use required either irrigation or dependable rains. Manure from village
stock was in short supply for three reasons: many peasants had few draft
animals, sheep, or goats, and those they had were insufficient to provide
the amount of manure required; peasants used cow and ox dung for

TABLE 17
Per Capita Grain Yields, Imports, and Consumption, 1927–1939
(total of wheat, barley, and durra, in kg)

Year	Yield Per Capita	Imports Per Capita	Consumption Per Capita
1927	237	1	211
1928	185	13	177
1929	206	18	205
1930	223	3	172
1931	161	47	198
1932	104	50	152
1933	96	107	203
1934	209	70	274
1935	229	35	261
1936	156	65	219
1937	263	63	310
1938	170	55	225
1939	207	85	292

Sources: Computed from data on grain yields, imports and population, Government of Palestine, *Statistical Abstract*, various years.
Note: consumption = yields + imports − exports

cooking and for mixing with mud for building; many peasants sold manure to agents who in turn resold it to the citrus growers whose need for fertilizer was continually increasing along with the expansion of their groves.

But there was another reason, which has been insufficiently stressed, for the prevalence of short fallow. According to the Johnson-Crosbie report, 63 percent of the total field crop was planted with winter growths, and 37 percent with summer, a ratio of approximately 2:1. Winter crops were sown in November–December and harvested in May and June. Summer crops were sown in April and May and harvested in August and September. It was impossible to follow a winter by a summer crop in the same field in the same season, but a winter crop could follow a summer crop after an interval of two or three months fallow.

Had the Arab cultivators sufficient land, it would have been profitable for them to undertake a two-year rotation, in which a winter crop of wheat and barley alternated every other year with a crop of leguminous grains such as sesame or durra, sown in the spring following the wheat harvest and picked at the end of the summer. The ground could then have been prepared for sowing wheat and barley in November. A two-year rotation, which according to Volcani was widely used in the 1920s, compensated somewhat for the lack of manuring, as the leguminous summer crop aided in the replenishment of the soil, and the repeated plowing and hoeing it required reduced the spread of weeds and inhibited the field mice.

Peasants had to bring in a wheat or barley harvest each year, in order to feed themselves and their families, to repay loans, pay tithes and taxes, cover the rent if the land belonged to someone else, and pay the wages of hired laborers, if any. Thus, they had to divide their holdings so that the two-year rotation could be staggered and they would be assured of a grain crop each year. Peasants could plant fodder to be turned under as green manure, a good substitute for animal manure, but in order to do so they needed enough land for a three-year rotation instead of two: winter wheat and barley the first year; summer grain the next; and a green fallow the following summer which could then be turned under in preparation for sowing wheat again.

Given the average holding size, the two-thirds to one-third distribution of crops reported by Johnson and Crosbie was apparently necessary in order to provide a yield sufficient for the peasants' needs. They could maintain this ratio annually on a three-year rotation only if they left a short fallow between two out of the three winter crop years. The alternative would have been to skip the winter crop on one-third of the land (i.e., reduce the total winter crop by half). There would have been no point in doing so, however; it would have been better to divide the fields equally between winter and summer crops and move to a two-year rotation. But a two-year rotation would probably not have given the farmers an annual return sufficient for their needs during the year. Nor could the farmer include a green manure as part of the rotation, since it would come at the expense of part of the winter wheat or barley crop.

Insufficient land combined with the social organization of village agricultural production to inhibit change in traditional cropping practices. In the early 1950s, peasants in Kufr al-Ma, Jordan, had difficulty changing from a two-year to a three-year rotation, despite encouragement by government agricultural agents:

> For a cultivator to follow a three-crop system while other villagers were following a two-crop system would be to court disaster, for the whole

area is thrown open to grazing after the general harvest. The man who
did not follow the village planting regime would run the risk of having
his crops eaten by grazing animals. More important, growing three
crops simultaneously presumes a large enough piece of land to allow
this division. Most land holdings in Kurf al-Ma are under twenty-five
dunums. . . . Most peasants in Kufr al-Ma are primarily concerned
with producing enough wheat to assure a year's supply of flour for
bread. . . . Even under the two-crop rotation system peasants do not
fulfill their yearly bread requirements. It is this same necessity to produce enough bread that prevents the peasant in Kufr al-Ma from fallowing for a longer period than seven months. . . . Certain prosperous
farmers in Kufr al-Ma could undoubtedly afford to work a three-crop
system. But their sharecroppers are reluctant to work for them unless a
substantial portion of the acreage is devoted to wheat.[6]

The considerations affecting the preferences of cultivators in Kufr al-
Ma in the 1950s could not have been so different from those affecting
Palestinian peasants two decades earlier. Figure 1 summarizes land
utilization under the three-year rotation, and demonstrates the peasant's
predicament. Only one of the three fields could in any year be left fallow
for a period of time long enough to allow some of the soil's fertility to be
restored naturally. For two out of the three years the peasant was demand-
ing from the land more than it was able to give, and both suffered. If it
was true that a gradual shift from a two-year to a three-year rotation
occurred during the Mandate, this would be evidence for the decline in
the amount of land available to the average household, and the consequences of that decline for peasant agricultural practices.
     The development of Arab agriculture is summarized in tables 18 to
22, which present data for the six main Arab crops: wheat, barley, durra,
vegetables, olives, and citrus.[7] In 1937 citrus fruits represented almost
half the value of all Palestinian produce, and the five other crops represented almost two-thirds of the remainder. Their share in Arab crop
production was even greater, since most of the grains and almost all the
olives were grown by Arabs. As table 18 shows, the relative share of
grains in the value of Palestinian produce (other than citrus) declined
between 1937 and 1944, and the relative share of vegetables increased,
although some of the differences are due to the inherent annual fluctuations in the size of the olive crop. By 1944/45 the Arab share of the major

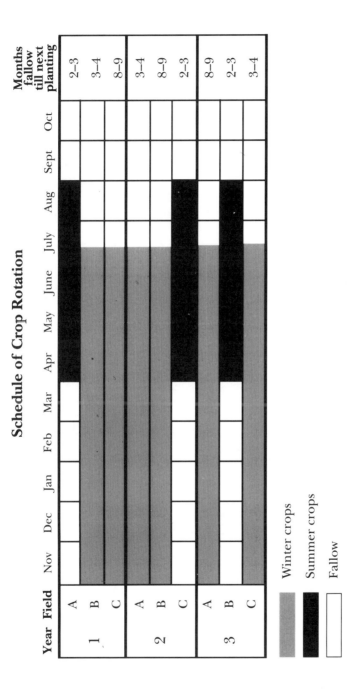

FIGURE 1: Three-Year Crop Rotation on Unirrigated Land

TABLE 18

A. Value of Agricultural Production and of Principal Crops, 1937–1944

	1937	1938	1939	1940	1941	1943	1944
Total agricultural production (£P)	8,221,739	7,721,758	5,582,352	5,980,274	8,898,541	22,240,170	20,340,799
Citrus (%)	49.2	58.6	35.0	1.0	2.6	5.2	9.6
Of total production (excluding citrus)							
Wheat, barley, durra (%)	45.3	32.2	36.4	40.5	40.1	17.0	13.7
Olives (%)	9.4	10.7	11.0	11.3	5.0	17.7	4.0
Vegetables (%)	11.5	18.0	18.4	19.3	25.3	34.0	40.9
Total	66.2	60.9	65.8	71.1	70.4	68.7	58.6

B. Arab Share of Production and Value of Principal Crops, 1944–1945

Crop	Arab Share	
	Production	Value
Grains	92.1	89.9
Vegetables	77.2	74.6
Fodder	10.5	14.2
Fruits (excl. citrus)	77.4	69.5
Olives	98.5	98.3
Melons	95.0	92.0

Sources: For production figures: Government of Palestine, *Statistical Abstract,* various issues; for Arab share of production: Government of Palestine, *Survey of Palestine,* pp. 323, 327.

crops produced was at least 75 percent, except for fodder, and their share of the value of these crops was almost as great.

The decline in the share of grains in the total value of Arab agricultural production throughout the entire period of the Mandate was, of course, even greater than the decline in their share after 1937, since the continuing development of Arab agriculture led to a diversification of production and a growing emphasis on crops other than cereals. The increase in village population that could not be employed in local agricultural work, the lack of vacant cereal lands to which cultivation could be extended, and the great dependence on climate for crop success transformed the traditional character of Arab agriculture, although the true extent of this transformation was not always stressed even by those who were in a position to see it clearly. The chapter on agriculture in the *Survey of Palestine*, after briefly describing the climatic factors affecting Palestinian cultivation, continued: "Cereal growing is the most important activity of the majority of Arab cultivators,"[8] even though the cereals, legumes, and sesame grown in 1944 comprised less than 25 percent of the total agricultural production, excluding citrus.[9] In terms of number, of course, the authors of the *Survey* were correct, for cereal-growing engaged more hands than did any other crop, because of the extensive methods employed.

There was considerable variation in the production of the three major cereal crops—wheat, barley, and durra—throughout the Mandate (table 19). Between 1924–1927 and 1939–1944 the production of wheat declined by 7.5 percent, while barley and durra production increased by almost 70 percent and more than 48 percent, respectively. The share of wheat in the production total of the three grains declined during the same period from 55.6 to 41.8 percent. Local production never sufficed for local needs, and wheat imports rose from about one-third of local production during 1928–1938, to more than 85 percent of local production during 1939–1944. Barley imports remained stable throughout the same period at about one-fourth of local production, and a small amount of barley, some 6 percent of the crop, was even exported during 1928–1938. There was a moderate annual increase in the production of barley and of durra between 1928 and 1938 (measured by the correlation between total production and year), but no similar systematic relationship held with respect to local wheat production. Except for durra exports, the price of both imports and exports of wheat, barley, and durra was lower in

TABLE 19

A. Production, Import and Export of Wheat, Barley, and Durra, 1924–1944 (annual averages in tons)

	Wheat				Barley			Durra		
	Total Production	Production	Imports as % of Production	Wheat Flour Imports	Production	Imports as % of Production	Exports as % of Production	Production	Imports as % of Production	Exports as % of Production
1924–1927	176,126	97,925	(a)	(a)	46,737	(a)		31,464	(a)	(a)
1928–1938	165,048	77,345	34.0	23,801	53,398	23.9	5.9[b]	34,305	16.4 (b)	21.1
1939–1944	216,560	90,585	85.7	23,625	79,313	26.3	—	46,662	(a)	(a)

B. Distribution of Total Production (%)

	Total	Wheat	Barley	Durra
1924–1927	100.0	55.6	26.5	17.9
1928–1938	100.0	46.9	32.4	20.8
1939–1944	100.0	41.8	36.6	21.5

Sources: Government of Palestine, *Statistical Abstract*, 1936, p. 32; ibid., 1939, pp. 41, 62; ibid., 1940, pp. 41, 62–63; ibid., 1942, p. 46; ibid., 1944/45, pp. 68, 223, 226; Gurevich, *Statistical Abstract*, p. 127.

Notes:
a. Incomplete data.
b. Includes maize.

1938 than it had been ten years earlier. Imports of wheat flour of a better grade than could be obtained from milling the local grain remained stable from 1928 to 1944, averaging less than 24,000 tons per year. In short, production of the three main cereal crops increased by only 23 percent from 1924–1927 to 1939–1944.

The data for vegetable production are less complete than for cereals, but the dramatic increase in local supplies is clear from table 20. Mean annual production increased almost twelvefold from 1924–1927 to 1939–1944, and about three-quarters of this production came from fields owned by Arabs. Arab vegetable production probably doubled between 1939 and 1944. In 1944/45, Arabs had 107,000 dunums of irrigated vegetables, almost 45 percent of their total vegetable production, while the 38,000 dunums of irrigated vegetables cultivated by Jews that season represented 95 percent of the area devoted by them to these crops.[10] While vegetable imports averaged more than 40 percent of local production during 1928–1938, they averaged less than 7 percent of local production during the next five years and declined absolutely from an annual average of some 19,000 tons in the earlier period to some 13,700 tons in the later one.[11]

The development of olive cultivation and the production of olives and olive oil was also evident during the Mandate. Since there are large natural fluctuations in the olive crops of successive seasons, however, there was no steady annual increase in production. As table 21 shows, mean annual olive production rose from 17,000 tons in 1921–1928 to 40,000 tons in 1939–1944. This increase was due to a combination of factors: an increase in the area planted with olive trees; distribution by the government of improved plants for propagation; improvement in methods of cultivation and of picking; and pest control. Between 1928 and 1938 annual exports of olive oil averaged 525 tons. There were villages in the Galilee in which a substantial portion of the land was devoted to olive groves, even at the expense of grain cultivation. Since olive-growing was much less labor intensive than raising field crops, men from these villages would have been more likely to seek outside employment that those whose land was under field crops.[12]

The most valuable crop Palestine produced was citrus, primarily oranges. Table 22 presents the basic statistics for the development of the citrus industry during the Mandate. The area of Arab-owned citrus groves increased more than sevenfold between 1925 and 1939, and

TABLE 20
A. Vegetable Production and Imports, 1924–1944

	Mean Annual Production (tons)	Imports as Percent of Production
1924–1927	17,467	NA
1928–1938	46,086	41.4
1939–1944	204,574	6.7

B. Vegetable Production by Subdistrict, 1939 and 1944[a]

	1939	1944	Percent Increase
1. Arab village production (Nazareth, Beisan, Tiberias, Haifa, Jaffa, Ramle subdistricts)	39,823	59,782	50.1
2. Total production in 1939; Arab village production in 1944 (Safad, Acre, Tulkarm, Gaza subdistricts)	41,473	106,884	157.7
3. Total production (Jenin, Nablus, Jerusalem, Hebron, Ramallah subdistricts)	17,805	29,105	63.5
Total	129,373	271,329	110.0
Arab[b]	99,101	195,771	97.5
Jewish	30,272	75,558	150.0

C. Vegetable Production and Imports, 1937, 1944 (tons)

	1937	1944	Percent Increase
Production			
According to Gurevich, *Statistical Handbook*, p. 166	12,500	57,500	360.0
According to the *Survey of Palestine*[c]			
Arab	NA	189,104	
Jewish	NA	55,730	
Imports	28,843	9,737	−66.2

Sources: Government of Palestine, *Statistical Abstract*, various issues.
Notes:

a. Subdistricts are grouped according to availability of separate data on Arab vegetable production.

b. The estimate in 21B is based on the assumption that all production in line 1 is Arab, almost all production in line 3 is Arab, and the proportion of production in line 2 which is Arab is not greater in 1939 than it is in 1944. In 1944 an additional 20,723 tons of vegetables were produced in Jewish settlements in category 2, representing 16.2 percent of the vegetable production in those subdistricts. The discrepancy between the total vegetable production reported in the 1944/45 *Statistical Abstract* (271,329 tons), which I allocated between Arab and Jewish production, and the total reported in the *Survey of Palestine* (279,940 tons), as well as the discrepancies regarding the totals for each community, are probably due to production by neither Arabs nor Jews which was not included in these tables of the *Statistical Abstract*.

c. Figures are for 1944/45 (p. 323).

TABLE 21
Olive Cultivation and Production, and Olive Oil Exports, 1929–1944

A. AREA UNDER OLIVE CULTIVATION,
1937–1944

	Dunums
1937	535,190
1938	546,181
1939	571,731
1940	582,952
1941	600,444
1942	NA
1943	592,388
1944	595,405

B. MEAN ANNUAL OLIVE PRODUCTION

	Tons
1921–1927	17,312
1928–1938	19,864
1939–1944	40,415
Mean annual export of olive oil, 1928–1938	525
Correlation (r) between annual production and export, 1928–1938	0.71

C. OLIVE OIL PRODUCTION,
1940/41–1944/45

Season	Tons
1940/41	10,535
1941/42	1,618
1942/43	9,414
1943/44	9,912
1944/45	2,738

Sources: Government of Palestine, *Statistical Abstract*, various issues.

TABLE 22
Citrus Planting and Export, 1925–1945

A. AREA OF CITRUS CULTIVATION *(dunums)*

	Total	Arab-owned	Jewish-owned
Planted by the end of 1925	30,500	19,000	11,500
Planted 1926–1939	269,000	125,000	144,000
Total planted by end of 1939	299,500	144,000	155,500
Total planted at end of 1945	250,000	120,000	130,000

B. EXPORTS OF ARAB CITRUS PRODUCTION *(cases)*

Total exports, 1930/31–1938/39	66,917,926
Percent Arab production of total exports	42.7%
In 1930/31	63.0%
In 1938/39	35.0%
Arab production exported	
1930/31	1,605,406
1938/39	5,342,672
Increase, 1930/31–1938/39	232.8%

Source: Gurevich, *Statistical Handbook*, pp. 179–80.

exports of citrus from Arab-owned groves between 1930/31 and 1938/39 more than tripled. However, the relative proportion of Arab production in the total Palestinian citrus export market declined in the same period from 63 to 35 percent because Jewish growers achieved greater productivity and a better quality fruit, as well as benefiting from a superior marketing operation in the countries of destination. But Jewish and Arab growers had much to do to improve their practices. In 1930, the government's chief horticultural officer listed the changes he believed were necessary to expand the English market for Jaffa oranges. These included improvement in cultivation practices, in grading and packing the fruit, and in shipping. The citrus export industry was seriously damaged by the Second World War; local production plummeted and many groves were left untended. [13]

A summary prepared after World War II by Jewish Agency economists clearly demonstrates the rise in Arab agricultural output between 1931 and 1945 (table 23). Production increased of crops which had long been grown in Palestine (bread cereals, melons, grapes, figs, sesame,

TABLE 23
Gross Output for Direct Human Consumption in Arab Agriculture,
1931–1945 (excluding citriculture and fisheries)

Commodity	Tons		Percent		Percent Change, 1931–1945
	1931	1945	1931	1945	
Bread cereals	100,000	140,300	53	23	+40
Vegetables[a]	12,000	189,100	6	30	+1,476
Melons	22,000	135,600	12	22	+516
Grapes	10,000	34,900	5	6	+249
Figs	6,700	19,600	4	3	+193
Almonds	500	4,000	(b)	1	+700
Apples, plums	—	3,500	—	1	—
Bananas	—	4,100	—	1	—
Other fruit	1,500	7,200	1	1	+380
Sesame	2,000	4,700	1	1	+135
Olives	34,000	78,300	18	13	+130
Total	188,700	621,300	100%	102%	+229

Source: CZA/S90/633, L. Samuel, "Arab Agriculture and Its Development Between 1931 and 1945," p. 1.
Notes:
   a. Including potatoes
   b. Less than 1 percent.

and olives), and new crops were introduced and found ever greater acceptance (vegetables, including potatoes, on a commercial scale, and fruit trees of various kinds).

Agricultural Innovation and Change

The two best-known analyses of Arab peasant agriculture in Palestine are Volcani's *The Fellah's Farm* and the Johnson-Crosbie report.[14] Both refer to roughly the same period, the late 1920s, and provide the most comprehensive description available of the details of peasant economy. While the Johnson-Crosbie report focused on peasant indebtedness, Volcani, the director of the Jewish Agency's agricultural research institute, presented a detailed analysis of peasant farming methods.

Underlying Volcani's discussion of peasant cultivation was the issue of transforming Arab agricultural methods in order that peasants obtain a higher yield from their land. Though there were clear political implications to such a goal—by reducing the size of the holding required by peasants to support themselves, land could be freed for additional Jewish purchases and settlement—Volcani did not refer to them in his monograph. His discussion had four main themes: a description of Arab agriculture carried out on moderate-sized holdings; an analysis of the suitability of existing techniques to the resources of land and climate available to the fellah; consideration of alternative policies which might be implemented in order to improve Arab peasant agriculture; and a brief discussion, at the very end of the monograph, of what would be required in order to implement the policy that Volcani considered to be necessary.

Volcani dealt with a particular type of Arab farm—the independent peasant owning about 80 to 100 dunums, whose major income came from the sale of surplus grain. He included tenants or sharecroppers in his discussion only to the extent of mentioning the portion of the crop due to the landowner (p. 54). He obtained his data on farm expenditures and income from two sources. The first were records kept by the administrators of lands bought in the Jezre'el Valley by the JNF before the First World War; they continued to be worked by the Arab tenant cultivators who had previously farmed them, the JNF serving as landlord and receiving rental payments until Jewish settlements could be established. The second source were the results of experiments on different crop rotations which Volcani directed at the Jewish Agency's agriculture station at Gevath, also in the Jezre'el Valley. In one of the treatments, 60 dunums of land were given to be farmed in the traditional manner by a local peasant who cultivated 200 dunums of other land, and his expenses, yields, and income were recorded.

Volcani's discussion assumed a holding of moderate size. Under the conditions of fellah grain cultivation, a holding of 80–100 dunums was adequate only in years when the rain fell at the right times and with the proper intensity, and the market prices for produce were good. In such circumstances, the peasants might be able to avoid increasing their indebtedness, or even reduce its burden somewhat, while at the same time retaining enough grain for sowing in the coming season and for household consumption until the next crop was harvested. Most peasants, however, did not possess holdings of this size, and many of those who did had debts to repay which reduced their ability to support themselves only on the income from agriculture. It was clear to Volcani that the larger the holding, the less able were peasants and their families to cultivate it without hired help. If, in order to increase their income, peasants could contract to farm an additional area, they and the members of their households could not do so by relying solely on their own labor, and were obliged to hire a *harrath*, an agricultural laborer, hired by the season, usually with no land of his own. But, as Volcani recognized, in such a situation "the surplus income of the owner [or principal tenant] is only made possible by a ruthless exploitation of the harath who is in consequence living below the poverty line" (p. 84).

Volcani did not believe that it was possible to bring about rapid improvements in Arab peasant agriculture by massive capital investment and a radical transformation of the traditional cropping patterns. In his view, the expense of investment in modern farm buildings and machinery would be totally disproportionate to the anticipated short-term gains from increased production and would quickly lead the peasant family to disaster (p. 98). Nor was a total transformation of Arab peasant agriculture necessary, for the cultivators had, over the years, developed techniques of production that were well suited to their physical and economic environment. Volcani noted in particular the nail plow, which, since it did not expose the soil too deeply and thereby allow moisture to evaporate, was appropriate to unirrigated cultivation in a climate characterized by a long, hot, rainless summer, alternating with a winter whose rains, while often abundant, were unreliable in their timing.[15]

Volcani did not romanticize the peasant's most important agricultural implement, though his lyrical opening chapters, in which he alternates description of the fellah's yearly agriculture round with citations from biblical and talmudic sources, created a nostalgic atmosphere at variance with his subsequent analysis of the practical alternatives available to peasants for improving their standard of living. So long as they were dependent for their main source of income on extensive grain cultivation and were tied to a system of agricultural production relationships from which they could not unaided extricate themselves, the traditional nail plow was eminently suitable. It was not, however, a value to be preserved at all costs.

Volcani argued that the condition of the peasant farm could be improved by three measures that would not require a radical transformation of agricultural practices and the farm economy: increasing the fertility of the soil; increasing the production of existing crops; diversification (pp. 111–15). Soil fertility was to be improved by green manure, with one-sixth to one-fifth of the farm area devoted to its cultivation; part of the crop would be used for fodder and the remainder would be turned under. Crop yields would be increased by the choice of an appropriate rotation crop; the use of fertilizer; and more careful selection of seeds. Production would be diversified by planting a small area with trees—olives, figs, citrus—or with grapes; expanding production of onions or eggs and marketing the surplus; dairying on a small scale based on stock produced by crossing imported pure-bred bulls and local cows; improving the poultry in a similar way to increase egg production. Once underway, these changes would provide peasants with additional income that would enable them and their families to make further improvements.

Volcani distinguished between improvements for which peasants had to pay and those which should not require expenditure of money on their part (pp. 124ff). This final section of his monograph thus dealt with the link between the fellah's household economy and the national economic and political structure in which it operated. Volcani believed that minimal expense was involved in improving soil fertility through better crop rotation; more careful selection of seeds; setting aside land for planting fruit trees; and acquiring stud bulls for improving livestock. On the other hand, investment was necessary to expand irrigation and cover the temporary losses resulting from withdrawal of part of the land from grain production in order to use it for growing fodder and green manure. At this point he referred to the question of peasant debt and the need for government action to permit the necessary improvements to be made.

Volcani's study was weakened by his postponement to a later work any systematic discussion of agriculture policy and credit. Although he was certainly aware of the widespread existence of peasant debt, his analysis of household income and expenditure ignores expenses resulting from loan repayments. But Volcani's decision to treat agricultural policy and credit in a separate work (p. iv) affected not only the validity of the peasant budgets he presents. Peasants are unlikely to make changes in their agricultural practices if the practical effect of these changes is to enable them to make larger debt payments but not to liquidate their obligations. There was little incentive for peasants to make even those innovations which apparently cost them little or nothing, since in the absence of a program of protection against creditors, or the establishment of government-run agriculture credit institutions that would lend to small cultivators, any increased income they might gain would go straight to the moneylender.

The ability of Arab cultivators to benefit from technical developments as a result of the establishment of the Mandatory government and the example of the Jewish settlements was quite uneven. Most of the systematic effort directed to assist Arab farmers was carried out by the government Department of Agriculture. Abcarius, who criticized the inadequacy of government policies toward the Arabs, summarized the scope of its activities which included: demonstrations at agricultural stations of deep-plowing and the use of tractors and machinery for sowing and reaping, experiments, and seed selection; the sale of suitable seed to farmers; the sale of grafted fruit seedlings; the establishment of plots to demonstrate crop rotation, manuring, and weeding; and the provision of experts in grading citrus, establishment of a citrus inspection service, and arranging for the fumigation of trees. Abcarius complained that not all the efforts were carried through; the program of experimental plots was abandoned; and not enough was done to improve the olive yield nor to improve the quality of the local tobacco so it would be suitable for export and thereby reduce the dependence of the local Arab growers on the "good will" of the Palestinian cigarette manufacturers.[16]

The major change in Palestinian Arab agriculture during the Mandate was the tremendous expansion of vegetable production. Although the value of the vegetable crop was much lower than that of citrus, which also expanded greatly until the outbreak of the Second World War, the expansion of vegetable production had potentially greater significance for the structure of Arab agriculture than did the extension of citriculture. Orange growing required capital investment and did not provide an immediate return, since it was necessary to wait a number of years until the trees began bearing. Although no information seems to be available on the distribution by size of Arab citrus groves, many were owned and operated by wealthy individuals who ran them not as family farms but as medium and large-scale capitalist enterprises. Moreover, Arab citrus production was restricted to the coastal plain, and its extension to other areas of the country was difficult. It was much easier for a small cultivator to begin to raise vegetables than to introduce citrus. Irrigation was required for vegetable growing to be profitable, and between 1927 and 1939/40 the area of Arab irrigated mixed farming rose from 3,000 to 36,500 dunums; a similar increase occurred in Jewish irrigated mixed farming.[17] Specific information is unavailable regarding the sources of the funds required for introducing irrigation, though a portion may have been earned by family members seasonally employed in towns or on government public works projects, while another portion may have come from land sales to Jews. In any case, the investment necessary to sink a well, to purchase water from a well operating nearby, or to establish cooperative arrangements among adjacent villages, would not have been beyond the reach of an owner-cultivator with 20 dunums or more who had access to credit, especially considering the income anticipated from the crop.

Nevertheless, innovations in crops, in techniques, or in equipment were almost impossible for the vast majority of Arab cultivators because they lacked capital, did not receive technical assistance, or because their holdings were too small or they had no land at all. However well meaning they might have been, the efforts of the Department of Agriculture, and its budget, were inadequate to the needs of Arab agriculture. Consequently, development was very uneven. Arabs with capital or with the possibility of pooling their resources (as in cooperative societies) were better able to take advantage of modern methods and equipment. The rest, whose access was more limited, continued in their former condition, which improved if the agricultural situation in general improved, but which could rapidly decline again in the wake of a poor harvest caused by the vicissitudes of climate. All the information available regarding innovation and change in Arab agriculture during the Mandate is consistent with the conclusion that differentiation on the basis of access to resources restricted the extent to which most Arab cultivators could participate in development. How such participation occurred in practice depended on the interaction between village resources and social structure, on the one hand, and the requirements of the new techniques, on the other. This can be seen in the examples of the use of tractors, the introduction of fodder crops and potatoes, the use of manure, and other available innovations. Access to agricultural credit was similarly affected.

Tractors

Only a small proportion of the tractors used in Palestine agriculture were employed on Arab lands. Even as late as 1940, only about 10 percent of the 500 tractors in the country were owned by Arabs. A combination of factors hindered the wider use of agricultural machinery by Arab farmers, and they reflected the familiar problems of peasant agriculture in the country.[18]

Tractors provided a source of power much greater than that obtainable from plow animals. They made possible the cultivation of larger tracts of land in a given period of time. Tractors were employed in the various stages of cultivation, including plowing, harrowing, reaping, and baling. They could also be used to power agricultural machinery used in postharvest processing, such as threshing and chaff-cutting. The application of increased power which they made possible not only speeded the work of the farmer but, in the case of plowing, made it possible to break up the ground more effectively, to plow under stalks and stubble which would then enrich the soil, and permitted farmers to make more efficient use of the land at their disposal.

The advantages of tractors, however, were vitiated by the conditions of Arab peasant cultivation, which made their use unprofitable. The deep plowing which tractors made possible was a dangerous technique in a region where the rains were uncertain. The traditional peasant nail plow scratched the surface of the ground, making a narrow furrow only deep enough to receive the seed without exposing the lower layer of the soil to the heat of the sun and permitting evaporation of the moisture it contained. Deep plowing, by overturning the lower layers in which moisture was stored, made sense only if the rain could be counted on, which was not the case in Palestine.

Deep plowing was an appropriate technique where land could be irrigated, either naturally or from wells. But serious obstacles existed to the introduction of irrigation to Arab holdings. It was difficult, if not impossible, to establish an efficient irrigation scheme on small holdings, beyond watering of small vegetable plots from a private well. A larger scheme, designed to cover hundreds of dunums, required either that the land be in the hands of a single owner, or that the owners cooperate. This was often very difficult to achieve. In the 1940s villages in the Hula area had their lands plowed by tractors in connection with government efforts to increase the production of cereals and vegetables for the large numbers of servicemen stationed in the country.[19] Though the file does not indicate who owned the tractors, farmers in the Huleh region had access to surface water that could be diverted to fields relatively inexpensively. Apparently some of the Arab lands were plowed by tractors hired by the government from Jewish settlements.

In addition to the topographical difficulties, tractors were expensive; they were economical only if they freed cultivators to engage in other income-producing activities or reduced an unbearable labor burden. Most smallholders, however, could neither afford to purchase tractors nor make efficient use of them even had their acquisition been possible. The small size of most of the holdings, the inconvenient layout of the fields, with irregularly shaped plots and lack of access for tractors, and the brief plowing and harvesting seasons, greatly reduced the likelihood that a tractor could be efficiently employed. Moreover, there was no alternative employment readily available for most peasant cultivators, and the introduction of tractors would have increased rural underemployment. That, in turn, would have put greater pressure on the towns to which displaced peasants came seeking work, as well as on the government to provide work in the countryside.

The Second World War could have provided a great impetus for the spread of tractors and other agricultural machinery among Arab farmers. Food requirements increased substantially because of the presence of large numbers of British troops in the country, and the government encouraged the expansion of grain and vegetable cultivation through "lease/lend" agreements with Arab and Jewish cultivators. Twenty-five tractors, twenty-seven plows, one combine, one mower, and one sweep rake were distributed to Arab cultivators in 1943, in various parts of the country. The recipients of the equipment included a municipality (Shafa 'Amr), village cooperative societies, individual farmers, and business associations. In the same year Jewish cultivators received fifty-nine tractors, forty-eight plows, thirty-one combines, twenty-nine mowers, and four sweep rakes.[20]

Jewish agriculture was much more mechanized than Arab farming before the war, and the organization of the *Yishuv*'s agriculture made it easier to demonstrate that machinery could be effectively used. Allocation of lease/lend tractors to Jewish farming was based on the recommendation of a special committee established by the Jewish organizations. Arabs received tractors based on individual applications, since no special countrywide committee was established to represent Arab farmers. This probably reduced the likelihood that Arab cultivators would get equipment; a countrywide committee could have publicized the program and encouraged applications; it could also have represented applicants and improved their chances of being approved.

The lease/lend program was established primarily in order to increase agricultural production and not principally as a means of agricultural development. Rising prices for agricultural produce may have enabled some of the peasants to buy power implements. But wartime conditions made it extremely difficult to obtain additional tractors. Plants in the United States and in England that manufactured agricultural equipment had been turned over to war production; most of the tractors manufactured were earmarked for military purposes; transport shortages and shipping dangers resulted in a low priority for tractors intended for use in Middle Eastern agriculture. In response to Arab complaints in 1944 that the distribution of tractors was insufficient, the controller of agricultural production, Steadman Davis, replied that machinery had been made available under "rigid conditions"; he had tried to obtain more machinery for Arabs but had been told "that they must continue, as in the past, to use working animals. Even in the U.S.A., tractors were not being issued to replace working animals."[21]

Davis had only been transmitting the reply he had received, and local cultivators could not have taken much consolation from the comparison with the United States. As we will see in the discussion of fodder growing, the typical work animal found on an Arab holding was not strong enough, because of breed and inadequate diet, to pull a heavy plow. The Department of Agriculture report for 1934 noted that expensive agricultural machinery and modern labor-saving devices were not recommended for the smallholder: "The Arab cultivator has neither the power to work nor the money to purchase them."[22] The Department of Agriculture encouraged Arabs to replace their nail plows with modern, steel implements, but the lack of strong animals hampered their introduction. Still, the department's annual report for 1935 noted "a decided increase" among Arab farmers in the use of light steel plows, though this was apparently characteristic of "the more wealthy and progressive landowners."[23]

The department also recommended the acquisition of modern cultivators and harrows and maintained a stock of implements at the government agricultural stations which could be loaned to cultivators. In 1934, thirteen Arab cooperative farmers in the Jaffa and Ramleh subdistricts borrowed a variety of such implements (plows, harrows, chains, fenceposts, a maize husker; grain cleaning machines, chaff cutters, hammers, iron pegs). Ten or eleven of the borrowers were farmers who had agreed to have demonstration plots for fodder-growing placed on their land, and

the same was true for three of the twenty-three borrowers in the Beersheba subdistrict. The department lent "native ploughs" as well as those
made of steel, perhaps to farmers who had hired temporary workers and
did not have animals who could pull a steel plow. It seems strange,
however, that a nail plow (assuming that was what was meant) would have
to be borrowed from the agricultural station. [24]

Table 24 summarizes the information available regarding the number, power, distribution, and ownership of tractors in Palestine between
1921 and 1940. Agricultural officers in the various districts and
subdistricts were required to submit each year a detailed list of the
tractors "employed" in agriculture in their jurisdictions. The returns in
the files are neither completed nor totally consistent, but they provide
some basic information regarding the use of tractors by Arab and Jewish
cultivators.

Between 1921 and 1940 the total number of tractors in agricultural use
increased more than twelvefold but, as noted, only about 10 percent of
them were in Arab hands at the start of the 1940s. Arab-owned tractors
were concentrated in the Ramleh and Jaffa subdistricts, where the coastal
plain widens and provides relatively large areas of level land suitable for
grain cultivation. It seems as if a number of Arab tractors were owned by
contractors who went from village to village and plowed the fields prior to
sowing. This would have required the villagers to agree among themselves
to hire such a contractor and to allocate the expense among themselves.
Such arrangements might have been more likely in villages having cooperative societies, which would have provided a framework for joint effort
which could have been adapted to additional endeavors.

There are fluctuations from year to year in the number of tractors in
use, due to incomplete reporting and to variations in economic conditions. In 1937, for example, the agricultural officer in the Jaffa
subdistrict noted a great decrease in the employment of tractors (68 in
the Jaffa and Ramleh subdistricts, down from 106 in 1936), and attributed it to "the crisis in the citrus culture and difficult financial
situation"—a reference to the consequences of the Arab revolt between
1936 and 1939. [25] Tractors in Arab ownership were more powerful than
those in Jewish localities, which suggests that they were likely to be
bought not only for the owner's lands but also to be hired out.

That the Department of Agriculture report for 1935 found it "worthy
of record" to identify two tractor purchases in the Jenin subdistrict, one

by the Agricultural Committee of Yamoun village, and the other in Beit Qad, purchased by the Abboushi family of Jenin, suggests how rare such acquisitions still were (the department helped train operators for these tractors).[26] The following year witnessed, according to the department's annual report, a "marked increased in the use of tractors purchased by Arab farmers on a cooperative basis,"[27] though given the presumed number of tractors hitherto in cooperative Arab ownership, the absolute increase was probably quite small. Of forty-seven Caterpillar and International Harvester tractors sold in 1932, one was bought by an Arab; two years later the two firms sold thirty-four tractors in Palestine, eleven to Arabs.

Fodder

Government Efforts to Encourage the Growing of Fodder Crops

Since techniques of peasant cultivation common in Palestine made it difficult for the fellah to improve agricultural production, one of the areas in which the government Department of Agriculture attempted to intervene was the growing of fodder for livestock. Normally village cattle, sheep, goats, camels, and donkeys foraged for themselves on the grasses that grew naturally in the winter and spring, and on the stubble remaining in the fields after the crops were harvested in the summer and autumn. Only the plow animals were fed supplementary rations during the months they were working, in order to help them maintain their strength. No systematic attempt was made to improve the quality of livestock, and the local breeds were poor.[28]

In seasons of regular rainfall, the natural forage and stubble were more or less adequate, though they did not provide the nutrients necessary for dairy cattle.[29] But when the rains failed, the quantity of natural forage and of stubble available for grazing both declined, and livestock reached a condition repeatedly characterized as "semi-starvation."[30] Since the rainfall was not equally distributed throughout the various regions of the country, there were years in which one area had sufficient stocks of fodder and no fear of a shortage, whereas in others farmers faced serious deficiencies. In the autumn of 1932, for example, a review of the fodder supplies in the southern half of the country indicated that no fodder was available in the Beersheba subdistrict; that fodder stocks were in immediate danger of exhaustion in the Jerusalem and Ramallah

TABLE 24

Tractors Employed in Agriculture in Palestine, 1921–1940

	1921	1922	1924	1926	1927	1931	1932	1934	1935	1936	1937	1938	1940
Total Palestine													
Number	40	45	52	113	105		190	288					500
Hp	735		1318	3973	3869		3022	5059					
Hp/tractor	18.4		25.3	35.2	36.8		15.9	17.6					
Arab*													50
Jewish*													450
Northern District													
Number	27		38	50	56		95	134					
Hp	477		1048	1691	1848		1813	2631					
Hp/tractor	17.6		27.6	33.8	33.0		19.1	19.6					
Arab*				6			5–9	3					
Jewish*				44									
Subdistricts													
Acre*								1					
Jenin* (all Arab)								2					
Tulkarm*											3	3	
Hp											60	60	
Hp/tractor											20	20	
Southern District													
Number	13		14	63	49		95	154		113	94	102	
Hp	258		270	2282	2021		1907	2428		2612	2661	2901	
Hp/tractor	19.8		19.3	36.2	41.2		23.0[a]	15.8		23.1	28.3	28.4	

		5–10[b]			
Arab*	4	6	21		
Hp			714		
Hp/tractor			34		
Jewish*	25	53	85		
Hp			1638		
Hp/tractor			19.3		
German*		9	7		
Subdistricts					
Jaffa and Ramleh*	142	80	106	68	76
Hp	2038	2006	2352	1771	2011
Hp/tractor	14.4	25.1	22.2	26.0	26.5
Arab*		2–6	21	15	15
Hp			714	491	491
Hp/tractor			34.0	32.7	32.7
Jewish*			85	53	61
Hp			1638	1280	1520
Hp/tractor			19.3	24.2	24.9
Gaza*[c]	12	16	7	23	23
Hp	390	590	260	830	830
Hp/tractor	32.5	36.9	37.1	36.0	36.0
Jerusalem District					
Number (all Arab)	1	4	3	4	3

Sources: ISA/RG7/Box 633/Ag 14, and ISA/RG7/Box 635/Ag 19/4, "Returns of Tractors Purchased and Employed in Palestine," various years.

Notes:

* = number.

a. Based on 83 tractors for which hp is known.

b. Five in Arab villages; five owned by touring contractors all or most of whom were probably Arab.

c. Gaza subdistrict includes Majdal and Beersheba subdistrict.

subdistricts; that the villages in the Hebron subdistrict (but not the Bedouin) had sufficient supplies; that shortages were anticipated in the Gaza subdistrict by the end of the year; and that in the Jaffa and Ramleh subdistricts supplies were generally adequate, except for some of the hill areas.[31]

Officials of the Department of Agriculture sought solutions to immediate fodder needs and also tried to bring about permanent changes in cultivation practices that would provide farmers with an assured supply of more nutritious feed for livestock. Estimates were prepared of the cost of growing maize, alfalfa (lucerne), and berseem (a succulent clover) as emergency measures. Maize, if cut while still green, could provide two crops each season; if thinned while green it could provide green fodder as well as grain from the plants left to reach maturity. Lucerne could be repeatedly cut and used for green fodder, or dried and made into hay (which, however, could not meet immediate needs). Berseem was intended to be used for grazing following the maize crop. The quality of both green maize and lucerne deteriorated rapidly after being cut; they were also bulky and expensive to transport. These crops were therefore most valuable when grown in the same localities with the starving livestock, especially since in their weakened condition the cattle could not be expected to walk long distances to distribution centers. Unless the crops were irrigated, however, their yields were poor and uncertain, which restricted their cultivation to plots with access to water. But that raised the cost of production and made it difficult for income from sales to farmers to cover the expense of growing the fodder. Comparisons among various combinations of green maize, grain, lucerne, and berseem, taking into account the rent of land and the cost of water, in addition to the difficulty of locating suitable plots in the regions of greatest need, led to the conclusion that the cheapest solution was to import fodder—grain and *tibn* (cut straw remaining after threshing)— rather than to grow it.[32]

Difficulties in Expanding Cultivation of Fodder Crops

An early attempt to convince Arab farmers of the value of growing fodder crops was made in the fall of 1932 by a Mr. Yazdi, an agricultural officer in the Tiberias subdistrict, who "by personal persuasion, induced certain landowners to lay down areas in maize from seed provided by the

Dept. of Agriculture and by manual and cattle labour provided in great part by the proprietors and public-spirited local cultivators."[33]

Although the crop was successful, and the Department of Agriculture officials who reported on their visit to the area praised the initiative of their local representative, the results of the experiment were "disappointing from the economical and the psychological aspect." The owners of the livestock were neither enthusiastic about feeding the green fodder to their animals nor were they prepared to transport it at their own expense to their farms. The officials suggested that animals probably were not yet dying of starvation, and thus no great need was felt for changing customary practices. But they wondered why the cultivators didn't themselves grow summer grain crops on the land, or put it under fodder, and suggested that "the answer would appear to be lack of initiative, laziness, the necessity to leave the land fallow, possibly a non-realization of the necessity to grow forage, or the fact that truck crops have no local market. It is to be noted that a green fodder crop like maize cut and removed from the land, is a very exhaustive [of soil fertility] one and that the result of similar green forage culture is bound to have a bearing on future crops over the area."[34]

The farmers would probably not have agreed with some of the explanations on this list. From their point of view, the fact that green maize for fodder was not a crop they were used to, one which depleted the soil and reduced the yield of the winter grain crop which would normally be sown in November or December, may have been sufficient reason to refrain from investing land and labor in the experiment. Yazdi's experiments were apparently carried out on land belonging to persons with fairly large holdings, who could forgo income from the usual crops for the duration of the experiment. One wonders about the motivations of these "public-spirited" farmers who agreed to the undertaking, and what they received in return.

From the government's point of view the conditions of the experiment were quite favorable, since land, labor, and water were obtained without cost. But had these costs been included, along with the price of transporting the fodder to Tiberias, the total cost of feeding the stock for two months would have exceeded the value of the animals fed. The alternative, bringing the livestock to the fodder, seemed to be out of the question because of the weakened condition of the animals as well as the unwillingness of the stock owners, "who are apparently not nomad Arabs," to move with their animals. Even such a temporary relocation would have meant a major change in stock-rearing practice, might have exposed the animals to theft, and would have required stationing someone at the feeding grounds, thereby complicating usual practices. In a broader accounting, even had stock owners been willing to trek to the fodder-growing area, that land might have been used to yield other, more profitable crops. Although the green forage would have prevented starvation, it would not have been an adequate diet for a working plow animal, which required supplements of concentrated dry food such as grains or *tibn*. Finally, the period of greatest need for such fodder, the end of the summer and the beginning of autumn, was also the period when the plow animals were needed at home to prepare the soil for the winter planting and could not be grazed elsewhere.

Three days after visiting Yazdi's experiment, G. G. Masson, chief agricultural officer of the Tiberias subdistrict, submitted a memorandum on stock-feeding that listed additional reasons why, from the fellah's perspective, it was disadvantageous to change customary practices: "Under the present condition of land tenure, and in view of the small area he has at his disposal from which to make a living and the small number of draught animals in his possession, the practice of growing green fodder is economically unsound. In even a season slightly below average he will harvest sufficient tibn and grain for his food, the animals' food for the forthcoming season, and perhaps a little to sell. If the late rains are good his dura and sesame, especially the latter, brings him in some income." According to Masson's figures, however, cultivating fodder might be more profitable than growing grain. Assuming a holding of eighty dunums, were the cultivator to devote twenty to oats and vetch he would obtain six to eight tons of dry fodder which, after being made into hay (an operation which the farmer would have to learn), would have an "intrinsic value" of £P18–£P24. The twenty dunums would yield about one and one-half tons of grain, and four and one-half tons of *tibn*, together worth about £P20.[35]

However, as Yazdi discovered, and for reasons similar to those Masson enumerated, there was no market for fodder, and thus no incentive for the Arab farmer to cultivate it. Moreover, "in an emergency, that is to say, in a year of general drought, the necessity for the growing of fodder for stock is not apparent until mid-March," when the size of the cereal crop could be known. But if no rain fell at the end of March or the beginning of April it was impossible to grow a good maize crop, except under irrigation, and "it is then that the need for the production of fodder for animals which may possibly be starving from the following October to January becomes a matter of urgency."[36]

Masson proposed a number of possible measures, including preparation of silage;[37] planting large areas of lucerne which could be repeatedly cut, part stored as hay and part used for grazing; sowing with forage grasses all government plains lands irrigable by gravity and not leased for cultivation, and fertilizing them to obtain higher yields; inducing private farmers to grow crops that could be cut and stored as hay; improvement of natural pasture by distribution of grass seed and by fertilization at the expense of landowners; inducing cultivators to substitute maize for durra in areas where rainfall is "not precarious"; and teaching farmers who keep milch cows the benefits of storing and preserving green fodder as silage.[38]

During the following year, demonstration plots for maize, clover, oats, and vetch were initiated in various locations, and agricultural inspectors talked to mukhtars and villagers about the advantages of growing forage. S. Antebi, the government's agricultural officer for the southern half of the country, believed that the efforts had met with a satisfactory response, considering the nature of the difficulties encountered. Many had been noted the previous year: the fellahin were not used to growing fodder; they preferred growing cereals for their family's needs and selling the surplus; poor yields in the past two years made farmers even more reluctant to remove land from grain production; farmers might recognize the need for special feeding of dairy cattle, but few kept them; where water for irrigation was available, and fodder crops could be grown, farmers preferred raising vegetables which found a ready market and met an increased demand; durra, more drought-resistant, was preferred to maize, especially in the southern areas where rainfall was less certain.[39]

A month later Dawe, the director of agriculture, responded to a message from the chief secretary of the Palestine Administration conveying the dissatisfaction of Sir Arthur Wauchope, the high commissioner, that the Department of Agriculture had neglected fodder-growing. Wauchope had four reasons for wanting maize grown for fodder: anticipation of shortages of fodder in parts of the country; spending funds in Palestine rather than on imported fodder; demonstrating to the villagers that fodder-

growing was possible; fodder shortages were hard to forsee, and maize
could be planted as late as August and still give a crop.[40] Wauchope
complained that "nothing was done in this direction two years ago: little
last year: and . . . little again this year."[41] Dawe defended his department's record, and presented reasons for the apparent slow progress:

> It must be realized . . . that the difficulties encountered in trying to
> persuade the local Arab farmer to sacrifice part of a crop which pro-
> duces an assured income, or at least keeps him from actual starvation,
> for the—to him—very problematical benefits bestowed by a fodder
> crop on his animals, are enormous. It will take years of continued,
> successful demonstration before any progress on a large scale can be
> registered. . . . The ultimate success . . . of any given system of farm-
> ing is the result stated in terms of cash and it is difficult to convince
> the fellah that initial increased expenditure is going to benefit him.
> Deeper ploughing, made possible by stronger animals, will in course of
> time improve his crops, but the increase is so gradual that in its earlier
> stages it will be hardly perceptible to the rough and ready methods of
> accounting employed by the average fellah.[42]

Despite such arguments, Wauchope continued to press for greater
efforts. In November 1933 he asked what had been done with regard to
improving grazing on hillsides; whether the department had consulted
Jewish agricultural experts regarding the best grasses to grow for pasture;
and what evidence was available regarding the claim that many farmers
sold their livestock after the end of the plowing season to avoid having to
feed them during the months they were not working. Wauchope particularly questioned the argument that one of the principal difficulties preventing the spread of fodder-growing was the fellah's resistance to innovation. Wauchope's own impression, based on conversations with district
officers and mukhtars, was that "the great majority of the fellaheen feed
their plough cattle to some extent with barley and kersenneh [vetch],"
and that the job of the administration was not to persuade farmers to do
something that was unknown to them, but rather "to enlarge [their]
present practice and . . . to do it in the wisest manner."[43]

Wauchope's memorandum was circulated to agricultural officers in
the field, and Antebi responded to the points raised. He noted that
because of the reclamation and terracing of hillsides the area under

natural grazing was steadily decreasing; although farmers always grew kersenneh, in years of poor rainfall its success was even less assured than wheat; in normal years only poor or old working cattle were sold after threshing, but in bad years, when the cost of feed was high, it did not pay the farmer to keep bullocks worth between £P4 and £P6 when they were not working, and when he might have to borrow money to pay for their feed. With respect to the question of peasant conservatism, Antebi distinguished between growing kersenneh, a legume, and forage crops such as oats and vetch for hay, or green forage such as berseem or maize. Apparently farmers grew kersenneh only when they did not believe that it would be profitable to grow wheat; thus, the high commissioner was incorrect in his assumption that the extension of such crops was simply a matter of inducing farmers to do more of what they were already doing. Kersenneh was not being grown for forage, but because conditions were unfavorable for wheat. The implication was that this was not a firm basis on which to build a program of expansion.[44]

The conditions of Arab cultivation were such that impediments existed to the extension of forage crops in good years as well as in bad. In bad years, farmers were reluctant to forgo the possibility of raising a crop that could be used by the household for food (such as durra), and perhaps sold (sesame). In good years, however, there were also "great difficulties to be overcome, such as the presence of surplus supplies of tibben in all villages, the good prospects of a good summer crop making it exceedingly difficult for the farmer to sacrifice even the smallest portion of it for silo making, the absence of unemployment at this time of the year when every fellah is busy on harvesting, threshing, collection of vegetables from his field & marketing same, etc." The fact that there were relatively few dairy cattle in Arab villages was another reason for the lack of interest in producing green fodder; the Jewish and German colonies had dairy herds, and berseem, oats, vetches, and maize were available throughout the year.[45]

Demonstration Work

During the six seasons from 1932/33 through 1937/38, the Department of Agriculture was able to establish demonstration plots for growing fodder in at least 203 Arab towns and villages, as well as in 13 Jewish localities. Table 25 summarizes the data in the files. Most of the Arab

TABLE 25

**Arab Localities and Farmers with Fodder Demonstration Plots,
1932/33–1937/38**

Season	Number of Localities	Number of Farmers	Number of Farmers with Demonstration Plot in Previous Season	Number of Farmers with Plots for Two Different Crops
1932/33 (oats, vetch)	24	24[a]	—[d]	—[f]
1933 (maize)	33	38		—
1933/34 (oats, vetch)	20	22	} 5	—
1934 (maize)	11	11	—	—
1935/36 (oats, vetch, berseem)	47[b]	99[c]	10	11
1936/37 (oats, vetch, berseem)	59[b]	100[c]	24	5
1937/38[e] (oats, vetch, berseem)	9	14	—	—
Total	203	268[g]	31[g]	15[g]

Sources: From ISA/RG7/Box 638/Ag 22-12, the following documents:

1932/33: Berseem—"Supply of Fodder," 16.3.33. Oats/vetch—ibid., "Demonstration Plots for the Production of Oats and Vetch, Season Winter 1932" (tables).

1933: Maize—"Supply of Fodder," 16.3.33; "Demonstration Plots for the Production of Oats and Vetch, Season Winter 1932" (tables).

1933/34: Oats/vetch—"List of Fodder Plots Season 1933/34, Jaffa-Ramleh Area" (table).

1934: Maize—"Maize," 26.6.34.

1935/36: Berseem—"List of Distribution of Berseem for Ramleh S.D., 1935/36" (table); "Results of Berseem Plots—1935/6 Under Irrigation Jaffa Area," 11.7.36; "Results of Berseem Demonstration Plots," 21.9.36. Oats/vetch—"Results of Fodder Demonstration Plots at Beersheba S.D. 1935–36" (table); "Result of Fodder Demonstration Plots Vetch and Oats," 23.7.36; "Results of Fodder Plots (Oats and Vetch) 1935/6—Ramleh S/D," 31.7.36; "Fodder Plots 1936—Results," 11.7.36; "Results of Fodder 1935/36 Season, Gaza Area, Ramleh SD, Jaffa Area" (tables).

1936/37: Berseem—"Berseem Demonstration Plots in Southern District, Season 1936/37" (table). Oats/vetch—"Fodder Demonstration Plots Season 1936/37—Southern District" (table).

1937/38: Oats/vetch—"Distribution of Oats and Vetches, 37/38," 19.2.38.

Notes:

a. Some lists include only localities, but not names of individual farmers. I counted such localities as representing one farmer each.

b. "Quarters" (identified as "Q") in Gaza were not counted as separate localities.

c. Farmers having more than one plot in a given season are counted only once.

d. By definition, since this is the first season about which I have information.

e. Information only on plots in Tulkarm subdistrict.

f. Some localities without information on individual farmers had plots for more than one kind of crop.

g. An individual farmer can appear only once in the total. In villages where individuals were not identified I counted one farmer for any mention of oats/vetch or berseem, and one for any mention of maize.

localities were in the southern part of the country, in the Jaffa, Ramleh, and Gaza subdistricts, where the maritime plain gradually broadened to provide large stretches of land suitable for extensive fodder-growing, but where rainfall was less certain.

The costs of such demonstrations were not great, but the Department of Agriculture nevertheless had difficulty finding the necessary funds to carry them out. In 1933 the agricultural officers for the Northern and the Southern Circles submitted a proposal for demonstration plots in eighty-four villages, to be started in the fall. The total cost, including seed, manure, rental of land, transportation, labor for digging silage pits, and acquisition of hand-baling machines for the hay, was estimated at less than £P900. Dawe, the director of the department, objected to paying for rent and for labor, arguing that the cultivators would be keeping the crop; he also eliminated the baling machines. This was a good example of short-term penny-pinching at the expense of potential long-term gains. Government departments in Palestine were under constant pressure to keep expenses down, and the Department of Agriculture was never well staffed; despite the expressed concern of the high commissioner, Dawe was unable to find the extra funds that might have given the demonstration program a greater chance of succeeding.[46]

The requirement that administrative expenses in Palestine be covered out of current income hindered attempts to ameliorate fodder shortages in years that the rains failed. In March 1933 an analysis was prepared of six locations where fodder could be grown on an emergency basis, in anticipation of shortages later in the season. Five locations— Ras el Ain and Wadi Rubin (Ramleh subdistrict), Rakayik (Acre subdistrict), Bassets Sheikh Salah and Dalieh (Tulkarm subdistrict), and Sebiah and Ghower el Samira (Tiberias subdistrict)—required the installation of irrigation works; the sixth, on lands in the Huleh, could use the available surface water. Estimated costs of production and the value of yield were computed for each of the locations, and except for the Huleh lands the balance was negative. The reason for this was the government's desire to recoup the total investment, including the cost of irrigation works, during one growing season. Table 26 show the figures presented in the government memorandum, as well as my own estimate of the annual balance on the assumption that the cost of irrigation works was covered by a twenty-year loan. Under such conditions, fodder-growing would seem to be quite profitable. Distribution would have been the

TABLE 26

Cost and Income Estimates for Emergency Fodder Schemes

Item	Ras el Ain	Wadi Rubin	Rakayik	Bassets Sh. Salah Dalieh	Sebiah Ghower el Samira	Huleh
Total area (dunums)	3,000	2,000	300	500	100	1,000
Crop	Maize for grain and for fodder	Lucerne; 2 sowings, 4 cuttings	Maize for grain and for fodder	Maize for grain and for fodder	Maize for grain and for fodder	Maize; two grain crops
Rent, labor, seeds, fertilizer	£P3,560	£P3,796	£P470	£P1,367	£P196	£P1,298
Cost per dunum	£P1.187	£P1.898	£P1.567	£P2.734	£P1.96	£P1.298
Irrigation[a]	£P7,000	£P5,000	£P2,200	£P2,250	(natural irrigation)	
Yield per dunum (kg)	Grain: 200; green maize: 1,000	Green fodder: 1,800; hay: 125	Grain: 150; green forage: 1,083	Grain: 200; green forage: 1,050	Grain: 150; green fodder: 180	Grain: 360
Value of yield	£P7,200	£P6,600	£P477.5	£P950	£P114	£P2,520
Value of yield per dunum	£P2.400	£P3.300	£P1.592	£P1.900	£P1.140	£P2.520
Balance, according to memorandum	– £P2,360	– £P1,196	– £P1,205	–£P1,667	–£P82	£P1,222
Profit, assuming 20 year loan at:						
5%	£P3,106	£P2,423	–£P160	–£P955	[– £P82][b]	[£P1,222][b]
7.5%	£P2,934	£P2,357	–£P189	–£P984		
10%	£P2,843	£P2,292	–£P218	–£P1,014		

Source: ISA/RG 7/ Box 638/Ag 22-12, "Supply of Fodder, March 16, 1933."

Notes:

a. £P 2/dunum for leveling and canalization; £P 1000 (estimated) for pump, engine, and installation. Though the areas of the different plots vary, I used the same estimate for the cost of pump, engine, and installation. Where land is under natural irrigation the irrigation costs are recurring and assigned to labor.

b. Identical with the estimate in the memorandum, in the absence of costs for the installation of irrigation.

greatest obstacle, since the emergency plan was based on putting hundreds of dunums under fodder at each site. Because freshly cut fodder deteriorated quickly and was expensive to transport, emergency programs would not have been successful unless undertaken in regions with relatively dense populations. But the memorandum fails to mention such difficulties, and the most reasonable inference is that the government did not contemplate using the current emergency as an opportunity to establish fodder-growing by Arabs as a regular operation.

It is difficult, in the absence of comprehensive statistics, to evaluate the success of the department's efforts to encourage cultivation of fodder. Progress at the beginning of the 1930s was slow, as Antebi's summary shows with respect to results in the Southern Circle for the first three seasons of the decade (table 27). In later years the cultivation of maize for grain and green fodder became more widespread, though the available data do not separate Jewish and Arab localities (table 28).

Potato Cultivation

Potatoes were not an important component of the diet of Palestinian Arabs, and as late as 1933 there were only about 2,500 dunums planted

TABLE 27
Demonstration and Cultivation of Forage Crops, Southern Circle, 1930/31–1932/33

	1930/31	*1931/32*	*1932/33*
Dunums under oats and vetch, for hay	4,800	5,200	6,450
Dunums under maize, for fodder and seed	2,284	3,071	3,635
Demonstration plots under oats and vetch, for hay			
Number	8	—	18
Dunums	8	—	165
Demonstration plots under maize, for fodder and seed			
Number	2	—	28
Dunums	10	—	358
Demonstration plots under clover (berseem)			
Number	1	3	7
Dunums	1	3	13
Maize seed distributed (kg)	50	—	1,250
Dunums grown by private individuals under maize for green fodder (d.)	610	1,300	2,703

Source: ISA/RG 7/Box 638/Ag 22-12, "Growing Maize for Green Fodder, August 7, 1933."

TABLE 28
Maize: Cultivation and Estimates of Production, 1935–1937

	Dunums	Grain (tons)	Green Fodder (tons)
1935	70,436	500	8,000
1936	66,775	4,336	9,967
1937	86,286	8,673	17,742

Source: Himadeh, *Economic Organization of Palestine*, p. 136.

(table 29). Potatoes were a staple of Jewish diet in Europe, however, and as the Jewish population grew, so did potato consumption. Since local production was insufficient to meet the increased demand, potatoes were imported, mostly from Cyprus, in growing quantity. The rise in potato imports was especially sharp after 1932, as increased Jewish immigration from Germany heightened demand. Between 1927 and 1936 annual imports of potatoes almost tripled, from 6,078 tons to 17,604 tons. Between 1933 and 1937 total annual consumption of potatoes in Palestine (local production plus imports) rose from about 10,000 tons to more than 27,000 tons. Local production accounted for an increasing proportion of total consumption, and by 1940 two-thirds of the potatoes consumed in Palestine were locally grown. Arab cultivators raised most of the local potatoes, and although their share of the total gradually declined, by 1941 they still accounted for almost two-thirds of local production.

Potato-growing by Arabs was carried out primarily in the southern part of the country, with a large number of growers in and around Lydda. Potatoes grown in the south were lifted in April and May, while in the north they were lifted later, in June and July. Yields were not high, and despite an optimistic estimate made in 1933 by Antebi that farmers were obtaining 750 kilos per dunum, actual yields at the time were only about half that amount and did not rise much above 500 kilos per dunum before 1937.[47]

In July 1934 Masson expressed his surprise at the "very low" potato yields obtained due to the poor quality of the soil at the Majdal agricultural station. He recommended fertilization in order to compensate for the lack of natural nutrients.[48] Most Arab potato growers were probably obtaining lower yields than those Antebi specified because they failed to manure their lands. The optimal yields he expected depended on applying both animal manure and chemical fertilizers, which was not yet common practice, for reasons discussed above. Some Arabs were, however, obtaining much better results: in the 1930/31 season farmers in the villages of Salameh obtained 800 kilos per dunum, and those in Lydda and Ramleh lifted 750 and 600 respectively. The yields Jewish farmers obtained were also higher than the overall average.[49]

Only about 10 to 20 percent of Arab potato crops were irrigated, and unirrigated potatoes were quite susceptible, of course, to fluctuations in rainfall.[50] Growers in the Ramleh and Jaffa subdistricts planted fewer dunums of potatoes in 1932/33 than they did in the two previous years, in part because the low rainfall in those years had led to disappointing yields.[51]

Much of the difference between Arab and Jewish farmers in the yields they obtained was probably due to the greater prevalence of irrigation on the latter's fields. There were two potato-planting seasons in Palestine, in the spring and in the fall. Potatoes planted in the autumn on irrigated land matured by December or January, about four months earlier than potatoes dependent on the rains.[52] Growers whose plots were irrigated could bring their crops earlier to market and expect to obtain higher prices for them. Most Arab potato growers probably planted their crops in the fall, so they would be less dependent on the uncertain late rains.

Returns to Palestine potato growers were reduced, however, because of the competition of cheaper imports from Cyprus. Between 1935 and 1939, years for which I have comparative data, the value per ton for Cyprus potatoes was lower by 4 percent to 40 percent, depending on the year, than the value per ton of potatoes grown locally (table 30). The lower price of imported potatoes was seen even in earlier years as a brake on the development of local production. Not only insufficient rainfall, but also competition from imports was noted as a reason for the reduction of acreage devoted to the crop in the Ramleh and Jaffa subdistricts in the 1932/33 season, compared with those of the two preceding periods.[53]

Potato imports represented a considerable expense to the Palestine economy. Between 1927 and 1936 the cost of imports rose from £P48,147 to £P105,266, while the price per ton actually declined by 25 percent, from £P7.921 to £P5.924. The administration believed that the replacement of imported potatoes by locally grown varieties would save money as well as provide a new and potentially valuable cash crop for

TABLE 29
Production and Imports of Potatoes, 1927–1944

	1927	1928	1929	1930	1931	1932	1933	1934
Dunums under potatoes							*2,500	*5,000
Yield								
Total (tons)							1,000	*2,750
Per dunum (kg)							250	550
Value								
Total (£P)								
Per ton (£P)						9–10		
Imports								
Tons	6,078	6,697	6,548	7,431	6.822	7,780	9,753	12,349
Value (£P)	48,147	51,131	48,940	43,694	48,098	44,857	45,257	73,150
Per ton (£P)	7.921	7.635	7.474	5.880	7.050	5.766	4.640	5.924
Total consumption (tons)ᶜ							*10,000	*14,000
Local production as % of total consumption								
% by which price of local potatoes exceeds price of imports								
Jewish production (tons)								
% Arab production of total								

Sources: Government of Palestine, *Statistical Abstract*, 1937–38, pp. 44, 64–65; ibid., 1939, p. 41; ibid., 1940, pp. 41, 63; ibid., 1942, pp. 29, 33, 46; ibid., 1944/45, p. 226; Gurevich, *Statistical Handbook*, p. 166; ISA/RG7/Box 631/Ag 10-1, Antebi to CAO, April 27, 1934; ISA/RG7/Box 631/Ag 10-1, Agricultural Inspector, Jaffa, to Agricultural Office, Southern Circle, February 25, 1933.

Arab farmers. In 1931, Masson inquired as to the extent of potato cultivation in the country and the possibility of establishing potato growers' associations.[54] A special subcommittee to the Agricultural Economics and Marketing Committee, composed of government agricultural officers, British, Arab, and Jewish, met in February 1933 and advanced a number of arguments for encouraging potato cultivation: potatoes were valuable as a rotation crop; they could be grown among citrus trees in new groves until the trees matured and began giving fruit, thus providing small farmers who wished to plant citrus with an interim income; the money spent on imported potatoes could instead benefit local producers; potato exports from Palestine could replace exports of melons whose Egyptian market had lately been closed; potatoes could replace some of

1935	1936	1937	1938	1939	1940	1941	1942	1943	1944
6,142	9,654	9,454	7,837	8,410	17,661	17,552		26,777ª	37,916ª
2,850	5,000	9,536	8,760	10,480	20,891	20,736		30,707	53,259
464	518	1,009	1,118	1,246	1,182	1,181		1,147	1,405
20,339	30,992	49,928	57,951	72,720	168,774	399,729		1,468,018	2,283,538
7.136	6.198	5.236	6.615	6.939	8.079	19.277		47.807	42.876
15,774	17,604	17,695	18,879	16,454	10,646	2,636			
97,208	105,266	85,411	88,915	101,467	77,838	34,265			
6.162	5.980	4.827	4.710	6.167	7.311	12.999			
18,624	22,604	27,231	27,639	26,934	31,537	23,372		30,707ª	53,259ª
15.3	22.1	35.0	31.7	38.9	66.2	88.7			
15.8	3.6	8.5	40.4	12.5	10.5	48.3			
		2,000		2,918	7,581	7,294	6,782		(b)
		79.0		72.2	63.7	64.8			

Notes:

 *Indicates approximate figures.

 a. Includes sweet potatoes and potatoes for military contracts.

 b. Gurevich, *Statistical Handbook*, has 35,000 tons for 1944 production, which is not consistent with figures for earlier years and for total 1944 production.

 c. Production + imports.

the imported rice consumed, and additional money thereby be diverted to local cultivators.[55]

 Imported potatoes were in 1933 subject to a customs duty of £P1 per ton. That summer foreign potatoes were being sold for £P5 per ton. The subcommittee proposed the imposition of an additional, seasonal import duty of £P2 per ton, which would protect local producers during the period that Palestinian crops were lifted, between April and July. It considered that the duty should be set so that growers would receive a "fair price" of £P7 per ton. The increased duty was imposed for the 1933/34 season, and went into effect on April 1, 1934. But potato importers increased their purchases in January, February, and March 1934. While some of the increase might have been due to the cheaper

price of Cyprus potatoes because of the good harvest in that country, and
to the increase of demand for the vegetable by the growing immigrant
population, part of it was also attributed to the desire of importers to
avoid payment of the additional duty. In the following season the imposition of the supplementary duty began in February rather than in April.
Although administration officials were resigned to the increase in imports during the month preceding the imposition of the duty, whichever
month it was, the fact that potatoes could be kept for only one to two
months meant that the stock imported would only suffice for about one
and one-half months, by which time local potatoes would be coming onto
the market. They would then bring a good price and not be subject to
competition from cheaper imports.[56]

Potato prices in Palestine rose substantially during 1934, from
£P6.747 per ton in January to £P9.220 in December, and by April and
May 1935 they had reached £P12.131. They were thus much greater
than the "fair price" of £P7 per ton hoped for by those who supported the
increase in customs duty. Much of the price increase must have been due
to increased demand, both by Jewish immigrants and by the Arab population who had become "important consumers" of potatoes.[57] It was hoped
that imposition of an import duty in February rather than in April would
encourage local growers to increase their production of potatoes under
irrigation, but these hopes were not soon realized.[58] They seem to have
been unrealistic. Were irrigated land already under cultivation, and
growers choosing among alternative crops on the basis of their relative
profitability, it might have been reasonable to expect the higher duties to
have led cultivators to increase their acreage of potatoes. But few Arab
farmers had irrigated lands, nor did they have the necessary funds to
introduce irrigation or easy access to credit required to undertake such
an investment. Even if potato-growing under irrigation could be expected
to provide a good, stable return, most Arab farmers were unable to take
advantage of the opportunity.

Government efforts to encourage potato production were not limited to
the imposition of import surcharges. Unlike the grain crops, whose yield
provided seed for the next season's sowing as well as produce for current
consumption, the maintenance of good quality potato harvests depended
on the import of seed potatoes, primarily from Britain. Although potatoes
grown locally from imported seed tubers could themselves be used for
subsequent sowing, the quality of the crop deteriorated after three or four

seasons. The government therefore imported seed potatoes to be sold at cost to farmers and established demonstration plots in Arab localities. But it did not subsidize the cost of seed potatoes when their price was high, in order to overcome resistance to their purchase, and in at least one such year, 1937, Arab farmers withdrew their orders.[59]

Why was it not worthwhile to buy seed potatoes for £P7 per ton? Assuming that planting required 100 kilograms per dunum, the cost of seed for one dumun of potatoes was £P0.700. The average return from Arab potato cultivation was in 1937 probably between 600 and 700 kilograms (table 30); that is, an increase of six- or sevenfold compared with the amount of seed. Arab farmers were not obtaining such good yields from their grain crops. The Johnson-Crosbie report assumed that winter grains were sown ten kilograms per dunum; both Himadeh and Volcani concluded that average yields per dunum for wheat were 40 to 50 kilograms, and for barley between 20 and 40 kilograms per dunum.[60] In 1936, the year preceding the refusal of the farmers to buy seed tubers at £P7 per ton, the value of local potatoes averaged £P6.198 per ton, and the average yield per dunum was 518 kilograms (table 29). Farmers could have realized £P3.210 per ton, 4.6 times their seed costs. The calculation suggests that many Arab farmers were planting potatoes primarily because they could buy seed cheaply, but had more profitable uses for their land when the price of seed potatoes rose. What these uses might have been is difficult to know; perhaps they grew other vegetables instead.

It is not likely that all or most of the seed tubers planted in each season came from imported stock. In some years, such as 1937, the price of imported seed potatoes was too high. In most years, there may have been many cultivators who preferred to save the cost of imported seed and instead set aside part of their own harvests to be used the following season. That might have been an additional factor affecting yields, for care had to be taken in storing the seed potatoes until planting, in order to prevent their deterioration. Despite the establishment by the government of demonstration plots, many farmers must have lacked the necessary experience and equipment (sheds, storage trays, and so on). A 1937 circular from Masson to his district agricultural officers suggests that the department's field demonstrations were devoted to planting and cultivation, and not to storage of seed tubers, for he offered to distribute to demonstration farmers potatoes that had been stored at the Acre, Majdal, and Ain Aroub agricultural stations.[61]

Sixty-four Arab localities in the Tulkarm, Jaffa, Ramleh, and Gaza subdistricts are identified in the available files of the Department of Agriculture as places where potatoes were grown at some time between 1931 and 1938; twenty of them appear in more than one year. It is likely that the total number of localities was greater, as was the number in which growers cultivated potatoes during more than one season. In forty-six of these localities district agricultural officials had managed to establish at one time or another fodder demonstration plots sown with oats and vetch or maize. Most of the information about potato-growing does not include the names of the farmers. There were, however, twelve localities for which names of potato growers were available, as well as the names of farmers who agreed to the planting on their land of fodder demonstration plots. In seven of these localities, the same farmer appears on both lists.

Most of the potato growers and many of those with fodder plots were unnamed; there was often more than one fodder demonstration plot in a particular locality; and there could have been many potato growers. It would probably be an error to assume that the majority of potato cultivators were active participants in agricultural extension work and conclude that an "innovative" group of Arab cultivators was instrumental in spreading new cropping techniques. But the fact that the same names do reappear suggests that something of the sort may have been occurring, perhaps on a restricted scale, as has happened in other settings where traditional agriculture is exposed to pressures and opportunities stemming from European incursion. In fact, the agricultural inspector for the Tulkarm subdistrict had in 1937 visited twenty-seven villages to propagandize for potatoes; five of the villages appear in the lists of those cultivating the crop during the 1937–38 season.[62]

Agricultural Manure

Inadequate manuring of village lands was often cited as one of the factors contributing to the low yields from Arab cultivation. Many peasants failed to combine their fallow with a crop designed to enrich the soil, and much of the natural manure available was dried and used as fuel in the household. As early as 1923 the Department of Agriculture organized demonstrations of fertilizers on village lands,[63] and between 1922 and 1929 the import of chemical fertilizers increased from 1,177 to 6,911 tons,[64] most of it, however, for Jewish farms. A serious hindrance to the utilization of natural manures in the villages was the market for them in the citrus groves. In 1934 the Department of Agriculture noted that the farmers sought the prohibition of this trade, but "itinerant Bedouin, shepherds and landless villagers find a lucrative business in a wholesale collection of manure and sale thereof to agents."[65] Much of the manure collected was probably sold to Arab citrus growers, rather than to Jews.

The department's reports for 1934–1936 refer to the growing recognition by Arab cultivators of the importance of applying natural and chemical fertilizers, although the actual increase in their use was slow.[66] Throughout the war years a "serious shortage" of organic manure persisted, due to its continued use by villagers as fuel, although the wartime disruption of citrus exports had reduced the demand by orange growers.[67] There were two main impediments to the wider use of chemical fertilizers by many Arab cultivators: their cost, and the change their use required in agricultural techniques. The absence of a comprehensive agricultural extension program which could have effectively demonstrated the utility of the use of fertilizers contributed to the lack of demand and of incentive to seek ways of financing the cost of their use.

Other Innovations

Arab cultivators sought to diversify their production and were open to innovations which their resources could accommodate. In 1924 the Gaza, Nazareth, and Nablus municipalities allocated funds for the establishment of modern training farms for beekeeping and for poultry-raising.[68] The Department of Agriculture was in 1925 reprinting in Arabic for distribution to Arab farmers bulletins of the agricultural experimental station established by the Zionist Executive, though the number who could have used this information effectively must have been very small.[69] While many Arab farmers were willing to learn new methods and try new crops in order to increase their incomes,[70] officials of the Department of Agriculture continued to find "great difficulty . . . in inducing the farmer to grow crops other than those to which he is accustomed."[71] For example, efforts in 1935 to encourage the dry cultivation of maize in northern Palestine reportedly had little success,[72] for reasons already discussed. On the other hand, Arab poultry growers took advantage of government hatcheries which supplied chicks as well as diagrams for the construction of homemade, fireless brooders for them, and the 1941 report of the Department of Agriculture considered these two programs a success.[73] But by the end of

the war there had still been no improvement in the quality of the grain seed
used by "the more conservative" Arab farmers; crops from improved seed
become mixed on the threshing floor with the remainder, and no long-term
benefits were obtained.[74]

The preceding examples demonstrate the unevenness of Arab agricultural development, despite the large overall increase in the production of
major crops and in their value. Those most likely to benefit from the
economic and technical opportunities provided by the Mandate and by
the Jewish presence were most likely to be those who had surplus capital, or the means of obtaining it. A majority of Arab cultivators were not
in that situation, and little was done to change their condition.

Agricultural Credit and Rural Indebtedness

Most of the debts of the Arab cultivators were owed to private moneylenders, including landlords and merchants. The only systematic estimate of
the amount of peasant debt was made by Johnson and Crosbie in 1930; as
I will argue below, their estimate was flawed and did not in any case refer
to the ability of the cultivator to obtain needed financing. While the
annual reports of the Palestine government often noted the reduction of
the debt burdening the cultivators as a result of improved economic
conditions in the country, no later estimates of the average debt were
published, nor does it seem that they were even made. A small proportion of the total credit had been granted by public institutions.

Although moneylenders provided most agricultural credit prior to the
end of Ottoman rule, especially to small and medium cultivators, a
"semiofficial" institution, the Ottoman Agricultural Bank, also operated
in the country.[75] It succeeded the Caisse d'Utilité Publique in 1898,
taking over the latter's assets and supplementing its capital by a 1
percent (later halved) addition to the tithe. The bank had thirteen
branches in Palestine when British forces occupied the country. Its primary object was to grant seasonal, rather than long-term, credit to cultivators, thereby reducing their dependence on usurers. The bank charged 6
percent interest and an additional initial fee of 1 percent to cover expenses. Loans were secured by mortages on immovable property which
meant, of course, that only cultivators with title to their own land could
obtain credit. Tenants were thus ineligible for these loans, as were
applicants whose lands were held as shares in *musha'a* villages.

Fragmentary information regarding the condition of Arab cultivators is available from lists of loans outstanding to the Ottoman Agricultural Bank. It ceased to grant such loans during the First World War, and its records were for the most part removed before the British occupation. The liquidation of its assets was entrusted to the Public Custodian of Enemy Property, who attempted to reconstruct the accounts from whatever documentary evidence was available. As of 1936 the net amount realized from the liquidation had reached approximately £P20,000.[76] Data on the condition of debtors from the Northern Region of Palestine in 1933 and 1944 indicate that as of 1933 a total of £P5,504 was owned in the Nazareth, Safed, and Tiberias subdistricts; in 1944, debtors in the Acre, Tiberias, and Nazareth subdistricts owned £P4,065.[77] All of the debts, of course, predated the First World War, and many, if not most, had been undertaken before the turn of the century.

The government divided the debtors into those who it believed were able to pay, either at once or in a fixed number of yearly installments, and those who were "unable to pay the debt except by the sale of their land and the land owned by them is the minimum necessary for the maintenance of their families."[78] It recommended that in these latter cases the debt be remitted. A total of twenty-seven debtors were listed in 1934 for the Tiberias subdistrict; their average debt was £P34, and there was almost no difference in the average debt between those considered able to pay and those whose debt was to be remitted.[79] The average debt owed in 1933 by the sixty-eight debtors in the Nazareth subdistrict who were judged able to pay was almost twice as great as that owned by the nine recommended for remission—£P55.64 versus £P22.45;[80] while in the Safed subdistrict in the same year the five solvent debtors owed slightly more than half the sum owned by thirty-six others deemed unable to pay—£P8.58 versus £P15.41.[81]

The authorities recommended in 1933 remitting 93 percent of the debt owned in the Safed subdistrict, and 78 percent of that in the Nazareth subdistrict. Although the average debt per dunum seems low for those for whom information on landholding is available—£P0.19 in Safed and £P0.42 in Nazareth—the burden on the debtors or their heirs was apparently too great.[82] Interest payments on these debts in the Nazareth subdistrict represented 29 percent of the total amount owed, and were a lesser proportion of the smaller debts than of the larger ones.[83] The installment schedule proposed for Nazareth debtors who

were considered able to repay ranged between immediate repayment of
the total debt, for those owing the least, to nine years for a debt of £P316.
The larger the debt, the longer the repayment schedule, but the amount
of the proposed annual installment also increased with the size of the
debt.[84]

There were substantial differences between the Nazareth and Safed
subdistricts in the amount of debt still outstanding in 1933. Seventy-
seven Nazareth debtors owed an average of £P51.76, while forty-two
Safed debtors owned an average of £P14.62. Eighty-six percent of the
Safed debtors owed less than £P20, while 65 percent of those in Nazareth
owed £P20 or more.[85] Taken together, the average debt to the Ottoman
Bank in 1933 in the two subdistricts—£P38.65—was almost 50 percent
greater than the average debt owed three years earlier by cultivators in
the 104 villages surveyed by Johnson and Crosbie.[86]

The Palestine government summarized for the 1936 Royal Commission the efforts which had been made, first by military and then by civil
authorities, to ameliorate the condition of Arab cultivators by the provision of agricultural credit; the information appears in table 30. In 1918
the military administration issued what were known as "mule loans";
army mules no longer fit for active duty but still capable of normal
agricultural work were distributed to cultivators who were charged 6
percent interest on the purchase price; repayment schedules stretched
up to five years. Although the memorandum fails to indicate the number
of mules provided under the program, by 1921 a balance of £P8,590 was
still outstanding. Unfortunately, "many of the mules . . . never became
acclimatised to their new conditions of life, and a number of them died
shortly after their purchase by the cultivators."[87] Much of the outstanding balance was written off.

In 1919 the military administration reached an agreement with the
Anglo-Egyptian Bank by which the latter would provide up to one-half
million Egyptian pounds for loans to cultivators. The bank charged the
administration 6 percent, and borrowers were charged an additional 0.5
percent. By 1923 a sum equivalent to £P576,319 had been advanced;
the program was then stopped because the British government refused to
guarantee the repayment of additional sums. By 1936, 95 percent of the
loans had been repaid, 2 percent were still outstanding, and 3 percent
had been written off as a relief measure owing to the borrowers' inability
to pay. The agricultural loans of 1919–1923 comprised the only large-

scale, ongoing agricultural credit program undertaken by the military or civilian administration.

Loan schemes in subsequent years were put forward to meet what were defined as specific, temporary needs. These included loans to Bedouin in the Beersheba region in 1927 because of drought, seed loans in the Northern District because of crop failure in 1928, and fodder loans in 1933/34. Beginning in 1930, small annual loans, rarely exceeding £P10, were issued to cultivators in order to provide them with needed short-term credit, and were usually repaid in two equal installments after the crops were harvested at an interest rate of 5 percent. The total amount of loans issued by the government since 1919 exceeded £P800,000 (table 30).

In the 1930s there were about 75,000 Arab agricultural households engaged in what the 1931 census referred to as "ordinary cultivation." Some probably did not need loans; others, working as laborers for owners or sharecroppers, could not request them. Since the agricultural loans issued in the 1930s were normally no more than £P10 each, cultivators who could have benefited from them in the worst years, 1932–1934, probably numbered between 5,000 and 15,000. Assuming that about three-fourths of the agricultural households were cultivating land they

TABLE 30
Agricultural Loans Issued by the Administration Since 1919,
and Status of These Loans as of March 31, 1936 (£P)

	Total	Repaid	Written Off	Outstanding
Loans issued, 1919–1923	576,319	545,426	18,033	12,860
Beersheba loans, 1927	19,980	19,433	547	—
Seed loans, 1928	19,366	7,892	6,448	5,026
Agricultural loans				
1930	29,980	7,692	—	22,288
1931	17,137	12,070	—	5,067
1932/33	53,537	17,416	—	36,121
1933/34	57,259	3,064	—	54,195
1934/35	6,313	17	—	6,296
1935/36	4,988	—	—	4,988
Total, 1930–36	169,214	40,259	—	129,955
Fodder loans, 1933/34	20,720	406	—	20,314
Total	805,599	613,416	25,028	167,155

Source: CZA/S25/10.208, the section entitled "Measures Taken to Provide Agricultural Credit."

either owned or leased, the government loans could, in the worst years, have helped approximately 10 to 25 percent of ordinary cultivators. It is impossible to know how many others who might have needed assistance were unable to obtain it.

The agricultural loans issued during the 1930s were repayable after two years, so by 1936 all loans made up to and including the 1933/34 season should have been repaid. But the table shows that only about 25 percent of the loans had in fact been made good. Even if we assume that loans from 1933/34 were not yet overdue, 63 percent of the funds advanced between 1930 and 1932/33 had not yet been repaid in 1936. There were probably a number of reasons for this lag: some of the peasants might not have had enough left after covering other obligations to make the required payment; most of them were paying interest of 5 percent, and none were paying more than 9 percent, which was much less than the moneylender charged, providing a strong incentive to delay repayment as long as possible. Three-fourths of the debt incurred in the 1930 loans was still outstanding in March 1936.

After 1933, Barclay's Bank provided seasonal credit to cultivators and was assisted by government grants to enable it to open additional branches to serve those who might not have availed themselves of the new credit opportunities if they had to travel long distances to the existing branches. When the arrangement with Barclay's began, it had agents in Nazareth, Acre, and Nablus; additional offices were then opened in Hebron and Gaza (the opening of the Ramle office was postponed because of the 1936 strike and uprising). The bank lent to individuals at 8 percent interest, but agreed to lower the rate to 6 percent for loans to cooperative credit societies, who in turn charged their members 9 percent. Many of these members, of course, might not have been able to qualify for a loan from the bank, and the convenience for others of being able to obtain the funds locally might have made the premium worthwhile.

The only other source of credit to Arab cultivators, except for the moneylenders, were local cooperative credit societies. Following Strickland's 1930 report on the possibility of introducing a system of agricultural credit, the government began to encourage the formation of Arab societies. Although the annual statistics it published did not distinguish between Arab and Jewish organizations, its reports to the League of Nations provide some information about the Arab societies. Between 1936 and 1937 the number of Arab cooperative credit societies doubled, from 60 to 120, and their total membership grew from 3,078 to 5,121. The average loan issued per member was less than £P20.[88]

An investigation carried out in preparation for the visit in 1946 of the Anglo-American Committee of Inquiry reached members of Arab co-operative credit societies in eighty-eight villages. Nineteen percent of the male adults in these villages were members of such societies (since many households had more than one male adult, the proportion of house-holds represented by membership was probably somewhat lower). The 4,385 members held 6,629 loans; two-thirds of the loans were taken from credit societies, at 9 percent interest; 19 percent were taken from money-lenders at 15 to 30 percent interest, or more; and 13 percent were taken from banks at 9 to 12 percent. About half the members had no debts other than to the society; the others had multiple obligations which averaged £P111 per person. The report concluded that "the practice of borrowing from money-lenders is no longer followed by a majority, and . . . the tendency of the Arab *fellah* is to turn to sound forms of borrowing . . . even those members of co-operative societies who are still indebted to sources outside their societies are only indebted to the extent of one-half of a year's income."[89] Despite the authors' optimism, how-ever, only a small minority of Arab cultivators were members of coopera-tive credit societies, and it seems that the societies' resources were inadequate to meet many of their members' needs, else they would not have found it necessary to seek loans from other sources. Some of the loans might have been long-standing, incurred prior to the establishment of the village society, which might not have been able to provide the funds necessary to enable them to be refinanced.

Though seasonal loans to cultivators were undoubtedly important in enabling them to get through a difficult year without incurring a crushing debt burden, they were no solution to the basic credit problems facing Arab peasants. A large-scale development program that was supposed to get underway in the early 1930s was canceled because the British govern-ment was reluctant to spend large sums in Palestine while the population at home was suffering from the depression. In 1935 the Agricultural Mortgage Company of Palestine was established, whose purpose was to finance development by issuing long-term first mortgages on immovable property. The government encouraged the establishment of the company and advanced funds to secure loans that the latter might issue. But the company's activities were hindered by the start of the Arab strike in

1936, and in any case it could not have helped tenants nor owners of a holding inadequate to their needs. The latter could not raise sufficient money by mortgaging their property; and if it were *musha'a*, no mortgage could be had. The former, of course, had no land to mortgage.

Since loans could not be granted without the security provided by establishment of title to individual plots rather than shares in common land, and settlement of title in the hill districts lagged behind that in the plains, the company restricted its operations to the latter region. The government attempted to provide some long-term credit facilities for cultivators in the hills until settlement of title would allow them to obtain loans from private banking institutions, and to this end established a fund of £P50,000. Though applications in excess of this sum were received from eligible cultivators, the implementation of this scheme was also delayed by the strike and the revolt.

During World War II, government loans to farmers totaled more than £P3.6 million, average more than £P600,000 during each of the seasons from 1940/41 to 1945/46. During the first five years, more than ten thousand loans were made to Arab planters, and more than eighteen thousand to Jewish cultivators; many planters, of course, received loans during successive seasons. The amount of money that could be borrowed per dunum almost doubled between 1940/41 and 1944/45, from £P2.60 to £P5.00. In an average year some 3,600 Jews and 2,100 Arab farmers obtained loans; the Jews represented 63 percent of the borrowers and held a somewhat smaller proportion (54 percent) of the land on which the loans were made. The holdings on which Arabs obtained loans averaged about thirty-six dunums in area. The small number of loans to Arabs (compared to the number of Arab cultivators), and the size of the holding for which the money was lent, suggest that the borrowers were not grain farmers, but vegetable and fruit growers. They represented, therefore, the small number of Arab cultivators who had been able to take advantage of the market opportunities provided by the war.[90]

Johnson-Crosbie Report

The most systematic attempt made by the administration to obtain information on peasant indebtedness was made in 1930. Following the Shaw Commission's report on the 1929 Arab attacks on Jews, the Palestine government established a committee to investigate the economic conditions of the country's agriculturalists. Its chairman was William J.

Johnson, who served as deputy treasurer in the Palestine administration, and its ranking member was R.E.H. Crosbie, assistant district commissioner for the Southern District. The committee surveyed 104 Arab villages throughout Palestine, using Arab district officers to collect information from the mukhtars and elders of each of the villages. The authors of the Johnson-Crosbie report devoted most of their efforts to estimating the balance of income and expenditures in the villages they surveyed. They concluded that, while 84 of the 104 villages were able to meet their annual subsistence needs (20, it seemed, could not), decreasing numbers of them were able to pay additional, cumulating charges (70 villages, in addition to meeting their subsistence needs, could pay their taxes; only 56 could also make their rental payments; and as few as 31 of the 104 villages were able to meet all of the preceding charges and pay interest on debt as well).[91]

The report's conclusions regarding peasant indebtedness, however, were seriously flawed, methodologically and conceptually, and it is surprising that with all the attention paid to them there seems to have been no published analysis of the data on which they were based. The major methodological shortcoming was inconsistency in the computation of income and expenditures of the villages. The principal conceptual error was the imputation of rent payment on lands cultivated by their owners.

The total number of families in the 104 villages, according to the villagers' declarations, was 23,573, but the authors of the report preferred the Department of Health's estimate, 21,066 families. The data in the summary table presenting total income and expenditures for the villages (table XXXI in the report) were obtained as a result of computations which refer to two different bases. While the figures for cost of living were based on the total of 21,066 households, the figures for cost of production referred to only 12,476 households. The report gives a total of 15,530 families as owning land which, even if reduced to 13,878 by the ratio of 21,066/23,573, is 11 percent greater than my estimate of 12,476 families primarily engaged in cultivation.[92]

Johnson and Crosbie's table XXIV, in which the distribution of holdings by size is presented, also permits inferences to be made about the total area of cultivated land. This total area is inconsistent with data presented elsewhere in the report. If a feddan equalled 120 dunums, the 3,873 owner-occupiers holding more than two feddans would possess at least 929,520 dunums, which almost equals the total amount of cultivable land in the 104 villages, leaving an impossibly small area for the remaining owner-occupiers (1.24 million dunums).[93]

Whereas information on the cost of living is presented per household, the cost of production figures are given per 100 dunums. Though the report does not state specifically that 100 dunums are the equivalent of a single household's holding, both the language used and a comparison of cost estimates with those given by Volcani strongly suggests that the authors took their "standard" unit of 100 dunums as such an equivalent. Thus, the allocation of the cost of an ox refers to a plowing unit of 100 dunums, and it is clear from the context that the authors are writing of actual ownership of a yoke of oxen, rather than imputing to an average family a portion of some general total. They go on to assume that "the average family can do all the work of the holding except for the bulk of the harvesting of winter crops." Finally, their figures for the cost of forage for the plow animals (£P7) and of seed (£P6.50), which appear on p. 15, are identical with those given by Volcani for a family of 6–9 persons working a holding of 80–100 dunums.[94]

Because of the way in which income and expenditure were calculated, the report presents a misleading impression of the condition of the village *cultivators*, if we assume that the 12,476 households (59 percent of 21,066, the total number of households) to whom production costs were allocated were primarily engaged in agriculture as owner-cultivators, as tenants, or as lessees, while the remaining 8,590 households did not incur production costs because they were headed by agricultural laborers, by artisans, craftsmen, village tradespeople, and so on.

Let us look first at the way in which the report computes net income (Johnson-Crosbie, table XXVI), for the method it follows reflects both the methodological and conceptual errors. Table 31 presents a recomputation of the data for net income and divides it between cultivator families and non-cultivator families. The entry in table 31 for receipts from rent is adjusted to reflect the fact that most of the owner-cultivators were not in fact receiving rental income. The calculations in the table assume that most of the income gained from hired labor goes to noncultivating families, as does most of the income from transport and from other village sources, and I therefore allocated 90 percent of such income to them. To the extent this assumption is incorrect, and the owners of large holdings are also those who concentrate in their hands other sources of village income such as transport, shopkeeping, and so

TABLE 31
Allocation of Total Net Income (Johnson-Crosbie Table XXVI)
Between Cultivator Families and Noncultivator Families,
Adjusting Estimate of Rental Income Received

	To Cultivator Families	To Noncultivator Families
Net return from agriculture (at £P20/100 d., computed on 1,247,581 d.; 90% to cultivator families)	£P224,564	£P24,952
Rent[a]	21,919	—
Hired labor (computed on 1,247,581 d.; 90% to noncultivator families)	4,367	39,298
Transport (computed on 1,247,581 d.; 90% to noncultivator families)	2,495	22,357
Other village sources (90% to noncultivator families)	1,411	12,701
Total	£P254,756	£P99,308
Number of families	12,476	8,590
Average family income	£P20.420	£P11.561

Note:

a. The report computes rent at £P0.169/d. for the total cultivated and uncultivated land in village ownership (875,784 d.). But most of this land is cultivated by its owners, who receive no cash income from rent. To estimate the amount actually received in money rent, I applied to the total land in village ownership (see table XXIV) the proportion of households owning more than two feddans (3,873/23,573), less 25%, under the assumption that an average of 25% of these holdings are worked by the owners and the remainder rented. I assumed that households owning less than two feddans cultivated almost all the land themselves, and assigned to the income from rent of cultivator families only 5% of the proportional part of the total land in their possession [(1,604 + 1,657 + 8,396)/23,573) × Total income from rent].

The report gives total receipts from rent as £P148,157. My procedure reduces this figure to £P21,919, as follows:

Owners of more than 2 feddans: [£P148,157 × (3873/23,573)] × .75 = £P18,256.

Owners of 2 feddans or less: [£P148,157 × ((1604 + 1657 + 8396) / 23,573)] × .05 = £P3,663.

forth, a greater proportion of total village income will come to their hands and the difference between the average income of cultivating and noncultivating families will be even greater than shown in the table.

The authors of the report do not explain their decision to assign income from agricultural rent to all families in the villages. Since they are concerned with estimating total village income, it is not unreasonable to consider the rental payments as going to all the villagers. For the purpose of distinguishing among village families, however, it is impor-

tant to allocate rental payments to those who actually owned land. The
decision to impute rental income to all landowners is harder to justify.
Such imputation assumes that the village cultivators can be treated as
entrepreneurs seeking a satisfactory return on their invested capital. In
order to calculate the rate of return, a quantity must be assigned for the
rental value of the land, so that the rate of profit obtained from using the
land for agriculture can be compared with possible alternative uses for
the capital investment which the land represents. But as A. V. Chayanov
notes, the accepted definition of rent is

> *the part of income which the entrepreneur pays to the landowner for
> using the land.* In other words, we have before us a real social and
> economic phenomenon that exists in a specific setting of social rela-
> tions, arising on the basis of agricultural production and controlled by
> these relations. . . . This notion was frequently carried over into the
> analysis of farm income on the entrepreneur's land in the sense that
> part of the net income was separated out on the books, always by
> extremely notional methods. This part was what the farm might or
> ought to pay for the land if it were owned by someone else. In this
> sense, the "rent" was an accounting, "valuation" concept, depending
> on the bookkeeper's arithmetic, and not at all a real social and eco-
> nomic phenomenon dependent on the movement of social relation-
> ships. . . . The calculation of "rent," which is often very necessary and
> useful, bears to the *social and economic phenomenon of rent* as much
> relation as the valuation of produce circulating in kind on the farm
> bears to the phenomenon of market price."[95]

Were the authors of the report imputing the rental value of the land
for abstract analytic purposes, in order to arrive at some hypothetical
valuation of agricultural return, their procedure might be unobjection-
able. But the purpose of the Johnson-Crosbie report was to provide
information about the actual condition of the Arab and the Jewish cultivators in Palestine. Adding to the incomes of Arab peasant farmers a value
for imputed rent from the lands they owned distorts the analysis of
household income and expenditures by exaggerating the actual money
income they received. Since the imputed rental value of the land did not
enter into any practical calculations for most of the peasant cultivators,
adding it to their income only made their condition look better than it
really was. On the other hand, if the calculation of total net income is

carried out separately for cultivators and noncultivators, as I did in table 31, the former appear relatively better off than they did before.

The summary balance of income and expenditures presented in table XXXI of the report, before interest on debt is subtracted, totals £P14,758 for the 104 villages. This figure is based on computing income from agriculture and outlay on cost of production for 12,476 households, while computing cost of living expenses for 21,066 households. If the households not engaged primarily in agriculture are omitted from the computation, the balance rises to £P191,841, as in table 32. The mean household net annual income as computed by Johnson and Crosbie for 21,066 households, after all expenses except debt repayment are subtracted, comes to £P0.701 each, but it rises to £P15.377 if computed for only those households engaged in cultivation.

What about debt? Johnson and Crosbie state that the average debt per family was £P27, and deducted £P8 as the annual interest charge (29.6 percent) (table XXXI). They nowhere indicate how this figure was obtained, nor do they provide information about the distribution of debts among villagers. Most of the debts were probably incurred by cultivators whose crops were insufficient, because of poor yields, low prices, or too-small holdings, to allow them to pay the sums due for rent or taxes, or to provide both seed for the following season and family subsistence during the coming year. Those who lost their land because they failed to meet the interest payments could have continued to work the land as tenants of the new owner; supplemented their agricultural income by working as laborers, in transport, or some other nonagricultural employment; or abandoned agriculture altogether. It is unclear whether the total debts should be allocated to all the 21,066 village families, or only to those 12,476 households primarily engaged in cultivation. The Johnson-Crosbie report does the former, and the calculation results in a negative net balance per household of £P7.299. Thus, the average family ends the year in debt and requires additional credit in order to continue cultivation the following season.

If the debt is allocated only to the cultivating families, however, they end the year with a positive net balance. The size of that balance depends on whether each of the cultivating families is also assumed to have only £P8 of debt, or whether interest payments of £P168,528 are divided solely among the cultivating families. In the first case, the net income remaining would be £P7.377; in the second case it would be £P1.869

TABLE 32
Revision of Johnson-Crosbie Table XXXI,
"Total Income and Expenditure of 104 Villages" (£P)

	21,066 Households (original data)	12,476 Households (adjusted data)	
Income from agriculture	799,232	799,232	
Other income[a]	113,438	67,181[b]	
Total income	912,670	866,413	
Minus			
Cost of production	205,850	205,850	
Cost of living	547,716	324,376[c]	
Taxes[d]	81,449	81,449	
Rent payable outside village[e]	62,897	62,897	
Total expenditures	897,912	674,572	
Balance (income − expenditures)	14,758	191,841	
Net income per household (before debt repayment)	0.701[f]	15.377[g]	15.377[h]
Interest on debt	8.000[f]	8.000[g]	13.508[h]
Final household balance	7.299[f]	7.377[g]	1.869[h]

Notes:

    a. From village and from outside village.

    b. Portion of total allocated to households primarily involved in cultivation: (113,438) × (12,476/21,066).

    c. Only for the 12,476 households primarily involved in cultivation.

    d. Werko, tithe, and animal tax, almost all of which falls on actual cultivators.

    e. On 371,797 dunums in absentee ownership or leased from other villages; all the rent should be alloted to the cultivators.

    f. After assigning income and expenditures to 21,066 households, and using the report's figure of £P8 annual interest payment on debt.

    g. After assigning income and expenditures to 12,476 households, and using the report's figure of £P8 annual interest payment on debt.

    h. After assigning income and expenditures to 12,476 households, and dividing among them the total annual interest on debt.

(table 32, bottom). Neither sum is substantial, but if the harvest was sufficient to allow the cultivator to put seed aside for the coming season the household might avoid having to incur additional debt in order to plant new crops.

    Is it reasonable to assume that 41 percent of the households in the 104 villages were not primarily engaged in agriculture? The data in table 33, from the 1931 census of Palestine, provides some information on this question. According to the census, about 70 percent of the Moslems engaged as "earners" in "ordinary cultivation"—which excluded citrus, vegetable, and fruit cultivation, as well as raising of farm stock, and thus referred primarily to extensive cultivation of grain crops—were receiving their principal income from agriculture. If an earner is taken to represent a household, this figure is greater than the 59 percent I obtained in the adjusted computations for the number of households principally engaged in cultivation in the 104 villages. Much of the difference is probably accounted for by the fact that "earner" is not equivalent to "household," and that a certain proportion of the village households contained more than one earner principally involved in agriculture. Without trying to estimate the frequency of such households, taking into account the existence of more than one earner would reduce their number and make it more similar to the proportion I computed in the adjusted calculation.

The report ignores the income and expenditures on 371,827 dunums of cultivated land, about 32 percent of all the land cultivated by households in the 104 villages (p. 21). Of that total, 245,275 dunums belonged to absentee owners, and 126,522 dunums were leased from other villages. But these two kinds of land did not play the same role in the village economy. Lands in absentee ownership were contiguous with land owned by villagers, and in some cases may once have been owned by villagers but lost because of their inability to repay debts. Rent paid on such lands left the village. The rent paid for land leased from other villages, on the other hand, entered into the economy of the lessor village (except for land in those villages which was also in absentee ownership).

TABLE 33
Number of Earners in Agriculture, by Status (Moslems only)

	Total	As Principal Occupation	As Secondary Occupation
Ordinary cultivation	99,195	97,337	1,858
Of these			
Income from rent of agricultural land; ordinary			
cultivators	69,751	68,217	1,534
Farm servants, field laborers, watchers	29,397	29,077	320
Those having income from rent of land and ordi-			
nary cultivators (%)	70.3	70.1	82.6

Source: Census of Palestine, 1931, vol. 2, pt. 2, p. 282.

Very often villagers' holdings were combinations of land within and outside their home village; frequently particular cultivators owned part of the land they were working and leased another portion. The report included in the overall balance of income and expenditures the rent paid for land outside the village (table XXXI) but was incomplete so long as it failed to consider costs of production and income from this land. Omission from the calculations of land in absentee ownership or leased from other villages also unjustifiably reduced the size of the average holding, which increases from 51 to 73 dunums when the lands not in village ownership are included in the account.

The Johnson-Crosbie report, therefore, did not provide a firm basis for conclusions regarding the condition of Arab cultivators at the beginning of the 1930s. Not only did it give rise, inadvertently, to a misconception regarding the proportion of landless Arabs, but it created a misleading impression regarding the extent of indebtedness among many Arab farmers. By lumping together those whose principal source of income was from agriculture with others who were not primarily dependent on cultivation, the report arrived at too high a figure for total expenditures and too low a figure for net household income. Though its net income might have been very low, the average cultivating household did not end the season in debt.

It should be clear, however, that my revision of Johnson and Crosbie's computations does not undermine the conclusions they reached regarding the situation of the peasants. An average net income under £P2 conceals a range in which many cultivators ended the agricultural year with a negative balance. Without data on individual households, it is impossible to know what proportion of them ended the season with cash in hand. The analysis necessarily concealed the differentiation which in fact existed and strengthened the general impression of the uniformly depressed condition of Arab cultivators.

Conclusion

This review of Arab agricultural production during the Mandate demonstrates the importance of differentiating among cultivators in dissimilar situations, and the difficulty of doing so in the absence of more detailed information. It seems to be true that the majority of Arab farmers continued to own their land during the Mandate, while at the same time the average size of their holdings probably declined due to division among heirs. The great expansion in Arab agricultural production was not carried out on large estates, but on small and medium-sized holdings. The possibility of cultivating one's own holding and entering into leasing or tenancy arrangements to farm additional land was one way of overcoming the limitations imposed by the declining size of individual holdings. It is impossible, given the present state of information about the Arab land regime during the Mandate, to know the extent to which such combinations of ownership, rental, and tenancy were found, but they certainly were not rare.

It is also clear that, given the appropriate conditions, Arab farmers were ready to introduce new crops and try new techniques. The major obstacle to such innovations seems to have been the lack of any insurance for cultivators against the risk of losing a crop or making an investment which they could not expect to recoup. It is instructive to compare Volcani's proposals for relatively simple changes in Arab agricultural practices, such as the growing of green fodder, with the actual experiences of government agricultural agents who tried to introduce them. Many peasants did not have enough land to enable them to set some aside for fodder growing and could not afford to relinquish the portion of their grain crop that the fodder would supplant. Still, new crops such as potatoes were introduced and found acceptance. There also seems to have been a number of cultivators who were willing to cooperate with government agricultural agents and devote a portion of their land to extension crops. Although no information is available on the size of their holdings, they must have been larger landowners or they would not have been able to take part of their land out of normal production. Given the distribution of holding size, the paucity of government investment in agriculture, and its neglect of agrarian reform policies, innovation was beyond the reach of most cultivators, whatever the degree of their motivation.

Conclusions and Speculations

I BEGAN THIS book by asking again the question that served as a major theme in the argument over Palestine during the Mandate: What were the consequences of Jewish settlement for the Arab population of the country, and for peasants in particular? I think the answer must be that the social and economic structure of Arab agriculture was only marginally affected by Jewish settlement. Given the relatively short duration—less than three decades—of British rule, the constraints imposed on Zionist initiatives by government policy, the limited efforts made by government to alter the land regime, and the absence of concerted attempts by Palestinian Arabs to change what the government showed little interest in reforming, it is not surprising that many of the presumed consequences of Jewish settlement for the Arab village population turned out to be illusory. Jewish immigration did not release on a wide scale the latent potential for innovation of most Palestinian peasants by providing a model for new techniques of cultivation and new markets for products, as the Zionists often argued. Nor did it, by itself, seriously undermine the traditional basis of Arab rural society, as their opponents claimed. The Mandate was not in force long enough for these outcomes to occur, though there was clear evidence that such tendencies were developing.

This is not to say that changes did not occur, nor that they were unimportant. On the contrary, many aspects of Arab Palestine were transformed during the Mandate, and I have discussed some of them in the preceding chapters. But, as I have demonstrated with regard to agriculture, government opposition to fundamental change was too great to be overcome. Thus, considerable variation remained in the social and economic conditions in which Palestinian Arabs lived, and the majority of cultivators could not have been more than marginally better off at the end of the Mandate than they had been at its start, given the unequal distribution of holdings, the continued dependence on cereals, and plots too small to provide a living.

The very phrasing of the question regarding the effect of Jewish settlement, moreover, reflected the assumption of the participants in the conflict that Jews and Arabs comprised separate communities and would remain separate, despite ties of interest and affection among individuals. As a result, most contemporary and subsequent analysis of economy and society in Palestine has adhered to the view that there were two communities which, although in contact at various points, had nevertheless to be analyzed separately. This decision was a "political," not a "scientific," one, but it led to the creation of a particular approach to the study of Palestine and especially of Israel, one in which Jews are the major focus and Arabs, if they appear, are either of minor concern or viewed as a "minority" in a Jewish society.

The transformation of Arab Palestine during the Mandate was interrupted by the Arab-Israeli war of 1948, and tendencies visible prior to 1948 were overwhelmed by the disruption of Palestinian Arab society as a result of that war. The minority of Palestinian Arabs who remained in Israel were cut off for almost twenty years from their compatriots in Jordan and the other Arab countries of refuge. The Palestinian population of what became the West Bank of the Kingdom of Jordan comprised both persons who had already lived in that territory during the Mandate years, and refugees from the area that had become Israel. Most of the other displaced Palestinians were concentrated in refugee camps in Lebanon, Syria, and in the Gaza Strip under Egyptian administration.

The shock of that dispersal seems to have affected the study of Palestine between 1948 and 1967. Interest in the Palestinian Arabs was divided between those who remained in Israel and those who had fled or been forced out and not permitted to return. It was as if the physical and political separation of the two parts of the Arab population had created a barrier to considering them as constituting two parts of the same national entity. When this barrier was partially removed after the 1967 war, so that Palestinian Arabs from Israel could once again come into contact with those from the West Bank and other countries, the recognition that they represented portions of a single population with a common history slowly manifested itself in research. Moreover, the changed circumstances under which Arabs and Jews came into contact in the former territory of Palestine challenged not only the perceptions of Arabs, but those of Jews and others as well. The political consequences of that challenge have not yet been resolved.

In the remaining sections of this chapter, I discuss some of the ways in which my analysis affects our understanding of Arab agriculture and Arab society during the Mandate and conclude with a brief consideration of some implications for the study of the relations between Arabs and Jews in Palestine and Israel today.

The Changing Arab Agricultural Economy

Most Arab cultivators in Palestine were locked into an agricultural regime characterized by short fallow, seasonal peaks of intense labor activity alternating with longer periods during which there was little work to do on the farm, recurring harvest disasters, and increased pressure on the land as a result of population growth.[1] How, under these circumstances, could peasants cultivating cereals have raised their productivity? Labor power was limited to the members of the peasant's family, though workers might be hired to meet increased labor demands during ploughing and harvesting. Because of limited labor resources most peasants could not expand the area of cereal growing even though land might have been available. Therefore, their ability to produce a crop sufficient for their own subsistence and for seed reserves during the coming year was also limited. Had peasants been able to cultivate a larger area they might better have been able to insure themselves against a low per-dunum yield; had the rains been regular and dependable, peasants could have been fairly certain they could raise enough for their needs even on the limited amount of land that was in their power to cultivate. But they lacked the labor power to extend cultivation and the rains were not dependable, and so the size of their annual crop was uncertain.

The peasants' principal difficulty, moreover, was not poor yields, which were usually sufficient to enable them to survive. But when a substantial portion was paid in rent and taken away by tax collectors, peasants were left with an inadequate subsistence and driven into the hands of the moneylenders. It is in this context that Jewish land purchases represented a threat to the Arab peasant economy. The principal danger did not lie in the dispossession of current cultivators, though such cases, when they occurred, had serious consequences for the persons displaced as well as considerable political effect because of the publicity they generated. The greater danger was the closing-off to Arab cultivators of land resources for the future, thereby hastening the time when population pressure on existing land would require alteration of the cropping system.

Closing land to future cultivation by Arabs, however, was most threatening in circumstances where the majority of rural cultivators worked their holdings with minimal investment in innovations such as irrigation, fertilizers, crop rotation, production for the market, new crops, improved storage, and better seed varieties. But retaining land in "Arab" ownership by no means insured that it continued to be held by small cultivators working a family holding. There was evidence that Arab smallholders were selling all or part of their lands to other Arabs who were accumulating large amounts of property. The concentration of landed property by wealthy Arabs at the expense of smallholders could do little to improve the condition of the latter; indeed, the effects of such purchases were almost identical with those resulting from Jewish acquisitions. The principal difference was that the Jewish owners would sooner or later evict the Arab cultivators in order to settle Jews on the land, while Arab owners would retain them as tenants. Arab peasants would continue to be present on the land, but there would probably be little improvement in their circumstances. So long as the government of Palestine did nothing to bring about a more equitable distribution of landownership, the Arab tenants and many of the smallholders had, in practical terms, little to choose between Jewish and Arab ownership of the land they worked. In either case, their ability to make a living from their holding would continue to diminish.

The peasant's agricultural economy, to the extent that it remained subsistence-based, could be indifferent to the changes in agriculture occurring in the country so long as their consequences did not affect it. There was, of course, variation in the degree of such effects. The needs of the growing urban population provided opportunities for raising crops—primarily vegetables, but also eggs and dairy products—to be sold in the urban consumer market. Most of the peasants, however, were not involved in production for the urban market, but continued to depend on subsistence farming. When cereal yields were high, peasants had little incentive to change their methods of cultivation, since their livelihood was assured. When yields were poor there was no chance to make such changes; peasants had enough trouble maintaining themselves and their families.

Concern about agricultural backwardness which could be translated into policies designed to improve agricultural conditions came from outside the peasant economy—from the Palestine government and the Zionist organization. The government wanted to improve the peasant's standard of living; the Zionists wanted to free land for their own settlement. The government would have been satisfied with removing the debt burden and leaving the peasants on the land to continue their traditional cultivation, making slow improvements in crops, techniques, and implements in order gradually to improve yields. The Zionists required a restructuring of peasant agriculture in order to extend their own holdings.

During the Mandate, peasant producers in increasing numbers were slowly being drawn into active participation in the market for agricultural produce. Some cultivators, of course, had long depended on the market for their livelihood, but most were connected only through the fluctuations of prices for agricultural produce, which affected their ability to survive and determined the extent to which they would have recourse to moneylenders. The establishment of the Mandate over Palestine brought the country more fully into the network of international trade relations; but even without Jewish settlement there would most likely have developed an indigenous commercial sector with extensive trading links overseas, and a majority agricultural population whose condition may have been slowly ameliorated through technical and fiscal innovations.

The presence of Jewish settlements, and the inherently open-ended character of Zionist settlement activity, was more important than the activities of the Palestine government in altering the agricultural economy of the country. Though Arabs and Jews evaluated very differently the changes thus brought about, there is no question that Jewish settlement was one factor which provided an impetus to agricultural change that would otherwise have been much longer in coming. The nature of that impetus was not primarily in the opportunity offered to adopt modern farming practices introduced by Jewish settlers, although the Zionist organizations frequently made this argument, and it was true to a certain extent. Rather, the combination of an increasing Arab rural population, a growing urban population, both Arab and Jewish, and the relative and absolute reduction in the amount of cultivable land available to Arab peasants using traditional farming methods combined to create conditions favorable to an alteration of the cropping system. Because of the circumstances under which the Mandate was terminated, and the subsequent transformation of Palestinian economy and society, the full consequences of Jewish settlement for Arab society were never worked out in the context of Palestine. But it is clear that the Arab cultivators were being forced to make changes in the basis of their agricultural economy which would allow the expansion of Jewish settlement.

Reduction of the amount of cultivable land available to cereal growers as a result of Jewish settlement would have been likely to push them to decrease the period of fallow and thereby obtain a greater yield from a given area of land by more frequent cropping.[2] The price of such increase in yield, in the absence of capital investment in machinery and irrigation, would have been a reduction of output per hour of labor. This would have led to a change in cropping practices as a result of the increased pressure on the land, and probably would have involved the widespread adoption of leguminous crops to improve cereal yields. But such a change would have depended on the existence of yields sufficient to permit the peasants to subsist on them, taking into consideration that the total area devoted to grain would be reduced because of the extension of leguminous rotation crops.

In the view of Jewish agricultural planners, the solution to the problems of Arab agriculture was not an increase in the frequency of cropping, for that would have required continued utilization of the land currently under cultivation by Arabs. The Zionist view was that intensification of Arab agriculture should come about by increasing the labor input per unit of land by changing the crops grown from cereals to vegetables and plantations. Their view of the desired outcome affected the Jews' analysis of the shortcomings of the existing system and their prescription for change.

Maximization of value per unit of labor input is not the primary consideration for peasant cultivators. This is especially true where shortage of land does not permit the most optimal utilization of family labor power. Chayanov gave as an example Russian peasants who increased the growing of potatoes and hemp, which were often of lower profitability than oats, their former crop, but were more labor-intensive and thereby increased the farm family's gross profit.[3] They did so to take advantage of surplus family labor power which could not be utilized in oat cultivation because of the shortage of land. Even though the return per unit of labor from hemp and potatoes was lower than from oats, the gross return possible from a fuller use of family labor power was greater.

Palestinian Arab cereal cultivators were not in the same situation as were Russian oat farmers. Although their labor was underutilized, because of climatic conditions they did not have alternative crops to which they could easily switch. The long, dry, summer growing season could not support the kinds of crops requiring greater inputs of labor, and only irrigation would have enabled the peasant to introduce them. Irrigation, however, was beyond the resources of the ordinary cultivator. Moreover, it would have threatened the family's subsistence, which was still based in large measure on home-grown grains and not on produce purchased in the market.

One frequent criticism of the Arab agricultural economy in Palestine was that the absentee landlords with large holdings, those who lived outside the country as well as those residing in the main towns, took little or no interest in improving the productivity of their lands, but were concerned only with income derived from existing techniques of cultivation. It has been suggested that this behavior reflected an economically irrational attitude, one that viewed income from agricultural holdings not as a means of increasing wealth but as a way of maintaining a particular set of social, political, and economic relationships. There is a parallel between the behavior of large landowners in Palestine and that of landlords under feudal tenure, as described by Boserup: "If feudal tenures exist in regions where increasing rural populations are unable to find sufficient employment because of the survival of extensive forms of land use, it is often suggested as an explanation that the feudal landlords are behaving uneconomically, showing more interest in the prestige of land ownership than in the profits of intensive agriculture" (p. 101).

Though Palestine in the late nineteenth and early twentieth centuries was not a feudal society, large landowners acted in ways similar to those which presumably characterized feudal landlords, for some of the same reasons. Firestone, for example, describes how the 'Abdul Hadi family accepted lower rent shares on their lands in the vicinity of Jenin than might have been due them in order to maintain the "loyalty" of their tenants and protect their own local political interests and influence.[4] Boserup questions the explanation of such behavior as being the outcome of "traditional" attitudes:

When overall population growth promotes intensive land use and a change of the system of tenure in regions close to expanding urban centres, extensive land use is likely to continue to be more profitable than intensive in regions far from large urban centres. Feudal landlords in such regions may well be behaving economically when they refuse to change both land use and tenure, and it seems to me more pertinent to regard the rural migration which accompanies such divergent trends in land use and tenure as a necessary concomitant of the concentration of non-agricultural activities in particular regions, rather than to to interpret it as the result of non-economic behavior by feudal landlords. (p. 101)

Although the inland plains of Palestine were no great distance from the major towns—Haifa, Jaffa, Tel Aviv, Jerusalem—difficulties of road transport hampered access to urban markets and tended to isolate rural cultivators. For the large landowners to benefit economically from intensification of cultivation would have required easier access to markets. So long as this condition was not met, there was little point in undertaking the investments necessary to alter the cropping system.

There is a relationship between the system of cropping and the employment by peasant families of hired labor. In Palestinian villages, as elsewhere, most cultivators relied almost exclusively on family members for the labor required to plant and harvest the crop. Boserup argues that the seasonal pattern of the employment of hired workers in periods of peak labor demand provides an incentive for the intensification of cropping on holdings depending on such workers, "since the additional employment that goes with more intensive land use falls largely in the off-seasons" (when rural wages were low) (p. 108).

As the towns grew, increasing numbers of men from villages sought urban employment during the slack periods. The Palestine government, for a variety of reasons, did not wish to see a substantial migration from the countryside to the towns. As one way of preventing this, it provided rural employment on public works projects such as road construction. The effect of this was to establish a minimum off-season wage for the seasonally unemployed rural population, which may have prevented landowners from using their labor to make the changes in cropping techniques necessary for the intensification of cultivation.

Only in the first two decades of British rule in Palestine did changes in the structure of Arab agriculture proceed relatively free from direct governmental intervention, as a result of the dual process of Jewish settlement and Arab population increase. When the British severely restricted Jewish immigration after 1939, and limited the areas in which Jews could purchase land, the primary influence on the development of Arab agriculture was no longer the interaction between Jewish settlers and Arab cultivators, but the demands of the wartime economy represented by the substantial number of troops stationed in the country. The three years between the end of the war and the destruction of Arab Palestine were characterized by the need to adapt the economy to peacetime conditions and by disorder attending the preparations being made by the British, the Arabs, and the Jews for a new political order in the country. These three years were too short and too disorganized a period for the processes of agricultural change which had been underway during the first two decades after 1918 to continue in operation.

The History of Arab Palestine Comes to an End

The transformation of Arab Palestine as a result of the 1948 war made academic most discussions of the effects of Jewish settlement on the Arab population of the Mandatory territory. The potential that was felt at the time for Arab development following the end of the Second World War, which has been described both in contemporary and in later analyses of Palestinian Arab society, was never put to the test.[5] Though all the plans presented for the partition of the country, if carried out, would have seriously hampered the future development of Arab society and economy, whether in the Jewish, the Arab, or the "international" zone, the implementation of any of the plans would have been better for the Arab population than the outcome which actually occurred.

The elimination after 1948 of Palestine as a separate geographic, social, economic, and historical entity had certain consequences for the analysis of Palestine society, both as a whole and with regard to its two main components, the Arabs and the Jews. Analyses of the transformation of colonial or settler regimes in countries that subsequently gained their independence have typically devoted considerable attention to a description of the consequences of changes wrought by the colonial authority in the social and economic structure of the country. The assumption has usually been that understanding the colonial period is made possible in part by examining the consequences of policies carried out during that period, which only fully reveal themselves in later years. Since most of the research that considers the effects of colonial regimes on contemporary societies is necessarily historical, a natural component of such research is the tracing over time of the consequences of colonial policies.

Analysis of Mandatory Palestine has proceeded differently. The entire period of modern Jewish settlement in Palestine until 1948 was less than seventy years, and the Mandate was in effect only about half of that time. No one has argued that the structure of Palestinian Arab society after 1948, either in Israel, in the West Bank, or in the other countries of the Palestinian diaspora, was in any meaningful sense a continuation of social and economic developments during the Mandate, except in the broadest sense used by those Palestinians who attributed to the structure of Palestinian Arab society during the Mandate some of the blame for the disaster of 1948. Although some have identified in Palestinian social structure after 1948 the manifestation of tendencies that first became visible during the Mandate, most such analyses have begun with the new conditions created by the war and the dispersion.[6]

The consequences of this situation for the analysis of Palestinian Arab society during the Mandate have not always been recognized, particularly with regard to the effects of Jewish settlement on the Arab population. As time elapsed, these effects could be more clearly identified, but the circumstances under which the analysis was carried out did not facilitate objective understanding of them. As I argued in a earlier chapter, the socioeconomic analyses of Arab agriculture were aimed at providing support for political positions; it was not a situation in which dispassionate analyses were easily undertaken. After 1948 it was no longer possible to observe the effects of Jewish settlement on the development of Palestinian Arab society. Thus, the "natural experiment," if I may so call it, was prematurely ended. Historical analysis of the effects of Jewish settlement on Palestine Arab society has been unable to benefit from viewing the continuation of that process, and has been frozen in the limited period bounded by the beginning and the end of the Mandate.

One result of these circumstances has been that the analysis of Palestinian Arab society during the Mandate has only with difficulty been able to extricate itself from the terms of the discussion implicitly and explicitly set by the Jews, supported by the government. As I have

already noted, the Jews devoted much effort to demonstrating the beneficial effects of their colonization. Adequate data for examining the Jewish
claims was frequently unavailable; government officials tended to accept
the facts as presented by the Jews even if their evaluations of them did
not agree with those the Jews advanced; the Arabs did not undertake
statistical investigations of their condition. The 1948 war, by ending the
possibility of the continued development of Arab Palestine under the
conditions which had previously existed, also froze the analysis of Arab
Palestine that had been developed primarily under the aegis of the
government and of the Jews.

The Unequal Distribution of Landed Property

The preceding chapters of this work have dealt separately with two
interconnected topics: the analysis of the conditions of Arab agriculture
in Palestine, on the one hand, and the facts regarding aspects of those
conditions, on the other. I have tried to show how the views of government, the Jews, and the Arabs regarding the situation of Arab cultivators
were affected by the political positions of each of the parties to the
conflict, and were in turn utilized in support of these positions. By
examining one of the principal issues in the analysis of the social structure of Palestine—the effects of Jewish settlement on the Arab agricultural system—I have shown that some of the principal Jewish claims
regarding the beneficial effects of their settlement on Arab cultivators
were unsupported by the evidence available. The emphasis in discussions of the Mandatory period on the more easily noticed individual and
local effects of Jewish settlement on the Arab population has obscured
other effects of Jewish colonization which were equally important for the
development of rural Arab society.

All the evidence presented in the previous chapters points to the
considerable differentiation which existed in Arab agriculture during the
Mandatory period. Contemporary analyses of agricultural conditions
stressed the depressed condition of the peasantry, and in particular of
tenant cultivators. Much less emphasis was placed on the great inequality in the distribution of land and other agricultural resources which
existed throughout the same period. Though particular emphasis was laid
prior to and immediately after the First World War on the dramatic
contrast between the wealthy absentee owners of large estates and their

impoverished tenants, this emphasis faded following the completion of the major Jewish purchases of large tracts in the early 1920s. No corresponding concern ever became manifest regarding the inequality in the distribution of landholding among Arabs resident in Palestine. The reason for this, I have suggested, was twofold. The government had no intention of undertaking a land reform program, and the Jews were primarily interested in acquiring land for themselves, not in seeing it more equitably distributed among Arabs. The accumulating evidence regarding the great inequalities in access to land was not translated into a political program.

The data I have presented in the preceding chapters, as well as other evidence from contemporary sources, suggests that one effect of Jewish land purchases may have been to increase the inequality in the distribution of Arab landholding. This result could have come about in at least three ways. First, by creating a market for land which was, in certain periods, characterized by substantial price rises due to speculative activity, Jewish purchases encouraged Arabs to make speculative purchases of their own. Second, Jewish purchases of portions of Arab smallholdings (in those cases where the settlers retained sufficient land to cultivate) automatically had the effect of increasing the proportion of smaller holdings. Third, the displacement of owner-cultivators who sold their holdings, as well as of tenants whose holdings were sold by their owners, increased the size of the landless rural population. Since the majority of Arab holdings in Palestine were too small to enable a living to be made by those working them, and buyers could apparently be found for these lands, the temptation to sell was continually present.

The "Proletarianization" of the Rural Arab Labor Force

Contemporary observers as well as later researchers pointed to the gradual proletarianization of the Arab labor force in Palestine, attributing it to the inability of cultivators to support themselves on the land—either because they were displaced, or because they lacked the technology to compete in the market and did not have the resources to introduce it.[7] While perhaps not abandoning agricultural work entirely, it no longer provided the family's main income. The former peasants might remain in the countryside and find employment on government public-works projects or as landless agricultural laborers. The alternative was to seek jobs in the towns, and in particular in Haifa and in Jaffa, in the ports, the oil industry, construction, or other occupations.

Prior to the Second World War and the great expansion of nonagricultural employment provided by the British military installations in Palestine, the opportunities for Arab industrial employment were limited. Most Arab industrial establishments were small and employed no more than two or three workers; Jewish industrial enterprises were for the most part closed to Arabs. Government policy was designed to prevent the migration of rural Arabs to the towns. Unlike other colonial settings in which European settlers employed indigenous labor and thereby provided an outlet for the growing pressure of an underemployed rural population (whose growth had in many cases been due to the land policies of the colonial administrations themselves), the Jews in Palestine refused to provide industrial work for Arabs. The lack of substantial Arab investment in industrial undertakings, combined with the fact that the most progressive industrial sector in the country was closed to Arabs, made the public sector—ports, the railway, military workshops—and to a lesser degree the Haifa refinery installations the primary settings for the development of an Arab industrial working class. With the end of the Second World War the army workshops were disbanded, but the Arabs who were employed in them were not easily reabsorbed into the countryside.

Evidence of Progress

No agreed-upon indicators of Arab progress in Palestine during the Mandate were consistently employed to measure changes in the Arab population. This is one of the reasons that the series of reports issued by the government—with the exception of the *Survey of Palestine* in 1945— and by the investigatory commissions failed to include comparative statistics which would enable the reader to evaluate the Arabs' situation. The principal indicators were demographic: the unprecedented growth in the Arab population resulting from a decline in the death rate. The majority of the Arab population was rural and under the conditions of the Mandate was greatly dependent on government initiatives for improvement of its living standard. Since the efforts of the government to that end were limited, evidence of rural Arab progress was also necessarily limited.

It was, of course, possible to point to great changes in Palestine since the establishment of the Mandate, and not only in the areas of Jewish settlement. When the government reported annually to the Permanent Mandates Commission of the League of Nations it could point, for example, to the extension of the road system; to the establishment, at least in the early years, of scores of village schools; to land-reclamation projects which it had undertaken or supported; and to other activities such as afforestation which were designed to benefit the country as a whole. But Arab progress was most needed on the land, and since there were few comprehensive government programs designed to accomplish this the indicators presented annually referred to subsidiary activities of the various government departments, such as agricultural extension work, rather than to more fundamental endeavors. Comprehensive statistics on the situation of Arab cultivators are lacking for the same reason, since in the absence of government programs aimed at substantially bettering their condition there was little incentive to collect them.

The Jews measured their own progress in Palestine by the increase in their numbers and in the amount of land they owned, which were reasonable indicators given the goals of Zionist settlement. Additional indicators of progress referred to the increasing productivity of the Jewish agricultural economy and the expansion of urban Jewish enterprises, as well as a multitude of more specific topics. The emphasis, of course, was on growth, whereas the measures of Arab progress would necessarily have been those describing improvement in the existing situation: education, crop yields, health conditions, peasant debt, rural underemployment. As I have already noted, however, the necessary motive force and the resources for the encouragement of such changes were lacking.

The Jews were interested in the transformation of the Arab rural economy in order to free land for Jewish settlement; they wished to be granted the opportunity to undertake large-scale schemes which would have contributed to such changes. The government refused, for reasons of policy and its view of its obligations under the Mandate, to create the conditions that would have given the Jews the freedom they desired. Since the Jews had little interest in Arab development that did not contribute directly to their own settlement program, they had little reason to divert resources under their control to activities aimed at upgrading Arab agriculture if these brought no immediate benefits to themselves.

The Meaning of Arab Land Sales to Jews

Zionists often found it difficult to reconcile Arab opposition to Jewish settlement with the fact that Arabs were willing to sell land to Jews. Even more suspect was the fact that many prominent Arab political leaders were themselves engaged in surreptitious land sales. To most Jews, this seemed the height of hypocrisy, and further convinced the Zionists that their rights to the land were worthier than those of the Arabs. Yehoshua Porath has argued that land sales to Jews by prominent Arabs had a "devastating effect" on the Palestinian Arab national movement and damaged its image in the eyes of the government.[8] But this wholesale condemnation did not give sufficient weight to the internal differentiation of Arab society and imposed on its members standards of judgment which had developed in response to a situation very different from that confronted by most Arabs.

It was natural for Zionist ideology to emphasize the centrality of land purchase and to imbue Jewish landownership with a mystical significance. The "land of Israel" had long played a central role in Jewish lore and ritual; Jews were prevented from owning land in large areas of eastern Europe and Russia; as a practical matter, Jewish settlement in Palestine, an agricultural country, depended on obtaining land. The amount of available land was limited, and it rapidly became clear that the developing terms of the land conflict between Arabs and Jews meant that one side benefited at the expense of the other. Arab willingness to sell to Jews was defined by the latter as evidence for the weakness of the Arabs' attachment to the land, which was in turn seen as undermining the legitimacy of their claim to it.

Jews, who commonly referred to their land purchases as "redemptive" acts, condemned Arabs who sold for economic reasons, attributing to them baser motives than those which impelled their own actions. By doing so they sought to impose on Arab behavior the meanings they had created to justify their own. But Arabs who sold land did not see themselves as thereby relinquishing their patrimony. For some, the sale was a business transaction; for many others it was an unavoidable necessity. The sellers were not by their actions expressing their intention to leave Palestine. The force of the Zionist land mystique, however, was so powerful that Arab attempts to counter Jewish purchases—such as the Arab National Fund—were eventually couched in similar terms. They never attracted wide support, primarily because of the failure of Palestinian Arabs to create an effective national political organization which could provide a base for opposing land sales, but also, perhaps, because they were expressed in borrowed sentiments which were foreign to most Arabs.

Jewish land purchasers tended to reject as illegitimate politically motivated Arab resistance to land sales. The earlier purchases of large tracts were completed before organized opposition to Jewish land acquisition had begun to develop, and such opposition would have found it difficult to influence large landowners such as the Sursoqs, who did not live in Palestine. Later Jewish purchasers preferred to confront individual sellers, in order to complete the transaction with a minimum of publicity. This was one reason that they employed Arab middlemen to buy scattered plots and consolidate them for subsequent resale. They also claimed that Arab opposition was a ploy used to compel Jewish purchasers to pay a higher price. This may often have been true, and it reinforced the Jewish stereotype of Arab sellers as indifferent to the true interests of their people.

Jewish Settlement and Arab Development

The question has been repeatedly raised in writings dealing with Palestine of the extent to which Jewish immigration to the country contributed to Arab progress. I would like to suggest the opposite thesis: that in certain respects Jewish settlement, and in particular the Zionist policy of economic exclusiveness, hindered Arab economic development.

Colonial administrations often limited the access of indigenous peoples to positions of power and influence, and racist attitudes regarding the "capacities" of members of the local population served to justify policies restricting their employment in jobs requiring responsibility and skill, which could provide training and experience relevant to the operation of a capitalist economy. The situation in Palestine was complicated by the presence of two independent elements—the government and the organized Jewish community—whose policies were undermining traditional Arab rural society.

Arabs believed that the terms of the Mandate obligated the government to hire them, and they frequently complained of being underrepresented in senior civil service positions, compared with their proportion in the population and the relative number of Jews in such jobs. Such

accusations were part of the more general struggle between Arabs and
Jews over access to and control over public resources which was reflected in other controversies as well, such as the proportions hired on
public works; relative rates of pay; and the contributions of each community to government revenues compared to the relative benefits received
by each in return.

The encouragement of Arab development was clearly the responsibility of the government, and I am not proposing that the Zionist organizations had an obligation to substitute for its inaction. Continually short of
funds, the *Yishuv* had all it could do to provide jobs for Jews, and most of
its leaders would have been extremely surprised were it to be suggested
to them that a portion of their limited resources should be diverted to the
promotion of Arab technical progress.[9] The Jewish policy of economic
exclusiveness, however, imposed great obstacles to the creation of a
labor market in which "rational" and "universalistic" criteria of investment and employment would have permitted hiring Arabs as well as
Jews. One result of such nondiscriminatory hiring would have been the
more rapid transfer of knowledge, technical skills, and organizational
methods from Jewish enterprises to those run by Arabs. There were
industries in which such transfer did in fact occur. One of the examples
frequently mentioned was construction, in which Jews employed large
numbers of Arabs, who in turn learned methods of building with concrete
rather than with stone and subsequently applied this knowledge to the
erection of houses and other structures in Arab towns and villages.
Another Jewish source of employment for Arabs was in citrus cultivation,
but here Arabs tended to hold the more menial jobs, primarily those
requiring greater physical effort.[10]

The structure of Jewish agriculture also worked against an effective
transfer of methods and technology to Arab cultivators. The policy of
reserving for exclusive Jewish settlement land bought with money contributed through Zionist fund-raising activities abroad, and the desire to
restrict employment on such land to Jews, had both positive and negative consequences. On the one hand, it prevented the creation of an
economic stratification system in which ethnic and class characteristics
overlapped—the Jews as owners, the Arabs as laborers. The socialist
ideology of Labor Zionists made them especially determined to prevent
such an outcome, seeing it as indefensible morally and dangerous
practically.

On the other hand, restriction of Arab employment in many sectors of Jewish agriculture, because of the ideology which gave preference to hiring Jews and the practical necessity of providing employment for Jewish immigrants having no other means of support, closed off potential sources of income for underemployed Arab rural laborers. The Jews during the Mandate did not want to become rural capitalists. While their choice may well have prevented the addition of complications based on economic relations to the tensions already existing between the two nationalities, it did not ease the economic situation of the rural Arab population.

Jewish economic exclusiveness affected Arab development not only with respect to employment opportunities. The creation of separate co-operative organizations for production and marketing, reserved for individuals, groups, and settlements affiliated with the Histadrut, excluded Arabs from the organizational and technical benefits made possible by these forms of collective action. I am not claiming that cooperation between Arabs and Jews, and their participation in such undertakings, would have been widespread; indeed, given the history of the Mandate such common efforts would very likely have become increasingly rare. Nor am I arguing that had such joint endeavors been more prevalent they might have contributed to mitigating the national conflict.[11] But the radical separation of Jews from Arabs which became, for economic, political, cultural, and ideological reasons, a fundamental premise of Zionist policy, partly vitiated the claims often made by Zionist spokesmen that Jewish settlers were the bearers of progress. So long as Arab access to such progress was restricted by the policy of economic exclusiveness, the benefits to be gained were limited.

Toward a Reevaluation of Arab Palestine During the Mandate

I have tried to demonstrate in this work that the accepted ways of viewing the history of Palestinian Arab society during the Mandate are deficient, in that they give insufficient attention to actual developments and to the context in which they occurred. At the same time, stress on the underdevelopment which was most visible to European observers, whether government officials or Jewish settlers, weighted the analysis of Mandatory Palestine in favor of the Jewish view. Discussions of the history of Mandatory Palestine have typically focused either on the course of political developments, with occasional reference to social and economic changes as a way of providing a context,[12] or have taken the opposite course and stressed the social and economic structure, while merely noting contemporaneous political developments.[13]

The effect of these approaches has been an insufficient appreciation of the problems confronting Palestinian Arab society between the two world wars. The relationship between the Arabs' social and economic development, the policies carried out by the government, and the degree to which the Jews were successful in influencing these policies in accord with their own interests created a situation in which the social and economic progress of the Palestinian Arabs, to say nothing of their political advance, was dependent on a complex set of political and economic factors which have never been adequately analyzed. The absence of an appropriate understanding of Arab Palestine during the Mandate has also had consequences for the way in which Arab society in Israel has been viewed by researchers. By ignoring the complexity of the political economy of Mandatory Palestine, and stressing instead the contrast between the characteristics of Arab and Jewish society before 1948, such research perpetuates the stereotype of Palestinian Arab society which developed in part as a result of the political conflict over Palestine. But rural Arab households by the tens of thousands confronted an economic and political order that was changing dramatically, yet by virtue of the structure of their society most could expect neither to influence these changes nor benefit from them.

It is clear that political conflict was but one aspect of the relations among Jews, Arabs, and British, even though that aspect has received most scrutiny. The political events were the most dramatic and the most visible. But they occurred against the backdrop of fundamental social and economic changes whose significance has been insufficiently appreciated by later writers. The disruption of Arab society as a result of the 1948 war, and its subsequent transformation and rebirth, was preceded by fifty years during which the Arab population was exposed to what many of its members perceived as the threat of dispossession at the same time as they were unable to improve their economic circumstances sufficiently to permit them effectively to combat this threat. After 1948 their circumstances changed; many became refugees and unwelcome minorities, both in Arab lands and in Israel. But they surely remembered their past and, like the Jews, used their memories in evaluating their present and constructing their hopes for the future. If we are fully to comprehend the current conflict between Jews and Arabs in Palestine, we must exert ourselves to grasp as much of its past as we can. A reexamination of Arab Palestine during the Mandate is thus beneficial not only for our historical understanding, but for our contemporary understanding as well.

NOTES
BIBLIOGRAPHY
INDEX

NOTES

ISA   Israel State Archives, Jerusalem
CZA   Central Zionist Archives, Jerusalem

Document headings appearing in square brackets have been translated from Hebrew.

CHAPTER 1: *Introduction*

1. Morris, "The New Historiography," refers to some of these works, including Morris's own *Birth of the Palestinian Refugee Problem*. Other books include Shlaim, *Collusion Across the Jordan*, and Pappe, *Britain and the Arab-Israeli Conflict, 1948–1951*. A bitter exchange between Morris and Shabtai Teveth, an Israeli historian, over the legitimacy of the "new historiography," appeared in a series of Hebrew articles in the Israeli newspaper *HaAretz* (see bibliography).

2. J. Sawer, "Extracts from the Review of the Agricultural Situation in Palestine by the Director of Agriculture, dated March 16, 1922," CZA/Z4/5235, p. 2. Hereafter cited as Sawer, "Extracts."

3. See Metzer, "Fiscal Incidence and Resource Transfer," and Metzer and Kaplan, "Jointly but Severally."

4. Cf. Doukhan-Landau, *The Zionist Land-Purchasing Companies* (in Hebrew).

5. Cf. Mandel, *The Arabs and Zionism*, pp. 81, 85, and passim; Porath, *Emergence of the Palestinian-Arab National Movement*, pp. 20–30.

6. There are parallels here with the Afrikaner historiography of South Africa, whose history is seen to begin with the landing of the first Dutch settlers.

CHAPTER 2: *Arab Society in Palestine*

1. Government of Palestine, Department of Statistics, *Statistical Abstract*, 1944/45, p. 16.

2. Halevi, in "Political Economy of Absorptive Capacity," discusses the validity of utilizing "absorptive capacity" as a criterion for restricting immigration, and differentiates between immediate and long-term concepts of economic absorption: "The position taken by the Jewish Agency . . . was clearly correct in the long run: immigration and capital inflow combined to change the economic structure of the country and led to economic development which created potential for further immigration." The British view, on the other hand, "was a reasonable short-run approach, for it was based (at least officially) on evaluation of immediate employment opportunities" (p. 467).

3. These figures refer only to the "settled" population and exclude the Bedouin; they also include, for 1922, all Christians, whether or not ethnically Arab, and for 1944 all Christians except members of His Majesty's forces stationed in Palestine. The estimated number of "non-Jews" who were also non-Arab at the end of 1944 was 32,000 (cf. *Statistical Abstract*, 1944/45, pp. 16, 18), representing less than 3 percent of the population classified as "non-Jewish." The vast majority of them were Christians, either in religious establishments or in the Palestine government administration. I have included them among the Arab population since no information exists that would allow them to be subtracted from the totals for subdistricts, towns, etc. The largest number of non-Arab Christians was found in Jerusalem, followed by Haifa and Nazareth. For list of sources, see note to table 1.

4. I have not presented data for 1922 because the figures for that year included Bedouin within the boundaries of the towns. Enumeration of the Bedouin in 1922 was unsatisfactory (see Government of Palestine, *Census of Palestine, 1931*, vol. 1, pt. 1, p. 329), and it is unlikely that the figures are comparable with those of the 1931 census; moreover, 1931 population totals are presented exclusive of Bedouin, as are the 1944 estimates. It should also be noted that "changes in municipal boundaries throughout the period render the figures for the large towns somewhat uncertain" (Government of Palestine, *Survey of Palestine*, p. 146).

5. *Survey of Palestine*, pp. 150–51.

6. Ibid., p. 150.

7. The stability of the distribution of the Arab population between the towns and the villages was not an artifact of the methods used by the Department of Statistics to arrive at the 1944 estimates; see ibid., pp. 160 ff.

8. Ibid., p. 159.

9. Ibid., p. 153.

10. Mansur, *Arab Worker*, p. 14; ISA/CO.733/351, Wauchope to Ormesby-Gore, CF/223/37, June 1, 1937.

11. Cf. CZA/S9/1122, Shertok to Chief Secretary, Pol/30/38, March 2,

1938; Mansur, *Arab Worker*, p. 42. Both sources refer to existing wage differentials between Arab and Jewish workers.

12. CZA/S90/76, David Horowitz, "Jewish Colonization and Arab Development in Palestine," October 7, 1945, p. 8.

13. *Survey of Palestine*, pp. 157–58.

14. Gurevich, *Statistical Abstract*, p. 28, for 1922 tribal population by subdistrict (I assumed all Bedouin were Moslem); Government of Palestine, Department of Statistics, *Vital Statistics Tables, 1922–1944*, pp. 5, 8. Hereafter cited as *Vital Statistics*.

15. Official immigration statistics underestimated the number of Arab as well as the number of Jewish "travellers remaining illegally" in the country, as the Department of Statistics acknowledged (*Statistical Abstract*, 1944/45, p. 41).

16. Total to employment+[(dependents)×((total to employment)+(total −dependents))].

17. *Statistical Abstract*, 1944/45, p. 41.

18. A few years ago Joan Peters argued that a very large part of the growth in the size of the Arab population during the Mandate was the result of unregistered in-migration from neighboring countries. Her book made a considerable stir for a while, but its thesis has been widely rejected. While knowledgeable contemporary Jewish observers often expressed concern that Arabs coming into Palestine in search of seasonal employment were remaining permanently though unauthorized to do so, they never claimed that such illegal immigrants represented more than a fraction of the Arab population. Joan Peters, *From Time Immemorial* (New York: Harper Perennial Library, 1985); for critical reviews, see Ian Gilmour, *New York Review of Books*, January 16, 1986; Robert Olson, *American Historical Review* 90 (April 1985): 468; Joel S. Migdal, *Middle East Journal* 39 (Spring 1985): 376; Charles Glass, *The Spectator* 254 (March 2, 1985): 22; M. E. Yapp, *Times Literary Supplement*, February 15, 1985, p. 167.

19. Horowitz, "Colonization," p. 51, citing memo to DC Northern District from Palestine Arab Labourers Association, 9/2/32.

20. *Statistical Abstract*, 1944/45, pp. 26–28.

21. Ibid., p. 27.

22. Ibid., p. 28.

23. Ibid., p. 29.

24. *Census of Palestine, 1931*, vol. 2, pt. 2, pp. 294–95, 310–11.

25. One strategy sometimes used by Zionist writers to prove the beneficial consequences for local Arabs of Jewish settlement was to compare characteristics of rural Arab society, such as disease rates, or indices of agricultural modernization, in regions near the major urban Jewish population centers—

Haifa, Tel Aviv, Jerusalem—with the same characteristics in regions farther away from the main towns. See Horowitz, "Colonization," p. 8.

26. Great Britain, Colonial Office, *Palestine: Report on Immigration, Land Settlement and Development*, p. 22 (hereafter cited as Hope Simpson); Gurevich, *Statistical Handbook*, p. 143.

27. Estimate of cultivable land computed from Gurevich, *Statistical Handbook*, pp. 138–39.

28. See Stein, *Land Question in Palestine*, for a comprehensive discussion of government land policy and the difficulties it confronted.

29. For a discussion of the Arab nonagricultural labor force during the Mandate, see Taqqu, *Arab Labor*.

30. *Census of Palestine, 1931*, vol. 1, pt. 1, pp. 23–24.

31. Jewish Agency for Palestine, Economic Department, *Palestine Facts and Figures*, p. 96.

32. Granott, *Land System in Palestine*, p. 164. In addition to the villagers, there were in the 1940s about 70,000 Bedouin, mostly in the Beersheba subdistrict (Government of Palestine, Department of Statistics, *Vital Statistics*, p. 1).

33. Government of Palestine, Department of Statistics, "Survey of Social and Economic Conditions in Arab Villages, 1944," January–March 1946, p. 55. Hereafter cited as "1944 Survey."

34. The "principal" was not necessarily the household's only earner; additional earners were classified as "principals" if by their work they contributed an "increment" to the family income. It could not have been easy for enumerators to apply this definition in the field. The number of principal earners is not, therefore, equal to the number of households. "Ordinary cultivators" excluded citrus growers; fruit, vegetable, and viticulture; floriculturists; stock raisers; poultry farmers and beekeepers, etc. Ninety-five percent of all "ordinary cultivators" were Moslems. The discussion in this section is based on the *Census of Palestine, 1931*, vol. 1, pt. 1, pp. 289–92; vol. 2, pt. 2, pp. 282–83.

35. Ibid., vol. 1, pt. 1, p. 289.

36. See Gross, "Economic Policy of the Mandatory Government."

37. In a later chapter I discuss some of the consequences of this fact for our current understanding of Palestinian Arab society during the Mandate.

38. See Volcani, *The Fellah's Farm*, which I discuss below.

39. I often use the terms *peasants, farmers, cultivators* and *fellahin* interchangeably in this work when I speak about Arabs engaged in farming, though not when I am specifically discussing rural Arab society as a peasant society.

40. *Effendi* meant "a man of property, authority or education in an eastern Mediterranean country," but it became a term of opprobrium for some participants in the argument over the land; see Shanin's comments on the transforma-

tion of the meaning of *kulak,* and the displeasure some Arabs felt regarding the similar transformation of *effendi.* Shanin, *Russia as a "Developing Society,"* vol. 1, pp. 156–58; *Falastin,* English edition, July 26, 1930, p. 1.

41. See my discussion of the analyses by Greenbaum and by Flapan, below.

42. Firestone, "Crop-sharing Economics"; Graham-Brown, "Political Economy of the Jabal Nablus"; Miller, *Government and Society.*

43. I draw on Rosenfeld's writings below.

44. This characterization of peasant society is taken from Teodor Shanin's introduction to the collection he edited, *Peasants and Peasant Societies,* pp. 14–16.

45. Wolf, *Peasants,* pp. 3–4.

46. Foster, *Tzintzuntzan,* p. 8.

47. Scott, *Moral Economy of the Peasant,* pp. 4–5, 23.

48. The standard descriptions of Arab society in Palestine during the Mandate, on which almost all subsequent analyses have been based, include Granott, *Land System in Palestine;* the reports by the Johnson-Crosbie committee and by Sir John Hope Simpson; the *Survey of Palestine* prepared by the government in 1946; Himadeh, *Economic Organization of Palestine;* Volcani, *The Fellah's Farm.* Additional information is available from later anthropological studies of villages in Israel and Jordan: see Lutfiyya, *Baytin;* Antoun, *Arab Village;* Cohen, *Arab Border Villages in Israel;* and the writings of Rosenfeld, especially *Hem Hayyu Fallahim* [They Were Peasants] and "From Peasantry to Wage Labor."

49. It may seem perverse to argue that indebted fellahin living on the edge of subsistence were nevertheless producing a surplus. The resolution of this paradox lies in differentiating between the individual peasant household and the Arab agricultural economy as a whole. Although there seems to have been general agreement as to the depressed condition of the peasants, there is little evidence they were starving. Therefore, individual households must have had sufficient grain for their own needs, whether it remained from their own production after all the household's obligations were met, or was obtained from the landowner or in return for cash borrowed from a moneylender. Since, according to Schölch ("European Penetration," p. 12), prior to the First World War Palestine was a net wheat exporter, it is clear that the country's production was adequate for its needs, though the political economy of agricultural relations forced peasants into debt to replace grain they produced but which they had been forced to relinquish. Later, during the Mandate, local wheat production was insufficient for the country's needs, and Palestine became a net importer.

50. The only systematic ethnographic work on Mandatory Palestine was Hilma Grandqvist's study of the village of 'Artas, *Marriage Conditions in a Palestinian Village.*

51. The relevant studies of villages in the region of Palestine and adjoining territories include Antoun, *Arab Village;* Cohen, *Arab Border Villages in Israel;* Gulick, *Social Structure and Culture Change in a Lebanese Village;* and Lutfiyya, *Baytin.* The articles by Rosenfeld on which this section is based include "From Peasantry to Wage Labor," "Change, Barriers to Change, and Contradictions in the Arab Village Family," "The Contradiction Between Property, Kinship and Power as Reflected in the Marriage System of an Arab Village."

CHAPTER 3: *Arab Progress and Jewish Settlement*

1. Particularly with respect to the description of the underdeveloped character of Arab agriculture and the reasons for its condition; cf. Porath, *Palestinian Arab National Movement*, pp. 80–86. I am not suggesting that Jewish and government observers were usually in agreement on all matters of fact or of interpretation regarding the condition of Arabs, though there were many topics on which government and Jewish writers reached similar conclusions.

2. Sawer, "Extracts," p. 1.

3. Great Britain, Colonial Office, *Report of the Commission on the Palestine Disturbances of August, 1929*, pp. 113–24. Hereafter cited as Shaw Commission.

4. Government of Palestine, *Report of a Committee on the Economic Condition of Agriculturalists in Palestine and the Fiscal Measures of Government in Relation Thereto*, pp. 21, 57. (Cited hereafter as Johnson-Crosbie). This report also provided the basis for Hope Simpson's conclusion, based on a misunderstanding of its findings, that 29.4 percent of Arab peasant cultivators were landless; see Johnson-Crosbie, p. 21, and Hope Simpson, p. 26. This estimate of the proportion of landless Arabs appeared repeatedly in subsequent reports, despite the efforts of the Jewish Agency to demonstrate its inaccuracy.

5. For a discussion of *musha'a*, see chapter 4 below.

6. The data presented on the distribution of holdings by size appear to be incorrect. Johnson and Crosbie took the feddan, the amount of land that could be cultivated by a peasant with a yoke of oxen, as equivalent to 120 dunums and concluded that 16 percent of the owner-cultivators held two or more feddans of land. But the amount of land held by the 3,873 households in this category would, by this criterion, have amounted to at least 930,000 dunums, more than half the total amount of land owned by all the villagers in the survey, including those who cultivated smaller holdings.

7. Great Britain, Colonial Office, *Palestine Royal Commission Report*, p. 71. Hereafter cited as Peel Commission.

8. Government of Palestine, *Report by Mr. C. F. Strickland of the Indian Civil Service*, pp. 2, 4. Hereafter cited as Strickland.

9. Government of Palestine, *Agricultural Development and Land Settlement in Palestine*, pp. 31–32, 64. Hereafter cited as French.

10. Great Britain, Colonial Office, *Palestine Partition Commission Report*, p. 244. Hereafter cited as Partition Commission.

11. Horowitz and Hinden, *Economic Development of Palestine*, p. 203.

12. Ibid., p. 17.

13. CZA/S25/10.342, A. Bonné, "Arab-Jewish Economic Interrelations in Palestine," pp. 3–4.

14. Ibid., pp. 14–18.

15. CZA/S90/76, David Horowitz, "Jewish Colonization and Arab Development in Palestine," October 7, 1945.

16. CZA/S90/62, L. Samuel, "Agricultural Policy as an Instrument for the Promotion of an Understanding Between Jews and Arabs in Palestine," January 31, 1945, pp. 2, 9.

17. Peel Commission, p. 35.

18. CZA/A202/154, A. Granovsky, "Bemerkungen zu dem Bericht von Mr. Lewis French . . . ," July 5, 1932, p. 4.

19. Government of Palestine, *Palestine Royal Commission, Notes of Evidence*, par. 493. Hereafter cited as *Evidence*.

20. CZA/S25/10.065, Leonard Stein to Bernard Joseph, December 4, 1936.

21. Both the Shaw Commission and the Partition Commission agreed that only the land requirements of the *existing* Arab population needed to be considered. Shaw Commission, p. 123; Partition Commission, p. 30.

22. Jewish Agency for Palestine, *Land and Agricultural Development in Palestine. Memorandum Submitted to Sir John Hope Simpson*, p. 9. Hereafter cited as Jewish Agency memo to Hope Simpson.

23. Granovsky, *Land Problem and the Future*, p. 25.

24. Granovsky, *Land Issue in Palestine*, p. 80.

25. CZA/S25/4687, Hexter to Shertok, October 23, 1936.

26. Jewish Agency for Palestine, *Memorandum . . . on the Reports of Mr. Lewis French*, p. 70. Hereafter cited as Jewish Agency memo on French.

27. *Evidence*, par. 718.

28. CZA/A185/93, "Protection of Tenants and Cultivators," pp. 1–2; Jewish Agency memo on French, pp. 66–67.

29. Peel Commission, p. 64.

30. *Evidence*, par. 719–27.

31. CZA/S90/130, A. Bonné, "The Land Problem in Palestine," February 5, 1939, pp. 8–9.

32. Horowitz, "Colonization," pp. 73–97; CZA/Z4/17.009, D. Horowitz, "The Land Problem in Palestine," March 1939, p. 2.

33. CZA/S25/6916, "Land Policy in Palestine," n.d., pp. 41–42.

34. Horowitz and Hinden, *Economic Development of Palestine*, pp. 4–5.

35. Granovsky, "Bemerkungen," p. 7.

36. Samuel, "Agricultural Policy," pp. 4–7.

37. Jewish Agency memo on French, pp. 78–79.

38. "Land Policy," p. 41.

39. CZA/KKL5/4630, "Visit of Sir John Hope Simpson to the Keren Kayemeth Leisrael," June 17, 1930, p. 2; Jewish Agency memo to Hope Simpson, p. 6.

40. French, p. 19.

41. Horowitz and Hinden, *Economic Development of Palestine*, p. 204.

42. Samuel, "Agricultural Policy," p. 7.

43. French, p. 19.

44. Kisch, *Palestine Diary*, entry dated Aug. 17, 1930.

45. CZA/KKL5/4631, "Analysis of Hope Simpson's Report," chapter 1, p. 1 (in Hebrew); CZA/A202/154, A. Ruppin, "Bemerkungen zum French Report," p. 2; Jewish Agency for Palestine, *Memorandum to the Palestine Royal Commission*, pp. 168–70, for criticism of the concept of the lot viable (hereafter cited as Jewish Agency memo to Royal Commission).

46. Jewish Agency memo on French, p. 30.

47. Stein, *Memorandum on the "Report of the Commission on the Palestine Disturbances of August, 1929,"* p. 102. Hereafter cited as Stein memo.

48. CZA/KKL5/4631, Yosef Weitz, "Agricultural Colonization in the Hill Country," n.d., pp. 19–20.

49. "Land Policy," p. 41.

50. CZA/A107/299, A. Ruppin, "The Palestine Development Scheme—How Things Are Seen from the Jewish Side," 1932, p. 5.

51. Horowitz, "Colonization," p. 40.

52. CZA/S90/633, L. Samuel, "Arab Agriculture and Its Development Between 1931 and 1945," July 21, 1947, p. 8.

53. CZA/S25/6482, "Arab Evidence Submitted to United Nations Special Committee on Palestine," 1946. Cited hereafter as "Arab Case to UNSCOP."

54. CZA/S25/10.690, "Memorandum from Jamall Husseini to Permanent Mandates Commission," October 6, 1924.

55. CZA/S25/665, Palestine Arab Congress, "Report on the State of Palestine During Four Years of Civil Administration," submitted to the Permanent Mandates Commission, October 6, 1924, p. 7.

56. Cf. Shim'oni, *Arvei Eretz Yisrael*, pp. 407–08; Waschitz, *HaAravim BeEretz Yisrael*, pp. 260–61.

57. ISA/Daily Press Abstracts/*Falastin*, June 19, 1932.

58. *Falastin*, English edition, August 23, 1930, p. 2.

59. Ibid., February 21 and February 28, 1931.

60. Ibid., November 23, 1929.

61. Ibid., August 16 and August 30, 1930; May 16, 1931.

62. CZA/S25/10.690, Awni Abdul Hadi to High Commissioner, March 10, 1933, pp. 11ff.

63. Mansur, *Arab Worker*, p. 22.

64. "Arab Case to UNSCOP," C.32(v), p. 2.

65. *Evidence*, par. 5615.

66. "Arab Case to UNSCOP," C.32(v), p. 2.

67. Awni Abdul Hadi to High Commissioner, p. 4.

68. Ibid., p. 5.

69. "Arab Case to UNSCOP," C.32(v), p. 2.

70. Abcarius, *Palestine Through the Fog of Propaganda*, p. 14.

71. Ibid., p. 148.

72. Ibid., p. 146. A Lebanese participant in a 1951 University of Wisconsin conference on land tenure made a similar point: "Our farmer is tired, discouraged, desperate and helpless. He is in a complete state of apathy. Many writers have misunderstood this state of apathy in our part of the world and have erroneously called it fatalism. Fatalism is not the cause of the distress of our farmer. . . . His distress is caused by the various land tenure problems we have had. The hundreds of thousands of Lebanon farmers who have emigrated to the various parts of the world have certainly proved that they were not deterred by fatalism. They have proved that they are just as hard-working and industrious as their fellow-men." Najib Alamuddin, "Practical Proposals for the Solution of Land Tenure Problems in Lebanon," in Kenneth H. Parsons, et al., eds., *Land Tenure*.

73. Peel Commission, p. 218.

74. Ibid.

75. Ibid., p. 225.

76. Plans for a census in 1936 were abandoned because of the Arab general strike and rebellion, so that the 1931 census was the last carried out in Mandatory Palestine.

77. Hope Simpson, p. 69.

78. Ironically, the definition of "landlessness" adopted for the purpose of the landless Arab inquiry *restricted* the possible number of persons who could qualify for the category, thus working *against* the government's desire to keep Arabs on the land. The Jewish Agency's efforts to restrict the definition of "landlessness" as a way of supporting its claim that Jewish purchases had dispossessed few Arabs also had a paradoxical result: they reduced the number of Arabs who might have benefited from the compensation offered under the arrangement and thereby been able to establish themselves in nonagricultural

occupations rather than hoping to return to the land. Kenneth Stein claims that the restrictive definition represented a political victory for the Jews, who argued against a more inclusive definition. Stein, *Land Question in Palestine*, p. 148.

79. The deterioration of the political situation in Palestine following the end of the Second World War ultimately created the conditions that prevented most Arabs who had lived in the portion of Palestine that became Israel from returning home after the 1948 war. The contradictions in the Jewish proposals became irrelevant in the new situation, but the view of Palestinian Arab society which they implied affected the policies of the Israeli government toward the remaining Arab population after 1948.

CHAPTER 4: *Views of Palestine*

1. Owen, *Studies in the Economic and Social History of Palestine*, pp. 1, 4.

2. E.g., the surveys published by the Royal Institute of International Affairs, or the ESCO report.

3. Two recent works which appeared in Hebrew provide a great deal of information about alternate views of Arab society during the Mandate. Yosef Gorny's *HaShe'alah HaAravit Ve'HaBa'aya HaYehudit* [The Arab Question and the Jewish Problem] provides a comprehensive discussion of the range of political views, from right to left, held by the Jewish parties during the Mandate, but gives little attention to social and economic analysis. Tamar Gozansky, in *Hitpatchut HaKapitalism BePalestina* [Formation of Capitalism in Palestine], argues that the history of Palestine during the Mandate was an example of colonial development supported and underwritten by foreign interests—first British, and after 1948, American. I am unable to accept Gozansky's basic argument about the colonial nature of Mandatory Palestine, for the reasons I present later in this chapter.

4. HaShomer HaTza'ir was a pioneering youth movement established in Austria and in Russian Poland during the First World War. Its membership in Palestine had by the mid-1920s evolved an ideology which drew on Marxist thought and represented a synthesis between Zionism and socialism, between pioneering construction and class war.

5. Greenbaum, "On the Development of Agrarian Relations in Palestine," December 1, 1936, p. 11 (in Hebrew). The analysis of Ottoman Palestine is Greenbaum's.

6. Flapan, "On the Development of the Arab Village"; "The Arab Village and Jewish Settlement" (both in Hebrew). Flapan, also a member of kibbutz Gan Shmuel, was a prominent figure in MAPAM, the major left-wing Jewish political party, and director of its Arab Affairs Department after Israel was established.

The analysis which follows of feudal society in Palestine and its transformation is Flapan's.

7. Flapan, "The Arab Village and Jewish Settlement."

8. Ibid., p. 4.

9. Especially the section on Palestine during the late Ottoman era, pp. 264 ff.

10. Owen, *The Middle East*, pp. 178–79, 264–67, 272.

11. Schölch, "European penetration," p. 55.

12. Graham-Brown, "Political Economy of the Jabal Nablus, 1920–48."

13. See Zureik, *Palestinians in Israel.*

14. Lord Hailey, *African Survey*, p. 717. I refer frequently to Hailey's volume in the following discussion, since it provides a systematic account of the situation in Britain's African colonies during the same period that the Mandate over Palestine was in effect.

15. Gurevich, *Statistical Handbook*, pp. 138–39.

16. Hailey, *African Survey*, pp. 723 (table), 726, 730, 737, table 8, 741, table 9.

17. Ibid., p. 764, Tanganyika; p. 771, Northern Nigeria; p. 779, Gold Coast.

18. Taqqu, *Arab Labor*, pp. 42 ff. The discussion in the following paragraph also draws on Taqqu's work.

19. Brookfield, *Interdependent Development*, pp. 54–55.

20. Boeke, *Economics and Economic Policy of Dual Societies*, chaps. 1–3. As often happens to concepts in the social sciences, the notion of dualism was extended to situations which, although seemingly analogous to its original referent, were nevertheless different. Writing in 1970, H. W. Singer argued that "dualism in the sense of persistent and increasing divergencies exists on various levels, internationally in relations between richer and poorer countries, and internally within the developing countries themselves" ("Dualism Revisited," p. 60). The idea of dualism as referring to the internal differentiation of a national economy has also been used in studies of industrial societies (see Hodson and Kaufman, "Economic Dualism," p. 728). These reformulations, however, are not relevant to the situation in Palestine.

21. James C. Scott has noted that the apparently "economically irrational" behavior of peasants can be viewed as a special case of opportunity cost of peasant labor and the high marginal utility of income for those near the subsistence level (*Moral Economy of the Peasant*, pp. 14–15).

22. Even after 1948, economic separatism between Jews and Arabs remained Israeli government policy. After 1967, on the other hand, Arabs in the occupied territories of the West Bank and Gaza moved much more rapidly into the Jewish economy. Part of the difference might be due to the desire, immedi-

ately after 1948, to minimize the perceived "security risk" that would be posed by economic integration of Arabs in the Jewish economy, which would have meant a weakening of the territorial segregation of the two communities. Arabs from the West Bank and Gaza after 1967, on the other hand, had much less interest in and possibility to move into Jewish areas. It is interesting to speculate what might have happened, in terms of economic relations, had the terms of the Mandate led to Jewish control over a part of Palestine, or had a much larger Arab population remained in Israel after 1948. It may be that military considerations would have distorted the development of economic relationships, and that a development in a "colonial" economic direction would therefore have been less likely to occur.

23. Sussman, "The Determination of Wages"; Metzer, "Fiscal Incidence and Resource Transfer"; Metzer and Kaplan, "Jointly but Severally."

24. For example, although the proportion of the population which was urban was much greater for Jews than for Arabs throughout the Mandate, the absolute number of Arab and Jewish town dwellers was much more equal; thus, a substantial portion of the Jewish population, as well as many Arabs, lived in close proximity to each other, a situation which changed radically after 1948.

25. Their intention was different than the use I am making of their findings, which I am reinterpreting in a manner that stresses the economic links between Arabs and Jews rather than the differences.

26. Sussman, "The Determination of Wages," pp. 109–10.

27. Metzer and Kaplan, "Jointly but Severally," p. 334. Arabs and Jews sat together on a committee of citrus exporters.

28. Ibid., p. 338.

29. Ibid., p. 341. They go on to say that "both of these factors are much weaker in extent and effect in contemporary Israel and, indeed, the weight of Arab employment from the administered areas in the Israeli economy is very large. For example, in 1980 it made for no less than 35 and 20 percent of the administered areas' total employment and gross national product."

30. Metzer, "Fiscal Incidence and Resource Transfer," p. 119.

31. Ibid., pp. 102–04, 118.

32. Ibid., pp. 118–24.

33. It is extremely difficult, in any discussion of Mandatory Palestine, to avoid speaking of the Arab and Jewish "sectors" or "economies," since there were many areas of social and economic life in which there was little day-to-day contact between members of the two communities. I do not wish my usage of these terms to imply that I accept what I seem explicitly to reject. The real issue is whether Mandatory Palestine is viewed as a single economic entity, as I think it should be.

CHAPTER 5: *Landholding*

1. Wolf, *Peasants*, pp. 55–56.

2. Moses J. Doukhan, "Land Tenure," in Himadeh, *Economic Organization of Palestine*, p. 77.

3. Granott, *Land System in Palestine*, p. 174.

4. Patai, "Musha'a Tenure," p. 441.

5. *Evidence*, par. 594.

6. Government of Palestine, *Average Tithe Committee Report*, p. 8.

7. Johnson-Crosbie, p. 45. (This estimate was apparently misunderstood by Hope Simpson who transformed it into 46 percent of the villages, rather than the land; cf. Hope Simpson, p. 33. The error was subsequently perpetuated, though it had no practical consequences, unlike Hope Simpson's estimate of the proportion of landless Arabs.

8. French, p. 12.

9. CZA/A107/299, A. Ruppin, "The Palestine Development Scheme— How Things Are Seen from the Jewish Side," 1932, p. 12.

10. Patai, "Musha'a Tenure," p. 441.

11. Granott, *Land System in Palestine*, p. 174.

12. CZA/A202/154, M. Smilansky, "Comments on the French Report," p. 2 (in Hebrew).

13. Wolf, *Peasants*, pp. 78–80.

14. Antoun, *Arab Village*, p. 23.

15. Warriner, *Land and Poverty*, pp. 19, 66–67.

16. Firestone, "Crop-sharing Economics," pt. I, p. 18, n. 7.

17. Baer, *Mavo LeToldot HaYachasim HaAgrari'im BeMizrah HaTichon, 1800–1970*, pp. 69–71.

18. Granott, *Land System in Palestine*, pp. 72, 179.

19. Held, "Effects of the Ottoman Land Laws," pp. 190–93.

20. Lambton, *Landlord and Peasant in Persia*, p. 6.

21. Robinson, *Rural Russia Under the Old Regime*, pp. 74 ff.

22. Firestone, "Land Equalization."

23. Abcarius, *Palestine Through the Fog of Propaganda*, pp. 128–29.

24. Ibid., p. 19; Hyamson, *Palestine Under the Mandate*, p. 84.

25. Kolchin, *Unfree Labor*, p. 205.

26. Graham-Brown, "Political Economy of the Jabal Nablus," p. 125.

27. Himadeh, *Economic Organization of Palestine*, p. 106.

28. Abcarius, *Palestine Through the Fog of Propaganda*, pp. 128–29.

29. ISA/RG27/2689/T158, Thabet Khalidi to Settlement Officer, Haifa area, November 30, 1933.

30. CZA/S25/4687, Shertok to Chairman, Palestine Royal Commission, Pol/31/37, February 17, 1937.

31. ISA/RG27/2599/2/2, Land Settlement Taiyiba/Moledet.

32. CZA/A202/146 (this material was apparently prepared for Granott's analysis of the land system of Palestine; many of the examples in his book are drawn from this list).

33. Great Britain, Foreign Office, *Maps Relating to the Report of the Anglo-American Committee.*

34. Ibid.; Government of Palestine, *Village Statistics*, 1945. The data on Jewish *musha'a* holdings were taken from the map of lands in Jewish possession at the end of 1944.

35. ISA/RG27/2626/G216/III, Settlement Officer, Galilee, to Department of Land Settlement, April 4, 1946.

36. "1944 Survey," December 1945, pp. 762–63.

37. Since settlement of title had been carried out in this village a decade earlier, the biennial repartitioning of parcels was probably due to the particular circumstances of the plots and their owners.

38. For examples of fragmentation of holdings, see Granott, *Land System in Palestine*, pp. 202–12.

39. CZA/Z4/1260. One Turkish dunum equalled 0.919 metric dunums; thus, the total area of these estates was slightly more than 1.3 million metric dunums.

40. Total and cultivable area: Hope Simpson, p. 23; Peel Commission, p. 235.

41. Gurevich, *Statistical Handbook*, p. 136.

42. Not all the land on these estates was cultivable. The total estimate of cultivable land includes state lands; for the purpose of the computation I assumed that the uncultivable area of the large estates balanced the cultivable area of the state lands.

43. Ruppin, "Palestine Development Scheme," p. 9.

44. Ibid., p. 7.

45. "1944 Survey," January–March 1946, p. 55.

46. CZA/Z4/771-I, "List of Large Estates in Palestine."

47. Stein, *Land Question in Palestine*, p. 179.

48. Moshe Smilansky claimed in 1930 that 250 families owned large estates totaling more than 4 million dunums. He doesn't indicate his source for this claim, and it seems greatly exaggerated (Comments on the French Report, p. 2).

49. "List of Large Estates in Palestine."

50. "1944 Survey," January–March 1946, p. 55.

51. Gerber, *Social Origins of the Modern Middle East*, pp. 72–73.

52. Ibid., p. 79.

53. Ibid., p. 80. A few years ago Yoram Bar-Gal and Shmuel Shamai doubted whether the Jezre'el Valley was as marshy and deserted as it has usually been portrayed in Zionist writings (see "Bitzot Emeq-Yizra'el"). The more developed the land, of course, the better the deal made by the Sursoqs and similar purchasers—and by Jewish organizations who purchased the land from them in turn.

54. Kolchin's recent comparison of slavery in the American south and Russian serfdom was a fruitful source for many of the ideas which are developed in this section (Kolchin, *Unfree Labor*).

55. Jewish Agency for Palestine, *Financial Aspects of Jewish Reconstruction*, p. 6.

56. CZA/KKL5/1041/Statistiqa Qarqa'it, "List of P.J.C.A. Colonies and Lands Available for Settlement."

57. Ibid.

58. Stein, *Land Question in Palestine*, p. 60.

59. Peel Commission, p. 126.

60. *Financial Aspects of Jewish Reconstruction*, p. 12.

61. Stein, *Land Question in Palestine*, p. 181.

62. French, p. 19.

63. CZA/A202/154, A. Ruppin, "Bemerkungen zum French Report," p. 8.

64. Gurevich, *Statistical Handbook*, p. 135.

65. Ibid., p. 129.

66. Washitz, *HaAravim BeEretz Yisrael*, pp. 54–60.

67. Johnson-Crosbie, pp. 18–20. In a 1928 analysis Volcani estimated the cost of living at £P 49.50, without including debt (*The Fellah's Farm*, p. 49). My criticism in the next chapter of the Johnson-Crosbie estimates does not undermine the analysis in this paragraph.

68. The total number of Arab earners in these categories was 75,303; cf. *Census of Palestine, 1931*, vol. 2, pt. 2, pp. 282–83.

69. *Vital Statistics*, p. 5.

70. Peel Commission, pp. 127, 269.

71. 56,399 tons $\times$ 0.77 (the Arab share of the 1944/45 crop) $\times$ .788 (tons per dunum from Arab vegetable growing, 1944/45)

72. Mandel, *The Arabs and Zionism*, p. 229.

73. *Survey of Palestine*, p. 289.

74. Stein, *Land Question in Palestine*, p. 212.

75. Ibid., p. 158.

76. Ibid., pp. 156–57.

77. Ibid., p. 181.

78. *Survey of Palestine*, p. 244.

79. The problem with my estimate is the lack of evidence regarding the

relation between the size of the holding which was sold, and the likelihood that the holding supported a family of cultivators. The smaller areas sold could represent portions of family holdings, or they could be sales of the entire holding. Nor is there information regarding whether the larger holdings supported tenants who had no land elsewhere, or insufficient land to support them following the sales referred to here. If there was in fact no surplus cultivable land in Palestine, as the Arabs as well as many government officials argued, would it have been possible for more than 400,000 dunums to have been sold between 1930 and 1945 without displacing a number of Arabs which is extremely difficult to estimate? Most of the land sold during this period, especially in the latter part of it, was probably not only cultivable but under cultivation, since the major land-reclamation operations had been carried out by the Jews before 1930.

80. The estimate assumes, of course, that both the distribution of land sales by size and the mean size of sale remained constant during the entire period. In the data presented by Stein, the mean size of sale for the portions covered of the three years 1934, 1935, and 1936 was 17.1, 15.6, and 12.4 dunums, respectively. In 1938 there were 383 sales by Arabs to Jews of holdings less than 100 dunums each; the mean size of the holdings was 19.7 dunums (Government of Palestine, *Report on the Administration of Palestine and Trans-Jordan*, 1937, p. 76).

81. Stein, *Land Question in Palestine*, pp. 51–53.

82. *Survey of Palestine*, pp. 260, 289–93.

83. Peel Commission, p. 220.

84. Partition Commission, p. 28.

85. See Hexter's comments on Granovsky's 1936 memorandum, cited above, chapter 3, note 25.

86. *Statistical Abstract*, 1939, p. 162. The calculation is as follows:

Total land purchased by Jews	579,740 d.
Total land sold by Jews	314,043 d.
Balance (purchased from Arabs)	265,697 d.
Total land sold by Arabs	516,680 d.
Balance (purchased by Arabs from Arabs)	250,983 d.

Palestine Jews and Arabs together sold 830,723 dunums during 1932–1938, and bought 805,773 dunums. The difference was bought by the other three participants in the land market: foreigners, municipalities, and government. The total difference of 25,000 dunums is too small to affect my conclusion regarding the extent of land transfers among Arabs themselves.

87. The mukhtar was a villager appointed by the government to perform certain administrative and registration functions. He was usually the head of a principal *hamula* and often possessed considerable informal authority. Some larger villages may have had more than one mukhtar. *Waqf* land is land dedicated in perpetuity to some pious purpose; "the usufruct alone is applied for the benefit of human beings and the subject of the dedication becomes inalienable and non-hereditable in perpetuity" (Himadeh, *Economic Organization of Palestine*, p. 88).

88. The information was collected in the summer of 1936. Data from the Rural Property Tax records were entered onto cards which were sorted to determine the average holding in the country as a whole, and the figures were then given to the Statistical Department. Data were sorted by villages; thus, persons holding plots of land in more than one village were counted in each of them, and the data do not reflect the total holdings of a particular person. They also underestimate somewhat the average size of a holding. See *Evidence*, par. 408–16.

89. "1944 Survey," January–March 1946, p. 55.

90. Kendall, *Village Development in Palestine*, pp. 49–52, and in Granott's files, CZA/A202/146. It is noteworthy that both Kendall and Granott refer to the same region, but I do not know whether this is any more than a coincidence.

91. CZA/A202/150, "Number of Owners According to Holding Size in Metric Dunums" (in Hebrew).

92. Peel Commission, map 3.

93. Of the 14 localities excluded, 11 were in the Safed subdistrict: Marus (mean size of holding, 530 dunums), Jubb Yusuf (935), Zangariya (1,990), Al Shmalna (2,115), Kh. al Khakb (547), Esh Shuna (47.6), Ammuqa (515), Sab Al'an (0.7), Al Nebi Yusha' (226), and 'Abbasiyya (1,467). The remaining three were in Acre: Er Rein (1,995), Sameh (3,988), and Suwaneh (624). Sab Al'an was excluded because only 19 dunums were listed as being in private Arab ownership; this strongly suggests it was not actually a settled locality.

94. Cf. Great Britain, Colonial Office, CO 733/18, "Land Settlement Commission's Report," February 10, 1922, p. 615.

95. Using five for the mean household size is somewhat arbitrary; the 1944 village survey found 6.4 persons per household, and according to Granott (*Land System in Palestine*, p. 182) the 1931 census determined the size of an agricultural household as 4.5. No reasonable figure, however, will greatly reduce the difference shown in the table.

96. These findings also support the explanation of *musha'a* tenure as being connected with a more egalitarian peasant community.

97. *Evidence*, par. 409.

98. Ibid., par. 411.

99. Ibid., par. 414.

100. Villages for which Kendall provides information include Asita Esh-Shamaliya, Bazouriye, Beit Iba, Beit Umrin, Biet Wazan, Burqa, Deir Sharaf, Ijnisinya, Judeid, Ed Naqura, Nisf Jubeil, Qusin, Rafidya, Sabastya, and Zawata in the Nablus subdistrict; Anabta, Bal'a, Beit Lid, Danna[ba], Kafr el-Labad, Kafr Rumman, Famin, and Shuweika[t] in the Tulkarm subdistrict. Villages for which information appears in Granott's files include Atara, Beit Lid, Kh. Beit Lid, Bal'a, Foroun, Kafr El-Labad, Shufa, Zeita, Deir el Ghusun, Il'ar, Tira, Misr, Kafr Rumman, Qafin, Safarin, Atil, Qalqilya, Dannaba, Irtah, Anabta, Shuweikat and Qaqun in Tulkarm SD; Silat el Dahr, Sanur, and Sir in the Jenin subdistrict; and Burqa in the Nablus subdistrict.

101. See Abramowitz, "Wartime Development," p. 133.

102. Kendall is describing the situation in the "summer" of 1941, but he does not indicate whether harvesting has begun. Many of the jobs seem to be of a permanent character, though it may have been possible to take time off to return to the village and help bring in the crops.

103. Granott, *Land System in Palestine*, p. 182. According to the 1936 survey of 322 villages, almost 99 percent of the holdings were smaller than 500 dunums, while those 500 dunums or larger comprised about one-third of the total village area.

104. "1944 Survey," December 1945, p. 752; January–March 1946, p. 49.

105. Compare this with the figures for mean holding size in the "1944 Survey," January–March 1946, p. 56, which are slightly larger than those I obtain.

106. Ibid., p. 50.

107. Smilansky claimed that villages near Rehovot intensified cultivation after selling some of their lands to Jews. See "Comments on the French Report," pp. 11–15.

108. CZA/S25/10.065, Leonard Stein to Bernard Joseph, December 4, 1936.

109. *Evidence*, par. 2680.

110. Peel Commission, p. 269.

111. *Statistical Abstract*, 1942, p. 142; ibid., 1944/45, p. 272.

112. There are problems with using the *Village Statistics* to get evidence for upgrading of lands. Higher tax payments on land which was upgraded did not go into effect for a number of years, depending on the nature of the improvement— six years for land previously regarded as uncultivable being brought under cultivation, and ten years for land newly planted with fruit trees other than citrus or bananas (see *Survey of Palestine*, p. 253). It may nevertheless have been likely that not all cases of land being upgraded were brought to the attention of the relevant government departments so that the tax category could be changed. A second difficulty lies in the uncertainty concerning the exact area of land in Palestine and the extent of state lands. The continuation of survey and

settlement-of-title operations changed the categorization of land in many areas without the degree of its cultivability having changed, and this fact makes comparison of the 1937 and 1945 data questionable. Finally, the tax categories are fairly broad, and land in a particular classification (such as No. 8, "1st Grade ground crop land, 4th Grade irrigated land and 4th Grade fruit plantation," taxed in 1944/45 at 25 mils per dunum (*Statistical Abstract*, 1944/45, p. 272) could have been used for irrigated vegetable cultivation rather than cereals without this being reflected in the statistics.

113. It should be remembered that the tax category to which the land was assigned was not necessarily descriptive of the use to which it was being put at any particular time, but reflected its immediate productive potential. Thus, the data in table 13 should not be taken to represent the total area under production at any period. The best example of the relation between the tax categories and production was the case of citrus groves during the Second World War, when export was almost impossible and production was severely curtailed. The total amount of land in the "citrus" tax category remained unchanged between 1938 and 1944/45, but the tax on citrus lands was reduced in 1939/40 from 400 to 150 mils per dunum, and after 1940 was remitted annually for the entire country (*Survey of Palestine*, p. 253).

114. *Village Statistics*, 1937; ibid., 1945.

115. The 1937 *Village Statistics* do not present separately Arab and other lands held by non-Jews, nor do they show separately lands in government ownership. My calculations assume that practically all the land classified in the 1937 *Village Statistics* as owned by "non-Jews" was owned by Arabs. I am aware of the arguments regarding the existence of unrecorded land transfers from Arabs to Jews following the imposition of restrictions on Jewish land purchase in 1940; such transfers, which would not be reflected in the *Village Statistics*, make comparisons even more difficult.

116. Villages were included in the comparison if they met the following criteria: (1) Equal or almost equal total land in the period 1937–1945 or 1943–1945. (2) Either no public land in 1945, or an amount of public land which was considerably less than either the difference between the total land in the two periods, or the difference between the total amount of Arab land in the two periods. This minimizes the possibility that changes in the distribution of Arab cultivation might be due to reclassification of part of the village's lands as "public." (3) The amount of land in Jewish ownership in the later of the pair of years was greater than the amount of Jewish land in the earlier year; no lower limit was set on the amount of increase in Jewish land.

117. CZA/S90/62, L. Samuel, "Agricultural Policy as an Instrument for the Promotion of an Understanding Between Jews and Arabs in Palestine," January 31, 1945, p. 3.

118. Jewish Agency memo on French, p. 57.

119. "1944 Survey," January–March, 1946, p. 55.

120. CZA/S25/10.342, A. Bonné, "Arab-Jewish Economic Interrelations in Palestine," p. 18.

121. Avneri, *HaHitvashvut HaYehudit VeTa'anat HaNishul*, 1980.

122. Johnson-Crosbie, pp. 14, 26.

123. Other estimates of the average peasant debt put it as high as £P50 (Jewish Agency memo to Hope Simpson, p. 34). Volcani assumed that the cost of planting a dunum of orange grove was £P20, not £P10 as Ruppin believed; another Jewish Agency estimate concluded that £P192 was required for the development of seven dunums of groves.

124. Ibid., p. 18.

125. Ibid., pp. 33–34.

126. Ibid., p. 35.

127. Ibid.

128. CZA/A185/93, "Land Settlement Policy (continued). IV. Protection of Tenants and Cultivators," p. 11.

129. CZA/S55/155, Wilkanski to Ruppin, December 16, 1930, p. 4.

130. CZA/A202/154, A. Granovsky, "Bemerkungen zu dem Bericht von Mr. Lewis French . . . ," p. 6.

131. Gurevich, *Statistical Handbook*, p. 137.

132. CZA/Z4/3419A, Felix Green to Zionist Bureau, London, April 21, 1931.

133. CZA/Z4/3419A, Kisch, February 24, 1931; Smilansky to Kisch, March 1, 1931; Wilkansky to Kisch, March 2, 1931; Botkovsky to Kisch, March 3, 1931; Thon to Kisch, March 4, 1931, June 2, 1931.

134. Avneri, *HaHityashvut HaYehudit VeTa'anat HaNishul*, p. 249.

135. Gurevich, *Statistical Handbook*, p. 140.

136. Data on Jewish land purchases, 1920–1930, are in CZA/S19/158.

137. Granovsky, *Land and the Jewish Reconstruction*, p. 84.

138. CZA/KKL5/4631, PICA, Haifa office, to KKL, Jerusalem, AD/K/1, November 25, 1930.

139. Granovsky, *Land and the Jewish Reconstruction*, p. 84.

140. Granovsky, *Land Issue in Palestine*, p. 43.

141. Jewish Agency memo to Royal Commission, p. 139.

142. Granovsky, *Land Issue in Palestine*, p. 44.

143. Granovsky, *Land and the Jewish Reconstruction*, p. 85.

144. In *Land System in Palestine*, p. 182, Granott sets 500 dunums as the upper limit for a "medium" sized holding; larger areas would thus be considered "large holdings."

145. French, p. 19.

146. Stein, *Land Question in Palestine*, p. 179.

147. Ibid., p. 182.

148. CZA/S19/158, *Statistical Abstract*, 1939, p. 162; Ibid., 1944/45, p. 275; ISA/RG2/CS/L/189/46.

149. "1944 Survey," January–March, 1946, p. 55.

150. CZA/KKL5/4634, "Compensation Paid to Tenants on Lands Bought by PLDC in Jezre'el Valley and Acre Plain." Hereafter cited as "Compensation Paid to Tenants."

151. CZA/S25/10.065, "Lists of Persons Who Received Compensation for Jezre'el Valley and Acre Plain Land." Hereafter cited as "Lists of Persons."

152. My transliteration is based on the Hebrew spelling of the village names on the lists in the file. I don't know how dispossessed tenants could have settled in Mejdel, which was one of the villages whose lands had been bought by the Jews. Perhaps the reference is to Mujeidel, a village near Nazareth.

153. The computations regarding the fate of those dispossessed from lands in the Jezre'el Valley and in the Acre Plain are based on "Lists of Persons"; the total of 688 tenants which is usually taken to represented the number of those who received compensation seems to be an error based on a misnumbering of the names on the lists in the file. A summary of what became of 688 families appears in Granovsky, *Land and the Jewish Reconstruction*, p. 89, but the information presented there differs from that obtained from my computations based on the lists for individual localities.

154. Jewish Agency memo on French, p. 31.

155. £E = Egyptian pound, about 2 percent less than the Palestine pound which supplanted it as legal tender in Palestine.

156. CZA/S25/7622a through 7622d. The information on the application forms seems sometimes to be incorrect. Tenants who had already ploughed their holdings for sowing usually received compensation for the work they had done.

157. Granovsky, *Land and the Jewish Reconstruction*, pp. 91–92.

158. Ibid.

159. "Compensation Paid to Tenants."

160. "Lists of Persons."

161. See "Land Settlement Policy," p. 3.

162. CZA/S25/7622a through 7622d.

163. The comparison of the two lists of names was made difficult by the fact that the names of those who received compensation had been transliterated from Arabic into Hebrew, while the names of applicants to the register of landless Arabs had been transliterated into English. Nor was it certain that the identical form of the original Arabic name had been used in each of the lists. When in doubt about the identity of a pair of names, I counted them as different. This may have resulted in an underestimate of the number of persons appearing on

both lists. Of 111 applicants to the register whose names did not appear on the list of those receiving compensation, 35 had the same last names as others whose names did appear on the compensation lists.

164. CZA/L18/162/1, "List of Lands Offered for Sale, by Villages and Districts," July 15, 1923.

165. CZA/A238/16/7, "Accounting of Payments to Tenants, Yoqne'am" (in Hebrew). The mean compensation for the Yoqne'am lands was computed excluding twenty payments made as "expenses," which were almost certainly not intended as compensation, and the two final amounts on the list of £P300 each, which seem also to have been payments made for purposes other than compensation for land. Not all the tenants accepted compensation and left by 1936. Peretz Levinger describes the long process by which Arabs remaining on Yoqne'am's lands were finally removed. It was not until March 1948 that the remaining Arab cultivators fled after the failure of Kaukji's attack on Mismar HaEmeq. Levinger, "The Case of Land Purchases in the Yoqne'am Region," p. 153ff (in Hebrew).

166. CZA/Z4/771 II, Meeting Between Kisch and Stubbs, March 14, 1924.

167. CZA/S25/10.065, "The Situation of Those Who Sold Land to Jews in the Beisan Subdistrict" (in Hebrew), June 1936. W. P. N. Tyler recently showed how government policy hindered the development of the Beisan lands and raised their costs for Jewish purchasers (Tyler, "Beisan Lands Issue").

168. "The Situation of Those Who Sold Land."

169. Ibid.

170. CZA/S25/10.682, Yosef Weitz, "Regarding the Question of Dispossessing Arabs," March 1946 (in Hebrew).

CHAPTER 6: *Agriculture*

1. *Statistical Abstract*, 1939, p. 41; ibid., 1944/45, p. 226.

2. *Statistical Abstract*, 1944/45, p. 217.

3. *Survey of Palestine*, p. 310.

4. Volcani, *The Fellah's Farm*, p. 29.

5. Using the total Arab population as a basis for the computation, *Survey of Palestine*, p. 141 (Arab population taken as total population, including nomads, minus Jews).

6. Antoun, *Arab Village*, p. 14. "Kufr al-Ma" is a fictitious name.

7. The government statistical apparatus continually expanded during the Mandate, providing more detailed information in later years than it did earlier. The tables in this section are based on those published by the government at

different periods; hence, their coverage and the amount of detail they contain also varies.

8. *Survey of Palestine*, p. 310.

9. *Statistical Abstract*, 1944/45, p. 226.

10. *Survey of Palestine*, p. 326.

11. According to a summary published in 1947 by the Jewish Agency, Arab vegetable production increased from a three-year average of 11,000 tons in 1922–1924 to 205,000 tons in 1943–1945. Fruit crops, excluding citrus and olives, increased during the same period from 32,000 to 188,000 tons. See *Palestine Facts and Figures*, p. 376.

12. Yisra'eli, "On the History of Olive Cultivation and Oil Production in the Galilee and the Bet Kerem Valley," p. 105 (in Hebrew).

13. A. G. Turner, "Citrus Fruit," *Falastin* (English edition), August 23, 1930, p. 1.

14. All the other works prepared during the Mandate on Arab agricultural methods, whether they were official reports, scientific analyses, or popular accounts, relied in large measure on the data collected and presented by Volcani and by Johnson and Crosbie.

15. "The plough cannot be beaten for simplicity, lightness and suitability to the climate, to the condition of work and to the object in view. It performs at one stroke and without calling for any undue strain or effort the function of a plough, a roller and a harrow. It does not bring up clods, it makes the earth loose, it does not overturn it, it does not cause any of the moisture to evaporate, it does not bury any weeds in his passage, and of course, it does not make them grow or increase their number. When rain comes down for a long time continuously or with brief intervals, the Arab plough is the only one with which work can be done. In such conditions the European plow [with its broad iron share] does not cut the ground, but packs the dust together, makes bricks, rolls the earth into clods, and damages the ground for years. Hence in rainy years the Arab plough prolongs the working season" (pp. 47–48).

16. Abcarius, *Palestine Through the Fog of Propaganda*, pp. 151–55.

17. CZA/S53/127, Jewish Agency, D/W/12, Partition Commission, p. 35.

18. ISA/RG2/Box 16/A-10-42, Steadman Davis, document 92, July 13, 1944.

19. ISA/RG2/Box 16/A-14-4-42, "Hula Villages Tractor Ploughing Scheme"; *Palestine Agricultural Economy Under War Conditions*, p. 21.

20. ISA/RG2/Box 16/A-10-42, DC Galilee District from Controller of Agricultural Production, "Lease/Lend Tractors and Machinery Distributed to Arabs, 1943," June 17, 1944; ibid., "Distribution of Lease/Lend Tractors and Machinery Promised for 1943," June 17, 1944.

21. ISA/RG2/Box 16/A-10-42, Steadman Davis, July 13, 1944.

22. Government of Palestine, Department of Agriculture, Forests, and Fisheries, *Annual Report*, 1934, p. 23; ISA/RG7/Box 635/Ag-19-4, "Introduction: Note on the Use of Agricultural Machinery," May 28, 1935.

23. Department of Agriculture, *Annual Report*, 1935, p. 26.

24. ISA/RG7/Box 633/Ag 14, Department Agricultural Implements, October 10, 1934. The claim about the identity of the borrowers is based on comparisons of lists in this file with lists of Arab farmers having demonstration plots.

25. ISA/RG7/Box 633/Ag 14, Tractors, October 12, 1937 (Jaffa subdistrict).

26. Department of Agriculture, *Annual Report*, 1935, p. 26; ibid., 1936, p. 9.

27. ISA/RG7/Box 633/Ag 14, "Tractors Sold During 1933," n.d.; ibid., "List of Tractors Sold by British and Levant Agencies Ltd., Jaffa, During 1934."

28. Himadeh, *Economic Organization of Palestine*, p. 190.

29. ISA/RG7/Box 638/Ag 22-12, Veterinary Circular no. 700, January 27, 1934.

30. Ibid., Antebi to CAO, October 18, 1932.

31. Ibid., "Shortage of Fodder for Stock-grazing Situation," October 18, 1932. The grain harvest in 1932 was also very poor.

32. Ibid., "Forage Production in Times of Drought," December 1, 1932. The basic criterion was the feeding cost per day per animal. According to my calculations, based on the data in the memorandum, the cheapest method would have been to plant maize to be used as green fodder and as grain (8 mils per animal per day); imported fodder cost more than twice as much (17 mils per animal per day), and there were other alternatives which, though more expensive than maize as green fodder and grain were still cheaper than importing fodder. It is not clear from the memorandum how the calculations were carried out to arrive at the conclusions reached by its author.

33. Ibid., "Report of Administration, Forage Cultivation in Tiberias Subdistrict," p. 1.

34. Ibid., "Report of Administration, Forage Cultivation in Tiberias S.D.," November 30, 1932, pp. 2, 4.

35. Ibid., "Note on the Production of Fodder in Times of Drought," November 21, 1932, pp. 2, 3.

36. Ibid., p. 3.

37. Silage is a fodder produced from green maize by means of a process of anaerobic decomposition; suited particularly for dairy cattle, it would not provide the nutrition needed by plow animals, but it would prevent their starving.

38. Ibid., pp. 5–7.

39. Ibid., "Growing Maize for Green Fodder," August 7, 1933, pp. 3–4.

40. Ibid., "Fodder Committee, Minute by His Excellency the High Commissioner," June 26 and June 29, 1933.

41. "Growing Maize for Green Fodder."

42. Ibid., "Growing of Fodder," September 17, 1933, pp. 1–2.

43. Ibid., C. G. Eastwood to M. T. Dawe, November 8, 1933, p. 2.

44. Ibid., "H.E.'s Remarks Regarding Fodder," November 12, 1933, pp. 2–3.

45. Ibid., "Forage Experiments in Villages," June 25, 1934. My estimate of the number of villages is based on lists of farmers participating in fodder demonstrations. The existing files may not include all such demonstration plots on private land, either in the years covered or for additional years. The estimate of 203 localities is, therefore, probably too low. According to the government's annual report for 1932 to the League of Nations Permanent Mandates Commission, there were 57 village demonstration plots in 1931. Their number grew to 269 in the following year, 70 percent of which were in the Northern District. They included village nurseries, vegetable, potato, seed, and forage plots. See Government of Palestine, *Report on the Administration of Palestine and Trans-Jordan*, 1932, p. 179.

46. ISA/RG7/Box 638/Ag 22-12, "Propaganda for Fodder Growing," August 28, 1933; ibid., "Scheme of Fodder Demonstration Plots," September 20, 1933. Apparently demonstration schemes were sometimes initiated and then neglected; Abcarius refers to such a case involving crop rotation, manuring, and weeding (*Palestine Through the Fog of Propaganda*, pp. 151–55).

47. ISA/RG7/Box 631/Ag 10-1, Antebi to CAO, October 13, 1933; ibid., Antebi to CAO, March 8, 1933. In a circular he published in 1934, Antebi wrote that he expected yields of potatoes under dry cultivation to reach 600–800 kilos per dunum, and 800–1,000 under irrigation (*Potato Growing in Palestine*, p. 8).

48. ISA/RG7/Box 631/Ag 10-1, Masson to Superintendent, Majdal Agricultural Station, July 2, 1934.

49. Ibid., Agricultural Inspector, Jaffa, to Agricultural Officer, SC, February 25, 1933.

50. Ibid., "Potato Cultivation," April 16, 1934.

51. Ibid., "Areas Under Potatoes," March 8, 1933.

52. Ibid., "Customs Duty on Potatoes," October 13, 1933.

53. Ibid., "Areas Under Potatoes."

54. Ibid., "Potato Growing," March 3, 1931.

55. Ibid., "Customs Duty on Potatoes."

56. Ibid., "Potatoes: Increased Import Duty on," July 25, 1934; ibid., "Potatoes Increase Duty on" [sic], August 1, 1934.

57. Ibid., "Potatoes: Marketing and Prices," June 10, 1935.

58. Ibid., "Potatoes: Increased Import Duty on."

59. Himadeh, *Economic Organization of Palestine*, p. 161; ISA/RG7/Box 631/Ag 10-1, A/Agricultural Officer S.D. to Agricultural Inspector Tulkarm, August 29, 1937.

60. Johnson-Crosbie, p. 15; Himadeh, *Economic Organization of Palestine*, p. 131; Volcani, *The Fellah's Farm*, p. 55.

61. ISA/RG7/Box 631/Ag 10-1-1, "Potatoes Under Irrigation," August 30, 1937.

62. Ibid., "Potato Seed from United Kingdom," [August] 31, 1937.

63. Government of Palestine, *Report on the Administration of Palestine and Trans-Jordan*, 1923, p. 37.

64. Government of Palestine, *Commercial Bulletin*, v. 7 (n.s.), p. 105.

65. Department of Agriculture, *Annual Report*, 1934, p. 24.

66. Ibid., p. 24; ibid., 1935, p. 8; ibid., 1936, pp. 10, 23.

67. Ibid., 1944/45, p. 9.

68. Government of Palestine, *Commercial Bulletin*, V/56, 7.4.24, p. 263.

69. Government of Palestine, *Report on the Administration of Palestine and Trans-Jordan*, 1935, p. 42.

70. Department of Agriculture, *Annual Report*, 1931/32, p. 16.

71. Ibid., 1934, p. 28.

72. Ibid., 1935, p. 30.

73. Ibid., 1941, p. 9.

74. Ibid., 1944/45, p. 10.

75. My source for information on the Ottoman Agricultural Bank as well as the subsequent credit arrangements provided by the Palestine government is the memorandum which the government submitted to the 1936 Palestine Royal Commission. The government memoranda were printed; I used a typescript copy in CZA/S25/10.208, the section entitled "Measures Taken to Provide Agricultural Credit."

76. Ibid., par. 1.

77. ISA/RG27/2727/G228/48b-c (hereafter cited as Lists, A); ISA/RG27/2627/G228 (Lists, B).

78. Lists, A.

79. Lists, B.

80. Lists, A.

81. Lists, B.

82. Lists, B; ISA/RG27/2627/G228/26a-b.

83. Lists, A.

84. Ibid.

85. Ibid.; Lists, B.

86. Johnson-Crosbie, p. 26.

87. "Measures Taken to Provide Agricultural Credit," par. 3.

88. Himadeh, *Economic Organization of Palestine*, p. 499.

89. *Survey of Palestine*, pp. 367–68.

90. *Palestine Facts and Figures*, p. 147. The information provided in the footnotes to table for the amount loaned per dunum for the 1942/43 season and later is inconsistent with the amount per dunum calculated from the data presented in the table itself.

91. Johnson-Crosbie, p. 27.

92. I base this conclusion on a comparison of table XXXI, "Total Income and Expenditure of 104 Villages"; table XVIII, "Revised Costs of Production of 100 Dunums Field Crop"; and table XXII, "Revised Cost of Living of Family of Six." The following tables show the relevant computations.

Cost of Living for a Family of Six
(Johnson-Crosbie, Table XXII)

Wheat and durra	£P10.00	Other necessaries not	
Olives and olive oil	£P3.00	of village origin	£P3.00
Other village produce	£P4.00	Clothing	£P5.00
Total	£P17.00	Total	£P8.00

Total expenditure on village produce for all villages (table XXXI) comes to £P358,122. Dividing this amount by £P17 gives 21,066 households. Total expenditure on other requirements for living and on clothing comes to £P168,528, which divided by £P8 is again 21,066. The total for all households' share of communal expenditures, estimated at £P1 per household, is £P21,066.

Costs of Production and Expenditures
(Johnson-Crosbie, Tables XVIII, XXXI)

Cost of Production for 100 Dunums of Field Crop		*Expenditure of 104 Villages*	
Annual share of		Seed and forage	£P168,423
plough animals	£P2.0	Implements and an-	
Implements	£P1.0	nual share of cost	
Forage for plough		of plough animals	£P37,427
animals	£P7.0		
Seed	£P6.5		

Dividing the total expenditures in the 104 villages by the comparable per household expenditures for the same factors—168,423 / (7 + 6.5), and 37,427 / (2 + 1)—gives 12,476, the total number of households engaged in production.

93. The feddan was an area which could be cultivated by a peasant with one pair of oxen. The size of the feddan was not uniform throughout the country. Information about the number of families owning land and the area of the feddan appears on p. 21 of the report.

94. Revised costs of production of 100 dunums field crop (Johnson-Crosbie, table XVIII); cost of oxen: Johnson-Crosbie, p. 15; 80–100 dunums, Volcani, *The Fellah's Farm*, p. 49. Cf. note 92 above.

95. Chayanov, *Theory of Peasant Economy*, p. 227 (emphasis in original).

CHAPTER 7: *Conclusions*

1. My discussion in this section draws on ideas developed by Boserup in *Conditions of Agricultural Growth*.

2. This is the heart of Boserup's argument.

3. Chayanov, *Theory of Peasant Economy*, p. 8.

4. Firestone, "Crop-sharing Economics," pt. II, p. 185.

5. Shim'oni, *Arvei Eretz Yisrael*; Washitz, *HaAravim BeEretz Yisrael*; Taqqu, *Arab Labor*; Miller, *Government and Society*.

6. Cf. Rosenfeld, "From Peasantry to Wage Labor."

7. Ibid.; Taqqu, *Arab Labor*.

8. Porath, *Palestine Arab National Movement*, p. 86.

9. Jewish organizations and settlements did provide some health services and technical assistance to Arabs in nearby localities, and there were attempts on a national level to develop joint Arab-Jewish activities, such as the Palestine Labour League affiliated with the Histadrut. Much of this activity was politically motivated, in the sense that its supporters believed that it would help to lessen Arab resistance to Jewish settlement.

10. Cf. CZA/S9/1149, table (in Hebrew) headed "Results of the Agricultural Census (Arranged at the Beginning of April, 1938). Workers According to Sex and Type of Work," Organization of Agricultural Workers, Department of Statistics. Localities covered included Gan Yavne, Miqwe Yisrael, Ramatayyim, Ramat HaShavim, Kfar Mlal, Yarqona, Ramat HaSharon, Benyamina, Zichron Ya'aqov.

11. In fact, within the *Yishuv* itself the more general policy of exclusiveness vis-à-vis the Arabs found a parallel in the attempt by the Histadrut to establish the hegemony of the labor movement vis-à-vis the "private" sector, which was accompanied by deep divisions within the Jewish community.

12. Porath, *Palestinian Arab National Movement*, and *Emergence of the Palestinian-Arab National Movement*.

13. Shim'oni, *Arvei Eretz Yisrael*; Taqqu, *Arab Labor*; Washitz, *HaAravim BeEretz Yisrael*.

BIBLIOGRAPHY

This bibliography includes only published materials. The location of documents from the files of the Government of Palestine and the Central Zionist Archives is referred to in the notes.

Abcarius, Michel. *Palestine Through the Fog of Propaganda*. London: Hutchison, 1946.

Abramowitz, Ze'ev, "Arab Economy in Palestine in 1945." In Sophie A. Udin, ed., *The Palestine Yearbook*, vol. 2. New York: Zionist Organization of America, 1946, pp. 216–25.

———. "Wartime Development of Arab Economy in Palestine." In Sophie A. Udin, ed., *The Palestine Yearbook*. Washington, D.C.: Zionist Organization of America, 1945, pp. 130–44.

Abramowitz, Z., and Gelfat, I. *HaMesheq HaAravi* [The Arab Economy]. Tel Aviv: HaKibbutz HaMeuchad, 1944.

Antebi, S. *Potato Growing in Palestine*. Government of Palestine, Department of Agriculture and Forests, Agricultural Leaflets, Series VI: Staple Crops. January 18, 1934.

Antoun, Richard T. *Arab Village*. Bloomington: Indiana University Press, 1972.

Assaf, Michael. "Cultural Development of the Palestine Arabs in the Period of the Mandate." In Sophie A. Udin, ed., *The Palestine Yearbook*, vol. 2. New York: Zionist Organization of America, 1946, pp. 226–44.

Avneri, Arie L. *HaHityashvut HaYehudit VeTa'anat HaNishul* [Jewish Land Settlement and the Arab Claim of Dispossession]. Tel Aviv: HaKibbutz HaMeuchad, 1980.

Baer, Gabriel. *A History of Landownership in Modern Egypt, 1800–1950*. London: Oxford University Press, 1962.

———. *Mavo LeToldot HaYachasim HaAgrari'im BeMizrach HaTichon* [Introduction to the History of Agrarian Relations in the Middle East]. Tel Aviv: HaKibbutz HaMe'uchad Publishing House, 1972.

Bar-Gal, Yoram, and Shmuel Shamai. "Bitzot Emeq-Yizra'el—Agada VeMitzi'ut" [The Jezre'el Valley's Swamps—Legend and Reality]. *Qathedra* 27 (March 1983): 163–74.

Bergheim, Samuel. "Land Tenure in Palestine." *Palestine Exploration Fund Quarterly* (1894): 191–99.

Boeke, J. H. *Economics and Economic Policy of Dual Societies.* New York: Institute of Pacific Relations, 1953.

Boserup, Ester. *The Conditions of Agricultural Growth.* Chicago: Aldine, 1965.

Brookfield, Harold. *Interdependent Development.* London: Methuen, 1975.

Chayanov, A. V. *The Theory of Peasant Economy.* Homewood, Ill.: Richard D. Irwin, Inc., 1966.

Cohen, Abner. *Arab Border Villages in Israel.* Manchester: Manchester University Press, 1965.

Doukhan-Landau, Leah. *HaHavarot HaZiyoni'ot LeRichishat Qarqa BeEretz Yisrael, 1897–1914* [The Zionist Land Purchasing Companies in Palestine, 1897–1914]. Jerusalem: Yad Yitzhak Ben-Zvi, 1979.

Elyashar, Eliyahu. "Mifkad HaTa'asiya VeHaMelacha Shel Memshelet Eretz-Yisrael 1928" [The 1928 Government of Palestine Census of Industry and Handicrafts]. *Riv'on LeKalkala* 101–02 (1979): 248–62.

ESCO Foundation for Palestine, *Palestine: A Study of Jewish, Arab and British Policies.* New Haven, Conn.: Yale University Press, 1947.

Firestone, Ya'akov. "Crop-sharing Economics in Mandatory Palestine." Part I: *Middle Eastern Studies* 11, no. 1 (January 1975): 3–23; part II: *Middle Eastern Studies* 11, no. 2 (May 1975): 175–94.

———. "Land Equalization and Factor Scarcities: Holding Size and the Burden of Impositions in Imperial Central Russia and the late Ottoman Levant." *Journal of Economic History* 41 (1982): 813–33.

Flapan, Simha. "HaKfar HaAravi VeHaHityashvut HaYehudit" [The Arab Village and Jewish Settlement]. *HaShomer HaTza'ir* (Palestine edition), 9, no. 41 (October 9, 1940): 4–5; no. 42 (October 14, 1940): 7, 13.

———. "LeHitpatchuto Shel HaKfar HaAravi" [On the Development of the Arab Village]. *HaShomer HaTza'ir* (Palestine edition) 9, no. 20 (May 16, 1940): 12–14; no. 21 (May 23, 1940): 5–7.

Foster, George. *Tzintzuntzan.* Boston: Little, Brown, 1967.

Furlonge, Geoffrey. *Palestine Is My Country: The Story of Musa Alami.* London: John Murray, 1969.

Galeski, Boguslaw. *Basic Concepts of Rural Sociology.* Manchester: Manchester University Press, 1972.

Gerber, Haim. "Modernization in Nineteenth-Century Palestine: The Role of Foreign Trade." *Middle Eastern Studies* 18, no. 2 (April 1982): 250–64.

———. *The Social Origins of the Modern Middle East.* Boulder, Colo.: Lynne Rienner Publishers, 1987.

Gorny, Yosef. *HaShe'alah HaAravit VeHaBa'aya HaYehudit* [The Arab Question and the Jewish Problem]. Tel Aviv: Am Oved, 1985.

Government of Palestine. *Report on the Administration of Palestine and Trans-Jordan.* Jerusalem, various years.

Government of Palestine. *Agricultural Development and Land Settlement in Palestine* [French Report]. Jerusalem: Government Printing Press, 1931.

——. *Average Tithe Committee Report.* Jerusalem, July 26, 1926.

——. *Census of Palestine, 1931.* Alexandria, 1931.

——. *Commercial Bulletin.* Jerusalem, various years.

——. *Cooperative Societies in Palestine.* Report by the Registrar of Cooperative Societies on Developments During the Years 1921–1937. Jerusalem, 1938.

——. Department of Statistics. *Monthly Bulletin of Current Statistics.* Jerusalem, various issues.

——. Palestine Royal Commission. *Notes of Evidence.* Jerusalem: Government Printer, 1937.

Government of Palestine. *Report by Mr. C. F. Strickland of the Indian Civil Service on the Possibility of Introducing a System of Agricultural Cooperation in Palestine* [Strickland Report]. Jerusalem: Government Printer, 1930.

Government of Palestine. *Report of a Committee on the Economic Condition of Agriculturalists in Palestine and the Fiscal Measures of Government in Relation Thereto* [Johnson-Crosbie Report]. Jerusalem: Government Printer, 1930.

Government of Palestine. *Report of the Wage Committee.* Publication No. 9 for 1943. Jerusalem, 1943. In Hebrew.

Government of Palestine. Department of Statistics. "Survey of Social and Economic Conditions in Arab Villages, 1944." *General Monthly Bulletin of Current Statistics* (Jerusalem) (July 1945): 426–47; (August 1945): 509–17; (September 1945): 559–67; (December 1945): 745–64; (January–March 1946): 46–56; (October 1946): 554–73.

Government of Palestine. *A Survey of Palestine.* Jerusalem: Government Printer, 1946.

Government of Palestine. *Village Statistics.* Jerusalem, 1937, 1943, 1945.

Government of Palestine. Department of Agriculture, Forests, and Fisheries. *Annual Report.* Jerusalem, various years.

Government of Palestine. Department of Statistics. *Statistical Abstract of Palestine.* Jerusalem, annual volumes, 1936 to 1944/45.

Government of Palestine. Department of Statistics. *Vital Statistics Tables, 1922–1945.* Jerusalem: Government Printing Office, 1947.

Gozansky, Tamar. *Hitpatchut HaKapitalism BePalestina* [Formation of Capitalism in Palestine]. Israel: University Publishing Projects Ltd., 1986.

Graham-Brown, Sarah. "The Political Economy of the Jabal Nablus, 1920–

1948." In Roger Owen, ed., *Studies in the Economic and Social History of Palestine in the Nineteenth and Twentieth Centuries*. Carbondale: Southern Illinois University Press, 1982, pp. 88–176.

Grandqvist, Hilma. *Marriage Conditions in a Palestinian Village. Commentationes Humanarum, Societas Scientarium Fennica*, vol. 3. Helsingfors, 1931.

Granott, A. [A. Granovsky]. *The Land System in Palestine*. London: Eyre and Spottiswoode, 1952.

Granovsky, A. *Land and the Jewish Reconstruction in Palestine*. Jerusalem: Keren Kayemeth Leisrael, Ltd., 1931.

Granovsky, A. *The Land Issue in Palestine*. Jerusalem: Keren Kayemeth Leisrael, Ltd., 1936.

————. *The Land Problem and the Future*. Jerusalem: Jewish National Fund, 1945.

Great Britain. Colonial Office. *Palestine Partition Commission Report*. Cmd. 5854. London: HMSO, 1938.

————. *Palestine: Report of the High Commissioner on the Administration of Palestine, 1920–1925*. Colonial No. 15. London: HMSO, 1925.

————. *Palestine: Report on Immigration, Land Settlement and Development* [Hope Simpson Report]. Cmd. 3686. London: HMSO, 1930.

————. *Palestine Royal Commission Report* [Peel Commission]. Cmd. 5479. London: HMSO, 1937.

————. *Report of the Commission on the Palestine Disturbances of August, 1929* [Shaw Commission]. Cmd. 3530. London: HMSO, 1930.

————. *Report to the Permanent Mandates Commission of the League of Nations on the Administration of Palestine and Trans-Jordan*. London: HMSO, various years. Title varies.

————. Foreign Office. *Maps Relating to the Report of the Anglo-American Committee of Inquiry Regarding the Problems of European Jewry and Palestine*. London: HMSO, 1946.

Greenbaum, Binyamin. "LeHitpatchut HaYachasim HaAgrari'im BeEretz-Yisrael" [On the Development of Agrarian Relations in Palestine]. *HaShomer HaTza'ir* (Palestine edition) 5, no. 22 (November 11, 1936): 12–14; no. 23 (December 1, 1936): 9–11; no. 24 (December 15, 1936): 9–11.

Gross, Nachum T. "The Economic Policy of the Mandatory Government in Palestine." *Research in Economic History* 9 (1984): 143–85.

Gulick, John. *Social Structure and Culture Change in a Lebanese Village*. Viking Fund Publications in Anthropology 21. New York, 1955.

Gurevich, David. *Statistical Abstract of Palestine*. Jerusalem: Keren HaYesod, 1930.

———. *Statistical Handbook of Jewish Palestine, 1947.* Jerusalem: Jewish Agency for Palestine, Department of Statistics, 1947.

Hadawi, Sami. *Land Ownership in Palestine.* New York: The Palestine Arab Refugee Office, 1957.

Hailey, Lord. *An African Survey.* London: Oxford University Press, 1938.

Halevi, Nadav. "The Political Economy of Absorptive Capacity: Growth and Cycles in Jewish Palestine Under the British Mandate." *Middle Eastern Studies* 19 (1983): 456–69.

Hancock, W. K. *Survey of British Commonwealth Affairs.* Vol. 1. London: Oxford University Press, 1937.

HaVa'ad HaLe'umi. *Sefer HaKalkala HaYishuvit LeShnat 1947* [The Economic Book of Jewish Palestine for 1947]. Tel Aviv: 1947.

Held, Joanne Dee. "The Effects of the Ottoman Land Laws on the Marginal Population and Musha' Villages of Palestine." M.A. thesis, University of Texas, Austin, 1979.

Himadeh, Said, ed. *Economic Organization of Palestine.* Beirut: The American University of Beirut, 1938.

Hodson, Randy, and Robert L. Kaufman. "Economic Dualism: A Critical Review." *American Sociological Review* 47 (December 1982): 727–39.

Hoofien, S. *Immigration and Prosperity.* London: Jewish Agency for Palestine, 1929.

Horowitz, David, and Rita Hinden. *The Economic Development of Palestine.* Tel Aviv: Jewish Agency for Palestine, Economic Research Institute, 1938.

Hyamson, Albert. *Palestine Under the Mandate.* London: Methuen, 1950.

Issawi, Charles, ed. *Economic History of the Middle East, 1800–1914.* Chicago: University of Chicago Press, 1966.

Jewish Agency for Palestine. *Financial Aspects of Jewish Reconstruction in Palestine.* Palestine Papers 5. London: 1930.

———. *The Jewish Case Before the Anglo-American Committee of Inquiry on Palestine: Statements and Memoranda.* Jerusalem, 1947.

———. *Land and Agricultural Development in Palestine. Memorandum Submitted to Sir John Hope Simpson.* London, July 1930.

———. *Memorandum Submitted by the Executive of the Jewish Agency on the Reports of Mr. Lewis French, C.I.E., C.B.E., on Agricultural Development and Land Settlement in Palestine.* London, 1933.

———. *Memorandum to the Palestine Royal Commission.* London, 1936.

———. Economic Department. *Palestine Facts and Figures.* May 1947. Mimeographed.

Keen, B. A. *The Agricultural Development of the Middle East.* London: Middle East Supply Centre, HMSO, 1946.

Kendall, Henry. *Village Development in Palestine During the British Mandate.* London: Crown Agents for the Colonies, 1949.

Khalidi, Walid. *Before Their Diaspora.* Washington, D.C.: Institute for Palestine Studies, 1984.

———, ed. *From Haven to Conquest.* Beirut: Institute for Palestine Studies, 1971.

Kisch, F. *Palestine Diary.* London: Victor Gollancz, 1938.

Kolchin, Peter. *Unfree Labor: American Slavery and Russian Serfdom.* Cambridge, Mass.: Harvard University Press, 1987.

Ladurie, LeRoy. "Peasants." In *The New Cambridge Modern History,* vol. 13. Cambridge: Cambridge University Press, 1979, pp. 116–63.

Lambton, Ann K. S. *Landlord and Peasant in Persia.* London: Oxford University Press, 1953.

Leo, Christopher. *Land and Class in Kenya.* Toronto: University of Toronto Press, 1984.

Levinger, Peretz. "Parashat Rechishat HaQarqa'ot BeAzor Yoqne'am" [The Case of Land Purchases in the Yoqne'am Region]. *Qathedra* no. 42 (January 1987): 153–70.

Lutfiyya, Abdulla M. *Baytin: A Jordanian Village.* The Hague: Mouton, 1966.

Mandel, Neville J. *The Arabs and Zionism Before World War I.* Berkeley and Los Angeles: University of California Press, 1976.

Mansur, George. *The Arab Worker Under the Palestine Mandate.* Jerusalem, 1937.

Maoz, Moshe. *Ottoman Reform in Syria and Palestine, 1840–1861.* Oxford: The Clarendon Press, 1968.

———, ed. *Studies on Palestine During the Ottoman Period.* Jerusalem: Magnes Press, 1975.

Metzer, Jacob. "Economic Structure and National Goals: The Jewish National Home in Interwar Palestine." *Journal of Economic History* 38, no. 1 (March 1978): 101–19.

———. "Fiscal Incidence and Resource Transfer Between Jews and Arabs in Mandatory Palestine." *Economic History* 7 (1982): 87–132.

———. *Technology, Labor and Growth in a Dual Economy's Traditional Sector: Mandatory Palestine, 1921–1936.* Maurice Falk Institute for Economic Research in Israel, Discussion Paper 82.01. Jerusalem, January 1982. Mimeographed.

Metzer, Jacob, and Oded Kaplan. "Jointly but Severally: Arab-Jewish Dualism and Economic Growth in Mandatory Palestine." *Journal of Economic History* 45, no. 2 (June 1985): 327–45.

Miller, Ylana N. *Government and Society in Rural Palestine, 1920–1948.* Austin: University of Texas Press, 1985.

Mogannam, Matiel. *The Arab Woman and the Palestine Problem.* London: Herbert Joseph, 1937.

Morris, Benny. *The Birth of the Palestine Refugee Problem.* Cambridge: Cambridge University Press, 1988.

————. "The New Historiography: Israel Confronts Its Past." *Tikkun* 3, no. 6 (November–December 1988): 19 ff.

————. "The New History and the Old Propagandists." *HaAretz*, May 9, 1989. In Hebrew.

Nathan, Robert E., Oscar Gass, and Daniel Creamer. *Palestine: Problem and Promise.* Washington, D.C.: American Council on Public Affairs, 1946.

Owen, Roger. *The Middle East in the World Economy, 1800–1914.* London: Methuen, 1981.

————, ed. *Studies in the Economic and Social History of Palestine in the Nineteenth and Twentieth Centuries.* Carbondale: Southern Illinois University Press, 1982.

Palestine Agricultural Economy Under War Conditions. Prepared for visitors to Jewish agricultural settlements during the Second World War. n.d.

Pappe, Ilan. *Britain and the Arab-Israeli Conflict.* London: Macmillan, 1988.

Parsons, Kenneth H., et al., eds. *Land Tenure.* Madison: University of Wisconsin Press, 1956.

Patai, Raphael. "Musha'a Tenure and Cooperation in Palestine." *American Anthropologist* 51, no. 3 (July–September, 1949): 436–45.

Popkin, Samuel. *The Rational Peasant.* Berkeley and Los Angeles: University of California Press, 1979.

Porath, Yehoshua. *The Emergence of the Palestinian-Arab National Movement, 1918–1929.* London: Cass, 1974.

————. *The Palestinian Arab National Movement: From Riots to Rebellion, 1929–1939.* London: Cass, 1977.

Post, George E. "Essays on the Sects and Nationalities of Syria and Palestine: Land Tenure, Agriculture, Physical, Mental, and Moral Characteristics." *Palestine Exploration Fund Quarterly* (1891): 99–147.

Robinson, Geroid Tanquary. *Rural Russia Under the Old Regime.* London: Longmans, Green, 1932.

Robinson, Kenneth. *The Dilemmas of Trusteeship.* London: Oxford University Press, 1965.

Rosenfeld, Henry. "Change, Barriers to Change, and Contradictions in the Arab Village Family," *American Anthropologist* 70, no. 4 (1968): 732–52.

Rosenfeld, Henry. "The Contradictions Between Property, Kinship and Power, as Reflected in the Marriage System of an Arab Village. In J. G. Perestiany, ed., *Contributions to Mediterranean Sociology.* Paris: Mouton & Co., 1968, pp. 247–260.

———. "The Class Situation of the Arab National Minority in Israel." *Comparative Studies in Society and History* 20 (1978): 374–407.

———. *Hem Hayyu Fallahim* [They Were Peasants]. Tel Aviv: HaKibbutz HaMe'uchad Publishing House, 1964.

———. "An Overview and Critique of the Literature on Rural Politics and Social Change." In Richard Antoun and Iliya Harik, eds., *Rural Politics and Social Change in the Middle East.* Bloomington: Indiana University Press, 1972, pp. 45–74.

———. "From Peasantry to Wage Labor and Residual Peasantry: The Transformation of an Arab Village." In Robert A. Manners, ed., *Process and Pattern in Culture: Essays in Honor of Julian H. Steward.* Chicago: Aldine, 1964, pp. 211–34.

———. "Social and Economic Factors in Explanation of the Increased Rate of Patrilineal Endogamy in the Arab Village in Israel." In J. G. Peristiany, ed., *Mediterranean Family Structures.* Cambridge: Cambridge University Press, 1976, pp. 115–36.

Royal Institute of International Affairs. *Great Britain and Palestine, 1915–1936.* London, 1937.

———. *Great Britain and Palestine, 1919–1945.* London, 1946.

Ruedy, John, "Dynamics of Land Alienation." In Ibrahim Abu-Lughod, ed., *The Transformation of Palestine.* Evanston, Ill.: Northwestern University Press, 1971, pp. 119–38.

———. *Land Policy in Colonial Algeria.* University of California Publications, New Eastern Studies 10. Berkeley, 1967.

Samuel, Ludwig, *Jewish Agriculture in Palestine.* Jerusalem: Jewish Agency for Palestine, Economic Research Institute, 1946.

Schölch, Alexander. "European Penetration and the Economic Development of Palestine." In Roger Owen, ed., *Studies in the Economic and Social History of Palestine in the Nineteenth and Twentieth Centuries.* Carbondale: Southern Illinois University Press, 1982, pp. 10–87.

Scott, James C. *The Moral Economy of the Peasant.* New Haven, Conn.: Yale University Press, 1976.

Shanin, Teodore. *Russia as a "Developing Society."* 2 vols. New Haven, Conn.: Yale University Press, 1986.

———, ed., *Peasants and Peasant Societies.* Harmondsworth: Penguin Books, 1971.

Shapira, Anita. *HaMa'avak HaNichzav* [Futile Struggle]. Tel Aviv: HaKibbutz HaMeuchad, 1977.

Shim'oni, Ya'akov. *Arvei Eretz Yisrael* [The Arabs of Palestine]. Tel Aviv: Am Oved, 1947.

Shlaim, Avi. *Collusion Across the Jordan.* New York: Columbia University Press, 1988.

Singer, H. W. "Dualism Revisited: A New Approach to the Problems of the Dual Society in Developing Countries." *Journal of Development Studies* 7 (1970): 60–75.

Smilansky, Moshe. *HaHityashvut HaIvrit VeHaFalah* [Jewish Settlement and the Fellah]. Tel Aviv: Mischar veTa'asiya, 1930.

Smith, Pamela Ann. *Palestine and the Palestinians, 1876–1983.* New York: St. Martin's Press, 1984.

Stein, Kenneth. *The Land Question in Palestine, 1917–1939.* Chapel Hill: University of North Carolina Press, 1984.

———. "Legal Protection and Circumvention of Rights for Cultivators in Mandatory Palestine." In Joel S. Migdal, ed., *Palestinian Society and Politics.* Princeton, N.J.: Princeton University Press, 1980, pp. 233–60.

Stein, Leonard. *Memorandum on the "Report of the Commission on the Palestine Disturbances of August, 1929."* London: Jewish Agency for Palestine, May 1930.

———. *Memorandum: The Palestine White Paper of October, 1930.* London: Jewish Agency for Palestine, November 1930.

Sussman, Zvi. "The Determination of Wages for Unskilled Labor in the Advanced Sector of the Dual Economy of Mandatory Palestine." *Economic Development and Cultural Change* 22 (October 1973): 95–113.

Taqqu, Rachel. *Arab Labor in Mandatory Palestine, 1920–1948.* Ph.D. dissertation, Columbia University, 1977.

———. "Peasants Into Workmen: Internal Labor Migration and the Arab Village Community Under the Mandate." In Joel S. Migdal, ed., *Palestinian Society and Politics.* Princeton, N.J.: Princeton University Press, 1980, pp. 261–85.

Teveth, Shabtai. "The New Historians." *HaAretz,* April 7, April 14, April 21, 1989. In Hebrew.

———. "Blossoming Doves and Colored Rabbits." *HaAretz,* May 19, 1989. In Hebrew.

Tyler, W. P. N. "The Beisan Lands Issue in Mandatory Palestine." *Middle Eastern Studies* 25, no. 2 (April 1989): 123–62.

van Zwanenberg, R. M. A., and Anne King. *An Economic History of Kenya and Uganda, 1800–1970.* Atlantic Highlands, N.J.: Humanities Press, 1975.

Volcani, Eliezer. *The Fellah's Farm.* Jewish Agency for Palestine, Institute of Agriculture and Natural History, Agricultural Experimental Station, Bulletin 10. Tel Aviv, September 1930.

Warriner, Doreen. *Land and Poverty in the Middle East.* London: Royal Institute of International Affairs, 1948.

————. *Land Reform and Development in the Middle East.* 2d ed. London: Oxford University Press, 1962.

Washitz, Yosef. *HaAravim BeEretz Yisrael* [The Arabs in Palestine]. Merhavia: Sifriyat HaPo'alim, 1947.

Wolf, Eric. *Peasants.* Englewood Cliffs, N.J.: Prentice-Hall, 1966.

Yisra'eli, Amihud. "LeToldot HaZeytim VeHaShemen BaGalil U'Biqat Bet Kerem" [On the History of Olive Cultivation and Oil Production in the Galilee and the Bet Kerem Valley]. *Qathedra* 15 (April 1980): 95–105.

Yudelman, Montague. *Africans on the Land.* Cambridge, Mass.: Harvard University Press, 1964.

Zureik, Elia. *Palestinians in Israel.* London: Routledge and Kegan Paul, 1979.

INDEX

317